Numerical Methods

Robert W. Hornbeck, Ph. D.

Associate Professor of Mechanical Engineering
Carnegie-Mellon University

Prentice-Hall, Inc., E

To the memory of
my Father

O 80436

ISBN 0-13-626614-2

Copyright © 1975 by
QUANTUM PUBLISHERS, INC.

Printed in the United States of America

10 9   8   7   6   5   4   3

Preface

The purpose of this book is to present, in as clear a fashion as possible, a logically structured collection of the fundamental tools of numerical methods. The methods presented are all well suited to the digital computer solution of problems in many areas of science and engineering. Every effort has been made to include the most modern and efficient techniques available in the rapidly developing field of numerical methods, without neglecting the broad base of those older, well-established techniques which are still in widespread use.

Since the emphasis of the book is on the understanding and use of the various methods, proofs have been included only where they might enhance understanding or provide motivation for the study of a particular method. A number of illustrative example problems have been integrated into the main body of the text at points where the presentation of a method can best be reinforced by the immediate use of the method. In addition, an extensive assortment of detailed solved problems has been included at the end of each chapter, illustrating virtually every topic considered in that chapter and illuminating the fine points and potential difficulties of the various methods. The only mathematical background required of the reader is the usual introductory calculus sequence. This overall approach makes the book suitable not only as a text in a structured classroom situation, but also for self-study and as a supplement to all other texts in the subject.

This book does not follow the currently popular practice of providing a complete computer program for each method discussed. Based on the author's wide experience, this practice tends to encourage the student to simply reproduce and run the programs, rather than to actually attempt to understand the method in depth. In addition, such programs tend to restrict the scope of the book to a single computer language (usually FORTRAN), while for various reasons it may be desirable or convenient for the reader to employ other languages, such as PL/I, APL, or BASIC.

Although many of the examples and illustrative problems given in the text actually represent the results of the mathematical modeling of physical situations, they are usually presented in mathematical terms. Since the text is not cast in the rigid mold of any single discipline in engineering or science, this permits an instructor to show the relevance of the methods and problems to any desired area. However, the author would caution against the use of complex problems involving much physical insight until the basic numerical techniques have been mastered, since a student may become lost or misled in the physics, and hence not gain the desired experience in numerical methods.

Chapter 1 provides an introduction to the power (and limitations) of numerical methods, some motivation for the engineer or scientist to study these methods, and a short discussion of digital computing from the user's point of view. The basic building blocks of numerical methods, the Taylor series and the finite difference calculus, are presented in Chapters 2 and 3.

Interpolation is the subject of Chapter 4. Despite the fact that this topic continues to be of great practical importance, and also forms the theoretical basis for much of numerical analysis, many current texts for some reason either ignore it completely, or do not give it adequate attention. Chapter 5 is devoted to finding the roots of equations. Many methods of root solving can be developed directly from the Taylor series, but the concept of inverse interpolation is also useful.

Both direct and iterative methods are presented in Chapter 6 for solving sets of simultaneous linear algebraic equations. Particular attention is given to the problem of ill-conditioning and to the solution of very large sets of equations. In Chapter 7, the concepts of interpolation are extended to functional approximation, and using the tools gained in Chapter 6, least squares data fitting can be examined in an effective manner.

Numerical integration is considered in Chapter 8. Several highly accurate and efficient techniques are included, and methods of dealing with singularities are examined in some detail.

In Chapter 9, a wide variety of numerical techniques is presented for solving ordinary differential equations. Approaches are considered for solving both initial value and boundary value problems. The accuracy and efficiency of each of the methods is carefully considered.

The subject of Chapter 10 is the algebraic eigenvalue problem. Much emphasis is given to the selection of the most efficient technique to deal with the particular problem at hand.

In Chapter 11, the book is concluded with an introduction to the numerical solution of partial differential equations, particularly of the parabolic and elliptic types. The power and potential of finite element methods are also discussed briefly.

This material is more than ample for a one-semester course at the junior or senior level in any of the engineering or science disciplines. If sufficient time is not available to cover all of the subject matter, it is suggested that Section 7.2, the more advanced portions of Chapter 10, and Chapter 11 be considered as possible omissions which would still leave the logical structure of the book intact.

The author wishes to express his gratitude to all of his students and colleagues who, through their encouragement and suggestions, have made this book possible. Particular thanks are due to Jean Stiles, who deciphered the author's handwriting and typed the manuscript in her usual expert manner, and to Earl Feldman, who independently verified the flow charts by writing and running computer programs from them. Finally, the author would like to thank Nicolas Monti and Michael Schaum of Quantum Publishers for their continuing interest, advice, and encouragement.

ROBERT W. HORNBECK

Contents

CONTENTS

Chapter 1

Introductory Topics

1.0 INTRODUCTION

We will begin this introductory chapter by briefly discussing the purpose and power of numerical methods as well as their limitations, and then presenting a justification for the detailed study of these methods.

1.1 WHAT ARE NUMERICAL METHODS?

Numerical methods are a class of methods for solving a wide variety of mathematical problems. These problems can, of course, have their origins as mathematical models of physical situations. This class of methods is unusual in that only arithmetic operations and logic are employed, thus the methods can be employed directly on digital computers.

Although in the strictest sense of the term, anything from the fingers to an abacus can be considered as a digital computer, we will use the term here to refer to electronic stored program computers which have been in reasonably widespread use since the middle 1950's. Numerical methods actually predate electronic computers by many years, and in fact, many of the currently used methods date in some form from virtually the beginnings of modern mathematics. However, the use of these methods was relatively limited until the advent of the mechanical desk calculator and then increased dramatically as, in a real sense, the methods came of age with the introduction of the electronic digital computer.

The combination of numerical methods and digital computers has created a tool of immense power in mathematical analysis. For example, numerical methods are capable of handling the nonlinearities, complex geometries, and large systems of coupled equations which are necessary for the accurate simulation of many real physical situations. Classical mathematics, even in the hands of the most ingenious applied mathematician, cannot cope with many of these problems at the level required by today's technology. As a result, numerical methods have displaced classical mathematical analysis in many industrial and research applications to the extent that (for better or for worse) classical analytical approaches are seldom considered, even for problems where analytical solutions could be obtained, since the numerical methods are so easy and inexpensive to employ and are often available as prepackaged programs.

1.2 ARE THERE LIMITS TO THE CAPABILITY OF NUMERICAL METHODS?

The answer to this question is an emphatic "yes." It is the view of many laymen and of entirely too many scientists and engineers who should know better, that if a problem cannot be solved in any other way, all one has to do is "put it on the computer." This state of affairs is undoubtedly due to the enormous power of numerical methods which we have discussed in the preceding section. However, it is unfortunately true that there are many problems which are still impossible (in some cases we should use the word "impractical") to solve using numerical methods. For some of these problems no accurate and complete mathematical model has yet been found, so obviously it is impossible to consider a numerical solution. Other problems are simply so enormous that their solution is beyond practical limits in terms of current computer technology. For example, it has been estimated that to obtain a detailed time-dependent solution to turbulent fluid problems, including the effects of the smallest eddies, would require on the order of 30 years. This estimate was based on 1968 technology and is probably off by no more than a factor of 5 or so based on today's technology. Of course, the entire question of practicality is strongly dependent upon how much one is willing to pay to obtain an answer. Some problems are so important that industry or government is willing to spend many millions of dollars to obtain the necessary computing capacity and speed to make it practical to solve problems which had previously been considered impractical to solve. In any case, although the boundaries are constantly being pushed back, there remain many problems which are beyond the reach of present technology, either in the formulation of the mathematical model or in terms of actual computing capability.

1.3 WHY STUDY NUMERICAL METHODS?

It may seem strange, in view of their widespread use in virtually every facet of science, technology, and government, that the author should feel an obligation to justify the study of numerical methods. For present and prospective numerical analysts and computer scientists, certainly no justification is necessary.

For engineers and scientists, however, the justification might appear to some to be less apparent. In recent years many large computer programs, each requiring several man-years of work, have been developed to simulate complex physical problems. These programs are usually designed to be used by those without extensive knowledge of their inner workings. In addition, there are ever-expanding libraries of subprograms to perform a wide variety of mathematical tasks using sophisticated numerical methods. In the face of these facts, one might indeed wonder whether there is a need for engineers and scientists to acquire a working knowledge of numerical methods. However, the engineer or scientist who expects to be able to locate a prepackaged program or library subprogram to perform every desired task will be sadly disappointed. The selection and application of a numerical method in any specific situation is still more of an art than a science, and the computer user who does not have the ability and knowledge to select and tailor a numerical method for the specific problem at hand, and to carry out the actual programming of the method, will find severe limitations on the range of problems which can be handled.

Obviously, when proven prepackaged programs or subprograms are available which are suited to the task at hand, it is by far the most efficient course to employ them. A working knowledge of numerical methods is highly valuable even in these cases, however, since the user of such programs and library subprograms will inevitably encounter difficulties. These difficulties can stem from many causes, including the following:

(a) No complex physical situation can be *exactly* simulated by a mathematical model. (This is an extremely crucial point, but is outside the scope of the present discussion.)

(b) No numerical method is completely trouble-free in all situations.

(c) No numerical method is completely error-free.

(d) No numerical method is optimal for all situations.

(There can be considerable overlap among (b), (c), and (d). We will not be concerned with precise definitions here, only broad concepts.) The difficulties with the numerical methods can result in a prepackaged program or library subprogram yielding erroneous results, or no results at all. In addition, the user searching for a library subprogram to perform a certain task may find an overwhelming variety and number of subprograms which appear generally applicable, but the descriptive material will seldom give any indication of the efficiency of the subprogram or its suitability for solving the specific problem at hand.

The user with any of these problems, but no knowledge of numerical methods, must then seek out someone with the necessary information (perhaps a numerical analyst), if indeed such a consultant is available. In this situation, however, it may be difficult for the user to ask the right questions and for the consultant to give useable answers, since the background of the two may be vastly different.

We can thus see that there is a strong justification for the scientist or engineer to acquire a working knowledge of numerical methods. This knowledge enables the computer user to select, modify, and program a method suitable for any specific task, aids in the selection and use of prepackaged programs and library subprograms, and makes it possible for the user to communicate with a specialist in an efficient and intelligent way when seeking help for a particularly difficult problem. Finally, it should be recognized that the bulk of what has come to be known as "methods development" (which is to all intents and purposes the writing of large programs to simulate complex physical problems) is done by engineers and scientists, and not by numerical analysts. Obviously, however, the most efficient and accurate numerical techniques must be employed in such work, and a thorough knowledge of numerical methods is essential for the engineers and scientists involved in such a project.

We now turn briefly to a discussion of several computer-related topics which are not numerical methods in themselves, but which are of considerable interest to anyone who must actually implement numerical methods on a digital computer.

1.4 COMPUTER LANGUAGES

Most of the readers of this book will have had some experience in programming in a "high level" computer language such as FORTRAN, ALGOL, or BASIC. These languages allow the user to write programs in a form which includes algebraic formulas and English-like logical and input-output statements. Such high level languages are virtually independent of the machine on which the programs will be run. Through the use of a computer program called a *compiler* (or translator), the high level program can then be converted into the fundamental machine code of the particular machine on which the program will actually be executed.

By far the most widely used algebraic language for scientific purposes is FORTRAN IV or minor modifications thereof. With a few exceptions, ALGOL is seldom used for scientific computation today, but is widely used as a universal international language for describing algorithms. BASIC is quite popular as a language for use on time-sharing systems and is usually used for relatively simple programming tasks. Other high level languages which the scientific user may encounter are APL (also reasonably widely used on time-sharing systems and suitable for tasks ranging from the very simple to the highly sophisticated), MAD (an obsolescent ALGOL-like language), and PL-1 (a powerful language currently of interest primarily to computer scientists).

The appearance of each new language is greeted with some trepidation by the average user since it means a new set of rules which may have to be learned, and possible confusion with other languages. However, any reasonably flexible person will find little difficulty in adapting to a new language if necessary. A much more important issue is the economic one, since the development of large computer programs is very expensive, and the conversion of large programs from one language to another can be a major task involving many months of work. This is one of the primary reasons why FORTRAN IV is the current scientific "standard" and is unlikely to be displaced in the near future.

1.5 THE VERIFICATION PROBLEM

One of the most vital and yet most difficult tasks which must be carried out in obtaining a numerical solution to any problem is to verify that the computer program and the final solution are correct. First it must be established that the program is working as the programmer intended, i.e., that the coding is correct. This can usually be established by generous printing of intermediate results, and if necessary by making spot checks by hand or desk calculator computations. The second part of the verification procedure is to establish that the algorithm being employed will yield the correct solution. Since the correct solution to the problem is presumably not known beforehand (or we would not bother to obtain a numerical solution), this portion of the verification procedure will usually be indirect. This indirect approach could consist, for example, of looking at various limiting cases of the problem for which known solutions are available. These limiting cases might be simulated with the program under consideration by setting certain terms to zero, letting certain constants or conditions become very large or very small, or by bypassing temporarily certain sections of the program and/or inserting other small temporary sections.

In many cases the verification procedure can actually be more expensive and time consuming than obtaining the final desired answer. However, the confidence which one can place in the final results is directly related to the time and care which are invested in the verification process. In estimating the time and cost required to obtain a numerical solution, it is essential that allowance be made for the verification process.

Up to this point we have been concerned with the verification of a program written by the average user to solve a specific problem. The process of verification for a general program or library subprogram, which would be employed by many users to solve a wide variety of problems, would be similar but necessarily even more extensive and painstaking, and would include a series of "worst case" trials to test the ability of the program to cope with known difficult problems.

1.6 DO COMPUTERS MAKE MISTAKES?

Of course, in one sense or another, computers can and do make mistakes. We should note, however, that the vast majority of errors encountered in the course of computation are the user's own errors. It is sometimes very difficult to accept that a hard-to-locate error is one's own. Nevertheless, the most efficient procedure in tracking down errors is invariably to assume that this is the case, until the possibility has essentially been eliminated.

If computer errors are encountered, they can be characterized as either hardware or software errors. True hardware errors are relatively rare, and we are not in a position to discuss them here. Software errors (which are really just some other programmer's errors) are more common, and could typically include errors in the computer executive system, errors in the compiler which result in incorrect object (machine language) code, and errors in library subprograms.

Errors in the computer executive system (also variously called the exec, monitor, operating system, supervisor, and other names) can be quite confusing to the user. Modern systems usually incorporate the capability of handling several programs at once in order to most effectively utilize the hardware (this is often called multiprocessing) or of allowing a number of users to compute and "converse" with the system from remote terminals (often called time-sharing). Some systems even combine these capabilities. Most of the difficulties which the user encounters from the executive system come from unforeseen interactions of one program with another. These can result in anything from total system failure (a "crash") to erratic behavior and incorrect results from the individual user's program. These errors are seldom repeatable, and simply rerunning the program will usually rectify matters.

Errors in compilers are particularly frustrating to the user, since a high level program which is perfectly correct can produce incorrect machine code and hence incorrect results. Fortunately, due to extensive verification, serious compiler errors are usually not encountered (and a list of known minor errors is usually available from the computer systems personnel). However, with those compilers which incorporate optimization, serious and almost unpredictable errors can occur. Optimization can be interpreted in this context as an effort to generate the most efficient possible machine code from a given program written in the high level language. This optimization effort includes changing the order of operations from that specified in the high level code in order to (hopefully) obtain the same answers in less computer time. Optimization can result in remarkable savings in computing time in many cases, but the better the optimizer (in the efficiency sense) the more likely it is to result in incorrect machine code. In most cases it is possible to "turn off" the optimization facility of the compiler or to find a similar compiler without optimization or with relatively simple and error-free optimization.* It is recommended that this course be followed if possible in debugging and for the initial runs of a program, and that a compiler with a very high degree of optimization be employed only for production runs where efficiency is all-important. The highly optimized version should of course be verified by comparison with results obtained without optimization.

---

*It is sometimes remarkably difficult to obtain information about whether a given compiler is an optimizing compiler, and whether or not it is possible to "turn off" the optimization. However, a diligent search through the manufacturer's manuals will usually yield the information in some form.

Errors in library subprograms are generally the product of ineffective verification procedures, and usually cannot be dealt with by the user except by reporting the faulty routine to the responsible systems personnel.

Finally, we should note that, although the errors are not mistakes in the usual sense, any computation carried out with a finite number of decimal places will result in roundoff error, and any numerical method has error which is inherent in the application of the method. These errors are best discussed with the presentation of each method, and we will not consider them further at this point.

1.7 THE NEED TO GET INVOLVED

Numerical methods cannot be simply read about, they must be *used* in order to be understood. Accordingly, it is vital that the reader actually solve problems using the numerical methods described in this book. In closing this introductory chapter, the author would like to point out from personal experience that the best test of whether one understands a method is not to carry out a hand calculation (although this can be useful in the early stages of attempting to understand the logic) but to write a computer program, and thus to relinquish personal decision making to the impersonal computer. It is remarkable how hazy concepts can become clear under the resulting pressure to be completely precise and unambiguous.

Chapter 2

The Taylor Series

2.0 INTRODUCTION

The Taylor series is the foundation of numerical methods. Many of the numerical techniques are derived directly from the Taylor series, as are the estimates of the errors involved in employing these techniques. The reader should be acquainted with the Taylor series from his earlier studies, but we shall make a brief presentation of the subject here since our emphasis will be somewhat different from that of the conventional calculus.

If the value of a function $f(x)$ can be expressed in a region of x close to $x = a$ by the infinite power series

$$f(x) = f(a) + (x - a)f'(a) + \frac{(x - a)^2}{2!} f''(a)$$
$$+ \frac{(x - a)^3}{3!} f'''(a) + \cdots + \frac{(x - a)^n}{n!} f^{(n)}(a) + \cdots \qquad (2.1)$$

then $f(x)$ is said to be *analytic* in the region near $x = a$, and the series (2.1) is unique and called the *Taylor series expansion* of $f(x)$ in the neighborhood of $x = a$. It is difficult to specify general conditions under which the series (2.1) will exist and be convergent, but it is evident that all derivatives of $f(x)$ at $x = a$ must exist and be finite. If the Taylor series exists, then knowing $f(a)$ and all of the derivatives of f at $x = a$, we can find the value of $f(x)$ at some x different from a, as long as we remain "sufficiently close" to $x = a$.

If as $|x - a|$ is increased, a point is reached where the power series (2.1) is no longer convergent, then we are no longer "sufficiently close" to $x = a$ and are outside the *radius of convergence* of the power series. Some series will converge for all $|x - a|$ (have an infinite radius of convergence) while others will converge only for values of $|x - a|$ below a certain limit. If the series is convergent, then the value of $f(x)$ will be exact if an infinite number of terms are taken in the series. It is much more interesting and useful to us, however, to find out how well we can approximate $f(x)$ near $x = a$ by taking only a few terms of (2.1).

This can be graphically illustrated by examining Fig. 2.1. Suppose we wish to find $f(b)$. From (2.1),

$$f(b) = f(a) + (b - a)f'(a) + \frac{(b - a)^2}{2!} f''(a) + \frac{(b - a)^3}{3!} f'''(a) + \cdots \qquad (2.2)$$

If only the first term of (2.1) is used, then the function is assumed to be a constant, $f(a)$, as shown in Fig. 2.1*a*. If the first two terms are used, then the slope of f at $x = a$ is taken

7

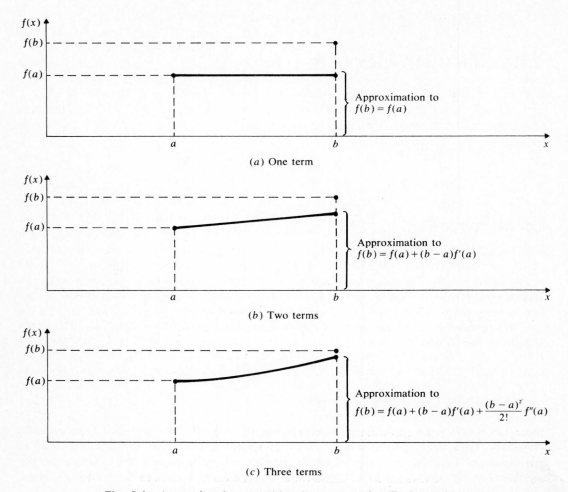

Fig. 2.1 Approximations resulting from truncating Taylor series.

into account by using a straight line from $f(a)$ with a slope $f'(a)$ as shown in Fig. 2.1*b*. Considering three terms allows the use of the curvature due to $f''(a)$ as shown in Fig. 2.1*c*, etc. Each additional term improves the accuracy in the approximation for $f(b)$.

It will be useful for us to adopt some standard terminology and conventions about the truncation of a Taylor series. We begin by examining the error made in truncating a Taylor series. The error in the Taylor series (*2.1*) for $f(x)$ when the series is truncated after the term containing $(x-a)^n$ is not greater than

$$\left|\frac{d^{n+1}f}{dx^{n+1}}\right|_{max} \frac{(|x-a|)^{n+1}}{(n+1)!} \tag{2.3}$$

where the subscript "max" denotes the maximum magnitude of the derivative on the interval from a to x.

It would seem that nothing can be gained from this error bound, since if the value of the $(n+1)$ derivative of f on the entire interval must be known to evaluate the error, then the value of $f(x)$ on this interval would also be known, and there would be no need to carry out the expansion in the first place.   This frustrating state of affairs is fairly common in numerical analysis, however, and much useful information can be gained from (2.3).   We have no control over the behavior of f (or any of its derivatives), nor over the constant $(n + 1)!$.   We do have control over how close x is chosen to be to a, or in other words on the quantity $(x - a)^{n+1}$.   Thus we use the terminology that the error (2.3) is *of the order of* $(x - a)^{n+1}$, or is $\mathcal{O}(x - a)^{n+1}$.   If the series expression for $f(x)$ is truncated after the first three terms, we say that $f(x)$ is accurate to $\mathcal{O}(x - a)^3$, since

$$f(x) = f(a) + (x - a)f'(a) + \frac{(x - a)^2}{2!}f''(a) + \mathcal{O}(x - a)^3 \tag{2.4}$$

It should be noted that the use of the notation $\mathcal{O}(x - a)^3$ implies nothing about the constants or derivatives multiplying $(x - a)^3$; for example, $7(x - a)^3$ is of $\mathcal{O}(x - a)^3$.   Thus the quantity $\mathcal{O}(x - a)^3$ might equally well be described as a quantity varying as $(x - a)^3$.

If we take a fourth term in the series (2.1) for $f(x)$ before truncating, we obtain

$$f(x) = f(a) + (x - a)f'(a) + \frac{(x - a)^2}{2!}f''(a) + \frac{(x - a)^3}{3!}f'''(a) + \mathcal{O}(x - a)^4 \tag{2.5}$$

In general, the four term representation (2.5) gives a more accurate approximation to $f(x)$ for a given value of x than does the three term representation (2.4).   Thus one would expect that for this function, the error term $\mathcal{O}(x - a)^4$ would be less than the error term $\mathcal{O}(x - a)^3$ in the three term series (2.4).   We can generalize this result to the statement that if we confine ourselves to a Taylor series for a given function, then the following relationship holds between the error terms of a series truncated at n terms and the same series truncated at $n + 1$ terms:

$$\mathcal{O}(x - a)^{n+1} < \mathcal{O}(x - a)^n \tag{2.6}$$

Note that this relationship will hold *whether or not* $|x - a| < 1$, as long as we are within the radius of convergence of the series.   (Strictly speaking, (2.6) may not hold for the first few terms of some series, particularly if $(x - a)$ is large in magnitude.   However, the relationship will be true for large n, and for our purposes (2.6) should be considered as the general trend.)

It should be noted that for certain series expansions some terms may vanish.   For example, a truncated series representation of $f(x)$ composed of the first four terms of (2.1) might have exactly the same error as a truncated series composed of the first five terms of (2.1).   See Problem 2.2 for an illustration of such a case.

Illustrative Problems

2.1   Find the Taylor series expansion for $\sin x$ near $x = 0$ using the series *(2.1)*.

Since we are expanding about $x = 0$, $a = 0$. The series *(2.1)* becomes

$$\sin(x) = \sin(0) + x \cos(0) - \frac{x^2}{2!} \sin(0) - \frac{x^3}{3!} \cos(0) + \frac{x^4}{4!} \sin(0) + \cdots$$

and since $\sin(0) = 0$ and $\cos(0) = 1$,

$$\sin x = x - \frac{x^3}{3!} + \frac{x^5}{5!} + \cdots$$

2.2   Truncate the Taylor series for the sine found in Problem 2.1 to give a representation of $\mathcal{O}(x)^4$. Show that this representation is in fact of $\mathcal{O}(x)^5$.

From Problem 2.1,

$$\sin(x) = \sin(0) + x \cos(0) - \frac{x^2}{2!} \sin(0) - \frac{x^3}{3!} \cos(0) + \mathcal{O}(x)^4$$

$$= x - \frac{x^3}{3!} + \mathcal{O}(x)^4$$

But if we carry one more term in the series,

$$\sin(x) = \sin(0) + x \cos(0) - \frac{x^2}{2!} \sin(0) - \frac{x^3}{3!} \cos(0) + \frac{x^4}{4!} \sin(0) + \mathcal{O}(x)^5$$

we see that this additional term is exactly zero since $\sin(0) = 0$. Therefore

$$\sin(x) = x - \frac{x^3}{3!} + \mathcal{O}(x)^5$$

This two term representation is thus actually of $\mathcal{O}(x)^5$ rather than $\mathcal{O}(x)^4$.

2.3   Using the Taylor series expansion for e^x about $x = 0$, find $e^{0.5}$ to $\mathcal{O}(0.5)^3$. Bound the error using the error expression *(2.3)* and compare your result with the actual error.

From equation *(2.1)*,

$$e^x = e^{(0)} + xe^{(0)} + \frac{x^2}{2!} e^{(0)} + \frac{x^3}{3!} e^{(0)} + \frac{x^4}{4!} e^{(0)} + \cdots$$

or

$$e^x = 1 + x + \frac{x^2}{2!} + \frac{x^3}{3!} + \frac{x^4}{4!} + \cdots$$

and if $x = 0.5$,

$$e^{0.5} = 1 + 0.5 + \frac{(0.5)^2}{2!} + \frac{(0.5)^3}{3!} + \frac{(0.5)^4}{4!} + \cdots$$

or, to $\mathcal{O}(0.5)^3$,

$$e^{0.5} = 1 + 0.5 + \frac{(0.5)^2}{2!} = 1.625$$

Now according to *(2.3)*, the error in this quantity should not be greater than

$$\left|\frac{d^3(e^x)}{dt^3}\right|_{max}\frac{(0.5)^3}{3!}=|e^x|_{max}(0.0208333)$$

where max denotes the maximum magnitude on $0\leq x\leq 0.5$. $|e^x|_{max}=e^{0.5}=1.6487213$, so the error is no greater in magnitude than

$$(1.6487213)(0.0208333)=0.0343831$$

The actual error is

$$e^{0.5}-1.625=1.6487213-1.6250000=0.0237213$$

which lies within the error bound. Notice that in this case the error which was $\mathcal{O}(0.5)^3$ was actually 0.0237213 or about $0.19(0.5)^3$.

2.4 Find the Taylor series expansion about $x=0$ for $f(x)=\log_e(1-x)$. What is the radius of convergence of this series?

The function and its derivatives are

$$f(x)=\log_e(1-x)$$
$$f'(x)=\frac{-1}{1-x}$$
$$f''(x)=\frac{-1}{(1-x)^2}$$
$$f'''(x)=\frac{-2}{(1-x)^3}$$
$$f^{iv}(x)=\frac{-6}{(1-x)^4}$$
$$\cdots\cdots\cdots$$

Using the series (2.1) with $a=0$, we obtain

$$\log_e(1-x)=\log_e(1)+x\left(\frac{-1}{1-0}\right)+\frac{x^2}{2!}\left(\frac{-1}{(1-0)^2}\right)$$
$$+\frac{x^3}{3!}\left(\frac{-2}{(1-0)^3}\right)+\frac{x^4}{4!}\left(\frac{-6}{(1-0)^4}\right)+\cdots$$

or

$$\log_e(1-x)=-\left(x+\frac{x^2}{2}+\frac{x^3}{3}+\frac{x^4}{4}+\cdots\right)$$

To find the radius of convergence of the series, we apply the ratio test. We take the limit

$$\lim_{n\to\infty}\left|\frac{x^{n+1}/(n+1)}{x^n/n}\right|=\lim_{n\to\infty}\left|\frac{nx}{n+1}\right|=|x|$$

The ratio test states that the series converges absolutely (even if all terms have the same sign) if this ratio is less than one. Thus the radius of convergence of the series is $|x|<1$. The ratio test tells us nothing if $|x|=1$, but we note that if $x=+1$, then we have the negative of

$$1+1/2+1/3+1/4+\cdots$$

which is the familiar divergent harmonic series. If $x=-1$, we have the series

$$1-1/2+1/3-1/4+\cdots$$

which is convergent. The series is thus convergent for $-1\leq x<1$.

2.5   Using the results of Problem 2.4, obtain the geometric series for $1/(1-x)$, $|x|<1$. This series is of great value in much numerical and approximation work.

From Problem 2.4,

$$\log_e (1-x) = -\left(x + \frac{x^2}{2} + \frac{x^3}{3} + \frac{x^4}{4} + \cdots\right)$$

Differentiating this series with respect to x, we obtain

$$\frac{d}{dx}(\log_e (1-x)) = \frac{-1}{1-x} = -\left(1 + \frac{2x}{2} + \frac{3x^2}{3} + \frac{4x^3}{4} + \cdots\right)$$

or

$$\frac{1}{1-x} = 1 + x + x^2 + x^3 + x^4 + \cdots$$

2.6   Find $e^{0.1}\sin (0.1)$ to $\mathcal{O}(0.1)^4$ by using the Taylor series expansion for each function and multiplying them.

From Problems 2.1 and 2.3, we have

$$\sin (0.1) = 0.1 - \frac{(0.1)^3}{3!} + \mathcal{O}(0.1)^5, \qquad e^{0.1} = 1 + 0.1 + \frac{(0.1)^2}{2} + \mathcal{O}(0.1)^3$$

We have taken sufficient terms in each series so that when the two series are multiplied together, the largest error term will be $\mathcal{O}(0.1)^4$. (This will come from the product of the first term in the sine series and the error term $\mathcal{O}(0.1)^3$ in the $e^{0.1}$ series. All other error terms will be smaller.) Then

$$e^{0.1}\sin (0.1) = \left[1 + 0.1 + \frac{(0.1)^2}{2} + \mathcal{O}(0.1)^3\right]\left[0.1 - \frac{(0.1)^3}{6} + \mathcal{O}(0.1)^5\right]$$

$$= 0.1 + (0.1)^2 + \frac{1}{3}(0.1)^3 + \mathcal{O}(0.1)^4$$

so

$$e^{0.1}\sin (0.1) = 0.110333 + \mathcal{O}(0.1)^4$$

2.7   Show that $f(x) = e^{x^{1/2}}$ cannot be expanded in a Taylor series about $x = 0$.

We have

$$f(x) = e^{x^{1/2}}$$

$$f'(x) = e^{x^{1/2}}\left(\frac{1}{2}x^{-1/2}\right)$$

$$f''(x) = e^{x^{1/2}}\left(\frac{1}{4}x^{-1}\right) - e^{x^{1/2}}\left(\frac{1}{4}x^{-3/2}\right)$$

. . . .

The function $f(x)$ is bounded at $x = 0$, but all of the derivatives of f involve negative powers of x which result in those derivatives becoming unbounded at $x = 0$. Thus $f(x)$ does not satisfy the conditions at $x = 0$ for an expansion in a Taylor series about $x = 0$.

2.8   Given the function $f(x) = e^x$, consider the following Taylor series expansions about $x = 0$:

$$f(x) = f(0) + xf'(0) + \frac{x^2}{2}f''(0) + \mathcal{O}(x)^3$$

$$f(x) = f(0) + xf'(0) + \mathcal{O}(x)^2$$

Let $x = 2$.   Show that the error term $\mathcal{O}(x)^3 < \mathcal{O}(x)^2$ despite the fact that $(2)^3 > (2)^2$.

The two series are

$$e^x = 1 + x + \frac{x^2}{2} + \mathcal{O}(x)^3$$

$$e^x = 1 + x + \mathcal{O}(x)^2$$

If we let $x = 2$,

$$e^2 = 1 + 2 + \frac{2^2}{2} + \mathcal{O}(2)^3$$

$$e^2 = 1 + 2 + \mathcal{O}(2)^2$$

From tables, $e^2 = 7.3891$, so

$$7.3891 = 5 + \mathcal{O}(2)^3$$
$$7.3891 = 3 + \mathcal{O}(2)^2$$

and thus the error terms are

$$\mathcal{O}(2)^3 = 2.3891$$
$$\mathcal{O}(2)^2 = 4.3891$$

Note that for this problem we have been able to evaluate exactly the error terms since we knew e^2.   In general, this would not be possible.

2.9   Using the Taylor series expansions about $x = 0$, evaluate $e^{\sin x}$ to $\mathcal{O}(x)^4$.

First, we use the Taylor series for the exponential:

$$e^{\sin x} = 1 + \sin x + \frac{\sin^2 x}{2!} + \frac{\sin^3 x}{3!} + \frac{\sin^4 x}{4!} + \cdots$$

Now we employ the Taylor series expansion for $\sin x$, taking enough terms each time to ensure that the result is accurate to at least $\mathcal{O}(x)^4$:

$$e^{\sin x} = 1 + \left[x - \frac{x^3}{3!} + \mathcal{O}(x)^5 \right] + \frac{[x + \mathcal{O}(x)^3]^2}{2} + \frac{[x + \mathcal{O}(x)^3]^3}{6} + \mathcal{O}(x)^4$$

$$= 1 + x - \frac{x^3}{6} + \mathcal{O}(x)^5 + \frac{[x^2 + \mathcal{O}(x)^4]}{2} + \frac{[x^3 + \mathcal{O}(x)^5]}{6} + \mathcal{O}(x)^4$$

$$= 1 + x + \frac{x^2}{2} + \mathcal{O}(x)^4$$

2.10 Show that $f(x) = (x - 1)^{1/2}$ cannot be expanded in a Taylor series about $x = 0$ or $x = 1$, but can be expanded about $x = 2$. Carry out the expansion about $x = 2$.

$$f(x) = (x - 1)^{1/2}$$

$$f'(x) = \frac{1}{2}(x - 1)^{-1/2}$$

$$f''(x) = -\frac{1}{4}(x - 1)^{-3/2}$$

$$f'''(x) = \frac{3}{8}(x - 1)^{-5/2}$$

. . . .

For an expansion about $x = 0$, the quantities $f(0)$, $f'(0)$, $f''(0)$, etc. are needed. These involve noninteger powers of (-1), e.g. $(-1)^{1/2}$. These cannot be evaluated to give real values and thus this expansion is impossible.

For an expansion about $x = 1$, we need quantities such as

$$f(1) = (0)^{1/2}$$

$$f'(1) = \frac{1}{2}(0)^{-1/2}$$

$$f''(1) = -\frac{1}{4}(0)^{-3/2}$$

. . . .

While $f(1)$ is bounded, all of the derivatives $f'(1)$, $f''(1)$, etc. are unbounded. Thus the expansion about $x = 1$ is impossible.

The Taylor series expansion about $x = 2$ is

$$f(x) = (2 - 1)^{1/2} + (x - 2)\left[\frac{1}{2}(2 - 1)^{-1/2}\right]$$

$$+ \frac{(x - 2)^2}{2}\left[-\frac{1}{4}(2 - 1)^{-3/2}\right] + \frac{(x - 2)^3}{3!}\left[\frac{3}{8}(2 - 1)^{-5/2}\right] + \cdots$$

All derivatives are bounded and finite and the series is

$$f(x) = 1 + \frac{(x - 2)}{2} - \frac{(x - 2)^2}{8} + \frac{(x - 2)^3}{16} - \cdots$$

This series is convergent for $|x - 2| < 1$.

2.11 By a technique entirely different from the Taylor series expansion, we find the following series:

$$\tan x = x + \frac{x^3}{3} + \frac{2x^5}{15} + \frac{17x^7}{315} + \cdots$$

Is this the Taylor series expansion about $x = 0$?

Yes, since the Taylor series expansion about $x = 0$ (i.e. in powers of x) is unique.

Problems

2.12   Find the Taylor series expansion for $\sinh x$ about $x = 0$.

2.13   Find $\sinh 0.9$ to $\mathcal{O}(0.9)^5$ by using the Taylor series expansion from Problem 2.12.

2.14   Bound the error on your answer to Problem 2.13 by using the error expression (*2.3*) and compare your result with the actual error. (*Note*: $\sinh 0.9 = 1.0265167$, $\cosh 0.9 = 1.4330864$.)

2.15   Find the Taylor series expansion of $\sin x$ about $x = \pi/4$.

2.16   Obtain the Taylor series expansion for $1/(1-x)^2$ by using the series for $1/(1-x)$ from Problem 2.5.

2.17   Is it possible to expand $\log_e x$ in a Taylor series about $x = 0$?   Discuss.

2.18   Find an expression for $\sin x \cos x$ accurate to $\mathcal{O}(x)^5$ by using the Taylor series for the individual functions about $x = 0$.

2.19   Evaluate $\cos(\sin x)$ to $\mathcal{O}(x)^6$ by using the known Taylor series for $\sin x$ and $\cos x$.

2.20   Examine the Taylor series about $x = 0$ for e^x when $x = 4$.   The fourth term in the series, $x^3/3!$, is larger than the third term, $x^2/2!$.   Does this mean the series is divergent?   Explain this apparent anomaly.

2.21   Consider two functions $g(x)$ and $h(x)$, related in such a way that $g'(x) = h(x)$ and $h'(x) = g(x)$ and that $g(0) = 0$ and $h(0) = 1$.   Find the Taylor series expansions for $g(x)$ and $h(x)$ using only this information.

2.22   Show that the Taylor series expansion of $f(x) = x^3$ about $x = 1$ simply reproduces x^3.

2.23   The error function $\operatorname{erf}(x)$ is defined as $\operatorname{erf}(x) = (2/\sqrt{\pi})\int_0^x e^{-t^2}\,dt$.   Find $\operatorname{erf}(1)$ to $\mathcal{O}(1)^4$ by expanding $\operatorname{erf}(x)$ in a Taylor series about $x = 0$.   (The value of $\operatorname{erf}(1) = 0.84270079$ to eight decimal places.)

Chapter 3
The Finite Difference Calculus

3.0 INTRODUCTION

In conventional calculus the operation of differentiation of a function is a well-defined formal procedure with the operations highly dependent on the form of the function involved.   Many different types of rules are needed for different functions.   In numerical methods a digital computer is employed which can only perform the standard arithmetic operations of addition, subtraction, multiplication, and division, and certain logical operations.*   Thus we need a technique for differentiating functions by employing only arithmetic operations.   The finite difference calculus satisfies this need.

3.1 FORWARD AND BACKWARD DIFFERENCES

Consider a function $f(x)$ which is analytic (can be expanded in a Taylor series) in the neighborhood of a point x as shown in Fig. 3.1.

We find $f(x + h)$ by expanding $f(x)$ in a Taylor series about x:

$$f(x + h) = f(x) + hf'(x) + \frac{h^2}{2!}f''(x) + \frac{h^3}{3!}f'''(x) + \cdots \qquad (3.1)$$

Solving equation (3.1) for $f'(x)$ yields

$$f'(x) = \frac{f(x + h) - f(x)}{h} - \frac{h}{2}f''(x) - \frac{h^2}{6}f'''(x) + \cdots \qquad (3.2)$$

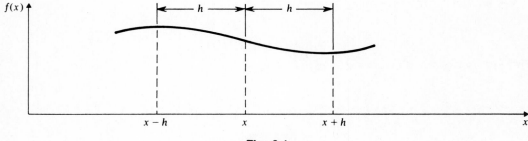

Fig. 3.1

---

*Certain sophisticated digital computer programs have been written which can perform formal, analytical differentiation of a rather wide variety of functions, but this topic is beyond the scope of this book.

Using the notation developed in Chapter 2,

$$f'(x) = \frac{f(x+h) - f(x)}{h} + \mathcal{O}(h) \tag{3.3}$$

In words, equation (3.3) states that we have found an expression for the first derivative of f with respect to x which is accurate to within an error order of h. We shall employ the subscript notation

$$f(x+h) = f_{j+1} \tag{3.4}$$
$$f(x) = f_j \tag{3.5}$$

Using this notation, (3.3) becomes

$$f'(x) = \frac{f_{j+1} - f_j}{h} + \mathcal{O}(h) \tag{3.6}$$

We define the *first forward difference of f at j* as

$$\Delta f_j \equiv f_{j+1} - f_j \tag{3.7}$$

The expression for $f'(x)$ may now be written as

$$f'(x) = \frac{\Delta f_j}{h} + \mathcal{O}(h) \tag{3.8}$$

The term $\Delta f_j/h$ is called a first forward difference approximation of error order h to $f'(x)$. Graphically, the expression $(f_{j+1} - f_j)/h$ approximates the slope of the function f at the point x by the slope of the straight line passing through $f(x+h)$ and $f(x)$.

We now use the Taylor series expansion of $f(x)$ about x to determine $f(x-h)$:

$$f(x-h) = f(x) - hf'(x) + \frac{h^2}{2!}f''(x) - \frac{h^3}{3!}f'''(x) + \cdots \tag{3.9}$$

Solving for $f'(x)$,

$$f'(x) = \frac{f(x) - f(x-h)}{h} + \frac{h}{2}f''(x) - \frac{h^2}{6}f'''(x) + \cdots \tag{3.10}$$

or

$$f'(x) = \frac{f(x) - f(x-h)}{h} + \mathcal{O}(h) \tag{3.11}$$

Using the subscript notation,

$$f'(x) = \frac{f_j - f_{j-1}}{h} + \mathcal{O}(h) \tag{3.12}$$

The *first backward difference of f at j* is defined as

$$\nabla f_j \equiv f_j - f_{j-1} \tag{3.13}$$

so that the expression (3.12) for $f'(x)$ may be written as

$$f'(x) = \frac{\nabla f_j}{h} + \mathcal{O}(h) \tag{3.14}$$

The term $\nabla f_j/h$ is called a first backward difference approximation of error order h to $f'(x)$. The geometric interpretation of the approximation is that of the slope of the straight line connecting $f(x)$ and $f(x-h)$.

Note from the error terms in (3.2) and (3.10) that both the forward and backward difference approximations are exact for straight lines (since the error term does not involve $f'(x)$) but are only approximations for any other function (where $f''(x)$ and higher derivatives are nonzero).

Now that we have obtained both forward and backward difference expressions of $\mathcal{O}(h)$ to the first derivative, we will proceed to find approximations to higher order derivatives. Returning to the forward Taylor series expansion (3.1) for $f(x + h)$,

$$f(x + h) = f(x) + hf'(x) + \frac{h^2}{2}f''(x) + \frac{h^3}{6}f'''(x) + \cdots \qquad (3.15)$$

Performing a similar expansion about x, $f(x + 2h)$ is found as

$$f(x + 2h) = f(x) + 2hf'(x) + 2h^2f''(x) + \frac{4h^3}{3}f'''(x) + \cdots \qquad (3.16)$$

Multiplying equation (3.15) by 2, and subtracting (3.15) from (3.16), the term in $f'(x)$ drops out, and we may solve for $f''(x)$ to yield

$$f''(x) = \frac{f(x + 2h) - 2f(x + h) + f(x)}{h^2} - hf'''(x) + \cdots \qquad (3.17)$$

or, employing the subscript notation,

$$f''(x) = \frac{f_{j+2} - 2f_{j+1} + f_j}{h^2} + \mathcal{O}(h) \qquad (3.18)$$

We have now found an expression for the second derivative of f with respect to x which is accurate to within an error order of h. The *second forward difference of f at j* is defined as

$$\Delta^2 f_j \equiv f_{j+2} - 2f_{j+1} + f_j \qquad (3.19)$$

and we may rewrite (3.18) for $f''(x)$ as

$$f''(x) = \frac{\Delta^2 f_j}{h^2} + \mathcal{O}(h) \qquad (3.20)$$

By using the backward expansion (3.9) to obtain $f(x - h)$ and a similar expansion about x to obtain $f(x - 2h)$, we can find a backward difference expression for $f''(x)$ which is accurate to $\mathcal{O}(h)$:

$$f''(x) = \frac{f_j - 2f_{j-1} + f_{j-2}}{h^2} + \mathcal{O}(h) \qquad (3.21)$$

The *second backward difference of f at j* is defined as

$$\nabla^2 f_j \equiv f_j - 2f_{j-1} + f_{j-2} \qquad (3.22)$$

Equation (3.21) may then be written as

$$f''(x) = \frac{\nabla^2 f_j}{h^2} + \mathcal{O}(h) \qquad (3.23)$$

We may now define the procedures for finding higher forward and backward differences and for approximating higher order derivatives. Any forward or backward difference may be obtained starting from the first forward and backward differences (3.7) and (3.13) by using the following recurrence formulas:

$$\Delta^n f_j = \Delta(\Delta^{n-1} f_j) \tag{3.24}$$

$$\nabla^n f_j = \nabla(\nabla^{n-1} f_j) \tag{3.25}$$

In words, we can find any difference by taking the differences of the next lower differences. For example, the second backward difference of f at j may be found as

$$\nabla^2 f_j = \nabla(\nabla f_j) = \nabla f_j - \nabla f_{j-1} = f_j - f_{j-1} - f_{j-1} + f_{j-2} = f_j - 2f_{j-1} + f_{j-2}$$

Forward and backward difference expressions for derivatives of any order are given by

$$\left.\frac{d^n f}{dx^n}\right|_{x_j} = \frac{\Delta^n f_j}{h^n} + \mathcal{O}(h) \tag{3.26}$$

and

$$\left.\frac{d^n f}{dx^n}\right|_{x_j} = \frac{\nabla^n f_j}{h^n} + \mathcal{O}(h) \tag{3.27}$$

Note that each one of these expressions for the derivatives is of $\mathcal{O}(h)$.

Forward and backward difference expressions of $\mathcal{O}(h)$ are tabulated in Fig. 3.2 for derivatives of up to fourth order. It may be a convenient memory aid to note that the coefficients of the forward difference expressions for the nth derivative starting from j and proceeding forward are given by the coefficients of $(-1)^n(a-b)^n$ in order, while those for the backward difference expressions starting from j and proceeding backward are given by the coefficients of $(a-b)^n$ in order.

	f_j	f_{j+1}	f_{j+2}	f_{j+3}	f_{j+4}	
$hf'(x_j) =$	-1	1				
$h^2 f''(x_j) =$	1	-2	1			$+ \quad \mathcal{O}(h)$
$h^3 f'''(x_j) =$	-1	3	-3	1		
$h^4 f^{iv}(x_j) =$	1	-4	6	-4	1	

(*a*) Forward difference representations

	f_{j-4}	f_{j-3}	f_{j-2}	f_{j-1}	f_j	
$hf'(x_j) =$				-1	1	
$h^2 f''(x_j) =$			1	-2	1	$+ \quad \mathcal{O}(h)$
$h^3 f'''(x_j) =$		-1	3	-3	1	
$h^4 f^{iv}(x_j) =$	1	-4	6	-4	1	

(*b*) Backward difference representations

Fig. 3.2   Forward and backward difference representations of $\mathcal{O}(h)$.

3.2 HIGHER ORDER FORWARD AND BACKWARD DIFFERENCE EXPRESSIONS

The difference expressions for derivatives which we have thus far obtained are of $\mathcal{O}(h)$. More accurate expressions may be found by simply taking more terms in the Taylor series expansion. Consider, for example, the series (3.1) for $f(x + h)$:

$$f(x + h) = f(x) + hf'(x) + \frac{h^2}{2!}f''(x) + \frac{h^3}{3!}f'''(x) + \cdots \tag{3.28}$$

As before, solving for $f'(x)$ yields

$$f'(x) = \frac{f(x + h) - f(x)}{h} - \frac{h}{2}f''(x) - \frac{h^2}{6}f'''(x) + \cdots \tag{3.29}$$

But from equation (3.17) we have a forward difference expression for $f''(x)$ complete with its error term. Substituting this expression into (3.29), we obtain

$$f'(x) = \frac{f(x + h) - f(x)}{h} - \frac{h}{2}\left[\frac{f(x + 2h) - 2f(x + h) + f(x)}{h^2} - hf'''(x) + \cdots\right]$$
$$- \frac{h^2}{6}f'''(x) + \cdots \tag{3.30}$$

Collecting terms,

$$f'(x) = \frac{-f(x + 2h) + 4f(x + h) - 3f(x)}{2h} - \frac{h^2}{3}f'''(x) + \cdots \tag{3.31}$$

or in subscript notation,

$$f'(x) = \frac{-f_{j+2} + 4f_{j+1} - 3f_j}{2h} + \mathcal{O}(h^2) \tag{3.32}$$

We have thus found a forward difference representation for the first derivative which is accurate to $\mathcal{O}(h^2)$. Note also that the expression is exact for a parabola since the error involves only third and higher derivatives. A similar backward difference expression of $\mathcal{O}(h^2)$ could be obtained by using the backward Taylor series expansion for $f(x - h)$ and replacing $f''(x)$ by the backward difference expression of $\mathcal{O}(h)$ from equation (3.21). Forward and backward difference expressions of $\mathcal{O}(h^2)$ for higher derivatives can be obtained by simply replacing the first error term in the $\mathcal{O}(h)$ difference expressions by an $\mathcal{O}(h)$ approximation. Forward and backward difference expressions of $\mathcal{O}(h^2)$ for derivatives of up to fourth order are tabulated in Fig. 3.3.

Higher order forward and backward difference representations, although rarely used in practice, can be obtained by replacing successively more terms in the Taylor series expansions by difference representations of $\mathcal{O}(h)$. However, as each term is replaced, it generates an error term which contributes to the next higher order error term and this must be taken into account when that term is replaced by its difference representation (see Problem 3.2).

	f_j	f_{j+1}	f_{j+2}	f_{j+3}	f_{j+4}	f_{j+5}	
$2hf'(x_j) =$	-3	4	-1				
$h^2 f''(x_j) =$	2	-5	4	-1			$+ \quad \mathcal{O}(h)^2$
$2h^3 f'''(x_j) =$	-5	18	-24	14	-3		
$h^4 f^{iv}(x_j) =$	3	-14	26	-24	11	-2	

(*a*) Forward difference representations

	f_{j-5}	f_{j-4}	f_{j-3}	f_{j-2}	f_{j-1}	f_j	
$2hf'(x_j) =$				1	-4	3	
$h^2 f''(x_j) =$			-1	4	-5	2	$+ \quad \mathcal{O}(h)^2$
$2h^3 f'''(x_j) =$		3	-14	24	-18	5	
$h^4 f^{iv}(x_j) =$	-2	11	-24	26	-14	3	

(*b*) Backward difference representations

Fig. 3.3   Forward and backward difference representations of $\mathcal{O}(h)^2$.

3.3   CENTRAL DIFFERENCES

Consider again the analytic function shown in Fig. 3.1.   The forward and backward Taylor series expansions about x are respectively

$$f(x+h) = f(x) + hf'(x) + \frac{h^2}{2!}f''(x) + \frac{h^3}{3!}f'''(x) + \cdots \tag{3.33}$$

$$f(x-h) = f(x) - hf'(x) + \frac{h^2}{2!}f''(x) - \frac{h^3}{3!}f'''(x) + \cdots \tag{3.34}$$

Subtracting the backward expansion (*3.34*) from the forward expansion (*3.33*), we note that the terms involving even powers of h, such as $(h^2/2!)f''(x)$, cancel, yielding

$$f(x+h) - f(x-h) = 2hf'(x) + \frac{h^3}{3}f'''(x) + \cdots \tag{3.35}$$

or, solving for $f'(x)$,

$$f'(x) = \frac{f(x+h) - f(x-h)}{2h} - \frac{h^2}{6}f'''(x) + \cdots \tag{3.36}$$

or

$$f'(x) = \frac{f(x+h) - f(x-h)}{2h} + \mathcal{O}(h^2) \tag{3.37}$$

Employing subscript notation,

$$f'(x) = \frac{f_{j+1} - f_{j-1}}{2h} + \mathcal{O}(h^2) \qquad (3.38)$$

This difference representation, called a *central difference representation*, is accurate to $\mathcal{O}(h^2)$. Note that the point x itself is not involved, and that from the error term in (3.36), this expression is exact for polynomials of degree 2 (parabolas) and lower. An expression of $\mathcal{O}(h^2)$ for $f''(x)$ is readily obtainable from (3.33) and (3.34) by adding these equations and solving for $f''(x)$ to yield

$$f''(x) = \frac{f_{j+1} - 2f_j + f_{j-1}}{h^2} + \mathcal{O}(h^2) \qquad (3.39)$$

To obtain $f'''(x)$ and $f^{iv}(x)$ requires one additional Taylor series expansion in each direction and some manipulations similar to those carried out to obtain $f'(x)$ and $f''(x)$. The central difference expressions of $\mathcal{O}(h^2)$ for derivatives up to the fourth order are tabulated in Fig. 3.4a. Note that the value of $f(x)(f_j)$ itself is missing from all of the representations for odd derivatives. A convenient memory aid for these central difference expressions of $\mathcal{O}(h^2)$ in terms of ordinary forward and backward differences is given by

$$\frac{d^n f}{dx^n} = \frac{\nabla^n f_{j+n/2} + \Delta^n f_{j-n/2}}{2h^n} + \mathcal{O}(h^2), \qquad n \text{ even} \qquad (3.40)$$

$$\frac{d^n f}{dx^n} = \frac{\nabla^n f_{j+(n-1)/2} + \Delta^n f_{j-(n-1)/2}}{2h^n} + \mathcal{O}(h^2), \qquad n \text{ odd} \qquad (3.41)$$

	f_{j-2}	f_{j-1}	f_j	f_{j+1}	f_{j+2}
$2hf'(x_i) =$		-1	0	1	
$h^2 f''(x_i) =$		1	-2	1	
$2h^3 f'''(x_i) =$	-1	2	0	-2	1
$h^4 f^{iv}(x_i) =$	1	-4	6	-4	1

$+ \quad \mathcal{O}(h)^2$

(a) Representations of $\mathcal{O}(h)^2$

	f_{j-3}	f_{j-2}	f_{j-1}	f_j	f_{j+1}	f_{j+2}	f_{j+3}
$12hf'(x_i) =$		1	-8	0	8	-1	
$12h^2 f''(x_i) =$		-1	16	-30	16	-1	
$8h^3 f'''(x_i) =$	1	-8	13	0	-13	8	-1
$6h^4 f^{iv}(x_i) =$	-1	12	-39	56	-39	12	-1

$+ \quad \mathcal{O}(h)^4$

(b) Representations of $\mathcal{O}(h)^4$

Fig. 3.4 Central difference representations.

   Central difference expressions of $\mathcal{O}(h^4)$ may be obtained by employing many tedious operations with the Taylor series expansions which will not be repeated here.   These expressions for derivatives up to order four are tabulated in Fig. 3.4b.

   It should be noted that a complete operator approach to central differences can also be defined[1],* but this approach seems somewhat artificial and overly complicated for practical purposes.

3.4 DIFFERENCES AND POLYNOMIALS

Difference expressions for derivatives and polynomials have some distinct relationships which can be very useful.   The error term for an nth difference will involve only derivatives of order $n + 1$ or higher.   Thus if we consider a polynomial of order n, the nth difference representation taken anywhere along this polynomial will be constant and exactly equal to the nth derivative regardless of the mesh spacing h (since all of the error terms will be zero).

   This knowledge may be used to get some idea of how well a given polynomial will fit data obtained at a series of equally spaced points on the independent variable.   For example, if the third differences taken at various values of the independent variable are approximately equal and the fourth differences are close to zero, then a cubic should fit the data relatively well.   This will be discussed in more detail in Chapter 4.

   These relationships between difference expressions and polynomials may be used in an inverse fashion to find difference expressions from polynomials.   For example, the forward difference expression for $f'(x)$ of $\mathcal{O}(h^2)$ should be exact for a parabola since the first error term involves $f'''(x)$.   Thus we should be able to find this difference expression by fitting the parabola

$$f(x) = Ax^2 + Bx + C \tag{3.42}$$

to the points $x = 0$, h, $2h$ (these points may be chosen without loss of generality; why?) and then evaluating $f'(0)$:

$$f'(x) = 2Ax + B \tag{3.43}$$

$$f'(0) = B \tag{3.44}$$

Fitting the parabola to the three points gives

$$f_j = C \tag{3.45}$$

$$f_{j+1} = Ah^2 + Bh + C \tag{3.46}$$

$$f_{j+2} = 4Ah^2 + 2Bh + C \tag{3.47}$$

Solving for B yields

$$f'(0) = B = \frac{-f_{j+2} + 4f_{j+1} - 3f_j}{2h} \tag{3.48}$$

which is identical to the forward difference expression (3.32).   This polynomial approach can be particularly worthwhile in finding difference expressions for nonuniform values of h (see Problem 3.3).

---

*Numbers in brackets designate References at end of book.

Illustrative Problems

3.1   Find the fifth backward difference representation which is of $\mathcal{O}(h)$.

From the recurrence scheme for differences, the fifth backward difference can be expressed as

$$\nabla^5 f_j = \nabla(\nabla^4 f_j)$$
$$= f_j - 4f_{j-1} + 6f_{j-2} - 4f_{j-3} + f_{j-4} - (f_{j-1} - 4f_{j-2} + 6f_{j-3} - 4f_{j-4} + f_{j-5})$$
$$= f_j - 5f_{j-1} + 10f_{j-2} - 10f_{j-3} + 5f_{j-4} - f_{j-5}$$

and

$$\frac{d^5 f}{dx^5} = \frac{\nabla^5 f_j}{h^5} + \mathcal{O}(h)$$

3.2   Find a forward difference representation for df/dx which is of $\mathcal{O}(h^3)$.

The Taylor series expansion for $f(x + h)$ is

$$f(x + h) = f(x) + hf'(x) + \frac{h^2}{2}f''(x) + \frac{h^3}{6}f'''(x) + \frac{h^4}{24}f^{iv}(x) + \cdots$$

Now we represent $f''(x)$ and $f'''(x)$ by difference expressions accurate to $\mathcal{O}(h)$. Since the error in the representation for $f''(x)$ will contribute to the $f'''(x)$ term, we need to know the first error term in the $f''(x)$ representation. This is obtained from equation (*3.17*), which gives

$$f''(x) = \frac{f(x + 2h) - 2f(x + h) + f(x)}{h^2} - hf'''(x) + \mathcal{O}(h^2)$$

Substituting this in the expression for $f(x + h)$, and collecting coefficients of $f'''(x)$, yields

$$f(x + h) = f(x) + hf'(x) + \frac{h^2}{2}\left[\frac{f(x + 2h) - 2f(x + h) + f(x)}{h^2}\right] - \frac{h^3}{3}f'''(x) + \mathcal{O}(h^4)$$

The forward difference representation of $f'''(x)$ from Fig. 3.2*a* is

$$f'''(x) = \frac{f(x + 3h) - 3f(x + 2h) + 3f(x + h) - f(x)}{h^3} + \mathcal{O}(h)$$

Since no more derivatives are to be represented, the leading error term in the $f'''(x)$ representation is not needed.   Substituting for $f'''(x)$,

$$f(x + h) = f(x) + hf'(x) + \frac{h^2}{2}\left[\frac{f(x + 2h) - 2f(x + h) + f(x)}{h^2}\right]$$
$$- \frac{h^3}{3}\left[\frac{f(x + 3h) - 3f(x + 2h) + 3f(x + h) - f(x)}{h^3}\right] + \mathcal{O}(h^4)$$

Note that the $\mathcal{O}(h^4)$ term now has a contribution from the representation of $f'''(x)$.   Solving for $f'(x)$ and collecting terms yields

$$f'(x) = \frac{2f_{j+3} - 9f_{j+2} + 18f_{j+1} - 11f_j}{6h} + \mathcal{O}(h^3)$$

3.3 Given the function tabulated at the points j, $j+1$, and $j+2$ shown in Fig. 3.5, find a three-point difference representation for f'_j.

We pass the parabola $f(x) = Ax^2 + Bx + C$ through the points $x_j = 0$, $x_{j+1} = h$, $x_{j+2} = 3h$ and solve for $f'(0)$:

$$f_j = C$$

$$f_{j+1} = Ah^2 + Bh + C$$

$$f_{j+2} = 9Ah^2 + 3Bh + C$$

Now $f'(0) = B$, so solving for B yields

$$f'(0) = \frac{-8f_j + 9f_{j+1} - f_{j+2}}{6h}$$

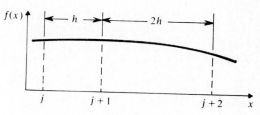

Fig. 3.5

3.4 Find a central difference representation of $\mathcal{O}(h^2)$ for d^5f/dx^5.

From Problem 3.1,

$$\nabla^5 f_j = f_j - 5f_{j-1} + 10f_{j-2} - 10f_{j-3} + 5f_{j-4} - f_{j-5}$$

$\Delta^5 f_j$ can be found in a similar manner as

$$\Delta^5 f_j = \Delta(\Delta^4 f_j)$$
$$= f_{j+5} - 4f_{j+4} + 6f_{j+3} - 4f_{j+2} + f_{j+1} - [f_{j+4} - 4f_{j+3} + 6f_{j+2} - 4f_{j+1} + f_j]$$
$$= f_{j+5} - 5f_{j+4} + 10f_{j+3} - 10f_{j+2} + 5f_{j+1} - f_j$$

Applying equation (3.41) directly:

$$\frac{d^5f}{dx^5} = \frac{\nabla^5 f_{j+2} + \Delta^5 f_{j-2}}{2h^5} + \mathcal{O}(h^2)$$

or

$$\frac{d^5f}{dx^5} = \{f_{j+2} - 5f_{j+1} + 10f_j - 10f_{j-1} + 5f_{j-2} - f_{j-3}$$
$$+ [f_{j+3} - 5f_{j+2} + 10f_{j+1} - 10f_j + 5f_{j-1} - f_{j-2}]\}/2h^5 + \mathcal{O}(h^2)$$
$$= \frac{f_{j+3} - 4f_{j+2} + 5f_{j+1} - 5f_{j-1} + 4f_{j-2} - f_{j-3}}{2h^5} + \mathcal{O}(h^2)$$

3.5 Given the following equally spaced data:

x	0	1	2	3	4
$f(x)$	30	33	28	12	-22

Find $f'(0)$, $f'(2)$, $f'(4)$, and $f''(0)$ using difference representations which are of $\mathcal{O}(h)^2$.

At $x = 0$, a forward difference representation must be used since no points are available in the backward direction:

$$f'(0) = \frac{-f(2) + 4f(1) - 3f(0)}{2(1)} + \mathcal{O}(1)^2$$

$$f'(0) = \frac{-28 + 4(33) - 3(30)}{2} = 7 \text{ to } \mathcal{O}(1)^2$$

At $x = 2$, we have a choice of several representations. We arbitrarily select a central difference representation of $\mathcal{O}(h)^2$:

$$f'(2) = \frac{f(3) - f(1)}{2} + \mathcal{O}(1)^2$$

$$f'(2) = \frac{12 - 33}{2} = -10.5 \text{ to } \mathcal{O}(1)^2$$

At $x = 4$, a backward difference representation must be employed:

$$f'(4) = \frac{3f(4) - 4f(3) + f(2)}{2(1)} + \mathcal{O}(1)^2$$

$$f'(4) = \frac{3(-22) - 4(12) + 28}{2} = -43 \text{ to } \mathcal{O}(1)^2$$

3.6   The following data represent a polynomial. Of what degree? What is the coefficient of the highest degree term?

x	0	1	2	3	4	5
$f(x)$	1	0.5	8.0	35.5	95.0	198.5

We will take forward differences at each point (backward differences could be used as well).

First differences:

$$\Delta f_0 = f_1 - f_0 = 0.5 - 1 = -0.5$$

$$\Delta f_1 = f_2 - f_1 = 8.0 - 0.5 = 7.5$$

$$\Delta f_2 = f_3 - f_2 = 35.5 - 8.0 = 27.5$$

$$\Delta f_3 = f_4 - f_3 = 95.0 - 35.5 = 59.5$$

$$\Delta f_4 = f_5 - f_4 = 198.5 - 95 = 103.5$$

Second differences:

$$\Delta^2 f_0 = \Delta f_1 - \Delta f_0 = 7.5 - (-0.5) = 8.0$$

$$\Delta^2 f_1 = \Delta f_2 - \Delta f_1 = 27.5 - 7.5 = 20.0$$

$$\Delta^2 f_2 = \Delta f_3 - \Delta f_2 = 59.5 - 27.5 = 32.0$$

$$\Delta^2 f_3 = \Delta f_4 - \Delta f_3 = 103.5 - 59.5 = 44.0$$

Third differences:

$$\Delta^3 f_0 = \Delta^2 f_1 - \Delta^2 f_0 = 20.0 - 8.0 = 12.0$$

$$\Delta^3 f_1 = \Delta^2 f_2 = \Delta^2 f_1 = 32.0 - 20.0 = 12.0$$

$$\Delta^3 f_2 = \Delta^2 f_3 - \Delta^2 f_2 = 44.0 - 32.0 = 12.0$$

Since the third differences are constant, the polynomial is of third degree.   The forward finite difference representation of the third derivative is, in general,

$$\frac{d^3 f}{dx^3} = \frac{\Delta^3 f}{h^3} + \mathcal{O}(h)$$

For a third degree polynomial, however, this expression is exact, so

$$\frac{d^3 f}{dx^3} = \frac{\Delta^3 f}{h^3} = \frac{12}{1} = 12$$

Integrating,

$$\frac{d^2 f}{dx^2} = 12x + C_1$$

$$\frac{df}{dx} = 6x^2 + C_1 x + C_2$$

$$f = 2x^3 + C_1 \frac{x^2}{2} + C_2 x + C_3$$

So the coefficient of the highest order term is 2.

3.7   The following function represents physical data taken at equally spaced intervals:

x	0	0.5	1.0	1.5	2.0	2.5	3.0
$f(x)$	1.00	0.80	0.20	0.25	0.31	0.38	0.44

Find $f'(1.5)$ to $\mathcal{O}(0.5)^2$.

In Problem 3.5 we simply chose forward, central, or backward difference expressions for the derivatives, depending on whether we were near the beginning, center, or end of the table.   In practice, this approach is often too naive, depending on the behavior of the function.   Plotting $f(x)$ for the present problem, we obtain the curve in Fig. 3.6.

We wish to find $f'(1.5)$ to $\mathcal{O}(h)^2$, which means a three-point representation will be needed.   A three-point backward representation would require $f(1.5)$, $f(1.0)$, and $f(0.5)$.   The value of $f(0.5)$ would obviously influence the answer in such a way as to give an incorrect result, and the use of $f(1.0)$ would also appear undesirable since there is apparently a drastic change in the behavior of $f(x)$ occurring very close to $x = 1.0$, and the behavior at $x = 1.0$ could be quite uncertain.   We must therefore reject a backward difference representation.   A central difference representation of $f'(1.5)$ would involve $f(1.0)$, which is undesirable for the reasons discussed before.   A forward difference representation would

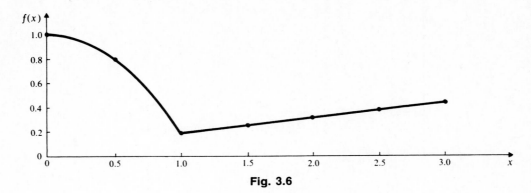

Fig. 3.6

involve $f(1.5)$, $f(2.0)$, and $f(2.5)$. Over this region the function is smooth and well behaved, so we choose this representation:

$$f'(1.5) = \frac{-f(2.5) + 4f(2.0) - 3f(1.5)}{2(0.5)^2} + \mathcal{O}(0.5)^2$$

$$f'(1.5) = \frac{-0.38 + 4(0.31) - 3(0.25)}{2(0.25)} = 0.22 \text{ to } \mathcal{O}(0.5)^2$$

3.8   Consider the function $f(x) = \sin 10\pi x$. Find $f'(0)$ using forward difference representations of $\mathcal{O}(h)$ and $\mathcal{O}(h)^2$ with $h = 0.2$. Compare these results with each other and with the exact analytical answer. Discuss the implications of these results.

The exact solution is

$$f'(x) = \frac{d}{dx}(\sin 10\pi x) = 10\pi \cos 10\pi x$$

$$f'(0) = 10\pi = 31.41593$$

Using $h = 0.2$, the forward difference representation for $f'(0)$ of $\mathcal{O}(h)$ is

$$f'(0) = \frac{f(0.2) - f(0)}{0.2} + \mathcal{O}(0.2) = \frac{\sin 10\pi(0.2) - \sin 10\pi(0)}{0.2} + \mathcal{O}(0.2)$$

$$f'(0) = \frac{\sin 2\pi - 0}{0.2} = 0 \text{ to } \mathcal{O}(0.2)$$

The forward difference representation for $f'(0)$ of $\mathcal{O}(h)^2$ is

$$f'(0) = \frac{-f(0.4) + 4f(0.2) - 3f(0)}{2(0.2)} + \mathcal{O}(0.2)^2$$

$$= \frac{-\sin 10\pi(0.4) + 4\sin 10\pi(0.2) - 3\sin 10\pi(0)}{2(0.2)} + \mathcal{O}(0.2)^2$$

$$= \frac{-\sin (4\pi) + 4\sin (2\pi) - 3\sin (0)}{2(0.2)} + \mathcal{O}(0.2)^2 = 0 \text{ to } \mathcal{O}(0.2)^2$$

It should be apparent that no matter what difference representation is chosen, the result will be zero, since the function will always be evaluated at intervals of 2π in its argument. Thus $h = 0.2$ is a very bad choice for a mesh size for this problem since it spans one complete period of the function as shown in Fig. 3.7.

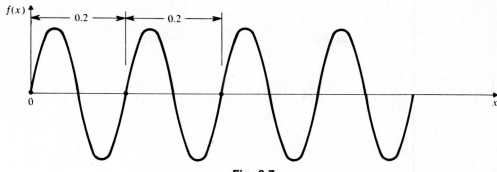

Fig. 3.7

In order to obtain a meaningful answer for a finite difference representation of $f'(0)$ it would be necessary to use a much smaller h, perhaps on the order of $h = 0.01$ or smaller.   It should be evident that the choice of a mesh size in numerically differentiating a function should be made only after careful examination of the behavior of the function.

3.9   Consider the function

x	0	1	2
$f(x)$	0	0.7071	1.0000

Find $f'(0)$ by using a forward difference representation of $\mathcal{O}(h)$ with $h = 1$ and $h = 2$.   Extrapolate these results to $h = 0$ and compare with the answer obtained by using a forward difference representation of $\mathcal{O}(h)^2$ with $h = 1$.

The representation of $\mathcal{O}(h)$ yields

$$f'(0) = \frac{f(2) - f(0)}{2} = \frac{1 - 0}{2} = 0.5 \text{ to } \mathcal{O}(2)$$

$$f'(0) = \frac{f(1) - f(0)}{1} = \frac{0.7071 - 0}{1} = 0.7071 \text{ to } \mathcal{O}(1)$$

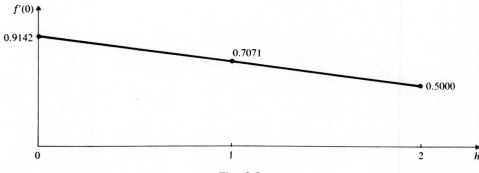

Fig. 3.8

Linear extrapolation to $h = 0$ yields (Fig. 3.8)

$$f'(0) \approx 0.7071 + (0.7071 - 0.5000) = 0.9142$$

Using a representation of $\mathcal{O}(h)^2$ with $h = 1$ yields

$$f'(0) = \frac{-f(2) + 4f(1) - 3f(0)}{2(1)} + \mathcal{O}(1)^2$$

$$f'(0) = \frac{-1.0000 + 4(0.7071)}{2} = 0.9142 \text{ to } \mathcal{O}(1)^2$$

Thus linear extrapolation to $h = 0$ of results obtained using representations of $\mathcal{O}(h)$ and $\mathcal{O}(2h)$ yields an answer which is accurate to $\mathcal{O}(h)^2$. This conclusion is true in general and can be very useful in certain circumstances as we shall see in later chapters.

3.10 Given the function $f(x) = x^{1/2} + 7x$, find $f'(0)$ by numerically differentiating the function. Use a difference representation of $\mathcal{O}(h)^3$ with $h = 1$.

A numerical answer will not be given. While we could readily carry out the numerical differentiation, the result would be meaningless as an approximation to $f'(0)$. Differentiating the function analytically,

$$f'(x) = \frac{1}{2}x^{-1/2} + 7$$

Hence $f'(0)$ is infinite. The only way in which we might recognize the true character of $f'(0)$ would be by taking the difference representation for a number of different values of h, each one smaller than the one before. We would find that the result would be larger each time h was reduced, and would not approach a limit. If there is doubt about the character of a function at the point of interest, this approach can be very valuable. It also provides the best way to decide if the chosen mesh size for a given problem is sufficiently small. (See the next problem.)

3.11 Given $f(x) = \sin x$. Find $f'(1)$ by using a central difference representation of $\mathcal{O}(h)^2$ with $h = 0.2$. Is this a sufficiently small mesh size for this problem?

It should immediately be apparent that the problem statement is ambiguous. What is meant by "sufficiently small"? Let us arbitrarily decide that we would like the result to be accurate to two decimal places. The central difference with $h = 0.2$ is

$$f'(1) = \frac{\sin(1.2) - \sin(0.8)}{2(0.2)} + \mathcal{O}(0.2)^2$$

$$f'(1) = \frac{0.932039 - 0.717356}{0.4} = 0.53671 + \mathcal{O}(0.2)^2$$

Now we must decide if the value of h chosen is sufficiently small. We have no way of knowing how good this result is since there is nothing to compare it with (presuming for the moment that we do not know how to differentiate $\sin x$ analytically). Thus we take another difference representation using $h = 0.1$, one-half of its previous value:

$$f'(1) = \frac{\sin(1.1) - \sin(0.9)}{2(0.1)} + \mathcal{O}(0.1)^2$$

$$f(1) = \frac{0.891207 - 0.783327}{0.2} = 0.53940 \text{ to } \mathcal{O}(0.1)^2$$

The change in the answer was approximately 3 in the third decimal place. To be sure of our answer to two digits, it would be safest to cut the mesh in half once more and examine the change. Using $h = 0.05$,

$$f'(1) = \frac{\sin(1.05) - \sin(0.95)}{2(0.05)} + \mathcal{O}(0.05)^2$$

$$f'(1) = \frac{0.867423 - 0.813416}{0.1} = 0.54007 + \mathcal{O}(0.05)^2$$

The change this time was only about 6 in the fourth decimal place and it would appear we can have confidence in the first two significant digits. (The exact answer is $\cos(1) = 0.54030$.) So while the original mesh size gave the answer correct to two places when rounded off, we could not be sure of this without also obtaining results for two smaller mesh sizes.

3.12 Evaluate the accuracy gained by using a central difference representation of $\mathcal{O}(h)^2$ as compared to a forward difference representation of $\mathcal{O}(h)$ in evaluating $(d/dx)(e^x)$ at $x = 1$. Use $h = 0.1$.

The forward difference representation is

$$f'(1) = \frac{e^{1.1} - e^{1.0}}{0.1} + \mathcal{O}(0.1) = \frac{3.004166 - 2.718282}{0.1} + \mathcal{O}(0.1)$$

$$= 2.85884 \text{ to } \mathcal{O}(0.1)$$

The central difference representation is

$$f'(1) = \frac{e^{1.1} - e^{0.9}}{2(0.1)} + \mathcal{O}(0.1)^2 = \frac{3.004166 - 2.459603}{0.2} + \mathcal{O}(0.1)^2$$

$$= 2.72282 \text{ to } \mathcal{O}(0.1)^2$$

The exact answer is, of course, $e^1 = 2.718282$. The error in the forward difference representation is

$$2.85884 - 2.71828 = 0.14056, \quad \text{or } 5.15\%$$

The error in the central difference representation with the same mesh size is

$$2.72282 - 2.71828 = 0.00454, \quad \text{or } 0.17\%$$

The very large gain in accuracy of the central difference representation over the simple forward difference representation is apparent.

3.13 Compare the central difference result of the preceding problem with a forward difference representation of $\mathcal{O}(h)^2$ with $h = 0.1$.

The forward difference representation of $\mathcal{O}(h)^2$ is

$$f'(1) = \frac{-e^{1.2} + 4e^{1.1} - 3e^{1.0}}{2(0.1)} + \mathcal{O}(0.1)^2$$

$$= \frac{-3.320117 + 4(3.004166) - 3(2.718282)}{0.2} + \mathcal{O}(0.1)^2$$

$$= 2.70855 \text{ to } \mathcal{O}(0.1)^2$$

The error is

$$2.70855 - 2.71828 = -0.00973, \quad \text{or } 0.36\%$$

The central difference representation of $\mathcal{O}(h)^2$ had an error of 0.17% so it is still the most accurate for this function, but the errors of the two $\mathcal{O}(h)^2$ representations are quite comparable.

3.14 Given the function $f(x) = \tan 40x$. Find $f'(0.175)$ using a backward difference representation of $\mathcal{O}(h)$ with $h = 0.075$.

$$f'(0.175) = \frac{f(0.175) - f(0.100)}{0.075} + \mathcal{O}(0.075) = \frac{\tan(7.000) - \tan(4.000)}{0.075} + \mathcal{O}(0.075)$$

$$f'(0.175) = \frac{0.87145 - 1.15782}{0.075} = -3.81831 \text{ to } \mathcal{O}(0.075)$$

The only problem with this result is that it is absolute nonsense.

Examining a plot of $\tan 40x$ near $x = 0.175$ (Fig. 3.9), we find that the differencing has spanned a discontinuity in $f(x)$, and the answer even has the wrong sign! As in Problem 3.8, the moral is to be aware of the character of the function before blindly using difference representations.

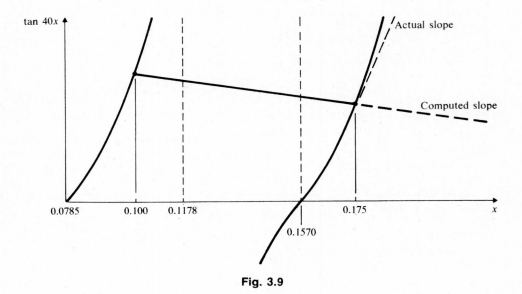

Fig. 3.9

3.15 When attempting to perform numerical operations with experimental data, one of the main concerns is the effect of the inevitable errors or noise in such data on the result. Consider the numerical differentiation of equally spaced experimental data when this error is of two very simple types: (a) a constant error, ϵ, in the data at each point, and (b) an error alternating in sign but constant in magnitude, e.g. $-\epsilon$ at one point, $+\epsilon$ at the next, $-\epsilon$ at the next, etc. Find the effect of such errors in the data on numerical differentiation. Consider examples of both low and high order derivatives.

A constant error ϵ (type a) will cancel out of all difference expressions for derivatives since the sum of the coefficients of all terms in any difference expression is zero.   For example,

$$f'(x_j) = \frac{-(f_{j+2}+\epsilon)+4(f_{j+1}+\epsilon)-3(f_j+\epsilon)}{2h} + \mathcal{O}(h)^2 = \frac{-f_{j+2}+4f_{j+1}-3f_j}{2h} + \mathcal{O}(h)^2$$

(Here we have denoted the "true" value of the function as f.)   This result would hold for any difference expression of any order.   Thus error of this type causes no problem.   If the error is alternating (type b), then the effect is entirely different.   Consider

$$f'(x_j) = \frac{-(f_{j+2}-\epsilon)+4(f_{j+1}+\epsilon)-3(f_j-\epsilon)}{2h} + \mathcal{O}(h)^2 = \frac{-f_{j+2}+4f_{j+1}-3f_j}{2h} + \frac{4\epsilon}{h} + \mathcal{O}(h)^2$$

Here the error is additive.   Consider the third derivative representation of the same order:

$$f'''(x_j) = \frac{-3(f_{j+4}-\epsilon)+14(f_{j+3}+\epsilon)-24(f_{j+2}-\epsilon)+18(f_{j+1}+\epsilon)-5(f_j-\epsilon)}{2h^3} + \mathcal{O}(h)^2$$

$$= \frac{-3f_{j+4}+14f_{j+3}-24f_{j+2}+18f_{j+1}-5f_j}{2h^3} + \frac{32\epsilon}{h^2} + \mathcal{O}(h)^2$$

The error in this representation is much higher.   This type of error is thus not only harmful, but also causes increasing difficulty when attempting to make difference representations of higher order derivatives.   This type of error also causes more difficulty with difference representations of high error order for a given derivative than with those of lower order, since the higher error order representations have more and larger coefficients.

3.16   In the course of performing many numerical calculations, roundoff error will inevitably occur.   This error tends to be quite random in nature.   What effect might this have on numerical differentiation?

Random error will obviously not always have the same sign, and tends to act more like the alternating error (type b) discussed in Problem 3.15.   Thus there is a tendency for the roundoff error to accumulate in a difference expression rather than to cancel.   In addition, the effect can be even more serious for representations of higher order derivatives as discussed in Problem 3.15.

Problems

3.17   Find a forward difference expression of $\mathcal{O}(h)$ for d^6f/dx^6.

3.18   Find a forward difference expression for $f'(x)$ which is of $\mathcal{O}(h)^3$ by fitting a cubic to four equally spaced points.   This expression should be the same as that obtained in Problem 3.2.

3.19   Given a function f defined at three unevenly spaced points x_j, x_{j+1}, and x_{j+2}.   The spacing of these points is such that $x_{j+1} = x_j + \theta h$, where θ is any positive number, and $x_{j+2} = x_{j+1} + h$.   Find a three-point difference representation for $f''(x_{j+1})$.

*3.20 Write a computer program to find the first derivative of $\sin x$ at $x = 5\pi/8$ using forward and backward difference representations of $\mathcal{O}(h)$ and $\mathcal{O}(h)^2$ and central difference representations of $\mathcal{O}(h)^2$ and $\mathcal{O}(h)^4$. Use $h = \pi/10$ and $h = \pi/20$. Compare the results with each other and with the exact answer.

3.21 The following tabulated function represents points on a polynomial. What is the degree of the polynomial?

x	0	1	2	3	4	5	6	7
$f(x)$	0	-2	-8	0	64	250	648	1372

*3.22 Given the function $f(x) = (\sin x)^{e^x}$. Write a computer program to find $f'(1)$ using a central difference representation of $\mathcal{O}(h)^2$. Begin with $h = 0.2$ and reduce the mesh size by a factor of 2 for each calculation until the third decimal place in the result does not change on successive calculations.

3.23 Suggest a reasonable mesh size (or sizes) for the numerical differentiation of the function $f(x) = \sin(x/100)$. Justify your selection.

3.24 For a function $f(x)$ at a point x_j, $\Delta f_j/h = 0.23751$ and $\nabla f_j/h = 0.24369$ with $h = 0.1$. Find the numerical values of the central difference representations of $\mathcal{O}(h)^2$ for $f'(x_j)$ and $f''(x_j)$.

3.25 For any given difference representation of a derivative, the coefficients must add to zero. Why?

3.26 A typical "biased" difference representation for $f'(x_j)$ might be $(\frac{1}{3}\nabla f_j + \frac{2}{3}\Delta f_j)/h$. Evaluate the first error term (not the error order) in this difference representation and compare with the first error term of a central difference representation using the same points.

3.27 Compare the actual error made by using the biased difference representation of Problem 3.26 with that of the central difference representation of $\mathcal{O}(h)^2$ in evaluating $d(\sin x)/dx$ at $x = \pi/3$. Use $h = 0.1$.

3.28 Averaging the forward and backward difference representations for $f'(x_j)$ of $\mathcal{O}(h)$ results in the central difference representation of $\mathcal{O}(h)^2$. What error order results if the forward and backward difference representations for $f'(x_j)$ of $\mathcal{O}(h)^2$ are averaged? (Note that it will be necessary to know or find at least the first error term in each of these representations.)

---

*In this chapter and all subsequent chapters the asterisk indicates problems for which a computer solution is recommended.

Chapter 4

Interpolation and Extrapolation

4.0 INTRODUCTION

Often scientific experimentation or numerical computation results in values for a function only at discrete points along the independent variable for that function.   Such a function is shown in Fig. 4.1.   These values of $f(x)$ may be spaced either evenly or unevenly along x.   In this chapter we shall discuss methods for finding the value of $f(x)$ between the tabulated points (interpolation) or outside the range in x of the tabulated points (extrapolation).   This chapter also serves as an introduction to the concept of functional approximation.   A more detailed treatment of functional approximation is reserved for Chapter 7.

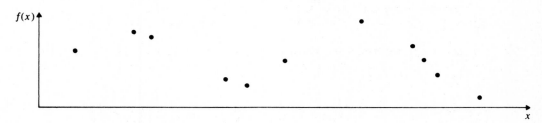

Fig. 4.1

4.1 GENERATION OF DIFFERENCE TABLES

We begin by considering data which are tabulated at evenly spaced intervals in x.   Consider, for example, Table 4.1.

Table 4.1

x	0	1	2	3	4	5
$f(x)$	-7	-3	6	25	62	129

A *forward difference table* can be generated by taking forward differences at each point in x, then taking differences of the differences, etc. A forward difference table generated from Table 4.1 would be Table 4.2. Note that the lower half of the table cannot be filled in since one entry is lost in each column every time a new set of differences is taken.

Table 4.2

x	$f(x)$	Δf	$\Delta^2 f$	$\Delta^3 f$	$\Delta^4 f$	$\Delta^5 f$
0	−7	4	5	5	3	1
1	−3	9	10	8	4	
2	6	19	18	12		
3	25	37	30			
4	62	67				
5	129					

In a similar manner, a backward difference table can be generated by taking backward differences at each point in x, then taking differences of the differences, etc. The result is Table 4.3. Note that the lower half of the table has been filled. The entries in the backward difference Table 4.3 are the same as those in the forward difference Table 4.2 except that they appear on different lines.

Table 4.3

x	$f(x)$	∇f	$\nabla^2 f$	$\nabla^3 f$	$\nabla^4 f$	$\nabla^5 f$
0	−7					
1	−3	4				
2	6	9	5			
3	25	19	10	5		
4	62	37	18	8	3	
5	129	67	30	12	4	1

A central difference table can be generated in a very similar fashion following a purely mechanical scheme. We leave a space between each line of data, and define the lines containing the original data as *full lines* and the lines between the full lines as *half lines*. We then take differences as in the forward and backward difference tables, but alternate the entries between half lines and full lines. The central difference operator δ is convenient to use in this context. The definition of the operator is

$$\delta f_{j+1/2} = f_{j+1} - f_j \tag{4.1}$$

Note also that

$$\delta(\delta^n f) = \delta^{n+1} f \tag{4.2}$$

The central difference table is Table 4.4.

Table 4.4

x	$f(x)$	δf	$\delta^2 f$	$\delta^3 f$	$\delta^4 f$	$\delta^5 f$
0	−7					
		4				
1	−3		5			
		9		5		
2	6		10		3	
		19		8		1
3	25		18		4	
		37		12		
4	62		30			
		67				
5	129					

We now fill in the gaps in the table by taking the arithmetic mean of the values above and below each gap. This results in Table 4.5.

Table 4.5

x	$f(x)$	δf	$\delta^2 f$	$\delta^3 f$	$\delta^4 f$	$\delta^5 f$
0	−7					
0.5	−5	4				
1	−3	6.5	5			
1.5	1.5	9	7.5	5		
2	6	14	10	6.5	3	
2.5	15.5	19	14	8	3.5	1
3	25	28	18	10	4	
3.5	43.5	37	24	12		
4	62	52	30			
4.5	95.5	67				
5	129					

It is worth noting that the difference Tables 4.2, 4.3, and 4.5 show that a polynomial would fit the data points fairly well since successively higher differences became smaller in magnitude.

It is possible to fill out the empty regions in any of the tables by assuming that the function is a polynomial. This will be discussed in detail in Sec. 4.2 in connection with interpolation.

4.2 GREGORY-NEWTON INTERPOLATION FORMULAS

We are now ready to consider methods of using a tabulated function and the difference tables to find values of the function between the tabulated points. Although the function is known only at the discrete tabulated points, we begin by *assuming* that the function is analytic over the entire range of interest. This is helpful in the development, and in any case, if "good" values are to be obtained for the function between the tabulated values, then the actual function represented by the discrete points should be reasonably smooth and well behaved.   If the function is analytic, then it should be possible to find the value $f(x)$ at any point between the tabulated points by using the Taylor series expansion of $f(x)$ about one of the tabulated points.   We arbitrarily designate this point at $x = 0$.   For the present, the discussion is restricted to evenly spaced points.   The function might appear as shown in Fig. 4.2.

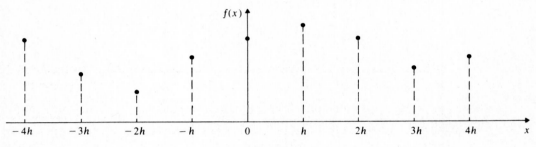

Fig. 4.2

The Taylor series expansion about $x = 0$ is

$$f(x) = f(0) + xf'(0) + \frac{x^2}{2!}f''(0) + \frac{x^3}{3!}f'''(0) + \cdots \qquad (4.3)$$

None of the values for the derivatives are known, but difference expressions are available for these derivatives as obtained in Chapter 3.   For example,

$$f'(0) = \frac{\Delta f_0}{h} - \frac{h}{2}f''(0) + \mathcal{O}(h^2) \qquad (4.4)$$

Substituting the difference representations for each one of the derivatives and keeping careful account of all of the error terms, (4.3) becomes

$$f(x) = f(0) + \frac{x}{h}\Delta f_0 + \frac{x(x-h)}{2!h^2}\Delta^2 f_0 + \frac{x(x-h)(x-2h)}{3!h^3}\Delta^3 f_0 + \cdots \qquad (4.5)$$

The remaining terms can be readily obtained by induction.   This formula is called the *Gregory-Newton forward interpolation formula*.   The differences are of course obtained from the forward difference table.   The x axis in the difference table can be shifted so that any desired point corresponds to $x = 0$.

An entirely similar formula may be found for backward differences as

$$f(x) = f(0) + \frac{x}{h}\nabla f_0 + \frac{x(x+h)}{2!h^2}\nabla^2 f_0 + \frac{x(x+h)(x-2h)}{3!h^3}\nabla^3 f_0 + \cdots \qquad (4.6)$$

This is the *Gregory-Newton backward interpolation formula*, which may be carried out by induction to as many terms as are needed.

The point chosen as $x = 0$ is called the *base line* in the difference table.   It is a widespread practice, which we shall follow, to eliminate h from the interpolation formulas by rescaling the independent variable x so that the spacing between lines in the table is 1 unit.   The variable x will be positive if below the base line in the table and negative if above the base line.

Employing the rescaled x, equations (4.5) and (4.6) become

Gregory-Newton forward formula:

$$f(x) = f(0) + x(\Delta f_0) + \frac{x(x-1)}{2!}\Delta^2 f_0 + \frac{x(x-1)(x-2)}{3!}\Delta^3 f_0 + \cdots \qquad (4.7)$$

Gregory-Newton backward formula:

$$f(x) = f(0) + x(\nabla f_0) + \frac{x(x+1)}{2!}\nabla^2 f_0 + \frac{x(x+1)(x+2)}{3!}\nabla^3 f_0 + \cdots \qquad (4.8)$$

We can now use these formulas together with the difference tables discussed in Sec. 4.1 to interpolate for intermediate values of $f(x)$.   The best accuracy will in general be obtained if the base line in the table has a relatively large number of entries (since more terms of the interpolation formulas can be used) and if x is less than 1 in magnitude (since each succeeding term in the series will tend to decrease more rapidly in magnitude).   The usual rule of thumb employed in interpolation is to pick the base line as the line in the table closest to the point of interest, thus resulting in the smallest value (in magnitude) of x.   In order to ensure a reasonably large number of entries in the base line of the table, we will usually want to use forward differences if near the top of the table and backward differences if near the bottom.   Interpolation near the center of the table is best achieved with central differences for several reasons which will be discussed in the next section.

Referring to the difference tables generated in Sec. 4.1, we shall present examples of interpolation and draw some general conclusions.   Suppose that we wish to find $f(1.1)$ for the following tabulated function:

x	0	1	2	3	4	5
$f(x)$	-7	-3	6	25	62	129

The forward and backward difference tables resulting from this function were given as Tables 4.2 and 4.3 respectively.   Note that since $x = 1.1$ is near the top of the table, there are many more entries in the forward difference Table 4.2 near this point.   Accordingly, we choose the Gregory-Newton forward formula (4.7).   We select $x = 1$ as the base line (shown as shaded in Table 4.6) and shift the origin in the forward difference table to this line.   The result is Table 4.6.

We now wish to find $f(0.1)$ in this table, since this was $f(1.1)$ before the origin was shifted.   The spacing between lines of the table is 1, so no rescaling is necessary.

Formula (4.7) becomes

$$f(x) = (-3) + x(9) + \frac{x(x-1)}{2!}(10) + \frac{x(x-1)(x-2)}{3!}(8)$$

$$+ \frac{x(x-1)(x-2)(x-3)}{4!}(4) \qquad (4.9)$$

Table 4.6

Old x	New x	$f(x)$	Δf	$\Delta^2 f$	$\Delta^3 f$	$\Delta^4 f$	$\Delta^5 f$
0	−1	−7	4	5	5	3	1
1	0	−3	9	10	8	4	
2	1	6	19	18	12		
3	2	25	37	30			
4	3	62	67				
5	4	129					

The series must stop at this point since there are no more entries in the base line of the table. Thus (*4.9*) is actually a polynomial of degree four rather than an infinite series. Interpolation of the type being carried out here is thus often called *polynomial interpolation*. In fact, it may be easily shown (see Problem 4.1) that the polynomial (*4.9*) is the one which fits exactly all of the points $f(0), f(1), \ldots, f(4)$ from the base line to the bottom of the table. (A fourth degree polynomial is required to fit five arbitrary points.)

Substituting $x = 0.1$ into (*4.9*) yields

$$f(0.1) = (-3) + (0.1)(9) + \frac{(0.1)(-0.9)}{2}(10) + \frac{(0.1)(-0.9)(-1.9)}{6}(8)$$
$$+ \frac{(0.1)(-0.9)(-1.9)(-2.9)}{24}(4)$$
$$= -3 + 0.9 - 0.45 + 0.228 - 0.08265 = -2.40465$$

Now that a value for $f(0.1)$ has been obtained by interpolation, the question of the accuracy of this value immediately arises. Accuracy in this context means the difference between the number $f(0.1) = -2.40465$ which we have calculated by polynomial interpolation, and the "true" value of $f(0.1)$. This "true" value would be the value of $f(0.1)$ determined by the same means as the tabulated values of $f(x)$ were obtained, e.g. from an experiment, as the result of numerical calculations, etc. In the present case, since we have no knowledge of the origin of the tabulated values of $f(x)$, we cannot even speculate as to what the true value of $f(0.1)$ would be or as to the error in the interpolated value.* Even in the best of cases, we can only estimate the true behavior of $f(x)$ between the tabulated points, based on our knowledge of the physical or numerical situation. The answer to the original question concerning the accuracy of the interpolated value for $f(0.1)$ must then be that we simply do not know. However, if the true function $f(x)$ is well behaved, then the interpolated value will be reasonably accurate. One measure of this behavior which has been mentioned earlier is that if the higher order differences of a tabulated function become small, then polynomial interpolation will *usually* be quite accurate. Certainly, if we have any reason to suspect that $f(x)$ would not behave in a smooth, continuous fashion between the tabulated values, then we should not expect polynomial interpolation to provide meaningful values.

---

*It is possible to give an expression for the error in polynomial interpolation, but this expression is usually useless in a practical sense since it requires knowledge of the behavior of $f(x)$ between the tabulated points. We shall, however, find this error expression of value in a different context in Sec. 4.5.

In general, taking as many terms as practical in the Gregory-Newton interpolation formulas will give the most accurate interpolated value, although there is no guarantee that this is the case.   Each additional term in the interpolation formula actually increases the degree of the interpolating polynomial by one.   Since we have used all of the available entries in the base line of the difference Table 4.6 to obtain $f(0.1)$, it would appear that the fourth order interpolating polynomial (4.9) is the best we can do.   However, it is possible to increase the number of entries in the base line.   The highest difference in the table is $\Delta^5 f = 1$ in the top line.   If it is assumed that *all* 5th differences are constant at 1, the empty spaces in the table may be filled, and (4.9) results in Table 4.7.   If the Gregory-Newton forward interpolation formula (4.7) is applied to *any* line in Table 4.7 as a base line, the resulting 5th degree polynomial may be shown to be the polynomial which exactly fits *all* of the six points in the table (see Problem 4.2).

Table 4.7

New x	$f(x)$	Δf	$\Delta^2 f$	$\Delta^3 f$	$\Delta^4 f$	$\Delta^5 f$
−1	−7	4	5	5	3	1
0	−3	9	10	8	4	1
1	6	19	18	12	5	1
2	25	37	30	17	6	1
3	62	67	47	23	7	1
4	129	114	70	30	8	1

Recalculating $f(0.1)$ using the additional term now available due to the added entry in the base line yields

$$f(0.1) = -2.40465 + \frac{(0.1)(-0.9)(-1.9)(-2.9)(-3.9)}{120} \quad (1)$$

$$= -2.40465 + 0.01612 = -2.38853$$

The contribution of this additional term is relatively small.   The effect of filling out the table would be much greater if the base line were farther down in the table.

Interpolation using the Gregory-Newton backward difference formula and the backward difference table is identical in concept to the forward difference interpolation just discussed.

4.3   INTERPOLATION WITH CENTRAL DIFFERENCES

Interpolation near the center of a set of evenly spaced tabulated values is best accomplished by using central differences.   A central difference table is first generated as discussed in Sec. 4.1.   Then an interpolation formula must be chosen.   There are many interpolation formulas using central differences, but we shall present only two of the most commonly used.   These are

Stirling's formula (full lines as base):

$$f(x) = f(0) + x(\delta y_0) + \frac{x^2}{2!}(\delta^2 y_0) + \frac{x(x^2-1)}{3!}(\delta^3 y_0)$$

$$+ \frac{x^2(x^2-1)}{4!}(\delta^4 y_0) + \frac{x(x^2-1)(x^2-4)}{5!}(\delta^5 y_0) + \cdots \qquad (4.10)$$

Bessel's formula (half lines as base):

$$f(x) = f(0) + x(\delta y_0) + \frac{(x^2-1/4)}{2!}(\delta^2 y_0) + \frac{x(x^2-1/4)}{3!}(\delta^3 y_0)$$

$$+ \frac{(x^2-1/4)(x^2-9/4)}{4!}(\delta^4 y_0) + \frac{x(x^2-1/4)(x^2-9/4)}{5!}(\delta^5 y_0) + \cdots$$

$$(4.11)$$

In order to employ these formulas, the origin of x must be shifted to the base line, and x rescaled so that the spacing between *full lines* of the table is made 1. Since we have a choice as to whether the full lines or the half lines of the difference table will be used as the base line, x need never be larger than ± 0.25. This results in very rapid "convergence" of the interpolation formula in the sense that only a few terms are needed to obtain "accurate" polynomial interpolation. (This actually means that only a few terms are required to obtain a value which lies essentially on the highest order interpolating polynomial available from the base line entries.)

To illustrate central difference interpolation, we shall find $f(2.7)$ for Table 4.1 which resulted in the central difference Table 4.5. The spacing between full lines in this table is already 1, so no rescaling is necessary. The coordinate $x = 2.7$ is nearest $x = 2.5$, so this half line is chosen as a base line (shown shaded) and the coordinate shifted accordingly. The result is Table 4.8.

In the shifted coordinate, we wish to find $f(0.2)$. Since we are using a half line as a base, Bessel's formula (4.11) is used:

$$f(0.2) = 15.5 + 0.2(19) + \frac{(0.04 - 0.25)}{2}(14) + \frac{0.2(0.04 - 0.25)}{6}(8)$$

$$+ \frac{(0.04 - 0.25)(0.04 - 2.25)}{24}(3.5) + \frac{0.2(0.04 - 0.25)(0.04 - 2.25)}{120}(1)$$

$$= 15.5 + 3.8 - 1.47 - 0.056 + 0.06768 + 0.00077 = 17.84245$$

Note that the terms decrease rapidly in magnitude.

One point of caution should be mentioned concerning the values of $f(x)$ on the half lines in the central difference table. (These are the values at old $x = 0.5, 1.5, 2.5, 3.5,$ and 4.5 in Table 4.8.) These were determined by averaging the values above and below them in the difference table, and *are not* accurate values obtained by polynomial interpolation. Bessel's formula takes this into account when interpolation is done with the half lines as a base, but if a value of $f(x)$ directly on a half line is needed, it should be obtained by using Bessel's formula with that half line as a base and with $x = 0$.

As with the forward and backward difference tables, the empty regions of the central difference table can be filled out in order to provide additional entries in the base line, but it is often not necessary due to the rapid "convergence" of the central difference interpolation formulas.

Table 4.8

Old x	New x	$f(x)$	δf	$\delta^2 f$	$\delta^3 f$	$\delta^4 f$	$\delta^5 f$
0	−2.5	−7					
0.5	−2	−5	4				
1	−1.5	−3	6.5	5			
1.5	−1	1.5	9	7.5	5		
2	−0.5	6	14	10	6.5	3	
2.5	0	15.5	19	14	8	3.5	−1
3	0.5	25	28	18	10	4	
3.5	1	43.5	37	24	12		
4	1.5	62	52	30			
4.5	2	95.5	67				
5	2.5	129					

4.4   INTERPOLATION WITH NONEQUALLY SPACED DATA; LAGRANGE POLYNOMIALS

For various numerical or experimental reasons it is often inconvenient or impossible to obtain data at equally spaced intervals.   Since all of our previous interpolation theory is based on equally spaced intervals, we must adopt a different approach, but the concept of polynomial interpolation will be retained.

Consider a series of points $f(x_i)$ where the x_i are in general not evenly spaced, and i can take on all integer values from 0 to n (which means that there are $n+1$ such points).   One possible approach to polynomial interpolation between the x_i's is to simply fit a polynomial of degree n to these $n+1$ points.   A typical example is shown in Fig. 4.3 for $n=7$.

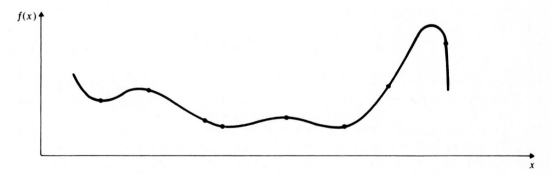

Fig. 4.3   Seventh degree polynomial fitted to eight unequally spaced points.

In order to find the $n+1$ coefficients of this nth degree polynomial so that it can be evaluated at any desired intermediate value of x, it would seem necessary to solve $n+1$ simultaneous linear equations.   Instead, we will not actually solve for these coefficients, but will construct the polynomial in a different way.

We can define a polynomial of degree n associated with each point x_j as

$$P_j(x) = A_j(x - x_0)(x - x_1)(x - x_2) \cdots (x - x_{j-1})(x - x_{j+1}) \cdots (x - x_n) \qquad (4.12)$$

where A_j is a constant, and where the factor $x - x_j$ is omitted. Equation (4.12) may be written in a shorter notation as

$$P_j(x) = A_j \prod_{\substack{i=0 \\ i \neq j}}^{n} (x - x_i) \qquad (4.13)$$

When x is equal to any of the x_i corresponding to a data point (except x_j), the value of this polynomial is zero since the factor $x_i - x_i$ will be zero. However, when $x = x_j$, the value of the polynomial is not zero since the factor $x - x_j$ is missing. Thus if we denote one of the data points as x_k,

$$P_j(x_k) = \begin{cases} 0, & k \neq j \\ A_j \prod\limits_{\substack{i=0 \\ i \neq j}}^{n} (x_j - x_i), & k = j \end{cases} \qquad (4.14)$$

If A_j is defined as

$$A_j = \frac{1}{\prod\limits_{\substack{i=0 \\ i \neq j}}^{n} (x_j - x_i)}$$

then (4.14) becomes

$$P_j(x_k) = \begin{cases} 0, & k \neq j \\ 1, & k = j \end{cases} \qquad (4.15)$$

Thus the $P_j(x)$ are a set of nth degree polynomials, defined in such a way that each one passes through zero at each of the data points except for the one point x_k where $k = j$. The $P_j(x)$ are called *Lagrange polynomials*.

We now form the following linear combination of the $P_j(x)$:

$$p_n(x) = \sum_{j=0}^{n} f(x_j) P_j(x) \qquad (4.16)$$

Since (4.16) is a linear combination of nth degree polynomials, it is also an nth degree polynomial. If we select any one of the points at which data are available, say x_2, then

$$p_n(x_2) = f(x_0)P_0(x_2) + f(x_1)P_1(x_2) + f(x_2)P_2(x_2) + \cdots + f(x_n)P_n(x_2)$$

But since each of the $P_j(x_2)$ is zero except for $P_2(x_2)$, which equals 1,

$$p_n(x_2) = f(x_2)P_2(x_2) = f(x_2)$$

At x_2, this nth degree polynomial yields the value $f(x_2)$. It can easily be seen that for any of the data points x_i, the polynomial becomes $f(x_i)$. Thus the polynomial $p_n(x)$ is the desired polynomial of degree n which exactly fits the $n + 1$ data points.

Interpolation with this polynomial can best be illustrated with an example. Consider the following set of data:

i	0	1	2	3
x_i	1	2	4	8
$f(x_i)$	1	3	7	11

Suppose we wish to interpolate for $f(7)$.   Then

$$p_3(7) = 1 P_0(7) + 3 P_1(7) + 7 P_2(7) + 11 P_3(7)$$

$$P_0(7) = \frac{(7-2)(7-4)(7-8)}{(1-2)(1-4)(1-8)} = 0.71429$$

$$P_1(7) = \frac{(7-1)(7-4)(7-8)}{(2-1)(2-4)(2-8)} = -1.5$$

$$P_2(7) = \frac{(7-1)(7-2)(7-8)}{(4-1)(4-2)(4-8)} = 1.25$$

$$P_3(7) = \frac{(7-1)(7-2)(7-4)}{(8-1)(8-2)(8-4)} = 0.53571$$

$$f(7) \approx p_3(7) = 0.71429 + 3(-1.5) + 7(1.25) + 11(0.53571) = 10.85710$$

This is the value of the interpolating polynomial at $x = 7$.

It should be noted that polynomial interpolation of this type can be dangerous toward the center of the regions where the independent variable is widely spaced. Although the polynomial is "tied down" at the data points, it is free to wander, possibly excessively, between widely spaced data points.

4.5   CHEBYSHEV INTERPOLATION; CHEBYSHEV POLYNOMIALS

When it is known beforehand that interpolation will be carried out on a certain interval of x, and if there is complete freedom of choice in the selection of the values of x where data will be obtained, then there are advantages to choosing these values of x in a certain way.   If the values of x are chosen properly, the effect is a very desirable tendency to minimize the maximum error in interpolation.

To show this, we quote without derivation the error made in polynomial interpolation.   (For the derivation, see Ref. 2.)

$$E(x) = \prod_{i=0}^{n} (x - x_i) \frac{f^{(n+1)}(\eta)}{(n+1)!} \tag{4.17}$$

The x_i are the $n + 1$ values of x at which data are available and $f(x)$ is the continuous function (generally unknown) which is to be approximated by the interpolating polynomial.   The $(n + 1)$th derivative of f in (4.17) must be evaluated at some η which is a function of x and which is within the range of the x_i, but is otherwise unknown.   In general, since $f(x)$ is fixed for a given problem and $f(x)$ and η are unknown, the only way in which we can influence this error is in the choice of the x_i at which data are taken.   We shall attempt to choose the x_i in such a way that the maximum value of $\prod_{i=0}^{n} (x - x_i)$ on the interval of interest is minimized (the so-called minimax principle). This *tends* to minimize the maximum value of the error $E(x)$, but since $f^{(n+1)}(\eta)$ may not peak at exactly the same value of x as does $\Pi_{i=0}^{n}(x - x_i)$, there is no guarantee of this overall minimax behavior.

Note first that $\Pi_{i=0}^{n}(x - x_i)$ is a polynomial of degree $(n + 1)$ with a coefficient of 1 for the term in x^{n+1}. We now restrict x to the interval $-1 \leq x \leq 1$. This is not a serious restriction since, as we shall see, any finite interval can be transformed into this interval. Consider next a set of polynomials called Chebyshev polynomials, which are defined by

$$T_n(x) = \cos(n \cos^{-1} x) \tag{4.18}$$

where $T_n(x)$ is the Chebyshev polynomial of degree n. The first few Chebyshev polynomials are

$$T_0(x) = 1$$

$$T_1(x) = x$$

$$T_2(x) = 2x^2 - 1$$

$$T_3(x) = 4x^3 - 3x \tag{4.19}$$

$$T_4(x) = 8x^4 - 8x^2 + 1$$

$$T_5(x) = 16x^5 - 20x^3 + 5x$$

$$T_6(x) = 32x^6 - 48x^4 + 18x^2 - 1$$

Since the generating function (4.18) is a cosine, these polynomials have a maximum magnitude of 1. We now define a new set of polynomials given by

$$\psi_n(x) = \frac{T_n(x)}{2^{n-1}} \tag{4.20}$$

By examining the Chebyshev polynomials (4.19) it is apparent that dividing by 2^{n-1} produces in the $\psi_n(x)$ a set of polynomials having a coefficient of 1 for the term in x^n. We state without proof (see Ref. 2 for proof) that the polynomial $\psi_n(x)$ has the *smallest* upper bound of all polynomials of degree n having a coefficient of 1 for the term in x^n.

Thus if we can make

$$\prod_{i=0}^{n}(x - x_i) = \psi_{n+1}(x) \tag{4.21}$$

we will have minimized the maximum value of $\Pi_{i=0}^{n}(x - x_i)$ on the interval $-1 \leq x \leq 1$ and as far as possible minimized the maximum error. Since both sides of (4.21) have a coefficient of 1 for x^{n+1}, we can satisfy the equality if the x_i are the roots of the polynomial $\psi_{n+1}(x)$. These are the same as the roots of the Chebyshev polynomial $T_{n+1}(x)$.

The roots of $T_{n+1}(x)$ are given by

$$x_m = \cos\left[\left(\frac{2m+1}{2n+2}\right)\pi\right], \qquad m = 0, 1, 2, \ldots, n \tag{4.22}$$

These roots tend to be packed more densely near the ends of the interval than at the center. For example, for $T_6(x)$, the roots are

$$x_0 = 0.96592583 \qquad x_3 = -0.25881905$$
$$x_1 = 0.70710678 \qquad x_4 = -0.70710678$$
$$x_2 = 0.25881905 \qquad x_5 = -0.96592583$$

The complete procedure for choosing the points at which to take data and for carrying out the interpolation can now be described. Suppose we wish to take data on the interval $a \leq z \leq b$ at $n + 1$ points. (Remember that x has been temporarily restricted to the interval $-1 \leq x \leq 1$.) These points should be located on the interval $-1 \leq x \leq 1$ according to (4.22). Their location on $a \leq z \leq b$ may be found from the equation

$$z_i = \frac{1}{2}[(b - a)x_i + b + a] \tag{4.23}$$

Taking the data on the z_i, $i = 0, 1, \ldots, n$, gives a set of values of $f(z_i)$. In order to interpolate for $f(z)$ at any arbitrary z, it is only necessary to carry out the Lagrange interpolation for nonequally spaced intervals discussed in Sec. 4.4. See Problem 4.10 for an example of Chebyshev interpolation.

4.6 INTERPOLATION WITH CUBIC SPLINE FUNCTIONS

One of the difficulties with conventional polynomial interpolation, particularly if the polynomial is of high order, is the highly inflected or "wiggly" character which it is possible for the interpolating polynomial to assume.

A smoother interpolating function can usually be produced by mechanical means such as a French curve or, more to the point of this discussion, by forcing a flexible elastic bar to pass through the desired points. The mathematical analog of this flexible elastic bar is the *cubic spline function.* Interpolation using the cubic spline is currently very popular, particularly for interpolation in relatively noise-free tables of physical properties.

The construction of a cubic spline interpolating function can be briefly described as follows[2]. As in Sec. 4.4, we are given a series of points x_i $(i = 0, 1, 2, \ldots, n)$ which are in general not evenly spaced, and the corresponding functional values $f(x_i)$. Now consider two arbitrary adjacent points x_i and x_{i+1}. We wish to fit a cubic to these two points and use this cubic as the interpolating function between them. We denote this cubic as

$$F_i(x) = a_0 + a_1 x + a_2 x^2 + a_3 x^3 \qquad (x_i \leq x \leq x_{i+1}) \tag{4.24}$$

There are clearly 4 unknown constants in (4.24), and only two conditions are immediately obvious, namely that $F_i(x_i) = f(x_i)$ and $F_i(x_{i+1}) = f(x_{i+1})$. We are free to choose the two remaining conditions as we like, to accomplish our desired objective of "smoothness." The most effective approach is to match the first and second derivatives (and thus the slope and curvature) of $F_i(x)$ to those of the cubic $F_{i-1}(x)$ used for interpolation on the adjacent interval $x_{i-1} \leq x \leq x_i$. If this procedure is carried out for all intervals in the region $x_0 \leq x \leq x_n$ (with special treatment at the end points as we will discuss later), then an approximating function for the region will have been constructed, consisting of the set of cubics $F_i(x)$ $(i = 0, 1, \ldots, n - 1)$. We denote this approximating function for the entire region as $g(x)$ and call it a *cubic spline.*

To actually construct $g(x)$, it is convenient to note that due to the matching of second derivatives of the cubics at each point x_i, the second derivative of $g(x)$ is continuous over the entire region $x_0 \leq x \leq x_n$. This second derivative might appear as shown in Fig. 4.4.

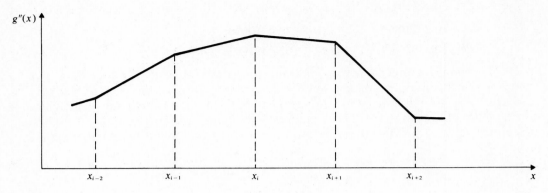

Fig. 4.4

Note that the second derivative varies linearly over each interval. (The second derivative of a cubic is a straight line.) Due to this linearity, the second derivative at any point x, where $x_i \le x \le x_{i+1}$, is given by

$$g''(x) = g''(x_i) + \frac{x - x_i}{x_{i+1} - x_i}[g''(x_{i+1}) - g''(x_i)] \tag{4.25}$$

Integrating this equation twice and applying the conditions that $g(x_i) = f(x_i)$ and $g(x_{i+1}) = f(x_{i+1})$, we find that for $x_i \le x \le x_{i+1}$,

$$g(x) = F_i(x) = \frac{g''(x_i)}{6}\left[\frac{(x_{i+1} - x)^3}{\Delta x_i} - \Delta x_i(x_{i+1} - x)\right]$$

$$+ \frac{g''(x_{i+1})}{6}\left[\frac{(x - x_i)^3}{\Delta x_i} - \Delta x_i(x - x_i)\right]$$

$$+ f(x_i)\left[\frac{x_{i+1} - x}{\Delta x_i}\right] + f(x_{i+1})\left[\frac{x - x_i}{\Delta x_i}\right] \tag{4.26}$$

where $\Delta x_i = x_{i+1} - x_i$. Equation (4.26) provides the interpolating cubics over each interval for $i = 0,1,\ldots,n-1$. Since the second derivatives $g''(x_i)$ $(i = 0,1,\ldots,n)$ are still unknown, these must be evaluated before we can use (4.26).

The second derivatives can be found by using the derivative matching conditions:

$$F_i'(x_i) = F_{i-1}'(x_i) \tag{4.27}$$

and

$$F_i''(x_i) = F_{i-1}''(x_i) \tag{4.28}$$

Equation (4.28) is simply equivalent to stating that $g''(x_i)$ is the same when x_i is approached from either side. Applying these conditions to (4.26) for $i = 1,2,\ldots,n-1$ and collecting terms yields a set of linear simultaneous equations of the form

$$\left[\frac{\Delta x_{i-1}}{\Delta x_i}\right]g''(x_{i-1}) + \left[\frac{2(x_{i+1} - x_{i-1})}{\Delta x_i}\right]g''(x_i) + [1]g''(x_{i+1})$$

$$= 6\left[\frac{f(x_{i+1}) - f(x_i)}{(\Delta x_i)^2} - \frac{f(x_i) - f(x_{i-1})}{(\Delta x_i)(\Delta x_{i-1})}\right] \quad (i = 1,2,\ldots,n-1) \tag{4.29}$$

If the x_i are evenly separated with spacing Δx, then (4.29) is considerably simplified and becomes

$$[1]g''(x_{i-1}) + [4]g''(x_i) + [1]g''(x_{i+1}) = 6\left[\frac{f(x_{i+1}) - 2f(x_i) + f(x_{i-1})}{(\Delta x_i)^2}\right] \qquad (4.30)$$

Whether the equations are of the form (4.29) or (4.30), there are $n - 1$ equations in the $n + 1$ unknowns $g''(x_0)$, $g''(x_1), \ldots, g''(x_n)$. The two necessary additional equations are obtained by specifying conditions on $g''(x_0)$ and $g''(x_n)$. It is usually simply specified that

$$g''(x_0) = 0 \qquad (4.31)$$

and

$$g''(x_n) = 0 \qquad (4.32)$$

The resulting $g(x)$ is then called a *natural cubic spline*. This corresponds physically to letting the elastic bar mentioned earlier assume a natural unrestrained straight line beyond the region of interest.

The set of equations (4.29) or (4.30) is now complete and can be solved for $g''(x_1)$, $g''(x_2), \ldots, g''(x_{n-1})$. The inconvenience of having to solve a set of simultaneous linear equations is tempered somewhat by the fact that the set seldom need be very large, and that each equation contains at most three unknowns. In Chapter 6, we will examine a very simple method for solving even very large sets of the form (4.29) or (4.30). Such sets are termed *tridiagonal*.

We will illustrate cubic spline interpolation with an example. Suppose the following unevenly-spaced tabulated function is given:

i	x_i	$f(x_i)$
0	1	4
1	4	9
2	6	15
3	9	7
4	10	3

We will approximate $f(5)$ by interpolation on a natural cubic spline. First, we set $g''(1) = g''(10) = 0$. Now, writing (4.29) for $i = 1$,

$$\left[\frac{(4-1)}{(6-4)}\right](0) + \left[\frac{2(6-1)}{(6-4)}\right]g''(4) + [1]g''(6) = 6\left[\frac{(15-9)}{(6-4)^2} - \frac{(9-4)}{(6-4)(4-1)}\right]$$

or

$$5g''(4) + g''(6) = 4$$

Similarly, we find for $i = 2$ that

$$0.66667g''(4) + 3.33333g''(6) + g''(9) = -11.33333$$

and for $i = 3$,

$$3g''(6) + 8g''(9) = -8$$

Solving these three equations simultaneously, we find

$$g''(4) = 1.56932, \qquad g''(6) = -3.84661, \qquad g''(9) = 0.44248$$

Since we wish to approximate $f(5)$, then we must use the cubic $F_1(x)$, which is appropriate for the interval $4 \le x \le 6$. From (4.26),

$$F_1(5) = \frac{g''(4)}{6}\left[\frac{(6-5)^3}{(6-4)} - (6-4)(6-5)\right] + \frac{g''(6)}{6}\left[\frac{(5-4)^3}{(6-4)} - (6-4)(5-4)\right]$$

$$+ 9\left[\frac{(6-5)}{(6-4)}\right] + 15\left[\frac{(5-4)}{(6-4)}\right]$$

Inserting the previously determined values for $g''(4)$ and $g''(6)$, we find

$$F_1(5) = 12.56932$$

This is the desired interpolated value.

4.7 EXTRAPOLATION

If a function $f(x)$ is known only on the interval $a \le x \le b$, but values of $f(x)$ are needed for $x < a$ or $x > b$, then extrapolation is required. Even under the best of circumstances, extrapolation contains a strong element of uncertainty. Unlike interpolation, where the function is firmly anchored on both sides of the point where a value is to be obtained, in extrapolation the function is fixed on only one side and is relatively free to wander on the other side.

If the function is known at discrete, evenly-spaced points, then the Gregory-Newton forward or backward polynomial interpolation formulas are commonly employed for extrapolation, with the last known point used as the base line. (The choice of a forward or backward formula will of course depend on whether $x > b$ or $x < a$.) In order to obtain meaningful answers using this type of extrapolation, it is particularly important that the function be well suited to polynomial interpolation. As discussed earlier, this means that higher order differences in the difference table must approach zero.

If the function is known at discrete, unequally-spaced points, then the Lagrange interpolation formula may be used directly for extrapolation by inserting the desired x. Since no difference table is available for evaluation of the character of the function, this type of interpolation requires particular care.

It is often necessary to extrapolate other types of functions, such as analytical functions defined only on a certain range or functions available only as curves on a graph (instrument calibration curves, experimental correlations, etc.). The many possible approaches to such problems are beyond the scope of this book, but a universal rule which should be applied to all extrapolation is not to accept extrapolated values without intelligent skepticism.

Some of the possible pitfalls of extrapolation are illustrated in Problem 4.8.

Illustrative Problems

4.1 In Sec. 4.2 it was stated that the application of the Gregory-Newton forward interpolation formula to any base line in a forward difference table would yield a polynomial which would fit exactly all data points below the base line in the table. Verify this for the polynomial (4.9) which resulted when $x = 0$ was used as a base in Table 4.6.

The polynomial (4.9) is

$$f(x) = (-3) + x(9) + \frac{x(x-1)}{2}(10) + \frac{x(x-1)(x-2)}{6}(8)$$
$$+ \frac{x(x-1)(x-2)(x-3)}{24}(4)$$

If $x = 1$, all terms drop out except the first two, since the factor $x - 1$ appears in all other terms. Thus

$$f(1) = -3 + (1)9 = 6$$

For $x = 2$, only the first three terms remain, yielding

$$f(2) = -3 + 2(9) + \frac{2(1)}{2}(10) = 25$$

Similarly,

$$f(3) = -3 + 3(9) + \frac{3(2)}{2}(10) + \frac{3(2)(1)}{6}(8) = 62$$

and

$$f(4) = (-3) + 4(9) + \frac{4(3)}{2}(10) + \frac{4(3)(2)}{6}(8) + \frac{4(3)(2)(1)}{24}(4) = 129$$

All of these values agree with the entries in Table 4.6.

4.2 Also in Sec. 4.2, it was stated that when all of the empty spaces in a difference table are filled in, the polynomial resulting from the Gregory-Newton interpolation formula using *any* line as a base would fit exactly *all* of the data points in the table. Partially verify this for the Table 4.7 by computing $f(-1)$ using the line $x = 3$ as a base.

Using the Gregory-Newton forward interpolation formula for $f(-1)$ with $x = 3$ as a base yields

$$f(-1) = 62 + (-4)(67) + \frac{(-4)(-5)}{2}(47) + \frac{(-4)(-5)(-6)}{6}(23)$$
$$+ \frac{(-4)(-5)(-6)(-7)}{24}(7) + \frac{(-4)(-5)(-6)(-7)(-8)}{120}(1)$$
$$= 62 - 268 + 470 - 460 + 245 - 56 = -7$$

which is the entry in Table 4.7 for $f(-1)$.

4.3   The following is the tabulation of an actual thermodynamic quantity:

x	0	0.2	0.4	0.6	0.8	1.0	1.2	1.4	1.6	1.8	2.0	2.2	2.4
f	1.000	0.916	0.836	0.740	0.624	0.40–0.29*	0.224	0.240	0.265	0.291	0.316	0.342	0.368

*The curve is essentially a vertical straight line at $x = 1.0$.

Find $f(0.23)$.

Since $x = 0.23$ is close to the top of the table, we choose to employ Gregory-Newton forward interpolation. Because the function $f(x)$ appears to behave smoothly for $0 \leq x \leq 0.8$, only this range of x will be used in generating the difference table. Because of the discontinuity in $f(x)$ at $x = 1$, the table should not include or span $x = 1.0$. We choose $x = 0.2$ as a base. Rescaling and shifting the x axis, the difference table is Table 4.9.

Table 4.9

Old x	New x	f	Δf	$\Delta^2 f$	$\Delta^3 f$	$\Delta^4 f$
0	−1	1.000	−0.084	+0.004	−0.020	0.016
0.2	0	0.916	−0.080	−0.016	−0.004	
0.4	1	0.836	−0.096	−0.020		
0.6	2	0.740	−0.116			
0.8	3	0.624				

The higher order differences tend to eventually decrease so that polynomial interpolation should be adequate. The point $x = 0.23$ on the old x scale is the same as $x = 0.15$ on the new x scale (0.03 is 3/20 of the interval between lines). Applying the Gregory-Newton forward interpolation formula for $f(0.15)$ yields

$$f(0.15) = 0.916 + (0.15)(-0.080) + \frac{(0.15)(-0.85)}{2}(-0.016)$$

$$+ \frac{(0.15)(-0.85)(-1.85)}{6}(-0.004)$$

$$= 0.916 - 0.012 + 0.00102 - 0.0001572 = 0.9049$$

4.4   Find $f(0.78)$ for the function of Problem 4.3.

Since $x = 0.78$ is near the bottom of the range $0 \leq x \leq 0.8$ where the function is smoothly behaved, we employ backward difference interpolation. As before, the point of discontinuity $x = 1.0$ should not be included or spanned in generating the difference table, which is given by Table 4.10.

Table 4.10

x	f	∇f	$\nabla^2 f$	$\nabla^3 f$	$\nabla^4 f$
0	1.000				
0.2	0.916	-0.084			
0.4	0.836	-0.080	$+0.004$		
0.6	0.740	-0.096	-0.016	-0.020	
0.8	0.624	-0.116	-0.020	-0.004	0.016

We choose $x = 0.8$ as the base line.   On this and all succeeding problems we will not explicitly rescale and shift x, since the x value to be used in the interpolation formulas is easily found.   The point $x = 0.78$ is 2/20 of the distance from $x = 0.8$ to $x = 0.6$ in the negative x direction.   Thus the x to use in the interpolation formula is $x = -0.1$.   The Gregory-Newton backward formula (4.8) then yields

$$f(0.78) = 0.624 + (-0.1)(-0.116) + \frac{(-0.1)(0.9)}{2}(-0.020)$$

$$+ \frac{(-0.1)(0.9)(1.9)}{6}(-0.004) + \frac{(-0.1)(0.9)(1.9)(2.9)}{24}(0.016)$$

$$= 0.624 + 0.0116 + 0.0009 + 0.000114 - 0.0003306 = 0.6363$$

4.5   Given the following tabulated function:

x	-1	0	1	2	3	4	5	6
$f(x)$	-0.93	1	3.07	5.40	11.95	41.32	144.75	431.32

Find $f(2.2)$ by using Gregory-Newton forward difference interpolation and central difference interpolation.   Compare the effectiveness of the two methods.

We first prepare forward difference Table 4.11.

Table 4.11

x	$f(x)$	Δf	$\Delta^2 f$	$\Delta^3 f$	$\Delta^4 f$	$\Delta^5 f$	$\Delta^6 f$
-1	-0.93	1.93	0.14	0.12	3.84	10.80	7.20
0	1	2.07	0.26	3.96	14.64	18.00	7.20
1	3.07	2.33	4.22	18.60	32.64	25.20	7.20
2	5.40	6.55	22.82	51.24	57.84	32.40	
3	11.95	29.37	74.06	109.08	90.24		
4	41.32	103.43	183.14	199.32			
5	144.75	286.57	382.46				
6	431.32	669.03					
7	1100.35						

At first glance, this table would seem to indicate that $f(x)$ is not well suited to polynomial interpolation, since through most of the table, the higher order differences increase in magnitude. However, one of the fifth differences decreases and the sixth differences are actually quite small. The two available sixth differences are also equal. This means that interpolating polynomials of degree five or six would probably give acceptable results, while polynomials of degree three or lower would probably be unacceptable.

If the table had been terminated, for example, at third differences, we would have concluded that polynomial interpolation would not be acceptable, and under the circumstances this conclusion would be correct. (The highest degree interpolating polynomials which could be generated with three differences would be third degree, and these would be inadequate.)

In order to be able to evaluate the two interpolation schemes which we will examine, we will disclose that the function from which the tabulation was prepared was a sixth degree polynomial, and that evaluating this polynomial at $x = 2.2$ yields $f(2.2) = 6.08078$.

We choose $x = 2$ as a base, and use the Gregory-Newton forward interpolation formula with $x = 0.2$. This gives

$$f(2.2) = 5.40 + 0.2(6.55) + \frac{0.2(-0.8)}{2}(22.82) + \frac{(0.2)(-0.8)(-1.8)}{6}(51.24)$$
$$+ \frac{(0.2)(-0.8)(-1.8)(-2.8)}{24}(57.84)$$
$$+ \frac{(0.2)(-0.8)(-1.8)(-2.8)(-3.8)}{120}(32.40)$$

or

$$f(2.2) = 5.40 + 1.310]_{6.710} - 1.8256]_{4.8844} + 2.45952]_{7.34392}$$
$$- 1.943424]_{5.400496} + 0.8273664]_{6.2278624} = 6.2279$$

The number at the base of the bracket on each new term is the partial sum of all terms up to and including that term. Note that the result is not a good approximation to the exact value of $f(2.2) = 6.08078$ until the final term (which corresponds to a fifth degree polynomial contribution) is included. The result would have been exact if there were one more entry in the base line of the difference table.

Now consider central difference interpolation. We first prepare central difference Table 4.12 near $x = 2$.

Table 4.12

x	$f(x)$	δf	$\delta^2 f$	$\delta^3 f$	$\delta^4 f$	$\delta^5 f$
-1	-0.93					
-0.5	0.035	1.93				
0	1	2.00	0.14			
0.5	2.035	2.07	0.20	0.12		
1	3.07	2.20	0.26	2.04	3.84	
1.5	4.235	2.33	2.24	3.96	9.24	10.80
2	5.40	4.44	4.22	11.28	14.64	14.40
2.5	8.675	6.55	13.52	18.60	23.64	18.00
3	11.95	17.96	22.82	34.92	32.64	
3.5	26.635	29.37	48.44	51.24		
4	41.32	66.40	74.06			
4.5	93.035	103.43				
5	144.75					

Since $x = 2.2$ is nearest to the full line $x = 2$, we choose this as a base line and employ Stirling's formula (4.10) with $x = 0.2$:

$$f(2.2) = 5.40 + 0.2(4.44) + \frac{(0.04)}{2}(4.22) + \frac{0.2(0.04 - 1)}{6}(11.28)$$

$$+ \frac{(0.04)(0.04 - 1)}{24}(14.64) + \frac{0.2(0.04 - 1)(0.04 - 4)}{120}(14.40)$$

$$= 5.40 + 0.888]_{6.288} + 0.0844]_{6.3724} - 0.36096]_{6.01144}$$

$$- 0.02342]_{5.98802} + 0.09124]_{6.07926}$$

$$= 6.07926$$

Not only is this answer more accurate than the forward difference formula with the same number of terms, but it is also notable that *each one* of the partial sums in this central difference formula is more accurate than *any* of the partial sums of the forward difference formula with the exception of the final value! The more rapid convergence of the central difference formula is obvious, and this method should be chosen whenever the value of x for which $f(x)$ is to be found is sufficiently far from the ends of the table to allow a reasonable numbers of entries in the base line. (Incidentally, both interpolation formulas would give exact results if one more term were included in each. Why?)

4.6 The following tabulated function represents data taken at equally-spaced intervals. It was thought that the data would result in a smooth function, generally similar in character to a second degree polynomial. However, there appears to be a significant error in one of the data points. Find this point and "correct" it.

x	1	2	3	4	5	6	7	8
$f(x)$	0.812	0.642	0.691	0.893	1.454	2.164	3.092	4.240

We first prepare forward difference Table 4.13.

Table 4.13

x	$f(x)$	Δf	$\Delta^2 f$	$\Delta^3 f$	$\Delta^4 f$
1	0.812	-0.170	0.219	-0.066	0.272
2	0.642	0.049	0.153	0.206	-0.416
3	0.691	0.202	0.359	-0.210	0.279
4	0.893	0.561	0.149	0.069	-0.067
5	1.454	0.710	0.218	0.002	
6	2.164	0.928	0.220		
7	3.092	1.148			
8	4.240				

The first impression of the table is that it shows little evidence that $f(x)$ could have the general behavior of a second degree polynomial. Many of the higher order differences increase instead of decrease, and the third differences, with the exception of the bottom entry, certainly are not close to zero. However, it should be noted that an error in a single entry in $f(x)$ propagates across and upward in the table, affecting two entries in the Δf column, three in the $\Delta^2 f$ column, etc. This tends to mask the true character of $f(x)$. We note that the top entry and the bottom two entries in the $\Delta^2 f$ column are approximately constant at 0.220. If we postulate that the entry for $f(x)$ at $x = 4$ is incorrect, then the remaining three entries in the $\Delta^2 f$ column are incorrect also as are all elements within the dotted lines. Setting the top two of these second differences to 0.220, and working back to the left to make all elements within the dotted lines consistent with these second differences, we obtain Table 4.14.

Table 4.14

x	$f(x)$	Δf	$\Delta^2 f$
1	0.812	-0.170	0.219
2	0.642	0.049	0.220
3	0.691	0.269	0.220
4	0.960	0.489	(0.221)
5	1.454	0.710	0.218
6	2.164	0.928	0.220
7	3.092	1.148	
8	4.240		

The remaining second difference (encircled) is given by $\Delta f|_{x=5} - \Delta f|_{x=4} = 0.710 - 0.489 = 0.221$. Since this is essentially the same as the assumed second differences, we can be reasonably confident we have found the error, and that $f(4) = 0.960$ is more nearly "correct" than the original value of 0.893. The function $f(x)$ now closely resembles a second degree polynomial since $\Delta^2 f$ is virtually constant. It should be noted that such "correction" can be very dangerous unless one is very certain that the point is actually in error.

4.7 It was stated in Sec. 4.4 that in Lagrange interpolation, if the spacing between any two points was large compared with the spacing of all other points in the table, then the polynomial could "wander" in that widely spaced region resulting in excessive error in approximating the actual function. Consider the function $f(x) = \sin x$, $0 \le x \le \pi$. Evaluate the effect of point spacing on the cubic approximation to $f(x)$ obtained by using four points in the Lagrange interpolation formula.

In order to keep the comparison as simple as possible, we will always use the two end points, $x = 0$ and $x = \pi$, and vary the spacing of the two interior points. Rather than plotting all of the polynomials, we will simply compare the peak value $f(\pi/2) = 1$ with the value for $x = \pi/2$ from the polynomial approximations. We first consider the following spacing:

i	x	$f(x)$
0	0	0
1	0.392699(π/8)	0.382683
2	2.748889(7π/8)	0.382683
3	3.141593(π)	0

(The values of $f(x)$ are of course obtained by evaluating $\sin x$ at the corresponding values of x.)

For this case the center spacing is 6 times the spacing between the interior points and the ends. Using the Lagrange interpolation formula (4.16) yields $f_{approx}(\pi/2) = 0.875$, which is in error by about 13%. Shifting the interior points to $x = \pi/4$ and $x = 3\pi/4$ results in a center spacing of 2 times the spacing between the interior points and the ends. The Lagrange formula for this case yields $f_{approx}(\pi/2) = 0.943$, which is in error by about 6%. Using $x = 5\pi/16$ and $x = 11\pi/16$ results in almost equal spacing of all points and yields $f_{approx}(\pi/2) = 0.968$, which is in error by about 3%. The results presented here should convey some impression of the errors involved when the function to be approximated is very smooth and well behaved. A function which might, for example, include inflection points between the widely-spaced data points would yield much more inaccurate polynomial approximations.

4.8   Given the following function:

x	1	2	3	4	5
$f(x)$	100.000	25.000	11.111	6.250	4.000

Extrapolate to find $f(5.7)$.

We first need a difference table. Since $x = 5$ will be used as a base, a backward difference table will provide the most entries in that line. The result is Table 4.15.

Table 4.15

x	$f(x)$	∇f	$\nabla^2 f$	$\nabla^3 f$	$\nabla^4 f$
1	100.000				
2	25.000	−75.000			
3	11.111	−13.889	61.111		
4	6.250	−4.861	9.028	−52.083	
5	4.000	−2.250	2.611	−6.417	45.666

It is clear upon examining the table that the differences all increase in magnitude toward the right of the table. The function is thus very poorly suited to polynomial interpolation (or extrapolation). We could simply stop and state that polynomial extrapolation is too dangerous in this case, but it is instructive to see just how bad such extrapolation can be, and also whether it is possible to salvage a reasonably accurate answer. If we apply the Gregory-Newton backward formula (4.8) to the line $x = 5$ as a base, and use all entries in the base line, the resulting fourth degree polynomial is the one which fits exactly all five points in the table.   (You can prove this to yourself if you wish; see Problem 4.1.)   Since $x = 5.7$ is 0.7 units below the base line, we use $x = 0.7$ in the interpolation formula.   This yields

$$f(5.7) = 4.000 + 0.7(-2.250) + \frac{(0.7)(1.7)}{2}(2.611)$$

$$+ \frac{(0.7)(1.7)(2.7)}{6}(-6.417) + \frac{(0.7)(1.7)(2.7)(3.7)}{24}(45.666)$$

$$= 4.000 - 1.575 + 1.554 - 3.436 + 22.620 = 23.163$$

This value for $f(5.7)$ certainly appears absurd in terms of the other tabulated values of $f(x)$, but in general it is impossible to estimate by how much an extrapolated value is in error.   However, in this case we have the advantage of being able to disclose the function which was used to make up the original table.   The function was $f(x) = 100/x^2$.   Using this function, $f(5.7) = 3.078$.   The extrapolation based on the fourth degree polynomial is thus completely worthless.   In order to decide whether polynomial interpolation is of any value in this case, consider the following table:

		$f(5.7)$
Original function		3.078
Type of polynomial	linear	2.425
	second degree	3.979
	third degree	0.543
	fourth degree	23.163

The linear extrapolation was obtained by taking two terms of the interpolation formula, the second degree by taking three terms, etc.   While none of the extrapolated values could be called accurate by any means, it is clear that the linear and second degree extrapolations are the "best."

If polynomial extrapolation must be done with poorly behaved functions, then very low degree extrapolation is usually the safest, but even this should be carried out only for values of x very close to the tabulated region.

4.9   If a function to be extrapolated cannot be well approximated by a polynomial, a useful device can be to plot $f(x)$ vs. x on log-log graph paper.   This reduces an amazingly large variety of functions to essentially straight lines or to smooth curves which are easy to extrapolate.   The numerical equivalent of this graphical procedure is to tabulate $\log_e f(x)$ vs. $\log_e x$, and then carry out polynomial extrapolation.   Describe this procedure and evaluate its accuracy for the function of Problem 4.8.

The tabulation of the function given in Problem 4.8 becomes

$x^* = \log_e x$	0	0.693	1.099	1.386	1.609
$f^*(x^*) = \log_e f(x)$	4.605	3.219	2.408	1.832	1.387

and we wish to find $f^*(\log_e 5.7) = f^*(1.740)$. This extrapolation could be accomplished by using the Lagrange interpolation formula (note that x^* is not equally spaced). However, we can first check to see if $f^*(x^*)$ is nearly linear. An estimate of the first derivative at $x^* = 1.609$ is the simple backward difference

$$\frac{1.387 - 1.832}{1.609 - 1.386} = \frac{-0.445}{0.223} = -1.996$$

A similar difference at $x^* = 1.386$ yields

$$\frac{1.832 - 2.408}{1.386 - 1.099} = \frac{-0.576}{0.287} = -2.007$$

These values are close enough to use linear extrapolation:

$$f^*(1.740) = 1.387 + (-1.996)(1.740 - 1.609) = 1.126 = \log_e f(5.7)$$

$$f(5.7) = 3.081$$

This extrapolated value is virtually identical to the value of the original analytical function at $x = 5.7$, which was 3.078. In fact, the error is due only to roundoff. If we consider the original function, $f = 100/x^2$, and take the natural log,

$$\log_e f = \log_e 100 - 2 \log_e x$$

$$f^*(x^*) = \log_e 100 - 2x^*$$

so $f^*(x^*)$ is linear in x^*, with a slope of -2.

4.10 Given the function

$$f(x) = \sin^2 x + 2 \cos(3x), \qquad 0 \le x \le \pi$$

This continuous function can be sampled at any value of x in the range $0 \le x \le \pi$ to provide data points. Construct two different fifth degree interpolating polynomials which approximate this function over the entire range by sampling the function at six points using the principles of (a) Chebyshev interpolation and (b) equally-spaced polynomial interpolation. The polynomials should, of course, fit the sampled points exactly. Plot the original function and the interpolating polynomials on the same graph and compare them.

We first employ Chebyshev interpolation. The function $f(x)$ must be sampled at the six roots of $T_6(x')$, $-1 \le x' \le 1$, converted to the interval $0 \le x \le \pi$. This conversion is accomplished by using (4.23). In the notation of the present problem,

$$x_i = \frac{1}{2}[(\pi - 0)x_i' + \pi + 0] = \frac{\pi}{2}x_i' + \frac{\pi}{2}$$

(Here x_i' has taken the role of x_i in (4.23) and x_i has taken the role of z_i.) The six roots of $T_6(x')$ were given in Sec. 4.5. These roots, the converted x_i, and the corresponding $f(x_i)$ are shown in Table 4.16.

The fifth degree interpolating polynomial can now be obtained from the Lagrange polynomial formula (4.16):

$$p_{5C}(x) = \sum_{j=0}^{5} f(x_j)P_j(x)$$

where the $P_j(x)$ are given by (4.14).

Table 4.16

i	x_i'	x_i	$f(x_i)$
0	-0.965926	0.053524	1.977134
1	-0.707107	0.460076	0.575988
2	-0.258819	1.164244	-1.034340
3	$+0.258819$	1.977347	2.721584
4	0.707107	2.681516	-0.181677
5	0.965926	3.088068	-1.971407

Rather than use the Gregory-Newton formula to generate the polynomial for equally spaced points, we shall employ the Lagrange formula. (The polynomial is unique and could be obtained either way.) To obtain six equally-spaced points, the spacing is $\pi/5$.

i	x_i	$f(x_i)$
0	0	2.000000
1	$\pi/5$	-0.272540
2	$2\pi/5$	-0.713530
3	$3\pi/5$	2.522538
4	$4\pi/5$	0.963531
5	π	-2.000000

The fifth degree interpolating polynomial obtained from these equally-spaced data is

$$p_{5E}(x) = \sum_{j=0}^{5} f(x_j)P_j(x)$$

Sample values from the two interpolating polynomials $p_{5C}(x)$ and $p_{5E}(x)$ are plotted in Fig. 4.5 along with the original function. Note that both functions approximate the original function very well except that $p_{5E}(x)$ becomes somewhat inaccurate near the ends of the interval, $x = 0$ and $x = \pi$. This concentration of the error near the ends of the interval is characteristic of polynomial interpolation which is based on equally spaced points. The error for the polynomial $p_{5E}(x)$ reaches a maximum magnitude of about 0.6, or 30%, near each end of the interval. The maximum magnitude of the error for the polynomial $p_{5C}(x)$ based on the Chebyshev zeros does not exceed about 0.3 (15%), or about one-half that of $p_{5E}(x)$. In order to prove that $p_{5C}(x)$ has the minimum maximum error of all fifth degree interpolating polynomials it would be necessary to examine an infinite number of other polynomials. However, $p_{5C}(x)$ is obviously better than $p_{5E}(x)$ in the minimax sense, and since it also seems to approximate the function just about as well as $p_{5E}(x)$ at points far from the ends of the interval, it would seem the better choice for this problem.

In this problem, as well as in Problem 4.7, we have actually illustrated the use of interpolating polynomials as simpler functional approximations to an originally rather complicated function. Interpolation theory is an excellent introduction to functional approximation, which will be treated in more detail in Chapter 7.

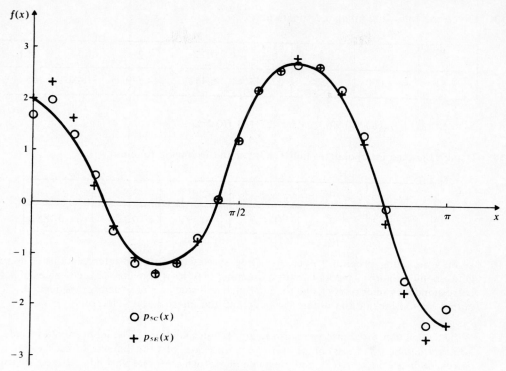

Fig. 4.5

Problems

4.11 Given the following tabulated function:

x	0	1	2	3	4	5
$f(x)$	-7	-4	5	26	65	128

This tabulated function is a polynomial. Find the degree of the polynomial and the coefficient of the highest power of x.

4.12 Prepare a forward difference table for the following function:

x	1	2	3	4	5
$f(x)$	6	10	46	138	430

Now, assuming the function is a polynomial, fill out all blanks in the table and interpolate for $f(4.31)$ using forward difference interpolation with $x = 4$ as a base line.

4.13 Given the following tabulated function:

x	0	0.3	0.6	0.9	1.2	1.5	1.8
f(x)	−3.000	−0.742	2.143	6.452	14.579	31.480	65.628

Find (a) $f(1.09)$, (b) $f(0.93)$, (c) $f(1.42)$, (d) $f(0.21)$.

4.14 Using Lagrange interpolation, find $f(4.3)$ for the following function:

x	0	1.0	2.0	3.8	5
f(x)	0	0.569	0.791	0.224	−0.185

*4.15 Write a computer program to perform Gregory-Newton forward interpolation. The program should require as input an arbitrary number (8 or less) of evenly-spaced values of x, the corresponding values of $f(x)$, and the intermediate value of x at which $f(x)$ is desired. The output should include the difference table and the interpolated value of $f(x)$.

*4.16 Write a computer program to perform Lagrange interpolation. The input should include an arbitrary number (8 or less) of arbitrarily-spaced values of x, the number of such values, the corresponding values of $f(x)$, and the value of x at which $f(x)$ is desired. (If you are using FORTRAN, remember that zero subscripts are not allowed, and some suitable adjustments will have to be made to the formulation in this chapter.)

*4.17 Employ the program written for Problem 4.15 to find $f(1.3)$ for the following function:

x	0	1	2	3	4	5	6	7
f(x)	4	−250	−881	−1667	−2357	−2493	−1295	2450

*4.18 Using the program written for Problem 4.16, find $f(6.3)$ for the following function:

x	0	1.2	1.7	2.8	4.4	5.8	7.0	8.0
f(x)	1.000	0.671	0.398	−0.185	−0.342	0.092	0.300	0.172

*4.19 Resolve Problem 4.13 by using the Lagrange interpolation program written for Problem 4.16. Should the results agree? How closely? Discuss the relative advantages and disadvantages of using polynomial interpolation based on difference tables as compared with Lagrange interpolation, assuming equally-spaced data.

*4.20 Using the principles of Chebyshev interpolation, construct a sixth-degree polynomial approximation to $f(x) = e^{-x/3\pi} \sin x$ on the interval $0 \le x \le 4\pi$. Plot the polynomial and the original function on the same graph and comment on the approximation.

4.21 Using a natural cubic spline, interpolate for $f(3.4)$ given the following equally-spaced function:

x	1	2	3	4	5
$f(x)$	11	9	12	15	11

4.22 Again using a natural cubic spline, find $f(9)$ given the following unequally-spaced tabulated function:

x	3	7	15	22	30
$f(x)$	1	-8	-22	-9	12

4.23 Given the following function:

x	0	0.5	1.0	1.5	2.0	2.5
$f(x)$	2.014	3.221	4.701	7.710	13.594	23.580

Find $f(3.0)$.

4.24 Given the following tabulated function:

x	1.0	2.0	3.0	4.0
$f(x)$	150	36.75	17.33	9.19

Find $f(5.0)$.

Chapter 5

Roots of Equations

5.0 INTRODUCTION

Root solving typically consists of finding the values of x which satisfy relationships such as

$$Ax^3 + Bx^2 = Cx + D$$

or

$$\tan Kx = x$$

These are not truly equations in the sense that they are only satisfied for certain values of x. Depending on the problem, these values of x may be real or complex and may be either finite or infinite in number.

The procedure for finding the roots will always be to collect all terms on one side of the equal sign; for example,

$$Ax^3 + Bx^2 - Cx - D = 0$$

or

$$\tan Kx - x = 0$$

For any values of x other than the roots, these equalities will not be satisfied, so that in general

$$Ax^3 + Bx^2 - Cx - D = f(x)$$

or

$$\tan Kx - x = g(x)$$

Finding the roots of these equations is now equivalent to finding the values of x for which $f(x)$ or $g(x)$ is zero. For this reason the roots of equations are often called the *zeros* of the equations.

We now examine methods of finding the roots of a general function $f(x)$. Unless otherwise stated, we shall deal only with finding the real roots of equations with real coefficients.

64

5.1   BISECTION

Bisection is a "brute force" technique for root solving which is too inefficient for hand computation but is ideally suited to machine computation.   Consider first the simplest possible case: a function $f(x)$ which is known to have one and only one real root in the interval $a < x < b$.   Such a function is shown in Fig. 5.1.

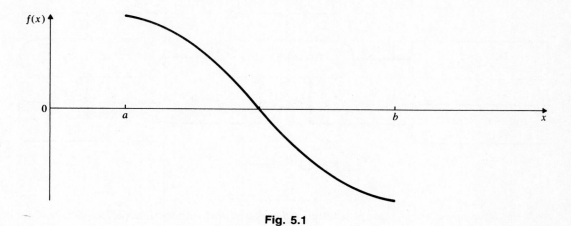

Fig. 5.1

The root may be located as accurately as desired by the following strategy.   Bisect the interval at its midpoint, $x_m = (a + b)/2$.   Now compute $f(x_m)*f(b)$.   If this product is negative, then the root is in the interval $x_m < x < b$ since $f(x)$ has changed sign in that interval.   If the product is positive, then $f(x)$ has not crossed the axis between x_m and b, and the root must be in the interval $a < x < x_m$.   Select the interval which contains the root, bisect it, and repeat the entire procedure.   The process is repeated until the root is located as accurately as desired.   If the root is assumed to be at the midpoint of the last interval found to contain it, the maximum error in the root will be no greater than one-half the size of this interval.   It is useful to represent this algorithm in flow chart form.   The left and right ends of the interval are designated as x_L and x_R respectively, and the final error acceptable in the root as ϵ.   The flow chart is shown in Fig. 5.2.

If there is the possibility of more than one real root in the interval $a < x < b$, then the strategy must be considerably more complex.   If $f(x_L)*f(x_R) < 0$, then there are an odd number of roots in the subinterval, while if $f(x_L)*f(x_R) > 0$, then there are an even number of roots in the subinterval (or none).   Bisection will always find a root if the subinterval chosen for the next bisection is one in which $f(x_L)*f(x_R) < 0$.   However, if there are several roots, several bisections may be necessary initially in order to find a subinterval with this behavior.   No generalized algorithm will be presented for bisection on an interval with an arbitrary number of roots.   It is seldom useful to find only one arbitrary member of a set of roots in an interval, and the complexity of a bisection algorithm to avoid finding the same root more than once would be very great.

As we shall see in our discussions of all of the root-solving methods, there is no substitute for a prior rough knowledge of the behavior of the function and the approximate location of the roots.   This makes it possible to use a small enough initial subinterval for bisection to isolate any desired root.   The approximate behavior of the function

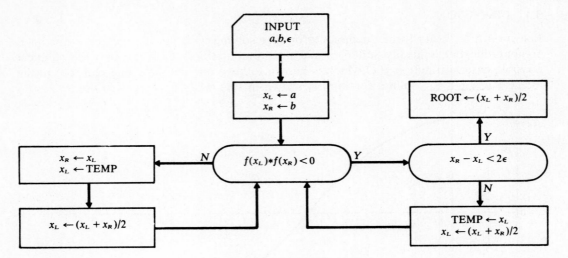

Fig. 5.2 Bisection.

can be determined from a graph plotted on a computer, either on a plotter or the line printer, or from a computer tabulation of the function at reasonably fine intervals. Often even simple hand computations or plotting will be sufficient to avoid such frustrating experiences as finding an unwanted root or missing the desired root. An additional advantage of a rough plot of the function is that such a plot often makes it possible to identify the presence of troublesome tangent points, where the function touches the x axis, but does not cross it, resulting in a multiple root. Bisection will neither locate these tangent points nor indicate their presence. Bisection will, however, find any multiple root at which the function crosses the axis.

5.2 NEWTON'S METHOD (NEWTON-RAPHSON)

Consider a point x_0 which is not a root of the function $f(x)$, but is "reasonably close" to a root. We expand $f(x)$ in a Taylor series about x_0:

$$f(x) = f(x_0) + (x - x_0)f'(x_0) + \frac{(x - x_0)^2}{2!} f''(x_0) + \cdots \tag{5.1}$$

If $f(x)$ is set equal to zero, then x must be a root and the right-hand side of (5.1) constitutes an equation for the root x. Unfortunately, the equation is a polynomial of degree infinity. However, an approximate value of the root x can be obtained by setting $f(x)$ to zero and taking only the first two terms of the right-hand side of (5.1) to yield

$$0 = f(x_0) + (x - x_0)f'(x_0) \tag{5.2}$$

Solving for x gives

$$x = x_0 - \frac{f(x_0)}{f'(x_0)} \tag{5.3}$$

or

$$x - x_0 = \delta = -\frac{f(x_0)}{f'(x_0)} \tag{5.4}$$

Now x represents an improved estimate of the root, and can replace x_0 in (5.3) to yield an even better estimate of the root on the next iteration. The general expression for Newton's method can thus be written as

$$x^{(n+1)} - x^{(n)} = \delta^{(n+1)} = -\frac{f(x^{(n)})}{f'(x^{(n)})} \tag{5.5}$$

where the superscript n denotes values obtained on the nth iteration and $n + 1$ indicates values to be found on the $(n + 1)$th iteration. This iterative procedure will converge to a root for most functions, and if it does converge, it will usually do so extremely rapidly. A flow chart of the algorithm is shown in Fig. 5.3.

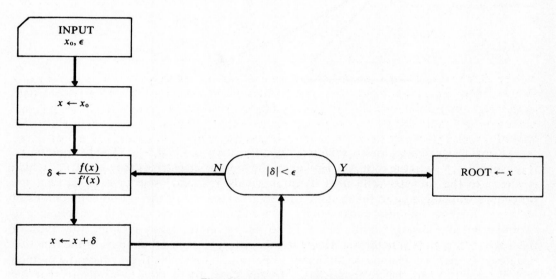

Fig. 5.3 Newton's method.

The algorithm is terminated when the magnitude of the computed change in the value of the root, δ, is less than some predetermined quantity ϵ. This does not guarantee an accuracy of ϵ in the root. Although more sophisticated convergence analyses are possible, a useful and conservative rule of thumb is to choose ϵ as one-tenth of the permissible error in the root. An additional point should be made concerning Fig. 5.3, and in fact all flow charts given in this chapter. No error exits have been provided in case the method diverges or does not find a root in a reasonable number of iterations. A computer program written from this flow chart should include such exits as the programmer feels necessary, but it should be noted that these exits require logic which will increase the running time of the program. If enough is known about the character of the function, such exits may not be necessary.

Despite its rapid convergence, Newton's method has some difficulties with certain types of functions. These difficulties can best be examined, and the most intelligent use made of this powerful method, by considering the graphical interpretation of the algorithm.   Figure 5.4 shows the first iteration for a typical function.   The next guess for the root, $x^{(1)}$, is the intersection with the x axis of a straight line tangent to the function at x_0.   The value $x^{(1)}$ is much closer to the root than the original guess x_0, and it is clear that succeeding iterations will converge rapidly to the root.

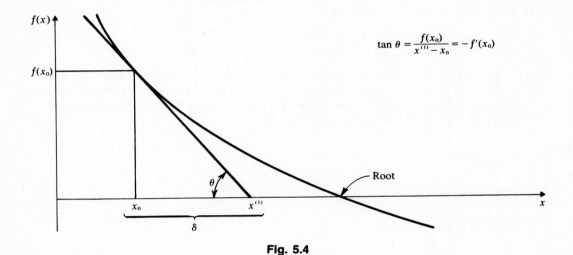

$$\tan \theta = \frac{f(x_0)}{x^{(1)} - x_0} = -f'(x_0)$$

Fig. 5.4

Consider next the simple oscillatory function shown in Fig. 5.5.   The first guess, x_0, is reasonably close to the root A.   However, the tangent line strikes the axis at $x^{(1)}$, which is closer to the root B.   The next iteration yields $x^{(2)}$, and it becomes clear that the procedure will converge to the root B.   This illustrates one of the possible difficulties of Newton's method; an initial guess which is close to one root may result in convergence to a different more distant root.   There is no simple method for avoiding this type of behavior with certain functions.   However, the rough plots or tabulations of the function discussed earlier will usually be sufficient to permit first guesses from which the method will eventually yield the desired roots.   In any case, these plots will ensure that the programmer is aware of the presence of any roots which the method may have missed.

Newton's method also has a tendency to home-in on a local minimum or maximum in a function (not a root) and then as the zero slope region is approached to be thrown far from any region of interest.   The algorithm can also occasionally oscillate back and forth between two regions containing roots for a fairly large number of iterations before finding either root.   These difficulties can be readily avoided with some prior knowledge of the behavior of the function.

It should be noted that some difficulty will be encountered in attempting to use Newton's method to find multiple roots.   For smooth functions, these multiple roots correspond to points where the function becomes tangent to the x axis and then may or may not cross the axis.   This behavior means that as $f(x)$ approaches zero, so does $f'(x)$.   While Newton's method can be shown to be formally convergent for such roots, the rate of convergence is slow, and in practice can make the computation of multiple roots difficult and expensive.   A modified Newton's method, which is very well suited to multiple roots, will be discussed in the next section.

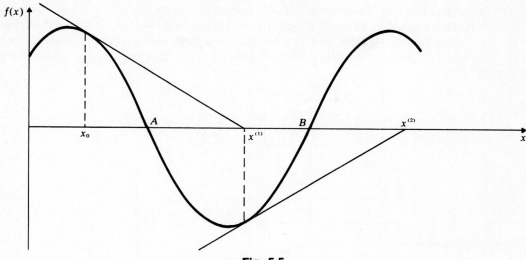

Fig. 5.5

In the illustrative problems at the end of this chapter, specific examples are presented which demonstrate some of the possible difficulties in the use of Newton's method for general root solving.

5.3 MODIFIED NEWTON'S METHOD

The difficulty of Newton's method in dealing with multiple roots leads us to consider a modification of the method discussed by Ralston[3].   As before, we wish to find the roots of a function $f(x)$.   Define a new function $u(x)$, given by

$$u(x) = \frac{f(x)}{f'(x)} \tag{5.6}$$

The function $u(x)$ has the same roots as does $f(x)$, since $u(x)$ becomes zero everywhere that $f(x)$ is zero.

Suppose now that $f(x)$ has a multiple root at $x = c$ of multiplicity r.   (This could occur, for example, if $f(x)$ contained a factor $(x - c)^r$.)   Then $u(x)$ may be readily shown to have a root at $x = c$ of multiplicity r, or a simple root.   Since Newton's method is effective for simple roots, we can apply Newton's method to $u(x)$ instead of $f(x)$.   Applying equation (5.5) gives

$$x^{(n+1)} - x^{(n)} = \delta^{(n+1)} = -\frac{u(x^{(n)})}{u'(x^{(n)})} \tag{5.7}$$

Equation (5.6) gives $u(x)$, and this can be differentiated to yield

$$u'(x) = \frac{(f'(x))^2 - f(x)f''(x)}{(f'(x))^2}$$

or

$$u'(x) = 1 - \frac{f(x)f''(x)}{(f'(x))^2} \tag{5.8}$$

The algorithm may be written in flow chart form as shown by Fig. 5.6. This algorithm is somewhat more expensive than the conventional Newton's method in the sense that it requires the computation of $f''(x)$, but the algorithm retains the same convergence rate as the conventional Newton's method regardless of the multiplicity of the root.

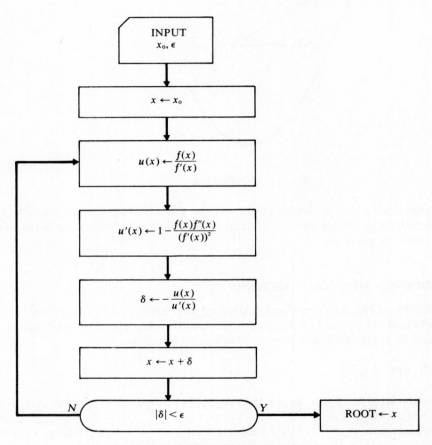

Fig. 5.6   Modified Newton's method.

The advantage of this method over the conventional Newton's method in finding multiple roots is illustrated in Problem 5.6.   See also Problem 5.7.

5.4   THE SECANT METHOD

The secant method is essentially a modification of the conventional Newton's method with the derivative replaced by a difference expression.   This is advantageous if the function is difficult to differentiate, and is also convenient to program in the sense that it is only necessary to supply a function subprogram to the method rather than subprograms for both the function and its derivative.   Replacing the derivative in (5.5) by a simple difference representation yields

$$x^{(n+1)} - x^{(n)} = \delta^{(n+1)} = -\frac{f(x^{(n)})}{[f(x^{(n)}) - f(x^{(n-1)})]/\delta^{(n)}}$$ (5.9)

To use this method, $f(x^{(n-1)})$ must be saved.   This is the value of f from two iterations previous to the present one.   Since no such value will be available for the first iteration, two different initial guesses for the root, x_0 and x_{00}, must be supplied initially to the algorithm.   This algorithm is shown in Fig. 5.7.

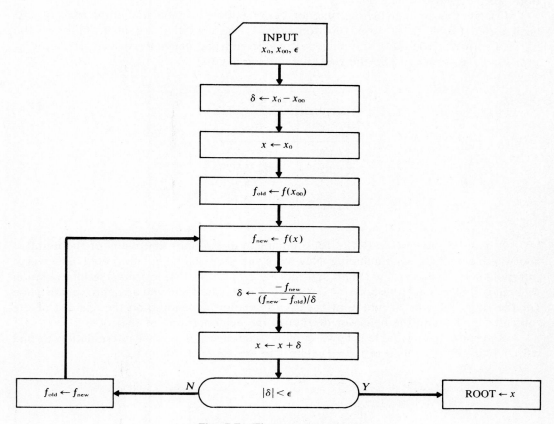

Fig. 5.7 The secant method.

For most functions, the secant method will not be as rapidly convergent as the conventional Newton's method, but its advantages may outweigh this somewhat decreased convergence rate.   If $f'(x)$ is very time consuming to evaluate, then the secant method may actually require less computer time than Newton's method.

5.5 ROOT SOLVING AS INVERSE INTERPOLATION

Suppose that in the neighborhood of a root of $f(x)$ we tabulate $f(x)$ at intervals of x (not necessarily evenly spaced).   Interpolation, as we have seen in Chapter 4, consists of finding a value for $f(x)$ at some predetermined x between the tabulated points.   Root solving, on the other hand, consists of finding the x at which $f(x)$ takes on a predetermined value (zero). Root solving thus may be thought of as inverse interpolation. However, in order to actually use interpolation methods, it is necessary that $f(x)$ be an *invertible* function of x. This means that in the region of interest, to every value of $f(x)$ there must correspond one and only one x. (This must be true for all points in the region, not just the tabulated ones.) The function $f(x)$ may be shown to be invertible if, in the region, $f(x)$ is continuous and differentiable and $f'(x)$ does not pass through zero. Under these conditions we may write x as $x(f)$.

Consider as an example the function $f(x) = \tan x - 2x$ tabulated at intervals of 0.05 near a root (Table 5.1). This function satisfies the conditions of invertibility on the interval shown. The table may thus be considered as an unevenly spaced tabulation of $x(f)$ vs. f. In order to find the root, we must find $x(0)$.

Table 5.1

x	$f(x)$
1.05	-0.3566846
1.10	-0.2352402
1.15	-0.0655030
1.20	$+0.1721513$

It may be shown (see Ref. 3 for a complete discussion) that many of the iterative root-solving techniques (including Newton's method) may be interpreted as inverse interpolation. However, we shall consider here only the simplest inverse interpolation technique, polynomial interpolation on $x(f)$. This method will find an approximate value for the root, with the accuracy of the approximation depending on the spacing of the tabulated points and the behavior of $f(x)$ in the neighborhood of the root.

Returning to the Table 5.1, we employ Lagrange polynomial interpolation to find $x(0)$. It is convenient to rewrite Table 5.1 in the form of Table 5.2.

Table 5.2

i	f	$x(f)$
0	-0.35668	1.05
1	-0.23524	1.10
2	-0.06550	1.15
3	$+0.17215$	1.20

Now,

$$x(0) \approx p_3(0) = 1.05 P_0(0) + 1.10 P_1(0) + 1.15 P_2(0) + 1.20 P_3(0)$$

where

$$P_0(0) = \frac{(0 + 0.23524)(0 + 0.06550)(0 - 0.17215)}{(-0.35668 + 0.23524)(-0.35668 + 0.06550)(-0.35668 - 0.17215)} = 0.14184$$

and similarly

$$P_1(0) = -0.47895$$

$$P_2(0) = 1.22976$$

$$P_3(0) = 0.10734$$

which yields

$$x(0) \approx p_3(0) = 1.16514$$

The exact root is 1.16556, so this answer is in error by about 4.2×10^{-4}.

5.6   A BRIEF NOTE ON SPECIAL METHODS FOR FINDING ROOTS OF POLYNOMIALS

All of the methods which have been discussed in this chapter will find most of the real roots of polynomials with real coefficients. (As has been mentioned, many of the methods do have difficulty in finding multiple roots corresponding to points where the function is tangent to the x axis.)   However, there exist techniques specifically suited to finding all of the roots, single or multiple, real or complex, of polynomials with real coefficients.

We shall not give the computational details for any of these methods, since the algorithms are quite complicated, particularly if provision is made to find all multiple and complex roots.   Ralston[3] gives complete descriptions of many of these methods with discussions of convergence rates and applicability to digital computation.   These techniques include Graeffe's root-squaring method, the Lehmer-Schur method, and various methods based on synthetic division.

Illustrative Problems

5.1   The function $f(x) = x^2 - 0.9x - 8.5$ has one real root in the interval $2 \le x \le 3$. How many bisections would be required to locate this root to an accuracy of $\epsilon = 10^{-6}$?

Since the root is originally known to be in an interval $3 - 2 = 1$ unit wide, after one bisection the root will be isolated to an interval 1/2 unit wide.   After two bisections the interval will be $1/2^2$ unit wide, and after n bisections the interval will be $1/2^n$ unit wide.   If the algorithm in Fig. 5.2 is used, then the root is assumed to be at the center of the last interval found, and the error in the root will be no more than one-half of that interval.   Thus the error criterion will be satisfied if

$$\frac{1}{2}\left(\frac{1}{2^n}\right) = \frac{1}{2^{n+1}} < \epsilon \qquad \text{or} \qquad \frac{1}{2^{n+1}} < 10^{-6}$$

Since $1/2^{20} = 0.9536 \times 10^{-6}$, $n = 19$ bisections will be sufficient.   Note that this answer is completely independent of the character of the function $f(x)$ (assuming that $f(x)$ crosses the axis once and only once in the initial interval).

5.2   Find the roots of $f(x) = e^{-x/4}(2 - x) - 1$.

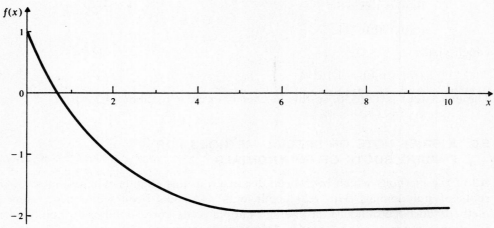

Fig. 5.8

A rough plot of this function is shown in Fig. 5.8.   The function has a root somewhere between $x = 0$ and $x = 2$, reaches a minimum somewhere near $x = 6$, and then appears to flatten out.   By looking at the analytical form of $f(x)$, it is apparent that $f(x) \to -1$ as $x \to \infty$.   It is also apparent that there are no negative roots.   We will employ Newton's method (Fig. 5.3) to find the root.   It would appear that $x = 1$ would be a good first guess, but to show the strong convergence rate of Newton's method, we shall pick a poorer guess, $x = 3$.   This gives

$$f(3) = -1.472366, \qquad f'(3) = -0.354275$$

so

$$\delta = -\frac{-1.472366}{-0.354275} = -4.155999$$

which yields an estimate for x of

$$x = x + \delta = 3.0 - 4.155999 = -1.155999$$

The next iteration yields

$$\delta = -\frac{f(-1.155999)}{f'(-1.155999)} = -\frac{3.213548}{-2.388477} = 1.345437$$

$$x = x + \delta = -1.155999 + 1.345437 = 0.189438$$

The next four iterations give

$$x = 0.714043, \qquad \delta = 0.52461$$
$$x = 0.782542, \qquad \delta = 0.06850$$
$$x = 0.783595, \qquad \delta = 0.00105$$
$$x = 0.783596, \qquad \delta = 0.890 \times 10^{-6}$$

The last value of x is the root accurate to six decimal places.

The rapid convergence rate with such a poor guess might tend to inspire such confidence in the method that one could question the need for the rough plot of $f(x)$. This false confidence can be dispelled by guessing $x = 8$. This gives

$$f(8) = -1.812011, \qquad f'(8) = 0.067668$$

and

$$\delta = -\frac{-1.812011}{0.067668} = 26.778107$$

$$x = x + \delta = 8 + 26.778107 = 34.778107$$

The next iteration yields

$$x = 869.1519$$

along with a computer underflow in the exponential routine. What has happened is that the guess was beyond the local minimum around $x = 6$, and the method is now proceeding vainly toward $x = +\infty$ attempting to find a root as the function asymptotically approaches $f(x) = -1$.

5.3   Find $\sqrt{7}$ by using root-solving methods.

This problem may be restated as finding the roots of $x^2 - 7 = 0$. The roots occur as positive and negative pairs. We shall seek only the positive root. Newton's method will be used:

$$f(x) = x^2 - 7, \qquad f'(x) = 2x$$

Since $3 = \sqrt{9}$, $x_0 = 3$ should be a reasonable guess. The first iteration is

$$\delta = -\frac{f(x_0)}{f'(x_0)} = -\frac{3^2 - 7}{2(3)} = -0.3333333$$

$$x = x_0 + \delta = 3 - 0.3333333 = 2.6666667$$

The second iteration is

$$\delta = -\frac{(2.6666667)^2 - 7}{2(2.6666667)} = -0.0208333$$

$$x = x + \delta = 2.6666667 - 0.0208333 = 2.6458334$$

The third iteration is

$$\delta = -0.0000820, \qquad x = 2.6457514$$

All eight digits of this value of x are correct! We have carried seven decimal places in this problem to illustrate the power of Newton's method in taking square root. In fact, Newton's method is used for virtually all square root routines for digital computers as well as on those desk calculators which include a square root capability.

5.4   Find the smallest positive root of the function

$$f(x) = x^2 |\sin x| - 4$$

A rough sketch of this function is shown in Fig. 5.9. The function closely approaches the x axis near $x = 2.4$, but a closely spaced tabulation of the function in this region indicates no root. The smallest positive root is thus between $x = 3$ and $x = 4$. This function has a

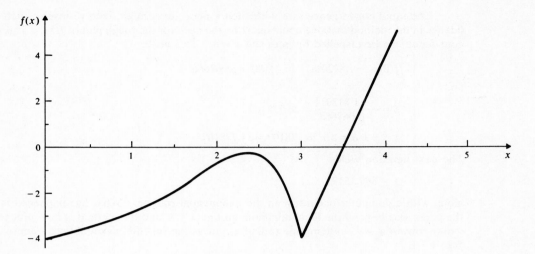

Fig. 5.9

discontinuous derivative at $x \approx 3$ (actually at $x = \pi$) and at various larger values of x as well. Root-solving methods based on the use of the derivative or difference approximations must be used with care for this function, not only because of the discontinuities but also because of the local maximum near $x = 2.4$. Bisection would thus seem to be the safest and simplest approach, since all of these factors can simply be ignored. With initial values of $x_L = 3.2$ and $x_R = 3.6$, the bisection algorithm (Fig. 5.2) produces a root of $x = 3.478508$ accurate to $\epsilon = 10^{-6}$ in 19 bisections.

For purposes of illustration, we will also apply the secant method (Fig. 5.7) to this problem. To begin this algorithm, we need two closely spaced initial guesses for the root; we choose $x_0 = 3.6$ and $x_{00} = 3.7$. Now,

$$f(3.6) = 1.735055, \qquad f(3.7) = 3.253452$$

The difference estimate of the derivative is

$$\frac{f(3.6) - f(3.7)}{-0.1} = \frac{-1.518397}{-0.1} = 15.18397$$

Then

$$\delta = -\frac{f(3.6)}{15.18397} = -\frac{1.735055}{15.18397} = -0.114269$$

and $x = x_0 + \delta = 3.6 - 0.114269 = 3.485730$. For the next iteration, the derivative is estimated by

$$\frac{f(3.485730) - f(3.6)}{3.485730 - 3.6} = \frac{-1.635724}{-0.114270} = 14.31455$$

and

$$\delta = -\frac{f(3.485730)}{14.31455} = -\frac{0.099331}{14.31455} = -0.006939$$

$$x = x + \delta = 3.485730 - 0.006939 = 3.478790$$

Two more iterations give $x = 3.478508$ with $\delta = 0.347 \times 10^{-6}$. This value of the root is identical with that obtained from bisection.

Suppose now that we had not bothered to find out the behavior of the function, but simply picked two values of x, say $x_0 = 2.8$ and $x_{00} = 2.9$, to use in applying the secant method. These values seem reasonably close to the root, but are actually far enough away to result in disaster, since they are to the left side of the discontinuity in the derivative at $x = \pi$. The first iteration produces $x = 2.576$. Many more iterations result in values of x scattered rather randomly from $x = 1.007$ to $x = 2.643$ and it becomes obvious that the method is attempting to find the nonexistent root at the local maximum near $x = 2.4$. This process will never converge to anything unless the method accidently hits a point on the function with a sufficiently small slope to throw the next guess far from the local maximum and into a region where a root exists.

5.5   Find the smallest positive root (other than zero) of

$$f(x) = \cos x \cosh x - 1$$

A rough sketch of this function in the range of the first positive root is shown in Fig. 5.10.

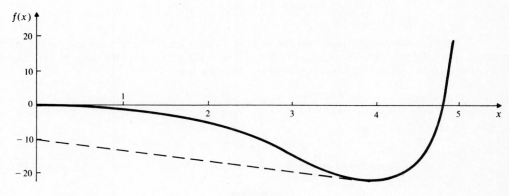

Fig. 5.10

We choose the secant method and pick two first guesses of $x_0 = 4.4$ and $x_{00} = 4.5$. Six iterations yield a value for the root of

$$x = 4.73004, \qquad \delta = 0.442 \times 10^{-6}$$

This root is correct to the five decimal places shown and was easily obtained.

Much more interesting is the failure of the secant method which occurs if we are slightly less accurate with our first two guesses. Suppose we guess $x = 3.8$ and $x_{00} = 3.9$. Four iterations with the secant method produce

$$x = -3.63597, \qquad \delta = -0.407 \times 10^{-56}$$

Our first impression would be that we have found a negative root (it is not unusual for a root-solving algorithm to produce a root rather distant from the initial guess) and that we have located this root extremely accurately since δ is so small. In fact, this value of x is *not a root* of $f(x)$ at all! We will follow the steps of the secant method algorithm to find out exactly what happened. We first note from Fig. 5.10 that the guesses $x_0 = 3.8$ and $x_{00} = 3.9$ are slightly to the left of the local minimum at $x \approx 4$. The difference approximation to the derivative is

$$\frac{f(3.8) - f(3.9)}{-0.1} = \frac{-18.68744 - (-18.93875)}{-0.1} = -2.5131$$

Since the points are so close to the local minimum, this is a relatively small slope, and corresponds to the dotted line shown in Fig. 5.10. The value of δ is

$$\delta = -\frac{f(3.8)}{-2.5131} = -\frac{-18.68744}{-2.5131} = -7.43598$$

and

$$x = x + \delta = 3.8 - 7.43598 = -3.63598$$

Graphically, this is the point at which the dotted line intersects the x axis. The function $f(x)$ is an even function, so $f(-x) = f(x)$. We would thus expect $f(-3.63598)$ to be reasonably close in value to $f(3.8)$, and we find

$$f(-3.63598) = -17.70966$$

The next difference approximation to the derivative becomes

$$\frac{f(-3.63598) - f(3.8)}{-3.63598 - 3.8} = \frac{-17.70966 - (-18.68744)}{-8.43598} = -0.11591$$

This is a very small slope, and corresponds to the virtually horizontal line joining $f(3.8)$ and $f(-3.63598)$. The intersection of this line with the x axis will obviously be very far out the negative x axis. To find the location, we compute

$$\delta = -\frac{f(-3.63598)}{-0.11591} = -134.68077$$

and thus

$$x = x + \delta = -3.63598 - 134.68077 = -138.31674$$

Due to the character of $\cosh x$, this could result in a very large value of $f(x)$, and in fact, we find

$$f(-138.31674) = 0.5655 \times 10^{60}(!)$$

The next value of δ is

$$\delta = -\frac{f(-138.31674)}{\left[\dfrac{f(-138.31674) - f(-3.63598)}{-138.31674 - (-3.63598)}\right]} = -\frac{0.5655 \times 10^{60}}{\left[\dfrac{0.5655 \times 10^{60} - (-17.70966)}{-134.68077}\right]}$$

The quantity 0.5655×10^{60} is so overpowering that this yields simply

$$\delta = 134.68077$$

$$x = x + \delta = -138.31674 + 134.68077 = -3.63598$$

which puts us back to where the previous iteration started. The next δ is

$$\delta = -\frac{f(-3.63598)}{\left[\dfrac{f(-3.63598) - f(-138.31674)}{-3.63598 - (-138.31674)}\right]} = -\frac{(-17.70966)}{\left[\dfrac{-17.70966 - 0.5655 \times 10^{60}}{134.68077}\right]}$$

$$= -0.4074 \times 10^{-56}$$

The method thus appears to have converged even though it obviously has not.   What has happened is that by beginning near a local minimum, we have been thrown far from the region of our initial guess.   Subsequent difference approximations to the derivatives span such large ranges of x that they do not in any way approximate local derivatives.   Eventually, we reach such a large value of $f(x)$ relative to the value from the preceding iteration that the difference approximation to the slope is essentially infinite, and the method appears to have converged regardless of the value of x which is finally reached.

Note that all of these meaningless computations could be avoided simply by initially sketching the function, and recognizing the problems which can be caused by a local minimum below the axis.

5.6   Find the positive real roots of the function

$$f(x) = x^4 - 8.6x^3 - 35.51x^2 + 464.4x - 998.46$$

A sketch of this function is shown in Fig. 5.11.   This sketch is based on a tabulation of $f(x)$ on the interval $0 \leqslant x \leqslant 10$ using a very coarse interval of 1 unit.

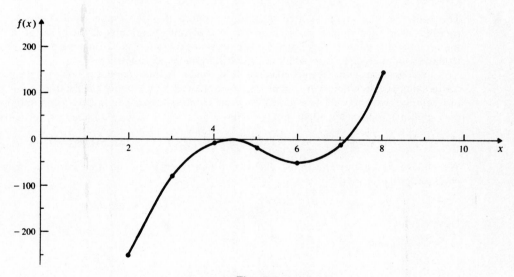

Fig. 5.11

It appears that there may be a multiple root (and a tangent point) near $x = 4$ and a simple root between $x = 7$ and $x = 8$.   The root(s) near $x = 4$ could also be two closely spaced real roots if the function crosses the axis, or perhaps no real root(s) at all if the function does not touch the axis (the tabulation is too coarse to tell for sure).

We begin by finding the simple root between $x = 7$ and $x = 8$.   Newton's method (in Fig. 5.3) should be suitable for this root.   We choose $x_0 = 7.0$ as the initial guess and ask that the final magnitude of δ be less than 10^{-6}.   We need the first derivative

$$f'(x) = 4x^3 - 25.8x^2 - 71.02x + 464.4$$

Now applying the algorithm of Newton's method,

$$f(7.0) = -36.4500, \qquad f'(7.0) = 75.0600$$

$$\delta = -\frac{-36.4500}{75.0600} = 0.485612$$

$$x = x + \delta = 7.0 + 0.485612 = 7.485612$$

The second iteration is

$$f(7.485612) = 20.6451, \qquad f'(7.485612) = 164.891$$

$$\delta = -\frac{20.6451}{164.891} = -0.125205$$

$$x = x + \delta = 7.485612 - 0.125205 = 7.36041$$

The next three iterations yield

$$x = 7.34857, \qquad \delta = -0.118 \times 10^{-1}$$

$$x = 7.34847, \qquad \delta = -0.102 \times 10^{-3}$$

$$x = 7.34847, \qquad \delta = -0.758 \times 10^{-8}$$

The root has now been located accurately. Note that the value of δ decreases very rapidly. For most simple roots, the value of δ on any iteration is of the order of $|\delta|^2$ from the previous iteration. This holds for the present problem. Newton's method is thus said to have a convergence rate which is *quadratic* for most functions.

We now turn to the possible multiple root. A finer tabulation of $f(x)$ near $x = 4$ reveals that $f(x)$ becomes very small but never changes sign. Since the function is simple to differentiate, we choose the modified Newton's method discussed in Sec. 5.3 in anticipation of a multiple root. We must supply subprograms to compute $f(x)$ and the derivatives

$$f'(x) = 4x^3 - 25.8x^2 - 71.02x + 464.4, \qquad f''(x) = 12x^2 - 51.6x - 71.02$$

We choose $x_0 = 4.0$ as the initial guess, and ask that $|\delta|$ on the final iteration be less in magnitude than $\epsilon = 10^{-6}$:

$$f(4.0) = -3.42, \qquad f'(4.0) = 23.52, \qquad f''(4.0) = -85.42$$

Now

$$u(4) = \frac{f(4)}{f'(4)} = \frac{-3.42}{23.52} = -0.145408$$

$$u'(4) = 1 - \frac{f(4)f''(4)}{(f'(4))^2} = 1 - \frac{(-3.42)(-85.42)}{(23.52)^2} = 0.471906$$

and

$$\delta = -\frac{u(4)}{u'(4)} = -\frac{-0.145408}{0.471906} = 0.308129$$

$$x = x + \delta = 4.0 + 0.308129 = 4.308129$$

Three more iterations yield

$$x = 4.300001, \qquad \delta = -0.812 \times 10^{-2}$$

$$x = 4.300000, \qquad \delta = -0.807 \times 10^{-5}$$

$$x = 4.300000, \qquad \delta = -0.660 \times 10^{-9}$$

Thus we have found the multiple root very accurately in four iterations. Note that the convergence rate of the modified Newton's method for this multiple root is quadratic.

For comparison, we can also find the multiple root by using the conventional Newton's method, with the same initial guess of $x = 4.0$ and the same ϵ of 10^{-6}:

$$f(4.0) = -3.42, \qquad f'(4.0) = 23.52$$

so

$$\delta = -\frac{f(4.0)}{f'(4.0)} = -\frac{-3.42}{23.52} = 0.145408$$

$$x = x + \delta = 4.0 + 0.145408 = 4.145408$$

The next four iterations produce

$$x = 4.22138, \qquad \delta = 0.075974$$
$$x = 4.26033, \qquad \delta = 0.038952$$
$$x = 4.28007, \qquad \delta = 0.019740$$
$$x = 4.29001, \qquad \delta = 0.009939$$

The method is obviously converging very slowly, with each δ only about one-half of the magnitude of the preceding δ. This convergence rate is termed *linear*. In all, 19 iterations are necessary to obtain

$$x = 4.300000, \qquad \delta = 0.612 \times 10^{-6}$$

The advantages of the modified Newton's method for multiple roots is obvious.

One very significant practical computational point should be mentioned. For the first attempt at finding this root, the function subprograms for f, f', and f'' used the standard integer exponentiation capability of the FORTRAN IV compiler to compute x^4 and x^3. It was not possible to obtain convergence to the desired accuracy even with the modified Newton's method, and in fact the estimates of the root varied from $x = 4.2777$ to $x = 4.5233$ with $|\delta|$ never smaller than 0.001. It was then determined that if x^4 was computed as $(x)(x)(x)(x)$, convergence could be readily obtained. The small amount of error involved in the compiler's use of the logarithm routine for exponentiation apparently resulted in the function never touching the axis at all. (Most compilers use products of x with itself for low integer powers of x, but shift to the log routine for high powers. The compiler used here shifted at x^4.) The solution for multiple roots can obviously be *very* sensitive to small errors in the computation of the function.

5.7 Find all roots of

$$f(x) = x^3 - 12.42x^2 + 50.444x - 66.552$$

in the interval $4 \leqslant x \leqslant 6$.

A rough sketch of the function is shown in Fig. 5.12.

If there are any roots of $f(x)$ in this interval, they are near $x = 4.8$ and consist of either a multiple root or two closely-spaced simple roots. A finely-spaced tabulation reveals that the function does go slightly negative, so there are apparently two closely-spaced simple roots. We apply the conventional Newton's method with a first guess of $x_0 = 4.5$ and $\epsilon = 10^{-6}$. The method requires eight iterations to reach convergence, yielding

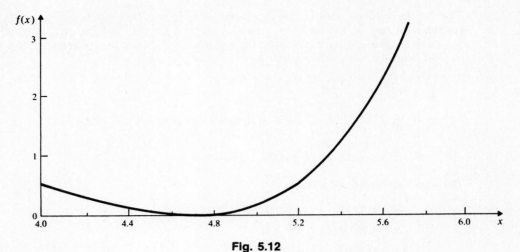

Fig. 5.12

$$x = 4.61263, \qquad \delta = 0.11263$$
$$x = 4.66228, \qquad \delta = 0.04966$$
$$x = 4.68541, \qquad \delta = 0.02313$$
$$x = 4.69574, \qquad \delta = 0.01032$$
$$x = 4.69937, \qquad \delta = 0.00364$$
$$x = 4.69998, \qquad \delta = 0.611 \times 10^{-3}$$
$$x = 4.70000, \qquad \delta = 0.184 \times 10^{-4}$$
$$x = 4.70000, \qquad \delta = 0.168 \times 10^{-7}$$

Note that the convergence rate is virtually linear, rather than quadratic, until the root is approached very closely. This is because the function approaches the axis with a very small and slowly varying slope, clearly very similar to the behavior near a multiple root. In order to find the other root, we use Newton's method with an initial guess of $x = 4.8$ and $\epsilon = 10^{-6}$. Seven iterations produce

$$x = 4.72000, \qquad \delta = -0.250 \times 10^{-7}$$

with essentially the same convergence rate as before.

Since the convergence rate of the conventional Newton's method corresponds more closely for this problem to the rate which usually results from multiple roots, it is reasonable to consider the suitability of the modified Newton's method (Fig. 5.3) in this case. Using an initial guess of $x_0 = 4.5$ with the modified Newton's method yields

$$x = 4.69258, \qquad \delta = 0.19258$$
$$x = 4.70134, \qquad \delta = 0.00876$$
$$x = 4.70010, \qquad \delta = -0.00123$$
$$x = 4.70000, \qquad \delta = -0.100 \times 10^{-3}$$
$$x = 4.70000, \qquad \delta = -0.507 \times 10^{-6}$$

This method needed five iterations to reach a $|\delta|$ of 10^{-6}, and while the convergence rate is clearly greater than that of the conventional Newton's method, note that the second iteration overshot the root.   This overshoot is due to the presence of the second derivative in the method.   In contrast, while the conventional method required three more iterations, the root was approached monotonically from below.   If we now attempt to find the larger root using the modified Newton's method with $x_0 = 4.8$ and $\epsilon = 10^{-6}$, we obtain on the first iteration

$$x = 4.71014, \qquad \delta = -0.08986$$

The first estimate has overshot the root to essentially the midpoint of the interval between the two roots.   The next four iterations yield

$$x = 4.71024, \qquad \delta = 0.106 \times 10^{-3}$$
$$x = 4.71045, \qquad \delta = 0.212 \times 10^{-3}$$
$$x = 4.71088, \qquad \delta = 0.422 \times 10^{-3}$$
$$x = 4.71171, \qquad \delta = 0.834 \times 10^{-3}$$

Note that the magnitude of δ is actually increasing on each iteration, as the method attempts to correct the overshoot.   It takes three more iterations until $|\delta|$ begins to decrease and a total of eleven iterations to converge to

$$x = 4.72000, \qquad \delta = 0.392 \times 10^{-6}$$

Since the conventional method took only seven iterations to converge to the same root with the same initial guess, the conventional method is clearly superior for this root.   As a matter of interest, if a first guess of $x_0 = 4.9$ is used for the modified Newton's method, the method overshoots so far that it converges to the *smaller* root ($x = 4.70000$) in only five iterations!

The conclusion must be that the conventional Newton's method is superior for simple roots, even if they are very closely spaced, if only because of its geometrically easily predictable behavior, and less costly computation per iteration.   The modified method may converge more rapidly than the conventional method in some cases and more slowly in others, but the presence of the second derivative makes it difficult to predict when it may be best, or even to which root it may converge.

Problems

*5.8   Write a computer program to use bisection to find a root of a general function $f(x)$ on the interval $a < x < b$.   Assume that there is one and only one simple root in this interval.   Input parameters should be a,b and the maximum allowable error in the root.   The program should be written in such a way that $f(x)$ can be supplied as a function subprogram.

*5.9   Write a computer program to use Newton's method to find one root of a general function $f(x)$.   Assume that the method will converge to a root.   (It may be a good idea to include intermediate printing of important quantities in order to recognize possible divergence.)   Input parameters should be an initial guess for the root and the magnitude of the final correction on the root (the value of δ at convergence).   The function $f(x)$ and its derivative $f'(x)$ should be assumed to be available from function subprograms.

*5.10   Repeat Problem 5.9 for the modified Newton's method discussed in Sec. 5.3.   The second derivative $f''(x)$ should also be assumed to be available from a function subprogram.

*5.11   Repeat Problem 5.9 for the secant method.   The input parameters should include two closely spaced but different first guesses for the root as well as the value of δ at convergence.   Only $f(x)$ will be needed from a function subprogram.

*5.12   Verify the general programs above by finding the positive root of $f(x) = x^3 - e^{-x}$.   This function has one and only one positive simple root located at $x = 0.77288$.

5.13   Find $\sqrt{3}$ accurate to six decimal places by using Newton's method with an initial guess of 2.

5.14   Find $\sqrt[3]{75}$ accurate to six decimal places by using Newton's method with an initial guess of 4.

5.15   Find a real root of $f(x) = x^3 - 3.23x^2 - 5.54x + 9.84$ by using the secant method with $x_0 = 0.9$ and $x_{00} = 1.0$.

5.16   Find a root of $f(x) = \cos x - x$ in the range $0 \leq x \leq \pi/2$ by using Newton's method.

5.17   The function $f(x) = x^2 - 2e^{-x}x + e^{-2x}$ has one multiple real root.   Find this root by using the modified Newton's method with $x_0 = 1$.   Also try the conventional Newton's method with the same initial guess and compare the number of iterations necessary to attain the same accuracy.

5.18   Show that the function of Problem 5.17 is a perfect square and that each of the factors has only one simple real root.   Find this root by any suitable method.   How should this root compare with the root found in Problem 5.17?

*5.19   Find the first five positive roots of $f(x) = \tan x - 2x$.   Be careful, since $\tan x \to \infty$ or $-\infty$ several times in the range of x which includes these roots.

5.20   Find the zero of the following function in the indicated range by inverse interpolation:

x	$f(x)$
3.6	0.0954655
3.7	0.0538340
3.8	0.0128210
3.9	−0.0272440
4.0	−0.0660433
4.1	−0.1032733

5.21   Find all the real roots of $f(x) = x^4 - 7.223x^3 + 13.447x^2 - 0.672x - 10.223$.

*5.22   Given the function $f(t) = e^{-1.5t}(3 \sin 3t) + 0.3 \sin 4t$.   Find the maximum value which $f(t)$ can attain, and the value of t at which it occurs.

*5.23   Find all of the real roots of $f(x) = x^4 - 12.2x^3 + 55.57x^2 - 111.996x + 84.2724$.   Watch for multiple roots.

*5.24   Find the first five positive roots of $f(x) = \cos x \cosh x + 1$.   Finding the larger roots will require some care since $\cosh x$ can get very large.

Chapter 6

The Solution of Simultaneous Linear Algebraic Equations and Matrix Inversion

6.0 INTRODUCTION

The solution of sets of simultaneous linear algebraic equations (and matrix inversion) consumes a significant fraction of the computer time at virtually all general purpose scientific computer installations. The solution of such sets arises in a wide variety of problems, including the numerical solution of ordinary and partial differential equations, structural analysis, network analysis, optimization, and data analysis. Sets consisting of large numbers of equations are commonly encountered, and the choice of a suitable method for any given problem which is both accurate and efficient is of prime importance. Since basic matrix techniques are needed in this chapter as well as later ones, we begin with a discussion of matrix terminology and operations.

6.1 BASIC MATRIX TERMINOLOGY AND OPERATIONS

A *matrix* is defined in this context as a rectangular array of numbers, with its size characterized by the number of rows and columns in the array. Thus

$$A = \begin{bmatrix} 1 & 7 & -1 & 4 & 8 & 7 \\ 2 & 0 & 5 & 4 & 3 & -1 \\ 1 & -1 & 2 & 3 & 1 & 9 \\ 6 & 2 & -1 & 4 & -1 & 1 \end{bmatrix}$$

is a 4 (row) by 6 (column) matrix. Any given element of the matrix A will be denoted by A_{ij}, where i is the row location and j the column location. Thus $A_{23} = 5$.

Our primary concern will be with square matrices and matrices of column dimension 1 or row dimension 1. Matrices with column dimension 1, such as

$$D = \begin{bmatrix} 2 \\ 7 \\ 3 \\ 5 \end{bmatrix}$$

are referred to as *column vectors*, while matrices with row dimension 1 such as

$$F = [1 \quad -3 \quad 5 \quad 2]$$

are called *row vectors*.

Square matrices can have certain special configurations which are of interest. We shall illustrate with a 4×4 matrix. All statements, of course, apply to square matrices of any size. Consider

$$C = \begin{bmatrix} c_{11} & c_{12} & c_{13} & c_{14} \\ c_{21} & c_{22} & c_{23} & c_{24} \\ c_{31} & c_{32} & c_{33} & c_{34} \\ c_{41} & c_{42} & c_{43} & c_{44} \end{bmatrix} \tag{6.1}$$

The diagonal consisting of c_{11}, c_{22}, c_{33}, and c_{44} is termed the *main diagonal* of the matrix. The matrix is termed *symmetric* if $c_{ij} = c_{ji}$. An *upper triangular* matrix is one in which all elements below the main diagonal are zero. Thus

$$C = \begin{bmatrix} c_{11} & c_{12} & c_{13} & c_{14} \\ & c_{22} & c_{23} & c_{24} \\ & & c_{33} & c_{34} \\ & & & c_{44} \end{bmatrix} \tag{6.2}$$

is upper triangular. Note that when large blocks of elements are zero they are simply left blank in the matrix representation. A *lower triangular* matrix is one in which all elements above the main diagonal are zero. A *diagonal* matrix is one in which all elements are zero except those on the main diagonal. A particularly important diagonal matrix is

$$I = \begin{bmatrix} 1 & & & \\ & 1 & & \\ & & 1 & \\ & & & 1 \end{bmatrix} \tag{6.3}$$

which is termed the *unit matrix* or the *identity matrix*. A *banded* matrix has all zero elements except for a band centered on the main diagonal. Thus

$$C = \begin{bmatrix} c_{11} & c_{12} & & \\ c_{21} & c_{22} & c_{23} & \\ & c_{32} & c_{33} & c_{34} \\ & & c_{43} & c_{44} \end{bmatrix} \tag{6.4}$$

is a banded matrix of bandwidth three, also called a *tridiagonal* matrix.

We can now define some of the basic matrix operations. Matrix addition is represented as

$$S = A + B \tag{6.5}$$

and defined as

$$s_{ij} = a_{ij} + b_{ij} \tag{6.6}$$

Thus each element of the matrix S is formed by adding the corresponding elements of A and B; for example,

$$s_{12} = a_{12} + b_{12}$$

Although A and B need not be square, they must have identical row dimensions and identical column dimensions. The matrix S will obviously have the same row and column dimensions as A and B. Matrix subtraction is simply the negative of matrix addition. These operations are commutative; that is,

$$A + B = B + A \tag{6.7}$$

and

$$A - B = -B + A \tag{6.8}$$

Matrix multiplication is represented as

$$P = AB \tag{6.9}$$

and defined as

$$p_{ij} = \sum_{k=1}^{n} a_{ik} b_{kj} \tag{6.10}$$

where n is the column dimension of A and the row dimension of B. These dimensions must obviously be the same in order for multiplication to be defined. The resulting matrix P will have the row dimension of A and the column dimension of B. Thus

$$P = \begin{bmatrix} 1 & 2 & 1 \\ -1 & 3 & 4 \end{bmatrix} \begin{bmatrix} 1 & 2 \\ 2 & -3 \\ 1 & 3 \end{bmatrix}$$

$$P = \begin{bmatrix} 6 & -1 \\ 9 & 1 \end{bmatrix}$$

and, for example,

$$p_{12} = a_{11} b_{12} + a_{12} b_{22} + a_{13} b_{32}$$
$$= (1)(2) + (2)(-3) + (1)(3) = -1$$

The unit matrix I acquires its other name, the identity matrix, from the property that for a square matrix A,

$$AI = A \tag{6.11}$$

It is also true that

$$IA = A \tag{6.12}$$

Matrix multiplication is obviously not in general commutative, i.e., in general,

$$AB \neq BA \tag{6.13}$$

In fact, for nonsquare matrices, if AB is defined, BA may not even be defined.

Matrix division is not defined. However, if C is square, another square matrix, C^{-1}, called the *inverse* of C, can usually be defined such that

$$CC^{-1} = I \tag{6.14}$$

(It is also true that $C^{-1}C = I$.)   The conditions under which C^{-1} exists and how it may be obtained will be explored in later sections of this chapter.   Note that if C^{-1} exists, then

$$(C^{-1})^{-1} = C \tag{6.15}$$

We may also define the *transpose* of a matrix.   The transpose of A is denoted as A^T and is obtained by replacing a_{ij} by a_{ji}.   Thus if

$$A = \begin{bmatrix} 1 & -1 \\ 2 & 4 \\ 3 & -2 \end{bmatrix}$$

then

$$A^T = \begin{bmatrix} 1 & 2 & 3 \\ -1 & 4 & -2 \end{bmatrix}$$

A square matrix C is termed *orthogonal* if

$$C^T = C^{-1} \tag{6.16}$$

The *determinant* of a square matrix C is denoted as det C and is defined as the sum of all possible products formed by taking one element from each row in order starting from the top and one element from each column, where the sign of each product depends on the permutation of the column indices.   Each product is multiplied by $(-1)^r$, where r is the number of times the column index *decreases* in the product.   Thus in a 4×4 matrix, one term would be

$$c_{13}c_{22}c_{31}c_{44}$$

and since the column index decreases three times (from 3 to 2, from 3 to 1, and from 2 to 1) the sign on this product would be the sign of $(-1)^3$, or $-$.   This definition is not practical as a method for evaluating determinants except for diagonal matrices and very small matrices.   For a diagonal $n \times n$ matrix,

$$\det C = \prod_{i=1}^{n} c_{ii} \tag{6.17}$$

For a 2×2 matrix,

$$\det C = c_{11}c_{22} - c_{12}c_{21} \tag{6.18}$$

The definition can also be used to evaluate the determinant for 3×3 matrices, but in general other methods should be used for larger matrices.   In particular, since some equation-solving methods are based on diagonalization of matrices, determinants can sometimes be easily evaluated as a by-product of equation solving.   This will be discussed further in Sec. 6.6.

6.2 MATRIX REPRESENTATION AND FORMAL SOLUTION OF SIMULTANEOUS LINEAR EQUATIONS

Consider a set of simultaneous linear equations (we arbitrarily choose four equations in four unknowns for illustrative purposes).   This set can be written as

$$c_{11}x_1 + c_{12}x_2 + c_{13}x_3 + c_{14}x_4 = r_1$$

$$c_{21}x_1 + c_{22}x_2 + c_{23}x_3 + c_{24}x_4 = r_2$$

$$c_{31}x_1 + c_{32}x_2 + c_{33}x_3 + c_{34}x_4 = r_3 \qquad (6.19)$$

$$c_{41}x_1 + c_{42}x_2 + c_{43}x_3 + c_{44}x_4 = r_4$$

An equivalent representation in matrix form is

$$\begin{bmatrix} c_{11} & c_{12} & c_{13} & c_{14} \\ c_{21} & c_{22} & c_{23} & c_{24} \\ c_{31} & c_{32} & c_{33} & c_{34} \\ c_{41} & c_{42} & c_{43} & c_{44} \end{bmatrix} \begin{bmatrix} x_1 \\ x_2 \\ x_3 \\ x_4 \end{bmatrix} = \begin{bmatrix} r_1 \\ r_2 \\ r_3 \\ r_4 \end{bmatrix} \qquad (6.20)$$

or

$$CX = R \qquad (6.21)$$

where C is the square matrix of coefficients, X is the column vector of unknowns, and R is the column vector of the right-hand sides.

The formal solution for the unknowns in (6.21) can be found by employing Cramer's rule. Any arbitrary unknown x_k is given by

$$x_k = \frac{\det C_k}{\det C} \qquad (6.22)$$

where C_k is the matrix C with its kth column replaced by R. The number of basic arithmetic operations (addition, subtraction, multiplication, and division) necessary to solve for all n of the unknowns in a set of n equations using Cramer's rule is of $\mathcal{O}(n^4)$. Thus if a certain amount of computer time is required to solve a set of equations of a given size, a set twice as large will require on the order of 2^4, or 16, times as long. In comparison with other methods which we shall discuss later in this chapter, this method is completely impractical since it is much too time consuming. However, equation (6.22) does provide some useful insight into the solution of sets of equations, regardless of the method employed. Clearly, if $\det C = 0$, no unique solution can be obtained.* In this event the matrix C is termed *singular*, and the same term is often employed for the set of equations as well. It might be expected that if $\det C$ is very close to zero, this might cause some difficulty in computing the solution, and this suspicion is confirmed by actual computational experience. This will be discussed further in Sec. 6.6.

The solution to (6.21) may also be written formally as

$$X = C^{-1}R \qquad (6.23)$$

In this chapter most of our attention will be devoted to methods of finding X directly, without solving for C^{-1} as an intermediate step, since this is usually the most efficient approach. However, in practice, (6.23) is used surprisingly often to solve sets of equations. Possible reasons for this approach include:

(a) In certain situations, solutions must be obtained for many different sets of equations in which C stays the same and only R changes. Thus once C^{-1} is found, new

---

*If all elements of R are zero, then $\det C_k = 0$ since one entire column is zero. Nontrivial solutions can only be obtained if $\det C = 0$ also. In this case, while no unique solutions are available, certain relationships exist between the unknowns. This case is of considerable value in the theory of eigenvalue problems. See Chapter 10.

solution vectors X can be obtained by using (6.23) with very little additional work.   In these cases, solving for C^{-1} is clearly advantageous.

(b) Information of value may be found, either directly or indirectly, from C^{-1}.   For example, information can often be gained from C^{-1} concerning the "conditioning" of the set of equations and thus the possible effects of roundoff error on the solution (see Sec. 6.6).

(c) "Stock" programs for matrix inversion which are very efficient and effective are sometimes available at computer installations even when equation-solving programs are not.   The net efficiency and accuracy of using such an inversion routine along with (6.23) may be better than the user can achieve by writing his own equation solver.   A philosophy concerning the use of such stock programs will be discussed further in the next section.

6.3   AN OVERVIEW OF EQUATION SOLVING

Before getting into the details of equation solving, it is worthwhile to discuss some of the overall concepts involved.

It has been noted by Ralston[3] that sets of simultaneous linear equations can usually be put into one of two categories: either the coefficient matrix is dense (few zero elements) but the set is not large, or the matrix is sparse (many zero elements) and the set is large.

Equation-solving methods can be generally categorized as either *direct* techniques, which yield answers in a finite, predictable number of operations, or as *iterative* techniques, which yield answers that become increasingly more accurate as the number of iterations becomes large.   Until fairly recently, it was commonly accepted that direct methods were most suitable for small sets of equations with dense coefficient matrices, while iterative methods were best for large sets involving sparse coefficient matrices.   The current viewpoint differs somewhat from this one.   Iterative techniques are still preferred for very large sets and for large sets with sparse but not banded coefficient matrices.   However, it has been found that direct methods are highly suitable for quite large sets of equations having banded coefficient matrices.   These banded matrices are usually the result of finite difference solutions for partial differential equations, or of finite element methods.

It should be noted that the meaning of "large" in describing the size of a set of equations is a strong function of the computer hardware available to carry out the solution.*   This includes such items as central processor speed, amount and access time of storage space, and word size.   For example, widely-used scientific and data processing computers which might readily be encountered by readers of this book could vary in CPU (central processor) speed by at least a factor of 100, could vary in available storage space from less than 8000 words to the essentially infinite space available using the virtual memory concept and some extended core configurations, and could vary in word size from less than 7 decimal digits to 15 decimal digits in a single precision word.

To give some frame of reference, the largest, fastest machines with large word sizes are capable of solving, by direct methods, a well-conditioned set of several hundred equations with a full coefficient matrix in a central processor time on the order of 1

---

*We have mercifully avoided much previous reference to computer hardware; however, for the present topic, hardware capability is of very great importance and cannot be neglected.

second.   The large word size is essential in order to obtain a reasonably accurate solution despite the strong tendency toward roundoff error which results from the many operations necessary to solve such a large set.   In comparison, combinations of all of the significant hardware factors might practically limit small machines with small word sizes to the direct solution of similar sets including no more than about 40 equations, and this might involve central processor times on the order of minutes.

The largest, fastest machines are similarly capable in a practical sense of the direct solution of a set of several thousand equations having a banded coefficient matrix with a reasonably narrow bandwidth and of solving by iterative methods sets on the order of hundreds of thousands.*   On the smaller, slower machines, practical limits might be in the range of several hundred equations for sets involving banded coefficient matrices, and several thousand equations by iterative methods.

In this chapter the commonly employed methods for the solution of sets of simultaneous equations will be discussed in detail, and exercises will be provided in using these techniques.   It is essential that the reader understand and actually use these techniques to solve problems.   This provides the necessary insight into the proper choice of a method for a given problem and into the difficulties which can be encountered with each of the methods.   However, it should be noted that virtually all computer installations have available stock computer codes for the solutions of sets of simultaneous linear equations and/or for matrix inversion.   These codes usually employ direct techniques and are best suited to sets of equations having dense coefficient matrices, although some stock codes are also available for the direct solution of sets having banded matrices.   When a suitable stock code of proven accuracy and efficiency is available, it is usually best to use this code in preference to writing a new one.   For various reasons, these codes usually are far more efficient than those which the user can write for himself, and are often particularly well suited to the specific machine on which they are employed.   The availability of highly efficient stock programs to perform many tasks is steadily increasing, and even the most enthusiastic do-it-yourself programmer should recognize their potential advantages.   These codes can only be used safely, however, if the user is aware of the techniques employed and the possible sources of error. Of course, special situations can often arise in which it is advantageous to write a program specifically suited to the problem at hand rather than to use an available code.

6.4   GAUSS ELIMINATION AND GAUSS-JORDAN ELIMINATION

In this section we shall examine the most commonly-employed direct methods for the solution of sets of simultaneous linear equations and for matrix inversion.   Despite the fact that these methods are among the oldest known, they are so efficient and straightforward that they are the standard for digital computation.

Consider as an example the following set of four equations:

$$
\begin{bmatrix}
c_{11} & c_{12} & c_{13} & c_{14} \\
c_{21} & c_{22} & c_{23} & c_{24} \\
c_{31} & c_{32} & c_{33} & c_{34} \\
c_{41} & c_{42} & c_{43} & c_{44}
\end{bmatrix}
\begin{bmatrix}
x_1 \\
x_2 \\
x_3 \\
x_4
\end{bmatrix}
=
\begin{bmatrix}
r_1 \\
r_2 \\
r_3 \\
r_4
\end{bmatrix}
\tag{6.24}
$$

---

*When necessary, it is possible to solve sets of several million equations by iterative techniques on such machines, but several hours of CPU time (and many dollars) are generally required.

The solution vector to this set remains unchanged if any of the following operations are performed:

1. Multiplication or division of any equation by a constant.
2. Replacement of any equation by the sum (or difference) of that equation and any other equation.

Gauss elimination is simply a sequential application of these basic row operations. The top equation is first divided by c_{11}:

$$
\begin{bmatrix}
1 & c'_{12} & c'_{13} & c'_{14} \\
c_{21} & c_{22} & c_{23} & c_{24} \\
c_{31} & c_{32} & c_{33} & c_{34} \\
c_{41} & c_{42} & c_{43} & c_{44}
\end{bmatrix}
\begin{bmatrix}
x_1 \\ x_2 \\ x_3 \\ x_4
\end{bmatrix}
=
\begin{bmatrix}
r'_1 \\ r_2 \\ r_3 \\ r_4
\end{bmatrix}
\tag{6.25}
$$

The primes denote elements which have been changed from their original values. The first equation is now multiplied by c_{21} and subtracted from the second equation. This yields

$$
\begin{bmatrix}
1 & c'_{12} & c'_{13} & c'_{14} \\
0 & c'_{22} & c'_{23} & c'_{24} \\
c_{31} & c_{32} & c_{33} & c_{34} \\
c_{41} & c_{42} & c_{43} & c_{44}
\end{bmatrix}
\begin{bmatrix}
x_1 \\ x_2 \\ x_3 \\ x_4
\end{bmatrix}
=
\begin{bmatrix}
r'_1 \\ r'_2 \\ r_3 \\ r_4
\end{bmatrix}
\tag{6.26}
$$

The first equation can now be multiplied by c_{31} and subtracted from the third equation, then multiplied by c_{41} and subtracted from the fourth equation. During these operations the first row is termed the *pivot row* and c_{11} the *pivot element*. The entire first column below c_{11} has now been cleared to zero and the set appears as

$$
\begin{bmatrix}
1 & c'_{12} & c'_{13} & c'_{14} \\
0 & c'_{22} & c'_{23} & c'_{24} \\
0 & c'_{32} & c'_{33} & c'_{34} \\
0 & c'_{42} & c'_{43} & c'_{44}
\end{bmatrix}
\begin{bmatrix}
x_1 \\ x_2 \\ x_3 \\ x_4
\end{bmatrix}
=
\begin{bmatrix}
r'_1 \\ r'_2 \\ r'_3 \\ r'_4
\end{bmatrix}
\tag{6.27}
$$

The second row now becomes the pivot row and c'_{22} the *pivot element*. The second equation is divided by c'_{22} to make the main diagonal element 1. Multiplication of the second equation by c'_{32} and subtraction from the third equation, and then multiplication by c'_{42} and subtraction from the fourth equation, clear the second column below the main diagonal to zero. Similar operations with the third and fourth rows as pivot rows finally yield

$$
\begin{bmatrix}
1 & c'_{12} & c'_{13} & c'_{14} \\
& 1 & c'_{23} & c'_{24} \\
& & 1 & c'_{34} \\
& & & 1
\end{bmatrix}
\begin{bmatrix}
x_1 \\ x_2 \\ x_3 \\ x_4
\end{bmatrix}
=
\begin{bmatrix}
r'_1 \\ r'_2 \\ r'_3 \\ r'_4
\end{bmatrix}
\tag{6.28}
$$

(For simplicity, we have shown only one prime on the elements which have been changed from their original values, even though some elements have been modified several times.) The method is sometimes termed triangularization since the coefficient matrix in (6.28) is upper triangular. The bottom equation in (6.28) now yields directly the value of x_4 as

$$
x_4 = r'_4
\tag{6.29}
$$

The third equation is

$$x_3 + c'_{34}x_4 = r'_3 \tag{6.30}$$

Since x_4 is known from (6.29), this may be solved for x_3 to yield

$$x_3 = r'_3 - c'_{34}x_4 \tag{6.31}$$

Repeated back substitution, moving upward, yields one new unknown from each new equation, and the unknown vector will have been completely determined when the top equation is solved for x_1.   The flow chart for Gauss elimination is shown in Fig. 6.1.

Gauss-Jordan elimination is an adaptation of Gauss elimination which is particularly well suited to digital computation.   The method can be illustrated by starting with the upper triangular form (6.28) which resulted from Gauss elimination:

$$\begin{bmatrix} 1 & c'_{12} & c'_{13} & c'_{14} \\ & 1 & c'_{23} & c'_{24} \\ & & 1 & c'_{34} \\ & & & 1 \end{bmatrix}\begin{bmatrix} x_1 \\ x_2 \\ x_3 \\ x_4 \end{bmatrix} = \begin{bmatrix} r'_1 \\ r'_2 \\ r'_3 \\ r'_4 \end{bmatrix} \tag{6.32}$$

Multiplying the second equation by c'_{12} and subtracting the second equation from the first yields

$$\begin{bmatrix} 1 & 0 & c''_{13} & c''_{14} \\ & 1 & c'_{23} & c'_{24} \\ & & 1 & c'_{34} \\ & & & 1 \end{bmatrix}\begin{bmatrix} x_1 \\ x_2 \\ x_3 \\ x_4 \end{bmatrix} = \begin{bmatrix} r''_1 \\ r'_2 \\ r'_3 \\ r'_4 \end{bmatrix} \tag{6.33}$$

(We use the double primes to denote values which have been changed from (6.28), no matter how many times they have been changed.)   The third and fourth columns can now be cleared in a similar manner to yield

$$\begin{bmatrix} 1 & & & \\ & 1 & & \\ & & 1 & \\ & & & 1 \end{bmatrix}\begin{bmatrix} x_1 \\ x_2 \\ x_3 \\ x_4 \end{bmatrix} = \begin{bmatrix} r''_1 \\ r''_2 \\ r''_3 \\ r''_4 \end{bmatrix} \tag{6.34}$$

Thus

$$\begin{array}{ll} x_1 = r''_1 & x_3 = r''_3 \\ x_2 = r''_2 & x_4 = r''_4 \end{array} \tag{6.35}$$

and the right-hand side vector has become the solution vector.

In practice, the upper triangular form (6.32) is not obtained as an intermediate step in Gauss-Jordan elimination.   Instead, the most efficient approach is to eliminate all elements both above and below the pivot element in order to clear to zero the entire column containing the pivot element, except of course for the 1 in the pivot position on the main diagonal.   This procedure is carried out by starting with the top row as the pivot row, and then moving downward through the matrix, using each row in turn as the pivot row.   The result is of the form (6.34).   A numerical example is presented in detail in Problem 6.1.   The flow chart for Gauss-Jordan elimination is shown in Fig. 6.2.

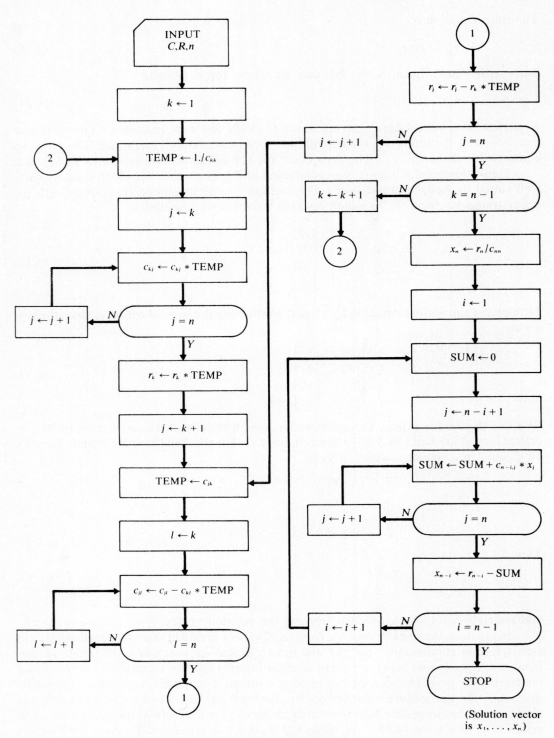

Fig. 6.1 Gauss elimination.

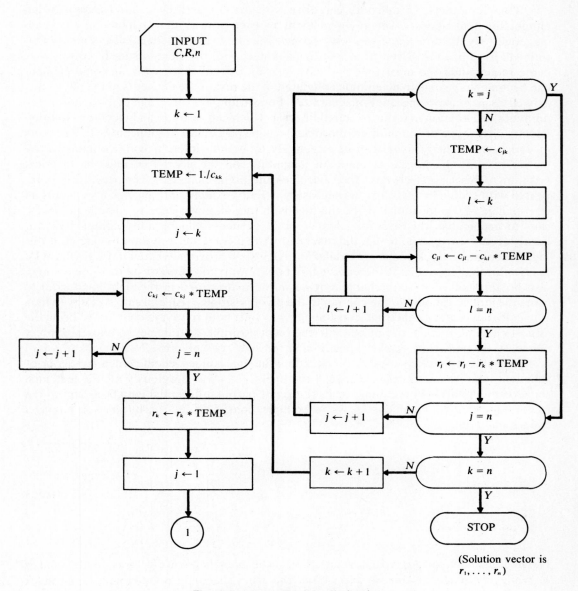

Fig. 6.2 Gauss-Jordan elimination.

The efficiency of Gauss and Gauss-Jordan elimination can be assessed by noting that the number of basic arithmetic operations necessary to carry out a solution to a set of n equations by either method is of $\mathcal{O}(n^3)$. Recall that Cramer's rule was of $\mathcal{O}(n^4)$.

One computational difficulty can arise with the standard Gauss and Gauss-Jordan elimination techniques. The pivot element in each row is the element on the main diagonal. By the time any given row becomes the pivot row, the diagonal element in that row will have been modified from its original value, with the elements in the lower rows being recomputed the most times. Under certain circumstances, the diagonal element can become very small in magnitude compared to the rest of the elements in the pivot row, as well as perhaps being quite inaccurate. For various reasons, this can create a very unfavorable situation in terms of roundoff error which can result in an inaccurate solution vector. This type of roundoff error problem can be particularly significant with large sets of equations. The problem can be effectively treated by interchanging columns of the matrix to shift the largest element (in magnitude) in the pivot row into the diagonal position. This largest element then becomes the pivot element. This operation is repeated with each new pivot row as necessary. Every column interchange also means an interchange of the locations of the unknowns in the unknown vector. The logic necessary to accomplish this maximization of pivot elements can be quite complex, and it hardly seems worthwhile to ask the reader to write a computer program to carry out this logic since many stock codes are available. One such program written in FORTRAN IV is given in the Appendix at the end of this book. Maximization of pivot elements may also be approached by interchanging rows in the matrix (and in the right-hand side) to bring the largest element in the column to the pivot position. An extreme strategy (which is usually unnecessary and time consuming) is to shift both rows and columns to bring the largest element in the entire matrix into the pivot position. Strategies to maximize pivot elements are sometimes called "positioning for size" or "pivoting."

The direct solution of sets of equations having banded coefficient matrices is of sufficient importance to deserve special treatment. As was previously mentioned, such sets commonly arise in the numerical solution of partial differential equations and in the use of finite element techniques. As an example, consider a set of arbitrary size having a tridiagonal coefficient matrix:

$$
\begin{bmatrix}
b_1 & c_1 & & & & & \\
a_2 & b_2 & c_2 & & & & \\
& a_3 & b_3 & c_3 & & & \\
& & & \ddots & & & \\
& & & & a_{n-1} & b_{n-1} & c_{n-1} \\
& & & & & a_n & b_n
\end{bmatrix}
\begin{bmatrix}
x_1 \\ x_2 \\ x_3 \\ \vdots \\ \vdots \\ x_{n-1} \\ x_n
\end{bmatrix}
=
\begin{bmatrix}
r_1 \\ r_2 \\ r_3 \\ \vdots \\ \vdots \\ r_{n-1} \\ r_n
\end{bmatrix}
\tag{6.36}
$$

Notice that we have adopted a new notation. The main diagonal elements are denoted as b, while the diagonals below and above the main diagonal are denoted as a and c respectively. Only a single subscript is thus needed on each coefficient to denote the row.

We now apply Gauss elimination to (6.36), starting from the top row. As the reader can verify by carrying out each step, only one element (one of the a's) will be eliminated in each column, since all remaining entries below the main diagonal are zero. Also, no entries outside of the tridiagonal band are changed from zero in the course of this elimination process. After the bottom row has been reached, (6.36) becomes

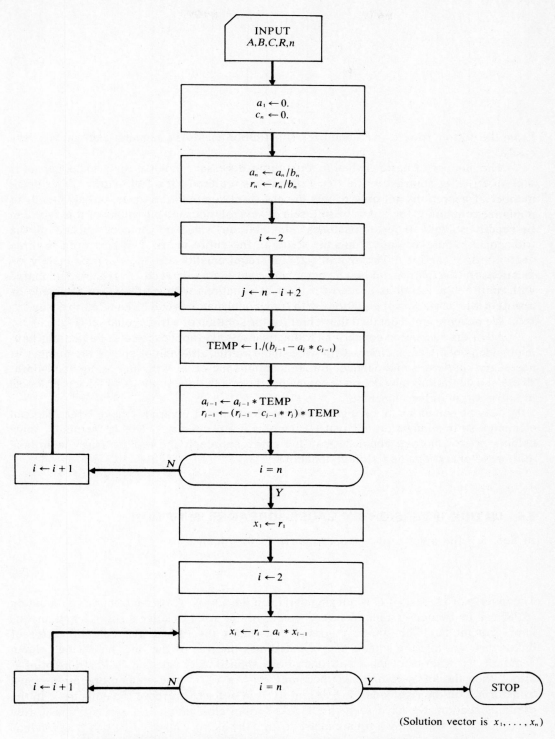

Fig. 6.3 Solution of tridiagonal set of equations by Gauss elimination.

$$\begin{bmatrix} 1 & c_1' & & & & \\ & 1 & c_2' & & & \\ & & 1 & c_3' & & \\ & & & \ddots & & \\ & & & & 1 & c_{n-1}' \\ & & & & & 1 \end{bmatrix} \begin{bmatrix} x_1 \\ x_2 \\ x_3 \\ \vdots \\ x_{n-1} \\ x_n \end{bmatrix} = \begin{bmatrix} r_1' \\ r_2' \\ r_3' \\ \vdots \\ r_{n-1}' \\ r_n' \end{bmatrix} \qquad (6.37)$$

From the bottom row, $x_n = r_n'$, and back substitution yields the remaining unknowns very easily.

The number of basic arithmetic operations necessary to solve this tridiagonal set is only of $\mathcal{O}(n)$, in contrast to the $\mathcal{O}(n^3)$ operations required for a full matrix. This small number of operations not only results in very short computation times, but also tends to minimize roundoff error. As a result, sets of several thousand equations of this type can be readily solved on most machines. In addition, since no element outside of the tridiagonal band ever enters into the solution, the entire matrix can be stored in three vectors: a, b, and c. The overall storage requirements are then approximately $5n$ locations for the matrix, unknown vector, and right-hand side vector. If this is compared with the $n^2 + 2n$ locations needed for a set of equations with a full matrix, it should be apparent why large sets of equations with tridiagonal matrices can be handled so easily.

We now present a detailed flow chart for the solution of a tridiagonal set (Fig. 6.3).

All of the discussion concerning tridiagonal sets also applies to sets of equations having banded coefficient matrices with wider bandwidths, although of course the number of necessary operations and needed storage locations increases with increasing bandwidth. These considerations may decrease somewhat the number of equations which it is practical to solve on any given machine.

Sets of equations involving banded matrices almost invariably have large diagonal elements, so maximization of pivot elements is not necessary. This is fortunate, since column or row shifting could destroy the entire approach and require many additional arithmetic operations and storage locations.

6.5 MATRIX INVERSION BY GAUSS-JORDAN ELIMINATION

In Sec. 6.1, the inverse of a square matrix C was defined by

$$CC^{-1} = I \qquad (6.38)$$

The inverse of C exists if C is not singular, i.e. if det $C \neq 0$. In order to find C^{-1}, equation (6.38) can be treated in a manner very similar to that used to solve a set of simultaneous linear equations. The square matrix C^{-1} assumes the role of the column vector of unknowns X, while the square matrix I assumes the role of the right-hand side column vector R. If a series of basic row operations applied to C and I in (6.38) transforms C into I, then the left side of (6.38) becomes IC^{-1} or C^{-1}. These same operations must transform I on the right side of (6.38) into C^{-1} in order to preserve the equality. In the previous section, we have seen that Gauss-Jordan elimination is a series of basic row operations that transform a square matrix C into the identity matrix I, so this is an obvious approach to matrix inversion.

The method is best illustrated with an example.   Consider the 3×3 matrix

$$C = \begin{bmatrix} 2 & 1 & 1 \\ 1 & 2 & 1 \\ 1 & 1 & 2 \end{bmatrix}$$

Now write C and I together, and perform the same basic row operations on each:

$$\begin{bmatrix} 2 & 1 & 1 \\ 1 & 2 & 1 \\ 1 & 1 & 2 \end{bmatrix} \begin{bmatrix} 1 & 0 & 0 \\ 0 & 1 & 0 \\ 0 & 0 & 1 \end{bmatrix}$$

Applying Gauss-Jordan elimination to C, we divide the first row of both matrices by 2:

$$\begin{bmatrix} 1 & 1/2 & 1/2 \\ 1 & 2 & 1 \\ 1 & 1 & 2 \end{bmatrix} \begin{bmatrix} 1/2 & 0 & 0 \\ 0 & 1 & 0 \\ 0 & 0 & 1 \end{bmatrix}$$

The first column of the left matrix can be cleared by subtracting the top row from the second row, and then from the third row:

$$\begin{bmatrix} 1 & 1/2 & 1/2 \\ 0 & 3/2 & 1/2 \\ 0 & 1/2 & 3/2 \end{bmatrix} \begin{bmatrix} 1/2 & 0 & 0 \\ -1/2 & 1 & 0 \\ -1/2 & 0 & 1 \end{bmatrix}$$

The second row of both matrices is now divided by the pivot element 3/2, then multiplied by 1/2, and subtracted from the top row and the bottom row.   This clears the second column of the left matrix and yields

$$\begin{bmatrix} 1 & 0 & 1/3 \\ 0 & 1 & 1/3 \\ 0 & 0 & 4/3 \end{bmatrix} \begin{bmatrix} 2/3 & -1/3 & 0 \\ -1/3 & 2/3 & 0 \\ -1/3 & -1/3 & 1 \end{bmatrix}$$

Finally, clearing the third column of the left matrix, we obtain

$$\begin{bmatrix} 1 & 0 & 0 \\ 0 & 1 & 0 \\ 0 & 0 & 1 \end{bmatrix} \begin{bmatrix} 3/4 & -1/4 & -1/4 \\ -1/4 & 3/4 & -1/4 \\ -1/4 & -1/4 & 3/4 \end{bmatrix}$$

Since the left matrix which was originally C has now been transformed into I, the right matrix which was originally I should now be C^{-1}.   To verify this, we multiply it by C:

$$\begin{bmatrix} 2 & 1 & 1 \\ 1 & 2 & 1 \\ 1 & 1 & 2 \end{bmatrix} \begin{bmatrix} 3/4 & -1/4 & -1/4 \\ -1/4 & 3/4 & -1/4 \\ -1/4 & -1/4 & 3/4 \end{bmatrix} = \begin{bmatrix} 1 & 0 & 0 \\ 0 & 1 & 0 \\ 0 & 0 & 1 \end{bmatrix} = I$$

Since C^{-1} is defined by $CC^{-1} = I$, we have found C^{-1}.   The similarity to solving a set of equations by Gauss-Jordan elimination should be apparent.

In computational practice, maximization of pivot elements is just as valuable in matrix inversion as in the solution of sets of equations.   In addition, as the inverse is computed, it can be stored on top of the original matrix so that virtually no additional storage space is needed over that required for the original matrix. The FORTRAN IV subroutine given in the Appendix incorporates these features, and there would seem to be little to be gained by asking the reader to carry out the logical details of the programming. Similar programs are available at virtually every computer installation.

6.6 ILL-CONDITIONED MATRICES AND SETS OF EQUATIONS

In this section we shall use the term "matrix" to apply equally to a matrix to be inverted and to the matrix of coefficients of a set of linear equations to be solved. Both will be denoted as C. As we have seen in previous sections, the operations for inversion and solution of a set are essentially the same.

There is no clear-cut and precise definition of ill-conditioning for a matrix. As the name might imply, ill-conditioning can potentially result in an inaccurate inverse or an inaccurate unknown vector for a set of simultaneous linear equations. The word "potentially" is used since we will distinguish carefully between the *presence* of ill-conditioning and the *effects* of ill-conditioning. This distinction is apparently seldom made. This may be partially due to the fact that it is not usually necessary to be concerned about ill-conditioning if the answers are accurate. However, it is difficult to tell if an inverse is accurate by looking at it, and an inaccurate unknown vector can satisfy an ill-conditioned set surprisingly well. Knowledge of the presence of ill-conditioning can thus put one on guard against its sometimes subtle effects.

We will discuss two of the many possible ways to recognize that ill-conditioning may be present. The first of these is to examine the inverse of the matrix directly. If there are elements in the inverse which are many orders of magnitude larger than the elements in the original matrix, then the matrix is probably ill-conditioned. (Some sources[3] *define* ill-conditioning by this criterion.) This situation can best be recognized if the rows in the original matrix are all normalized to have elements with a maximum magnitude of order 1.

The second method to be considered for detecting the presence of ill-conditioning involves the evaluation of the determinant of the matrix. If the magnitude of the determinant is small, then the matrix may be ill-conditioned. But what does small mean? Some normalization is necessary in order to provide a frame of reference. Conte[4] has suggested that the matrix C be considered as ill-conditioned if

$$\frac{\det C}{\sqrt{\sum_{i=1}^{n} \sum_{j=1}^{n} c_{ij}^2}} \ll 1 \qquad (6.39)$$

where n is the row and column dimension of the matrix. The quantity $\sqrt{\sum_{i=1}^{n} \sum_{j=1}^{n} c_{ij}^2}$ is called the *Euclidean norm* of C. The determinant of a matrix may be evaluated remarkably easily as a byproduct of Gauss-Jordan elimination. Since the determinant of a diagonal matrix is just the product of the diagonal elements, and since Gauss-Jordan elimination produces a diagonal matrix, it is only necessary to keep a running product of the pivot elements. (The product is recomputed at each new pivot row before the row is divided by the pivot element.) When the inversion or solution is complete, this running product is the determinant of the matrix. This determinant evaluation has been incorporated in the matrix inversion and equation-solving program given in the Appendix. The program also evaluates the normalized determinant (6.39).

There are many other criteria commonly used for evaluating the conditioning of matrices.   See, for example, Refs. 3 and 5.   Many of these criteria require the evaluation of one or more eigenvalues of the matrix.   Since eigenvalue problems will not be considered until Chapter 10, we are not able to meaningfully consider these criteria at this point.

We now turn to the evaluation of the *effects* of ill-conditioning.   These effects are due to roundoff error in the calculation of the inverse of a matrix or the solution to a set of equations.   There are two simple but quite effective tests which will detect whether this roundoff error will be significant for any given problem.   Both tests require the calculation of C^{-1}.   This inverse is, of course, the end result of an inversion problem.   If the effects of ill-conditioning on the solution to a set of equations are to be assessed, then C^{-1} must be obtained by the same method as the solution vector is to be obtained; that is, if Gauss-Jordan elimination would be used to obtain the solution vector, then it must also be used to obtain C^{-1} for these tests.   The two tests now consist simply of calculating $C^{-1}C$ (or CC^{-1}) and comparing the result to I, or of calculating $(C^{-1})^{-1}$ and comparing the result to C.   Significant deviation from the expected results indicates the presence of serious roundoff error.   Of the two tests, the calculation of $(C^{-1})^{-1}$ is the most critical, since roundoff is accumulated both on the original inversion and the reinversion.   This test also usually requires no additional storage space over that needed for C.   (The calculation of $C^{-1}C$ would in general require three times the storage space required for C.   This can exceed the available space in some cases.)

In closing our discussion of conditioning, we note that since the effect of ill-conditioning is roundoff error, then the best defense is a large word size (many decimal digits).   The word size is usually fixed by the computer being used, but many machines have available either hardware or software capability to provide much larger word sizes than the standard word.   This capability is usually obtained at the expense of computing speed and always at the expense of storage space, but the double precision hardware available on many scientific machines may result in only a 20–30% reduction in effective computing speed.   This can be a small price to pay for accurate answers from an ill-conditioned matrix.   We also note that except in the most pathological cases, it is possible to use an error correction technique to improve inaccurate answers to a set of linear equations.   The technique and its application are illustrated in Problem 6.3.

The effects of ill-conditioning are most serious with large dense matrices and with certain types of matrices which commonly arise in such problems as curve fitting by least squares (see Chapter 7).   In these cases the sizes of the matrices which can be handled accurately may be severely limited by roundoff error.   Problem 6.5 shows examples of ill-conditioning and its effects.

The sparse banded matrices which result from the numerical solution of partial differential equations and from finite element methods are usually quite well conditioned, and very large sets can be solved without excessive roundoff error problems.

6.7   GAUSS-SIEDEL ITERATION AND CONCEPTS OF RELAXATION

Gauss-Siedel iteration is the most popular and one of the most powerful iterative techniques for the solution of sets of linear equations.   Consider as an example a set of three linear equations:

$$c_{11}x_1 + c_{12}x_2 + c_{13}x_3 = r_1$$
$$c_{21}x_1 + c_{22}x_2 + c_{23}x_3 = r_2 \qquad (6.40)$$
$$c_{31}x_1 + c_{32}x_2 + c_{33}x_3 = r_3$$

We now solve the first equation for x_1, the second for x_2, etc. to yield

$$x_1 = \frac{r_1 - c_{12}x_2 - c_{13}x_3}{c_{11}}$$

$$x_2 = \frac{r_2 - c_{21}x_1 - c_{23}x_3}{c_{22}} \qquad (6.41)$$

$$x_3 = \frac{r_3 - c_{31}x_1 - c_{32}x_2}{c_{33}}$$

Initial guesses are needed for x_1, x_2, and x_3. Call these $x_1^{(0)}$, $x_2^{(0)}$, and $x_3^{(0)}$. From the first equation in (6.41) we can now find the value of x_1 on the first iteration as

$$x_1^{(1)} = \frac{r_1 - c_{12}x_2^{(0)} - c_{13}x_3^{(0)}}{c_{11}} \qquad (6.42)$$

The second equation in (6.41) gives $x_2^{(1)}$ as

$$x_2^{(1)} = \frac{r_2 - c_{21}x_1^{(1)} - c_{23}x_3^{(0)}}{c_{22}} \qquad (6.43)$$

Notice that $x_1^{(1)}$, which is the new value obtained from (6.42) on the current iteration, has been used instead of $x_1^{(0)}$. This use of the most recently obtained value of each of the unknowns is the distinguishing feature of Gauss-Siedel iteration.* The solution for x_3 from (6.41) is thus

$$x_3^{(1)} = \frac{r_3 - c_{31}x_1^{(1)} - c_{32}x_2^{(1)}}{c_{33}} \qquad (6.44)$$

The iterative process consists of repeatedly cycling through the solutions for the unknowns. As each new value of an unknown is computed, it replaces the old value. Only one computer storage location is thus required for each unknown. Programming is also greatly simplified, since whenever an unknown is used, it is automatically the most recently computed value. If the equations have the proper characteristics, then the iterative process will eventually converge to the solution vector.

The iteration is terminated when a convergence criterion is satisfied. The two commonly-used types of convergence criteria are *absolute* criteria and *relative* criteria.

An absolute convergence criterion is of the form

$$|x_i^{(l+1)} - x_i^{(l)}| \leq \epsilon \qquad (6.45)$$

If (6.45) is satisfied for all x_i, then the change in each unknown from the previous iteration (l) to the current iteration ($l + 1$) is no more than ϵ. This type of criterion is most useful when the approximate magnitudes of the x_i are known beforehand. With such a criterion

---

*A different iterative process, called Jacobi iteration, employs all of the old values of the unknowns until the sweep through all equations has been completed, and then replaces the old values with the newly-computed values in a block. Current opinion appears to be that Jacobi iteration has no significant advantages compared with Gauss-Siedel, and has a considerably slower convergence rate. We shall not discuss this method further.

it is possible to choose ϵ such that, for example, the solution is considered converged when the change in each x_i is less than 1 unit in the fourth decimal place on two successive iterations.   This of course does not mean that the fourth decimal place is accurate to 1 unit for each of the x_i; the actual accuracy of the x_i is dependent on the convergence rate of the process, which can vary widely for different sets of equations.   Some knowledge of the accuracy of the converged values in any given problem can usually be obtained by observing the results of several iterations near convergence.

A relative convergence criterion is of the form

$$\left| \frac{x_i^{(l+1)} - x_i^{(l)}}{x_i^{(l+1)}} \right| \leq \epsilon \tag{6.46}$$

This type of criterion is the safest choice if the magnitudes of the x_i are not known beforehand, and corresponds to specifying the maximum allowable percentage change in each unknown on two successive iterations.

For very large sets of equations, it may be impractical to test each unknown for convergence since excessive amounts of computer time may be involved in the testing procedure.   Convergence testing in such cases is usually individually tailored to the problem at hand and may consist of testing only certain critical unknowns or of using $\sum_{i=1}^{n}|x_i^{(l+1)} - x_i^{(l)}|$ or $\sum_{i=1}^{n}|x_i^{(l+1)} - x_i^{(l)}|^2$ as quantities to be compared with some predetermined convergence criterion.

Whether the iterative process is convergent or divergent does *not* depend on the initial guess supplied for the unknowns, but depends only on the character of the equations themselves.   However, if the process is convergent, then a good first estimate of the unknowns will make it possible for the convergence criterion to be satisfied in a relatively small number of iterations.   A poor first guess can prolong the iterative process considerably (but will not cause divergence).

The sets of equations which are best suited to iterative techniques are those in which the main diagonal elements are the largest elements (in magnitude) in each row.   In the example set (6.40) this would mean that c_{11}, c_{22}, and c_{33} would be the largest elements in their respective rows.   Convergence cannot be guaranteed unless

$$|c_{ii}| > \sum_{\substack{j=1 \\ i \neq j}}^{n} |c_{ij}| \tag{6.47}$$

for each value of i (each row).   However, in practice, convergence can be obtained with much weaker diagonal dominance than this.   In many cases convergence can even be obtained if a few of the equations have diagonal elements smaller than some other elements in those equations.   Examples of Gauss-Siedel iteration are shown in several problems at the end of the chapter.   We will defer the presentation of the flow chart until after the discussion of relaxation.

Relaxation originally evolved as a very sophisticated hand computation technique for solving large sets of simultaneous linear equations iteratively.   The overall approach is not well suited to digital computer use because of the extensive logic required.   However, some of the original concepts are embodied in the simple but powerful computer oriented method which we will now discuss briefly.

The method basically consists of calculating the value of each unknown by Gauss-Siedel iteration and then modifying the value before it is stored.   The fundamental operational equation for this so-called "point" relaxation is

$$x_i^{(l+1)} = x_i^{(l)} + \lambda(x_i^{(l+1)*} - x_i^{(l)}) \tag{6.48}$$

As before, we will consider iteration $(l + 1)$ as the current iteration and iteration (l) as the preceding iteration. The quantity $x_i^{(l+1)*}$ is the value of the unknown obtained on the current iteration by using Gauss-Siedel iteration. The quantity λ is a pure number in the range $0 < \lambda < 2$, which is called the *relaxation factor*. The effect of this factor can be seen more easily if (6.48) is rewritten as

$$x_i^{(l+1)} = \lambda x_i^{(l+1)*} + (1 - \lambda)x_i^{(l)} \qquad (6.49)$$

If $\lambda = 1$, then the Gauss-Siedel computed value of the unknown is stored as the current value. If $0 < \lambda < 1$, then the current stored value becomes a weighted average of the Gauss-Siedel value and the value from the previous iteration. This is termed *underrelaxation*. If $1 < \lambda < 2$, then the current stored value is essentially extrapolated beyond the Gauss-Siedel value. This is termed *overrelaxation*. (For $\lambda > 2$ the process diverges.) We might note that the term "Gauss-Siedel value" is a slight misnomer here (unless $\lambda = 1$), since the values from the current iteration which are utilized in its computation are not Gauss-Siedel values themselves, but have been modified by the relaxation formula (6.48) before they were stored.

Although definite exceptions can be shown, overrelaxation is usually employed to accelerate an already convergent iterative process, while underrelaxation is usually employed to make a nonconvergent iterative process converge. The same relaxation factor usually applies for all of the equations in a set, although it may occasionally be worthwhile to use different factors for blocks of equations within a set which are drastically different in character.

The choice of an optimum value of λ is a rather complex task which is beyond the scope of this text. See Ref. 6 for a discussion of this topic. In most circumstances it is practical to choose the value of λ by trial and error. The use of relaxation factors is particularly important and useful in solving iteratively the very large sets of equations which result from the numerical solution of partial differential equations. Several example problems at the end of this chapter illustrate the choice and use of relaxation factors.

A flow chart for Gauss-Siedel iteration including a relaxation capability will now be presented (Fig. 6.4). To obtain Gauss-Siedel iteration with this algorithm, set $\lambda = 1$. An absolute convergence criterion has been used in Fig. 6.4. A relative criterion can be substituted if desired.

In Sec. 6.3 it was stated that iterative techniques are used to solve the very largest sets of equations, perhaps sets as large as on the order of one hundred thousand equations. Very large sets of equations invariably have sparse coefficient matrices, and it is essential from a storage space standpoint that any solution technique to be used for such sets take full advantage of this sparseness, and only require the storage of those elements which are nonzero. Iterative techniques can easily satisfy this requirement in all cases, while direct techniques only satisfy the requirement if the coefficient matrix is banded, or in some cases if special programming techniques are used. However, the primary reason that such large sets can be handled with iterative techniques but not with direct techniques is that the roundoff characteristics of iterative techniques are much better. With direct techniques, roundoff error can be incurred with each mathematical operation, and simply accumulates until the final answers are obtained. When iterative techniques are used, the presence of roundoff error in the unknowns at the end of any given iteration simply results in those unknowns being somewhat poorer estimates for the next iteration. For practical purposes, the roundoff error in the final converged values is only that accumulated in the final iteration.

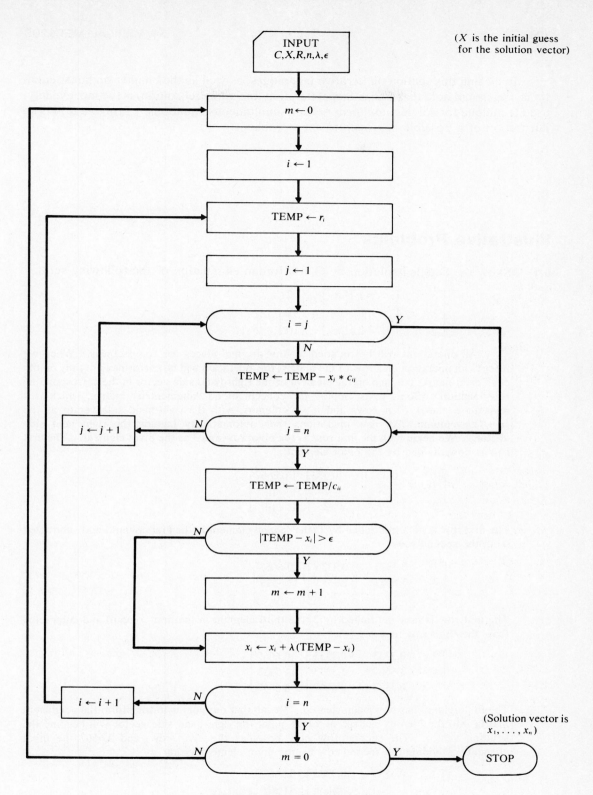

Fig. 6.4 Gauss-Siedel iteration.

In closing this section on iterative techniques, as well as the chapter on linear equations, we should note that Gauss-Siedel iteration (including relaxation) is the most widely-used technique for solving *nonlinear* sets of simultaneous equations. Problem 6.10 is an illustration of a possible approach to such problems.

Illustrative Problems

6.1   Show the detailed solution by Gauss-Jordan elimination of the following set:

$$\begin{bmatrix} 3 & 1 & -1 \\ 1 & 4 & 1 \\ 2 & 1 & 2 \end{bmatrix} \begin{bmatrix} x_1 \\ x_2 \\ x_3 \end{bmatrix} = \begin{bmatrix} 2 \\ 12 \\ 10 \end{bmatrix}$$

All operations will be rounded to four decimal places for compactness. When we refer to an operation on a row of the matrix, this operation will be performed not only on the coefficient matrix but also on the element of the right-hand side vector in the corresponding row location. (Some texts employ the concept of an "augmented" matrix, which is a nonsquare matrix of n rows and $n+1$ columns, with the right-hand side vector as the $(n+1)$th column. All row operations then automatically include the right-hand side vector.) We begin with the first row as the pivot row and 3 as the pivot element. The first row is now divided by the pivot element:

$$\begin{bmatrix} 1 & 0.3333 & -0.3333 \\ 1 & 4 & 1 \\ 2 & 1 & 2 \end{bmatrix} \begin{bmatrix} 0.6667 \\ 12 \\ 10 \end{bmatrix}$$

The first row is next multiplied by 1 (the second element in the first column) and subtracted from the second row:

$$\begin{bmatrix} 1 & 0.3333 & -0.3333 \\ 0 & 3.6667 & 1.3333 \\ 2 & 1 & 2 \end{bmatrix} \begin{bmatrix} 0.6667 \\ 11.3333 \\ 10 \end{bmatrix}$$

The first row is now multiplied by 2 (the third element in the first column) and subtracted from the third row to give

$$\begin{bmatrix} 1 & 0.3333 & -0.3333 \\ 0 & 3.6667 & 1.3333 \\ 0 & 0.3333 & 2.6667 \end{bmatrix} \begin{bmatrix} 0.6667 \\ 11.3333 \\ 8.6667 \end{bmatrix}$$

The first column has now been cleared. Recall that our goal is to transform the coefficient matrix into the identity matrix, at which point the right-hand side vector will become the solution vector. The second row now becomes the pivot row, and 3.6667 the pivot element. Dividing the second row by the pivot element yields

$$\begin{bmatrix} 1 & 0.3333 & -0.3333 \\ 0 & 1 & 0.3636 \\ 0 & 0.3333 & 2.6667 \end{bmatrix} \begin{bmatrix} 0.6667 \\ 3.0909 \\ 8.6667 \end{bmatrix}$$

The top element in the second column can be cleared to zero by multiplying the second (pivot) row by 0.3333 and subtracting the second row from the first:

$$\begin{bmatrix} 1 & 0 & -0.4545 \\ 0 & 1 & 0.3636 \\ 0 & 0.3333 & 2.6667 \end{bmatrix} \begin{bmatrix} -0.3636 \\ 3.0909 \\ 8.6667 \end{bmatrix}$$

The bottom element in the second column can be cleared next by multiplying the second row by 0.3333 and subtracting the second row from the third:

$$\begin{bmatrix} 1 & 0 & -0.4545 \\ 0 & 1 & 0.3636 \\ 0 & 0 & 2.5455 \end{bmatrix} \begin{bmatrix} -0.3635 \\ 3.0909 \\ 7.6365 \end{bmatrix}$$

The bottom row is now the pivot row and 2.5455 the pivot element. Dividing the bottom row by this element gives

$$\begin{bmatrix} 1 & 0 & -0.4545 \\ 0 & 1 & 0.3636 \\ 0 & 0 & 1 \end{bmatrix} \begin{bmatrix} -0.3635 \\ 3.0909 \\ 3.0000 \end{bmatrix}$$

Multiplying the bottom row by -0.4545 and subtracting it from the first row gives

$$\begin{bmatrix} 1 & 0 & 0 \\ 0 & 1 & 0.3636 \\ 0 & 0 & 1 \end{bmatrix} \begin{bmatrix} 1.0000 \\ 3.0909 \\ 3.0000 \end{bmatrix}$$

Finally, the second element in the third column can be cleared by multiplying the third row by 0.3636 and subtracting it from the second:

$$\begin{bmatrix} 1 & 0 & 0 \\ 0 & 1 & 0 \\ 0 & 0 & 1 \end{bmatrix} \begin{bmatrix} 1.0000 \\ 2.0001 \\ 3.0000 \end{bmatrix}$$

The solution vector is thus

$$X = \begin{bmatrix} 1.0000 \\ 2.0001 \\ 3.0000 \end{bmatrix}$$

The exact solution without roundoff error is

$$X = \begin{bmatrix} 1 \\ 2 \\ 3 \end{bmatrix}$$

6.2 Given the following set of equations:

$$\begin{bmatrix} 1.1348 & 3.8326 & 1.1651 & 3.4017 \\ 0.5301 & 1.7875 & 2.5330 & 1.5435 \\ 3.4129 & 4.9317 & 8.7643 & 1.3142 \\ 1.2371 & 4.9998 & 10.6721 & 0.0147 \end{bmatrix} \begin{bmatrix} x_1 \\ x_2 \\ x_3 \\ x_4 \end{bmatrix} = \begin{bmatrix} 9.5342 \\ 6.3941 \\ 18.4231 \\ 16.9237 \end{bmatrix}$$

Solve this set by using Gauss-Jordan elimination with and without maximization of pivot elements and compare the result.

The exact answers to this set are

$$x_1 = 1 \qquad x_3 = 1$$
$$x_2 = 1 \qquad x_4 = 1$$

The answers obtained by using Gauss-Jordan elimination in single precision on the IBM 360/67 are:

Without Maximization of Pivot Elements	With Maximization of Pivot Elements
$x_1 = 0.9991369$	$x_1 = 1.000006$
$x_2 = 1.000077$	$x_2 = 1.000003$
$x_3 = 1.000001$	$x_3 = 1.000000$
$x_4 = 1.000076$	$x_4 = 1.000001$

The gain in accuracy when the pivot elements are maximized (by column shifting) should be apparent.

This small set of equations has been deliberately formulated to produce rather poor results unless maximization of pivot elements is used. It should be clear that maximization of pivot elements may be necessary for small sets of equations as well as large sets, and that it is virtually impossible to identify the need for maximization by simply examining the coefficient matrix. The best practice is simply to employ maximization of pivot elements routinely for all equation solving unless there is some reason for not doing so (as is the case with sets having banded coefficient matrices).

6.3 Develop an error correction technique for simultaneous linear equations and demonstrate its use.

The matrix representation of a set of simultaneous equations is

$$CX = R$$

If we calculate the vector X by any method, it will naturally contain some error, even if only due to roundoff. Call this calculated vector X'. Now multiply this vector by C to yield

$$CX' = R'$$

where R' is a newly-calculated vector, somewhat different from R. If we now subtract this equation from the original equation, we obtain

$$C(X - X') = R - R'$$

If $(X - X')$ is denoted as E, then

$$CE = R - R'$$

Any standard technique can now be used to solve this equation for E. Then

$$X = X' + E$$

If E could be determined exactly, then the error would be completely corrected and we would now have the exact value of X. In fact, E will be in error for the same reasons (roundoff, etc.) that X' was, so that we have only accomplished a partial correction. If necessary, the process can be repeated as many times as necessary to obtain an accurate solution vector.

To illustrate the method, we reconsider Problem 6.2.   The calculated solution vector X' obtained for that problem when maximization of pivot elements was not used was

$$X' = \begin{bmatrix} 0.9991369 \\ 1.000077 \\ 1.000001 \\ 1.000063 \end{bmatrix}$$

as compared to the exact answer of all 1's.   We multiply this vector by the original coefficient matrix to form CX':

$$CX' = \begin{bmatrix} 1.1348 & 3.8326 & 1.1651 & 3.4017 \\ 0.5301 & 1.7875 & 2.5330 & 1.5435 \\ 3.4129 & 4.9317 & 8.7643 & 1.3142 \\ 1.2371 & 4.9998 & 10.6721 & 0.0147 \end{bmatrix} \begin{bmatrix} 0.9991369 \\ 1.000077 \\ 1.000001 \\ 1.000063 \end{bmatrix}$$

The result of this multiplication is the modified right-hand side vector R':

$$R' = \begin{bmatrix} 9.5337769 \\ 6.3939005 \\ 18.4206430 \\ 16.9230290 \end{bmatrix}$$

Now

$$R - R' = \begin{bmatrix} 9.5342000 - 9.5337769 \\ 6.3941000 - 6.3939005 \\ 18.4231000 - 18.4206430 \\ 16.9237000 - 16.9230290 \end{bmatrix} = \begin{bmatrix} 0.0004231 \\ 0.0001995 \\ 0.0024570 \\ 0.0006710 \end{bmatrix}$$

Using this vector as the right-hand side, we can solve the set

$$CE = R - R'$$

for E by Gauss-Jordan elimination to yield

$$E = \begin{bmatrix} 0.0008632 \\ -0.0000772 \\ -0.0000009 \\ -0.0000763 \end{bmatrix}$$

The improved estimate of X is given by

$$X' + E = \begin{bmatrix} 0.9991369 + 0.0008632 \\ 1.0000772 - 0.0000772 \\ 1.0000010 - 0.0000009 \\ 1.0000763 - 0.0000763 \end{bmatrix} = \begin{bmatrix} 1.0000001 \\ 1.0000000 \\ 1.0000001 \\ 1.0000000 \end{bmatrix}$$

The errors in the elements of this corrected unknown vector are no more than 10^{-7}.   The vast improvement is apparent, and no further correction is necessary.

In order to obtain the best results from this correction technique, the calculation of R' and $R - R'$ should be done using double precision arithmetic.   The remaining calculations can be done in single precision.

If it is known beforehand that error correction will be required, then the most efficient method is to calculate C^{-1} rather than to solve the set, since once C^{-1} is known, it can be used to calculate both X' and E.

6.4   Solve the following set of equations:

$$\begin{bmatrix} 4 & 3 & -1 \\ 7 & -2 & 3 \\ 5 & -18 & 13 \end{bmatrix} \begin{bmatrix} x_1 \\ x_2 \\ x_3 \end{bmatrix} = \begin{bmatrix} 6 \\ 9 \\ 3 \end{bmatrix}$$

For purposes of illustration, we begin by using a Gauss-Jordan program written from the algorithm in Fig. 6.2. This program does not employ maximization of pivot elements. The resulting solution vector is

$$X = \begin{bmatrix} 1.586206 \\ -0.4482759 \\ -1.000000 \end{bmatrix}$$

In order to check the accuracy of these answers, we substitute them into the first equation:

$$4(1.586206) + 3(-0.4482759) - 1(-1.000000) = 5.9999963$$

which is very close to the correct value of 6. Substitution into the other two equations shows that the solution vector also satisfies them to a high degree of accuracy. From all indications, we should feel secure that we have obtained an accurate solution. However, consider the following vector:

$$X = \begin{bmatrix} 0.6206896 \\ 2.1724137 \\ 3.000000 \end{bmatrix}$$

This is obviously very different from the original solution vector. If we substitute this vector into the first equation, we find

$$4(0.6206896) + 3(2.1724137) - 1(3.000000) = 5.9999995$$

which is again very close to the correct value of 6. Substitution in the other two equations yields similar accuracy. Something is obviously very wrong when two entirely different sets of unknowns satisfy (virtually exactly) the same set of equations. We might speculate that the set is very ill-conditioned, and perhaps in a sense that is true; however, the problem would seem to be more basic. In an effort to trace the difficulty, we employ the subroutine given in the Appendix which maximizes pivot elements, and also supplies the magnitude of the determinant of the coefficient matrix. This subroutine yields

$$X = \begin{bmatrix} -0.5000000 \\ 6.000000 \\ 16.00000 \end{bmatrix}$$

and $|\det C| = 2.7657 \times 10^{-5}$. This solution vector does not even come close to satisfying *any* of the three equations! The most informative piece of information, however, is the magnitude of the determinant. Recall that the determinant is defined as the sum of various products of elements in the matrix. No divisions are involved. For the present problem the coefficient matrix is composed entirely of integer elements, so the determinant *must* be an integer, or, practically speaking, as near to an integer as can be calculated using floating point arithmetic and allowing for a reasonable amount of roundoff error. The computed value for $|\det C|$ of 2.7657×10^{-5} can thus only mean that the determinant, if computed without roundoff error, is *exactly* zero. The set is thus singular, and no unique solution exists, which explains our earlier problem with multiple solutions.

The present problem was contrived by forming the third equation as a linear combination of the first two equations. In practice, it is quite common in certain physical problems to accidently form a singular set by applying a physical principle which is not independent of the other physical principles used to construct the set. This singular character of the set can sometimes be difficult to detect, particularly if the results of the solution happen to be physically reasonable. Maximization of pivot elements can often help, since the resulting "solution vector" will usually not satisfy the equations. Evaluation of the determinant of the coefficient matrix can also be helpful, as we have shown in the present problem.

6.5 A classical example of an ill-conditioned matrix is the so-called Hilbert matrix. This is a symmetric matrix of the form

$$H = \begin{bmatrix} 1 & 1/2 & 1/3 & 1/4 & \cdots & 1/n \\ 1/2 & 1/3 & 1/4 & 1/5 & \cdots & 1/(n+1) \\ 1/3 & 1/4 & 1/5 & 1/6 & \cdots & 1/(n+2) \\ \multicolumn{6}{c}{\dotfill} \\ 1/n & 1/(n+1) & 1/(n+2) & 1/(n+3) & \cdots & 1/2n \end{bmatrix}$$

Formulate and solve several problems involving the inverse of this matrix and the solution of sets having it as the coefficient matrix, in order to examine the signs and effects of ill-conditioning. Consider several values of n.

Consider the following set of three equations:

$$\begin{bmatrix} 1 & 1/2 & 1/3 \\ 1/2 & 1/3 & 1/4 \\ 1/3 & 1/4 & 1/5 \end{bmatrix} \begin{bmatrix} x_1 \\ x_2 \\ x_3 \end{bmatrix} = \begin{bmatrix} 11/6 \\ 13/12 \\ 47/60 \end{bmatrix}$$

The coefficient matrix of this set is the Hilbert matrix H with $n = 3$. The right-hand side vector has been chosen so that the exact solution vector is

$$X = \begin{bmatrix} 1 \\ 1 \\ 1 \end{bmatrix}$$

This permits easy observation of the effects of ill-conditioning on the solution vector as well as on the coefficient matrix. We begin by inverting the coefficient matrix, using the Gauss-Jordan subroutine given in the Appendix. The computed inverse is

$$H^{-1} = \begin{bmatrix} 9.000121 & -36.00063 & 30.00061 \\ -36.00069 & 192.0036 & -180.0034 \\ 30.00066 & -180.0034 & 180.0033 \end{bmatrix}$$

Recall that if the maximum elements in each row of a matrix are of order 1 (which is true of H in the present case) then the inverse of an ill-conditioned matrix will have elements which are much larger than 1 in magnitude. The ill-conditioning in this sense is obvious for the present problem. Another measure of the conditioning is to evaluate the normalized determinant of the matrix and compare the result to 1 (this criterion was given as equation (*6.39*), page 100). The subroutine used to obtain the inverse also supplies this information, and we find

$$\frac{|\det H|}{\sqrt{\sum_{i=1}^{3} \sum_{j=1}^{3} h_{ij}^2}} = 0.001319$$

which is another definite indication of the presence of ill-conditioning.   In order to examine the *effects* of ill-conditioning, we will use the same subroutine to reinvert the matrix and thus find $(H^{-1})^{-1}$.   If the effects of ill-conditioning are significant, then this reinverted matrix will show significant variations from the original matrix H.   The reinverted matrix is

$$(H^{-1})^{-1} = \begin{bmatrix} 0.9999908 & 0.4999933 & 0.3333282 \\ 0.4999948 & 0.3333294 & 0.2499971 \\ 0.3333294 & 0.2499973 & 0.1999979 \end{bmatrix}$$

which shows some error, but 5 decimal places of the original matrix have been retained.   The solution vector which results from multiplying H^{-1} by the right-hand side is

$$X = \begin{bmatrix} 1.000031 \\ 0.9999542 \\ 1.000046 \end{bmatrix}$$

The elements of this vector are in error in the fifth decimal place as compared to the correct solution vector of all 1's.   Thus for this case we have detected the *presence* of ill-conditioning, but have not found its *effects* to be very serious.

Consider next a similar set of 5 equations:

$$\begin{bmatrix} 1 & 1/2 & 1/3 & 1/4 & 1/5 \\ 1/2 & 1/3 & 1/4 & 1/5 & 1/6 \\ 1/3 & 1/4 & 1/5 & 1/6 & 1/7 \\ 1/4 & 1/5 & 1/6 & 1/7 & 1/8 \\ 1/5 & 1/6 & 1/7 & 1/8 & 1/9 \end{bmatrix} \begin{bmatrix} x_1 \\ x_2 \\ x_3 \\ x_4 \\ x_5 \end{bmatrix} = \begin{bmatrix} 137/60 \\ 87/60 \\ 459/420 \\ 743/840 \\ 1879/2520 \end{bmatrix}$$

For reasons of space we will not reproduce the entire inverse; however, the largest element in the inverse is 177807.6, or six orders of magnitude larger than the elements in the original matrix.   The normalized determinant is

$$\frac{|\det H|}{\sqrt{\sum_{i=1}^{5} \sum_{j=1}^{5} h_{ij}^2}} = 6.2638 \times 10^{-11}$$

These are indications of severe ill-conditioning.   To assess the effects, we examine

$$(H^{-1})^{-1} = \begin{bmatrix} 1.0049 & 0.5034 & 0.3361 & 0.2522 & 0.2019 \\ 0.5037 & 0.3360 & 0.2521 & 0.2017 & 0.1681 \\ 0.3363 & 0.2521 & 0.2016 & 0.1680 & 0.1440 \\ 0.2525 & 0.2018 & 0.1680 & 0.1440 & 0.1259 \\ 0.2021 & 0.1682 & 0.1440 & 0.1260 & 0.1119 \end{bmatrix}$$

The errors have clearly become significant for this case, since the third decimal place in almost all of the elements of this reinverted matrix are incorrect.   The solution vector, which should be all 1's, is found to be

$$X = \begin{bmatrix} 0.9992676 \\ 1.015625 \\ 0.9140625 \\ 1.2421875 \\ 1.0039063 \end{bmatrix}$$

The effects of ill-conditioning are apparent. Clearly, sets any larger than this will cause considerable trouble. It is interesting to examine the solution vector (which should be all 1's) for $n = 6$:

$$X = \begin{bmatrix} 0.9946289 \\ 1.285156 \\ 0.4375000 \\ 8.000000 \\ -6.000000 \\ 3.187500 \end{bmatrix}$$

This result is complete nonsense and the solution has been clearly overwhelmed by roundoff error. As might be expected, $(H^{-1})^{-1}$ for $n = 6$ looks quite different from H. If the solution vector is obtained directly by Gauss-Jordan elimination without finding H^{-1} as an intermediate step, then the number of arithmetic operations is smaller and the solution vector does not become complete nonsense until $n = 8$.

These results were obtained on the IBM 360/67 in single precision arithmetic (which uses essentially a seven digit word). Larger Hilbert matrices can be inverted with meaningful results if double precision arithmetic is employed, or if other machines with larger word sizes are used.

6.6   Carry out the first three iterations of the Gauss-Siedel method for the following set of equations:

$$8x_1 + 2x_2 + 3x_3 = 30$$

$$x_1 - 9x_2 + 2x_3 = 1$$

$$2x_1 + 3x_2 + 6x_3 = 31$$

The set is strongly diagonally dominant, so no rearrangement is needed and Gauss-Siedel iteration should converge. Solving each equation for the unknown which has the largest coefficient (in magnitude) gives

$$x_1 = \frac{30 - 2x_2 - 3x_3}{8}, \qquad x_2 = \frac{1 - x_1 - 2x_3}{-9}, \qquad x_3 = \frac{31 - 2x_1 - 3x_2}{6}$$

We use an initial guess of

$$X = \begin{bmatrix} 1 \\ 1 \\ 1 \end{bmatrix}$$

The first iteration is

$$x_1 = \frac{30 - 2(1) - 3(1)}{8} = 3.1250$$

$$x_2 = \frac{1 - 3.1250 - 2(1)}{-9} = 0.4583$$

$$x_3 = \frac{31 - 2(3.1250) - 3(0.4583)}{6} = 3.8959$$

Note that the most current estimate for x_1 of 3.1250 was used in solving for x_2, and that the most current estimates of x_1 and x_2 were used to solve for x_3. The second iteration is

$$x_1 = \frac{30 - 2(0.4583) - 3(3.8959)}{8} = 2.1745$$

$$x_2 = \frac{1 - 2.1745 - 2(3.8959)}{-9} = 0.9963$$

$$x_3 = \frac{31 - 2(2.1745) - 3(0.9963)}{6} = 3.9437$$

The third iteration gives

$$x_1 = \frac{30 - 2(0.9963) - 3(3.9437)}{8} = 2.0220$$

$$x_2 = \frac{1 - 2.0220 - 2(3.9437)}{-9} = 0.9899$$

$$x_3 = \frac{31 - 2(2.0220) - 3(0.9899)}{6} = 3.9977$$

The iteration is clearly converging. After three iterations, the estimate of the solution vector is

$$X = \begin{bmatrix} 2.0220 \\ 0.9899 \\ 3.9977 \end{bmatrix}$$

The exact answer is

$$X = \begin{bmatrix} 2 \\ 1 \\ 4 \end{bmatrix}$$

6.7   Solve the following set by Gauss-Siedel iteration:

$$\begin{bmatrix} 3 & -5 & 47 & 20 \\ 11 & 16 & 17 & 10 \\ 56 & 22 & 11 & -18 \\ 17 & 66 & -12 & 7 \end{bmatrix} \begin{bmatrix} x_1 \\ x_2 \\ x_3 \\ x_4 \end{bmatrix} = \begin{bmatrix} 18 \\ 26 \\ 34 \\ 82 \end{bmatrix}$$

At first glance the set does not seem to be suitable for an iterative solution, since the main diagonal elements are not the largest elements in each row. However, by simply reordering the equations this can be partially remedied:

$$\begin{bmatrix} 56 & 22 & 11 & -18 \\ 17 & 66 & -12 & 7 \\ 3 & -5 & 47 & 20 \\ 11 & 16 & 17 & 10 \end{bmatrix} \begin{bmatrix} x_1 \\ x_2 \\ x_3 \\ x_4 \end{bmatrix} = \begin{bmatrix} 34 \\ 82 \\ 18 \\ 26 \end{bmatrix}$$

The main diagonal elements are now the largest elements in magnitude in each row except for the last row. The diagonal dominance in the first three equations is sufficiently strong that the small diagonal element in the fourth equation may not cause divergence. We try an initial guess of

$$X^{(0)} = \begin{bmatrix} 1 \\ 1 \\ 1 \\ 1 \end{bmatrix}$$

with an absolute convergence criterion of $\epsilon = 0.0001$. The first iteration gives

$$X^{(1)} = \begin{bmatrix} 0.339286 \\ 1.230789 \\ 0.066725 \\ 0.144090 \end{bmatrix}$$

After 10 iterations,

$$X^{(10)} = \begin{bmatrix} -0.930569 \\ 1.901519 \\ 1.359500 \\ -1.729954 \end{bmatrix}$$

The process satisfies the convergence criterion after 35 iterations and gives

$$X = \begin{bmatrix} -1.076888 \\ 1.990028 \\ 1.474477 \\ -1.906078 \end{bmatrix}$$

The Gauss-Siedel procedure clearly converges with no problems for this set with $C_{44} = 10$. However, it is interesting to note that if C_{44} is 9 or smaller then the procedure is divergent. Clearly, the presence of any small main diagonal elements can pose a significant threat to the convergence of Gauss-Siedel iteration. However, if iterative techniques are indicated for other reasons, they are definitely worth trying even in the presence of a few small main diagonal elements. In some cases, underrelaxation of the offending equation(s) can turn a divergent procedure into a convergent one.

6.8 Given the following set of equations:

$$\begin{bmatrix} 5 & 4 & 4 & 4 \\ 5 & 6 & 5 & 5 \\ 6 & 6 & 7 & 6 \\ 7 & 7 & 7 & 8 \end{bmatrix} \begin{bmatrix} x_1 \\ x_2 \\ x_3 \\ x_4 \end{bmatrix} = \begin{bmatrix} 17 \\ 21 \\ 25 \\ 29 \end{bmatrix}$$

Using an initial guess of zero for all unknowns, and an absolute convergence criterion of $\epsilon = 0.0001$, carry out iterative solutions with various relaxation factors and compare the number of iterations necessary to attain convergence.

The exact solution to this set is

$$X = \begin{bmatrix} 1 \\ 1 \\ 1 \\ 1 \end{bmatrix}$$

For all iterative solutions considered here, the answers obtained were accurate to at least 3 decimal places. The relaxation factors employed and the corresponding number of iterations necessary to attain convergence are tabulated below:

λ	Iterations to Convergence
0.8	54
1.0	48
1.2	53
1.5	84
1.7	147

It is apparent that Gauss-Siedel iteration ($\lambda = 1$) is best for this set.   In fact, if an iterative scheme is to be employed for almost any problem, Gauss-Siedel iteration should be tried first.   The exception is for problems such as Problem 6.9, where previous experience makes it quite clear that overrelaxation will accelerate convergence in almost all cases.   Searching for a nearly optimum λ is clearly advantageous *only* if virtually the same set (perhaps with a slightly different coefficient matrix or right-hand side) is to be solved many times.

6.9   Given the following set of 10 equations:

$$\begin{bmatrix} -2 & 1 & & & & & \\ 1 & -2 & 1 & & & & \\ & 1 & -2 & 1 & & & \\ & & & \ddots & & & \\ & & & 1 & -2 & 1 & \\ & & & & 1 & -2 & 1 \\ & & & & & 1 & -2 \end{bmatrix} \begin{bmatrix} x_1 \\ x_2 \\ x_3 \\ \vdots \\ x_8 \\ x_9 \\ x_{10} \end{bmatrix} = \begin{bmatrix} -0.5 \\ -1.5 \\ -1.5 \\ \vdots \\ -1.5 \\ -1.5 \\ +0.5 \end{bmatrix}$$

Explore various solution methods.

This set (although quite small) is typical of the sets of equations which arise from the numerical solution of partial differential equations.   The matrix is tridiagonal, and in this case is clearly small enough that direct methods should be used.   However, similar (but much larger) sets are often solved by iterative methods, so we will explore the use of these techniques as well.

The most effective direct method for such a set is the Gauss elimination algorithm for tridiagonal sets (Fig. 6.3), which yields the following results:

$x_1 = 6.4091$	$x_6 = 20.9547$
$x_2 = 12.3183$	$x_7 = 19.3637$
$x_3 = 16.7274$	$x_8 = 16.2728$
$x_4 = 19.6365$	$x_9 = 11.6819$
$x_5 = 21.0456$	$x_{10} = 5.5909$

We now turn to the iterative methods.   Gauss-Siedel iteration with an initial guess of $x_i = 10$ for all x_i and with an absolute convergence criterion of $\epsilon = 0.001$ yields

$x_1 = 6.4054$	$x_6 = 20.9439$
$x_2 = 12.3113$	$x_7 = 19.3543$
$x_3 = 16.7181$	$x_8 = 16.2653$
$x_4 = 19.6258$	$x_9 = 11.6767$
$x_5 = 21.0344$	$x_{10} = 5.5883$

in 80 iterations.   These values are reasonably accurate (to 2 decimal places in most cases) and the accuracy could be improved as much as desired by using a smaller convergence criterion (at the expense of additional iterations).

Sets of this type are often well suited to overrelaxation.   Using a relaxation factor of $\lambda = 1.7$ and the same initial guess and convergence criterion as before yields essentially the same answers as does Gauss-Siedel iteration, but requires only 27 iterations.   Some additional searching might yield a more nearly optimal value of λ, which would mean that even fewer iterations would be required.   However, the advantage of overrelaxation as compared with Gauss-Siedel iteration for this set should be apparent from this example.   The reason that matrices of this type are encountered so often and their characteristics so well known will become more obvious when the numerical solutions of ordinary and partial differential equations are discussed in Chapters 9 and 11.

6.10   Given the following nonlinear set of algebraic equations:

$$4x + y^2 + z = 11$$

$$x + 4y + z^2 = 18$$

$$x^2 + y + 4z = 15$$

Solve this set by using Gauss-Siedel iteration.

Nonlinear algebraic sets can have multiple solutions and this could be true of the present problem.   However, the fortunate state of affairs with most sets of nonlinear equations is that the solution which is most easily obtained is the solution which is "wanted."   For example, if the set of equations comes from a physical problem, then the solution which is easiest to obtain is usually the only physically realizable solution.   The remaining solutions are often complex (have imaginary components) or are physically impossible or unlikely.

A solution to the present problem can be obtained by applying standard Gauss-Siedel iteration to the set which is already arranged in diagonally dominant form.   Thus

$$x = \frac{11 - y^2 - z}{4}, \qquad y = \frac{18 - x - z^2}{4}, \qquad z = \frac{15 - y - x^2}{4}$$

We use an initial guess of $x = y = z = 1$ and an absolute convergence criterion of $\epsilon = 0.0001$.   The first iteration yields

$$x^{(1)} = \frac{11 - (1)^2 - 1}{4} = 2.25$$

$$y^{(1)} = \frac{18 - 2.25 - (1)^2}{4} = 3.6875$$

$$z^{(1)} = \frac{15 - 3.6875 - (2.25)^2}{4} = 1.5625$$

After 67 iterations, the convergence criterion is satisfied, and we find

$$x = 1.000112, \qquad y = 1.999962, \qquad z = 2.999953$$

In fact, for this contrived problem, an exact solution is

$$x = 1, \qquad y = 2, \qquad z = 3$$

It must be emphasized that we had no guarantee that this iteration would converge despite the diagonal dominance of the set, since a general theory for the iterative solution of nonlinear equations is not available.

It is interesting to examine the effects of relaxation on this iterative process. Using the same convergence criterion and initial guess as before, we find the following for various relaxation factors:

λ	Iterations to Convergence
0.6	41
0.8	38
1.0	67
1.2	300 (not yet converged)

We find that underrelaxation accelerates convergence, with the optimum relaxation factor apparently near $\lambda = 0.8$. Even slight overrelaxation ($\lambda = 1.2$) slows the convergence enormously. No general conclusion should be drawn from these results (in fact, general conclusions can hardly ever be drawn from nonlinear problems), but the reversal of overall behavior in this case, as compared to most linear problems, is interesting and illustrates the degree of art rather than science which often must be exercised for the most effective solution of nonlinear problems.

Problems

*6.11 Write a computer program to solve a set of simultaneous linear equations by Gauss-Jordan elimination. Assume that no maximization of pivot elements is required. The program should be capable of solving sets of equations of arbitrary size, but no larger than 20×20.

*6.12 Write a computer program to solve a tridiagonal set of simultaneous equations by Gauss elimination. The three diagonals of the coefficient matrix should each be stored in one dimensional arrays to minimize storage and to eliminate unnecessary operations on zero elements. The program should be capable of solving sets of equations to arbitrary size, up to $n = 100$.

*6.13 Write a computer program to solve a set of simultaneous linear equations by Gauss-Siedel iteration or by point relaxation. The program should be capable of solving sets of arbitrary size, but no larger than 20×20. Input should include the initial guess for the unknowns, the convergence criterion (which may be absolute or relative, as you prefer), and the relaxation factor.

6.14 Solve the following sets by using Gauss-Jordan elimination:

(a)
$$\begin{bmatrix} 3 & -2 & 7 \\ -2 & 4 & -3 \\ -1 & 9 & 4 \end{bmatrix} \begin{bmatrix} x_1 \\ x_2 \\ x_3 \end{bmatrix} = \begin{bmatrix} 15 \\ 12 \\ 27 \end{bmatrix}$$

(b)
$$\begin{bmatrix} 2 & -5 & -9 \\ 7 & 1 & 1 \\ -3 & 7 & -1 \end{bmatrix} \begin{bmatrix} x_1 \\ x_2 \\ x_3 \end{bmatrix} = \begin{bmatrix} -4 \\ 8 \\ 2 \end{bmatrix}$$

*6.15 Solve the following sets by using the Gauss-Jordan program written for Problem 6.11:

(a)
$$\begin{bmatrix} 3 & -5 & 6 & 4 & -2 & -3 & 8 \\ 1 & 1 & -9 & 15 & 1 & -9 & 2 \\ 2 & -1 & 7 & 5 & -1 & 6 & 11 \\ -1 & 1 & 3 & 2 & 7 & -1 & -2 \\ 4 & 3 & 1 & -7 & 2 & 1 & 1 \\ 2 & 9 & -8 & 11 & -1 & -4 & -1 \\ 7 & 2 & -1 & 2 & 7 & -1 & 9 \end{bmatrix} \begin{bmatrix} x_1 \\ x_2 \\ x_3 \\ x_4 \\ x_5 \\ x_6 \\ x_7 \end{bmatrix} = \begin{bmatrix} 47 \\ 17 \\ 24 \\ 8 \\ 13 \\ -10 \\ 34 \end{bmatrix}$$

(b)
$$\begin{bmatrix} 1 & -1 & 2 & 5 & -7 & -8 \\ 3 & -9 & 1 & -1 & 8 & 1 \\ -1 & 1 & 9 & -9 & 2 & 3 \\ 1 & 7 & 2 & -3 & -1 & 4 \\ 7 & 1 & -2 & 4 & 1 & -1 \\ 2 & 3 & -9 & 12 & -2 & 7 \end{bmatrix} \begin{bmatrix} x_1 \\ x_2 \\ x_3 \\ x_4 \\ x_5 \\ x_6 \end{bmatrix} = \begin{bmatrix} -12 \\ 8 \\ 22 \\ 41 \\ 15 \\ 50 \end{bmatrix}$$

*6.16 Repeat Problem 6.15 by using the Gauss-Jordan subroutine in the Appendix to solve the sets.

*6.17 Solve the following tridiagonal set of 10 equations by using the Gauss elimination program written for Problem 6.12:

$$\begin{bmatrix} -4 & 1 & & & & \\ 1 & -4 & 1 & & & \\ & 1 & -4 & 1 & & \\ & & & \ddots & & \\ & & & 1 & -4 & 1 \\ & & & & 1 & -4 \end{bmatrix} \begin{bmatrix} x_1 \\ x_2 \\ x_3 \\ \vdots \\ x_9 \\ x_{10} \end{bmatrix} = \begin{bmatrix} -27 \\ -15 \\ -15 \\ \vdots \\ -15 \\ -15 \end{bmatrix}$$

*6.18 Construct a natural cubic spline which fits all of the following points, and interpolate for $f(7.3)$:

x	1	2	3	4	5	6	7	8	9	10
$f(x)$	0.995	0.980	0.955	0.921	0.878	0.825	0.765	0.697	0.622	0.540

(*Note*: This problem is not out of place. The matrix of coefficients of the set of equations which arises in the course of solving this problem is tridiagonal, and the program written for Problem 6.12 should be used.)

*6.19 Solve the following set by using the Gauss-Jordan subroutine in the Appendix. Examine the solution and the magnitude of the determinant, and comment.

$$\begin{bmatrix} 8 & 3 & -9 & 7 & 4 \\ 2 & -1 & 6 & 17 & 1 \\ 4 & 3 & -7 & 1 & 6 \\ 12 & -1 & 6 & 14 & 2 \\ 12 & 2 & 1 & 9 & 10 \end{bmatrix} \begin{bmatrix} x_1 \\ x_2 \\ x_3 \\ x_4 \\ x_5 \end{bmatrix} = \begin{bmatrix} 10 \\ 21 \\ 10 \\ 28 \\ 38 \end{bmatrix}$$

6.20   Solve the following sets by Gauss-Siedel iteration:

(a)
$$\begin{bmatrix} 7 & 1 & 2 \\ -1 & 4 & -1 \\ 3 & 15 & 20 \end{bmatrix} \begin{bmatrix} x_1 \\ x_2 \\ x_3 \end{bmatrix} = \begin{bmatrix} 47 \\ 19 \\ 87 \end{bmatrix}$$

(b)
$$\begin{bmatrix} 1 & -10 & 2 & 4 \\ 3 & 1 & 4 & 12 \\ 9 & 2 & 3 & 4 \\ -1 & 2 & 7 & 3 \end{bmatrix} \begin{bmatrix} x_1 \\ x_2 \\ x_3 \\ x_4 \end{bmatrix} = \begin{bmatrix} 2 \\ 12 \\ 21 \\ 37 \end{bmatrix}$$

*(c)
$$\begin{bmatrix} 17 & 1 & 4 & 3 & -1 & 2 & 3 & -7 \\ 2 & 10 & -1 & 7 & -2 & 1 & 1 & -4 \\ -1 & 1 & -8 & 2 & -5 & 2 & -1 & 1 \\ 2 & 4 & 1 & -11 & 1 & 3 & 4 & -1 \\ 1 & 3 & 1 & 7 & -15 & 1 & -2 & 4 \\ -2 & 1 & 7 & -1 & 2 & 12 & -1 & 8 \\ 3 & 4 & 5 & 1 & 2 & 8 & -19 & 2 \\ 5 & 1 & 1 & 1 & -1 & 1 & -7 & 10 \end{bmatrix} \begin{bmatrix} x_1 \\ x_2 \\ x_3 \\ x_4 \\ x_5 \\ x_6 \\ x_7 \\ x_8 \end{bmatrix} = \begin{bmatrix} 71 \\ 43 \\ -11 \\ -37 \\ -61 \\ 52 \\ -73 \\ 21 \end{bmatrix}$$

*(d)
$$\begin{bmatrix} 2 & -1 & 4 & -1 & 5 & 1 & 2 \\ 1 & -1 & 4 & 3 & 7 & 1 & 5 \\ -1 & 2 & -1 & -7 & 1 & -1 & 1 \\ 1 & 12 & 1 & -8 & 4 & -3 & 7 \\ 8 & 4 & 5 & -4 & 1 & -1 & 5 \\ 2 & 3 & 9 & -1 & 4 & 2 & 1 \\ 4 & 3 & 1 & 2 & -1 & 12 & -1 \end{bmatrix} \begin{bmatrix} x_1 \\ x_2 \\ x_3 \\ x_4 \\ x_5 \\ x_6 \\ x_7 \end{bmatrix} = \begin{bmatrix} 24 \\ 53 \\ -10 \\ 91 \\ 27 \\ 43 \\ 47 \end{bmatrix}$$

*6.21   Solve the tridiagonal set given in Problem 6.17 by using Gauss-Siedel iteration.

*6.22   Repeat Problem 6.21 by using relaxation with relaxation factors of 1.3, 1.6, and 1.8.   Compare the number of iterations required to the number needed for Gauss-Siedel iteration.   Which is best for this problem?

6.23   Carry out the error correction technique described in Problem 6.3 to improve the answers obtained in Problem 6.5 for $n = 3$.   Use the computed inverse of H given in Problem 6.5 to obtain the error vector E.

*6.24   Solve the following nonlinear set by Gauss-Siedel iteration:

$$5w + x^3 + y + z = 8.7$$
$$w^2 - 6x + 2y - z = 7.3$$
$$w - x + 4y + z^2 = 17.29$$
$$2w + x + y^2 + 11z = 34.7$$

Chapter 7

Least-Squares Curve Fitting and Functional Approximation

7.0 INTRODUCTION

In this chapter we will consider briefly the approximation of functions. The subject is much too long and complex to cover in detail here. Entire books devoted to the subject include Rice[7] and Meinardus[8]. However, we will attempt to provide enough information to enable the reader to construct some simple approximating functions, and to recognize and use the most common and effective approximating functions for digital computers. Methods will be examined for the approximation of both continuous functions and functions available only at discrete points.

In the case of functions available only at discrete points, we will consider approximation by simple continuous functions, such as polynomials. Actually, we have already introduced one variety of such approximations in Chapter 4. In that chapter, we constructed polynomial approximations to functions available at discrete points, and termed these polynomial approximations "interpolating polynomials." In the present chapter we will show how simple approximations can be constructed which can be used to smooth noisy experimental or numerical data, and to provide a simple analytical expression instead of a collection of scattered points.

In approximating continuous functions, the objective is usually to provide a "simpler" form than the original function. The approximation should be simpler than the original function either in the sense that it is easier to handle analytically, or (more to the point of this text) that it is easier and/or faster to evaluate on a digital computer. As was the case with functions available at discrete points, Chapter 4 also provided an introduction to the approximation of continuous functions. Polynomial approximations to continuous functions were constructed by using the concept of Chebyshev interpolation, in which the continuous function to be approximated was sampled at specific points (the zeros of the Chebyshev polynomials) and a polynomial was generated by using Lagrange interpolation. This approximating (or interpolating) polynomial tended to have minimum-maximum error in approximating the original function.

We reopen the discussion of functional approximation by again considering a function available only at discrete points.

7.1 LEAST-SQUARES FITTING OF DISCRETE POINTS

In constructing the interpolating polynomials of Chapter 4, the primary purpose was to provide information *between* tabulated points, and, as accurately as possible, to force the interpolating polynomial to assume exactly the value of the tabulated function at each of the points where the function was supplied. Consider, however, the nature of much experimental data. Typically, such data include noise due to many different effects. (Hopefully, if the experiment is well designed, the data do not include systematic error which would tend to shift all of the data in one direction.)* The noisy data from an experiment might appear as shown in Fig. 7.1. (We assume the x values are accurate.)

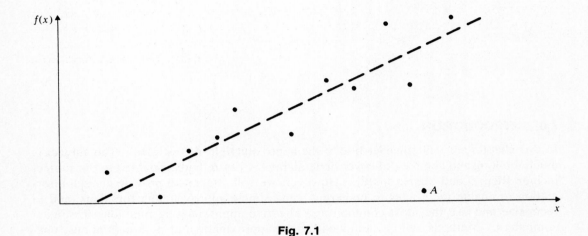

Fig. 7.1

Using our knowledge of interpolation, it would be possible to construct (perhaps using Lagrange interpolation) a polynomial which fits the data exactly at each of the points. However, such a polynomial would not only include all of the noise in the data, it would necessarily be of a very high degree, and would oscillate wildly, perhaps straying far from the immediate region which contains the data. Such a high degree polynomial would also be very unwieldy to use as a continuous function which is representative of the data.

A better functional approximation to the data would be one which is simple in form (perhaps a polynomial of relatively low degree) and which tends to "smooth" the data (reduce the noise). If the noise in the data is assumed to be essentially random in character, then a reasonable smoothing functional approximation to the data in Fig. 7.1 might be the straight line which we have drawn "by eye" through the points. We must, of course, have a more precise and automatic way of constructing such approximating functions than by eye.

If the function to be approximated is $f(x)$, and the approximating function is denoted as $g(x)$, then a measure of the accuracy of the approximation is the magnitude of the local distance between the two functions given by

---

*We will not attempt to discuss methods for recognizing or assessing noise or systematic error in experimental data. See any book on the analysis of data, such as Pugh and Winslow[9].

$$d(x) = |f(x) - g(x)| \tag{7.1}$$

The approximating function $g(x)$ should now be chosen such that, in some sense, $d(x)$ is minimized over the entire region of x where the approximation is to apply.

The sense in which $d(x)$ is minimized is clearly a vital factor in determining the character of the approximation.   We have previously encountered minimization of $d(x)$ in the Chebyshev sense: the minimization of the maximum value of $d(x)$ over the interval.   This criterion is usually *not* an effective one to use in selecting a continuous functional approximation to noisy data, simply because it permits individual points which may be badly in error to exert an overpowering influence on the approximating function.   A single point, such as the point labeled "A" in Fig. 7.1, can force the approximating function to shift drastically toward it in order to minimize the maximum error which would tend to occur at that point.   A much more favorable sense in which to minimize $d(x)$ for this type of approximation is in the *least-squares sense*.   If we denote the x coordinates at which data are available as the x_i, and if there are n such coordinates, then $d(x)$ is minimized in the least-squares sense if

$$E = \sum_{i=1}^{n} d^2(x_i) \tag{7.2}$$

is minimized.

For the approximation of functions known at discrete points, the most commonly-chosen form for $g(x)$ is the polynomial.   Thus if $g(x)$ is of degree l,

$$g(x) = a_0 + a_1 x + a_2 x^2 + \cdots + a_l x^l \tag{7.3}$$

and from (7.2),

$$E = \sum_{i=1}^{n} |f(x_i) - g(x_i)|^2 = \sum_{i=1}^{n} |g(x_i) - f(x_i)|^2 = \sum_{i=1}^{n} [g(x_i) - f(x_i)]^2 \tag{7.4}$$

Using (7.3), equation (7.4) becomes

$$E = \sum_{i=1}^{n} [a_0 + a_1 x_i + a_2 x_i^2 + \cdots + a_l x_i^l - f(x_i)]^2 \tag{7.5}$$

The parameters which can be varied in order to minimize E are the $(l + 1)$ coefficients of $g(x)$.   The minimization can be accomplished by setting equal to zero the partial derivatives of E with respect to each of these coefficients:

$$\frac{\partial E}{\partial a_0} = 0$$

$$\frac{\partial E}{\partial a_1} = 0$$

$$\frac{\partial E}{\partial a_2} = 0 \tag{7.6}$$

$$\vdots$$

$$\frac{\partial E}{\partial a_l} = 0$$

The proof that (7.6) indeed does provide a minimum can be found in many references, including [5].   The set of equations (7.6) provides $(l + 1)$ equations in the $(l + 1)$ unknowns

$a_0, a_1, a_2, \ldots, a_l$.   To illustrate the form of these equations, we will carry out the details of the differentiation for the first equation:

$$\frac{\partial E}{\partial a_0} = \frac{\partial}{\partial a_0} \sum_{i=1}^{n} [a_0 + a_1 x_i + a_2 x_i^2 + \cdots + a_l x_i^l - f(x_i)]^2$$

$$= \sum_{i=1}^{n} \frac{\partial}{\partial a_0} [\quad]^2 = \sum_{i=1}^{n} 2[\quad] \left\{ \frac{\partial}{\partial a_0} [\quad] \right\}$$

$$= \sum_{i=1}^{n} 2[a_0 + a_1 x_i + a_2 x_i^2 + \cdots + a_l x_i^l - f(x_i)](1) = 0$$

or, dropping the factor of 2 and summing term by term, we find

$$na_0 + \left[\sum_{i=1}^{n} x_i \right] a_1 + \left[\sum_{i=1}^{n} x_i^2 \right] a_2 + \cdots + \left[\sum_{i=1}^{n} x_i^l \right] a_l = \sum_{i=1}^{n} f(x_i) \tag{7.7}$$

Similarly, the second equation is

$$\left[\sum_{i=1}^{n} x_i \right] a_0 + \left[\sum_{i=1}^{n} x_i^2 \right] a_1 + \left[\sum_{i=1}^{n} x_i^3 \right] a_2 + \cdots + \left[\sum_{i=1}^{n} x_i^{l+1} \right] a_l = \sum_{i=1}^{n} x_i f(x_i) \tag{7.8}$$

It can be readily inferred from (7.7) and (7.8) that the complete set of simultaneous linear equations in the coefficients of the polynomial is

$$\begin{bmatrix} n & \sum x_i & \sum x_i^2 & \cdots & \sum x_i^l \\ \sum x_i & \sum x_i^2 & \sum x_i^3 & \cdots & \sum x_i^{l+1} \\ \sum x_i^2 & \sum x_i^3 & \sum x_i^4 & \cdots & \sum x_i^{l+2} \\ \cdots\cdots\cdots\cdots\cdots\cdots\cdots\cdots\cdots\cdots\cdots \\ \sum x_i^l & \sum x_i^{l+1} & \sum x_i^{l+2} & \cdots & \sum x_i^{2l} \end{bmatrix} \begin{bmatrix} a_0 \\ a_1 \\ a_2 \\ \vdots \\ a_l \end{bmatrix} = \begin{bmatrix} \sum f(x_i) \\ \sum x_i f(x_i) \\ \sum x_i^2 f(x_i) \\ \vdots \\ \sum x_i^l f(x_i) \end{bmatrix} \tag{7.9}$$

where Σ signifies $\Sigma_{i=1}^{n}$.

Standard equation-solving techniques, such as Gauss-Jordan elimination, may be used to solve the set (7.9), but unfortunately the set is *very* poorly conditioned.   The number of equations which can be solved (and thus the degree of the approximating polynomial) is severely limited in most cases by roundoff error, and $l = 7$ or 8 will usually produce meaningless results on most machines using single precision arithmetic.   One of the problems is the large variation in the magnitude of the coefficients in any given row; Σx_i^l is obviously much larger (or smaller) in magnitude than Σx_i for any reasonably large value of l.   Double precision arithmetic can be of enormous help in maintaining accuracy and is recommended where available for least-squares work.

Fortunately, relatively low order polynomials are usually the most useful for data fitting; higher order polynomials tend to simply reproduce the noise in the data and should not be used without good reason.   By far the most widely-used functions for data fitting are straight lines, and data are often replotted on different scales (such as log-log scales) until the data assume such a form that a straight line is a reasonably good approximation[9, 10].

The choice of the degree of polynomial to be used for the fitting of data can be somewhat difficult.   The best situation is one in which it is known a priori that the data should fall on a polynomial of a given degree.   This degree of polynomial is then the obvious choice.   Qualitative judgments can often be made by examining the data; for example, if the data appear to contain one inflection, then a cubic is the obvious choice.   Other methods of choice based on the observation of $\Sigma_{i=1}^{n} d^2(x_i)$ or on statistical analysis are also possible but are beyond the scope of this text.

Examples of the use of least-squares curve fitting are given in Problems 7.1–7.3.

It should be noted that functions other than polynomials can also be used to approximate data in the least-squares sense.   See Problem 7.2 for an example.

7.2 THE APPROXIMATION OF CONTINUOUS FUNCTIONS

The "best" approximations to continuous functions are usually considered to be approximations which minimize the error in the minimax (minimum-maximum error) sense. Unfortunately, it is often very difficult to find the best approximation of a certain class to a given function, and we must settle for an approximation to the best approximation.   For example, instead of finding the best quadratic to approximate a function, we might have to be satisfied with a quadratic which is reasonably close to the best quadratic.   Good approximations to continuous functions usually have an error $d(x)$ (defined by (7.1)) which oscillates about zero in the region of interest in such a way that the positive peaks are approximately equal to the negative peaks.   Such behavior is sometimes referred to as minimax behavior even if the approximating function is not the best in its class (i.e. even if the peaks do not have the minimum magnitude of all functions of that class).   The approximation methods to be examined here have this desirable behavior.

The simplest and most common form of approximation to a continuous function is some type of polynomial.   In fact, whenever a power series representation (such as a Taylor series) is used to calculate a function, then a polynomial approximation is actually being used since the power series must be truncated at some point, and a truncated power series is a polynomial.

We will begin our discussion of the approximation of continuous functions by examining a method for improving the efficiency of truncated power series, or, in other words, of obtaining better accuracy with fewer terms.   This is called *telescoping* a power series or *economization*.   As we will see, this method also has direct application to the approximation of any polynomial.

Chebyshev Economization

The Chebyshev polynomials were defined in Chapter 4, and the first few polynomials were given.   We require a somewhat expanded list for our present purposes:

$$T_0(x) = 1$$
$$T_1(x) = x$$
$$T_2(x) = 2x^2 - 1$$
$$T_3(x) = 4x^3 - 3x$$
$$T_4(x) = 8x^4 - 8x^2 + 1 \tag{7.10}$$
$$T_5(x) = 16x^5 - 20x^3 + 5x$$
$$T_6(x) = 32x^6 - 48x^4 + 18x^2 - 1$$
$$T_7(x) = 64x^7 - 112x^5 + 56x^3 - 7x$$
$$T_8(x) = 128x^8 - 256x^6 + 160x^4 - 32x^2 + 1$$

If more of these polynomials are needed, they can be obtained from the recurrence relationship

$$T_{n+1}(x) = 2xT_n(x) - T_{n-1}(x) \qquad (7.11)$$

Remember that these polynomials have a maximum magnitude of 1 on the interval $-1 \le x \le 1$.

For our purposes, it is also worthwhile to "invert" these polynomials by listing the powers of x in terms of the $T_n(x)$. These are

$$1 = T_0$$

$$x = T_1$$

$$x^2 = \frac{1}{2}(T_0 + T_2)$$

$$x^3 = \frac{1}{4}(3T_1 + T_3)$$

$$x^4 = \frac{1}{8}(3T_0 + 4T_2 + T_4) \qquad (7.12)$$

$$x^5 = \frac{1}{16}(10T_1 + 5T_3 + T_5)$$

$$x^6 = \frac{1}{32}(10T_0 + 15T_2 + 6T_4 + T_6)$$

$$x^7 = \frac{1}{64}(35T_1 + 21T_3 + 7T_5 + T_7)$$

$$x^8 = \frac{1}{128}(35T_0 + 56T_2 + 28T_4 + 8T_6 + T_8)$$

The $T_n(x)$ have been written simply as T_n.

Now consider a function which can be represented by a power series, such as

$$e^{-x} = 1 - x + \frac{x^2}{2!} - \frac{x^3}{3!} + \frac{x^4}{4!} - \frac{x^5}{5!} + \frac{x^6}{6!} - \cdots \qquad (7.13)$$

Since it simplifies this example, we shall restrict x to the interval $-1 \le x \le 1$. This restriction is not a serious one since any finite interval $a \le y \le b$ can be mapped onto the interval $-1 \le x \le 1$ by the formula

$$x = \frac{2y - b - a}{b - a} \qquad (7.14)$$

If the alternating series (7.13) is truncated after the term in x^5, the error will be no greater than 1.6152×10^{-3}. Using the Chebyshev polynomial representations of the powers of x, the truncated form of (7.13) can be written as

$$e^{-x} = T_0 - T_1 + \frac{1}{2}\left[\frac{1}{2}(T_0 + T_2)\right] - \frac{1}{3!}\left[\frac{1}{4}(3T_1 + T_3)\right]$$

$$+ \frac{1}{4!}\left[\frac{1}{8}(3T_0 + 4T_2 + T_4)\right] - \frac{1}{5!}\left[\frac{1}{16}(10T_1 + 5T_3 + T_5)\right] + \epsilon_1 \qquad (7.15)$$

where ϵ_1 has a maximum magnitude of 1.6152×10^{-3}.   Collecting coefficients of the various polynomials, we obtain

$$e^{-x} \approx 1.2656250 T_0 - 1.1302083 T_1 + 0.2708333 T_2$$
$$- 0.0442708 T_3 + 0.0052083 T_4 - 0.0005208 T_5 \qquad (7.16)$$

We can now take advantage of the fact that the maximum magnitude of $T_n(x)$ is 1 (on $-1 \le x \le 1$).   If we truncate the expression (7.16) after the term involving T_3, we will accumulate an additional error which will be no greater than the sum of the magnitudes of the coefficients of T_4 and T_5, or $0.0052083 + 0.0005208 = 0.0057291$.   Now

$$e^{-x} \approx 1.2656250 T_0 - 1.1302083 T_1 + 0.2708333 T_2 - 0.0442708 T_3 \qquad (7.17)$$

The magnitude of the maximum possible error in (7.17) is the sum of the maximum magnitude of the error in the truncation of the original series, which was 0.0016152, and the maximum magnitude of the error in truncating (7.16), which was 0.0057291.   This sum is 0.0073444.   The Chebyshev polynomials in (7.17) can now again be written in terms of powers of x, so that (7.17) becomes

$$e^{-x} \approx 1.2656250(1) - 1.1302083(x) + 0.2708333(2x^2 - 1)$$
$$- 0.0442708(4x^3 - 3x) \qquad (7.18)$$

Collecting the coefficients of the various powers of x, equation (7.18) may be written as

$$e^{-x} \approx 0.9947917 - 0.9973959x + 0.5416667x^2 - 0.1770832x^3 \qquad (7.19)$$

This four-term approximate expression is very similar to the first four terms of the original series (7.13) except that the maximum error of (7.19) is 0.0073444 as compared with a maximum possible error of 0.0516152 for the first four terms of the original series. In fact, if we take five terms of the original series, the maximum possible error will be 0.0099485, which is still greater than the maximum possible error in the four-term expression (7.19).   The expression (7.19) is called the *telescoped* or *economized* form of the power series.   If more terms of the original Taylor series are taken before the series is truncated, then the coefficients of the four-term approximation (7.19) will change slightly, and the approximation can be made more accurate.   However, this process eventually "converges" in the sense that a point is reached where additional terms in the Taylor series no longer affect the coefficients.*   It is important to note that there is no guarantee that the resulting cubic is the *best* cubic approximation to e^{-x} (in the minimax sense or any other sense) although it may indeed be a good approximation.

In the case of (7.19), the economized series for e^{-x} requires two terms less than the original series to attain essentially the same accuracy.   The savings in general are highly dependent on the character of the original power series.   The economization of rapidly convergent series (such as the present one for e^{-x}) provides relatively modest gains, while the economized form of very slowly convergent series can provide accuracy with a few terms that might require hundreds of terms of the original series.

This economization procedure can be used to approximate any polynomial by a lower order polynomial over any finite interval.   See Problem 7.4 for an example.

---

*This procedure can be automated; see Hamming[11].

We have now studied two ways to generate approximating polynomials for continuous functions: by Chebyshev interpolation on the original function (discussed in detail in Chapter 4) and by Chebyshev economization of the power series which represents the function. Polynomial approximations obtained by each of these methods are often used to compute continuous functions on digital computers. However, some functions are simply not well suited to polynomial approximation in the sense that high degree polynomials are needed to obtain reasonably accurate approximations. We will next briefly consider two types of approximating functions, the rational function and the continued fraction, which in many cases are much more powerful than polynomials.

Rational Functions

Rational functions are of the general form

$$r(x) = \frac{\sum_{i=0}^{n} a_i x^i}{\sum_{i=0}^{m} b_i x^i} \tag{7.20}$$

These functions are thus constructed as the quotient of two polynomials. Rational functions, however, are capable of behavior which is very difficult indeed to produce with reasonably low order polynomials. For example, low degree rational functions are capable of a single abrupt change in behavior (such as a localized bump or strong inflection) in the midst of an otherwise smooth, uninflected region. Any attempt to reproduce such behavior with a polynomial of reasonable degree will result in a series of ripples extending far into the regions where the function is supposed to be smooth and uninflected. Most of the rational approximations used for practical computing have polynomials of either the same degree or differing by one in the numerator and the denominator. It is beyond the scope of this text to consider the construction of rational approximations. See Meinardus[8] or Rice[7]. It should be noted that the efficiency of rational approximations can be improved by a Chebyshev economization procedure analogous to that previously discussed for power series[12]. A typical example of an economized rational approximation suitable for practical computation is given by Froberg[5] as

$$\frac{\sin x}{x} \approx \frac{1 - 0.1335639326x^2 + 0.0032811761x^4}{1 + 0.0331027317x^2 + 0.0004649838x^4} \tag{7.21}$$

This approximation is valid in the range $0 \leq x \leq 1$ with a maximum error of 4.67×10^{-11}. If the Taylor series for $(\sin x)/x$ were used, seven terms of the series would be needed to produce comparable accuracy in this range of x. Several different approximations (not necessarily of the same type) are often used in computer subroutines to provide accurate answers over the entire possible range of the argument.

Continued Fractions

Another powerful approximating function is the continued fraction. An infinite continued fraction is analogous to an infinite power series but usually has much better convergence properties. An infinite continued fraction can be written in the form

$$c(x) = \cfrac{a_0}{b_0 + \cfrac{a_1 x}{b_1 + \cfrac{a_2 x}{b_2 + \cfrac{a_3 x}{b_3 + \cdots}}}} \tag{7.22}$$

This is usually written as

$$c(x) = \frac{a_0}{b_0 +} \; \frac{a_1 x}{b_1 +} \; \frac{a_2 x}{b_2 +} \; \frac{a_3 x}{b_3 +} \cdots \tag{7.23}$$

although there are other commonly-used notations.   A typical example of such an infinite continued fraction is

$$e^x = \frac{1}{1 -} \; \frac{x}{1 +} \; \frac{x}{2 -} \; \frac{x}{3 +} \; \frac{x}{2 -} \; \frac{x}{5 +} \; \frac{x}{2 -} \cdots \tag{7.24}$$

Continued fractions of the form (7.22) can be cast into other forms which are usually more computationally efficient.   Acton[12] describes some of these conversions.   The expression (7.24) can thus be recast as

$$e^x = 1 + \frac{x}{(1 - x/2) +} \; \frac{3(x^2/4)}{1 +} \; \frac{15(x^2/4)}{1 +} \; \frac{35(x^2/4)}{1 +} \cdots \frac{(4n^2 - 1)(x^2/4)}{1 +} \cdots \tag{7.25}$$

The Choice between Continued Fractions and Rational Functions

When an infinite continued fraction is truncated to a finite continued fraction (as it must always be if numbers are to be obtained), the finite fraction can be readily converted to an algebraically equivalent rational function.   Conversely, a rational function can be converted to a finite continued fraction.   In computational practice, one is thus confronted with having to choose between a finite continued fraction and an algebraically equivalent rational function approximation.   Although roundoff characteristics can be important, the determining factor is primarily the amount of computer time required for the evaluation of the approximation.   Seemingly small differences in running time can be magnified enormously if the approximation might be evaluated many thousands of times in the course of a single computer run.

Interestingly enough, the best choice is dependent on the specific machine which will be used to evaluate the approximation.   There are significant variations from machine to machine in the relationships between the times required to perform addition, multiplication, and division in floating point arithmetic.   For those machines which have roughly comparable multiply and divide times, continued fractions are usually the best choice.   However, many machines require much longer time to perform a division than a multiplication (by a factor of 3 or more), which makes continued fractions much less desirable, and rational functions become the preferred form of approximation.   This subject is pursued further in Problems 7.7 and 7.8.

Illustrative Problems

7.1   Given the following noisy data:

x	2.10	6.22	7.17	10.52	13.68
$f(x)$	2.90	3.83	5.98	5.71	7.74

Fit a straight line to this data by using least squares.

For 5 data points and $l = 1$ (a first degree polynomial), the least-squares equations (7.9) are

$$\begin{bmatrix} 5 & \sum_{i=1}^{5} x_i \\ \sum_{i=1}^{5} x_i & \sum_{i=1}^{5} x_i^2 \end{bmatrix} \begin{bmatrix} a_0 \\ a_1 \end{bmatrix} = \begin{bmatrix} \sum_{i=1}^{5} f(x_i) \\ \sum_{i=1}^{5} x_i f(x_i) \end{bmatrix}$$

Each element in these equations can now be computed:

$$\sum_{i=1}^{5} x_i = 2.10 + 6.22 + 7.17 + 10.52 + 13.68 = 39.69$$

$$\sum_{i=1}^{5} x_i^2 = (2.10)^2 + (6.22)^2 + (7.17)^2 + (10.52)^2 + (13.68)^2 = 392.3201$$

$$\sum_{i=1}^{5} f(x_i) = 2.90 + 3.83 + 5.98 + 5.71 + 7.74 = 26.16$$

$$\sum_{i=1}^{5} x_i f(x_i) = (2.10)(2.90) + (6.22)(3.83) + (7.17)(5.98) + (10.52)(5.71) + (13.68)(7.74)$$

$$= 238.7416$$

The set of equations is

$$\begin{bmatrix} 5 & 39.69 \\ 39.69 & 392.3201 \end{bmatrix} \begin{bmatrix} a_0 \\ a_1 \end{bmatrix} = \begin{bmatrix} 26.16 \\ 238.7416 \end{bmatrix}$$

Gauss-Jordan elimination yields

$$a_0 = 2.038392, \qquad a_1 = 0.4023190$$

The required straight line is thus

$$g(x) = 2.038392 + 0.4023190x$$

The data and the straight line approximation are shown in Fig. 7.2.   The straight line appears to provide a good approximation to the data.

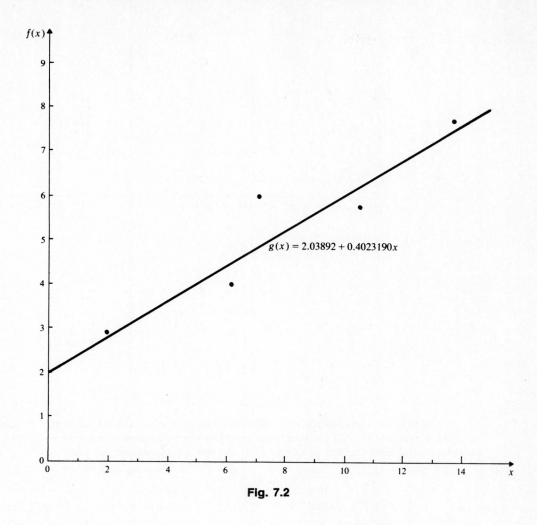

$g(x) = 2.03892 + 0.4023190x$

Fig. 7.2

7.2 Given the following data:

x	0	1.0	1.5	2.3	2.5	4.0	5.1	6.0	6.5	7.0	8.1	9.0
$f(x)$	0.2	0.8	2.5	2.5	3.5	4.3	3.0	5.0	3.5	2.4	1.3	2.0
x	9.3	11.0	11.3	12.1	13.1	14.0	15.5	16.0	17.5	17.8	19.0	20.0
$f(x)$	−0.3	−1.3	−3.0	−4.0	−4.9	−4.0	−5.2	−3.0	−3.5	−1.6	−1.4	−0.1

Choose the most suitable low order polynomial and fit it to this data using the
least-squares criterion.   Also examine methods of using the least-squares criterion
to fit other suitable nonpolynomials to the data.

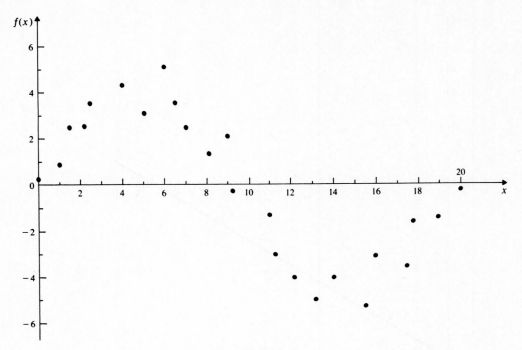

Fig. 7.3

The data are plotted in Fig. 7.3.   The data appear to show a maximum near $x = 5$ and a minimum near $x = 15$.   The lowest order polynomial which can reproduce such behavior is a cubic.   The least-squares equations (7.9) for this set of data ($n = 24$) and for $l = 3$ are

$$\begin{bmatrix} 24 & 229.6 & 3060.2 & 46342.79 \\ 229.6 & 3060.2 & 46342.79 & 752835.2 \\ 3060.2 & 46342.79 & 752835.2 & 12780148.0 \\ 46342.79 & 752835.2 & 12780148.0 & 223518120.0 \end{bmatrix} \begin{bmatrix} a_0 \\ a_1 \\ a_2 \\ a_3 \end{bmatrix} = \begin{bmatrix} -1.30 \\ -316.88 \\ -6037.242 \\ -9943.3597 \end{bmatrix}$$

Gauss-Jordan elimination (in double precision) yields

$$a_0 = -0.35934718$$

$$a_1 = 2.3051112$$

$$a_2 = -0.35319014$$

$$a_3 = 0.01206020$$

Thus

$$g_1(x) = -0.35934718 + 2.3051112x - 0.35319014x^2 + 0.01206020x^3$$

This is the desired cubic approximation.   (We should note that this set of equations is very ill-conditioned; the normalized determinant is 3.42×10^{-11}.   However, inverting the inverse of the coefficient matrix produces the original matrix very accurately, so the effects of this ill-conditioning are apparently not serious, due at least partly to the use of double precision arithmetic.)

We now turn to some other possible approximating functions. The character of the data suggests the use of a trigonometric function such as the sine. We might, for example, assume an approximating function of the form

$$g_2(x) = A + B \sin \frac{\pi x}{10}$$

We have specified the period of the sine as 20. This would appear to be reasonable from examination of the data, and, also important, attempting to solve for the period results in a nonlinear problem which is much more difficult. (We will consider this problem next.) Now applying the same least-squares method as we used in Sec. 7.1 for polynomials, we define

$$E = \sum_{i=1}^{n} \left[A + B \sin \frac{\pi}{10} x_i - f(x_i) \right]^2$$

The parameters which can be varied to minimize E are A and B. We obtain two equations in A and B by setting

$$\frac{\partial E}{\partial A} = 0 \qquad \text{and} \qquad \frac{\partial E}{\partial B} = 0$$

Inserting the expression for E,

$$\frac{\partial E}{\partial A} = 2 \sum_{i=1}^{n} \left[A + B \sin \frac{\pi}{10} x_i - f(x_i) \right](1) = 0$$

$$\frac{\partial E}{\partial B} = 2 \sum_{i=1}^{n} \left[A + B \sin \frac{\pi}{10} x_i - f(x_i) \right] \left(\sin \frac{\pi}{10} x_i \right) = 0$$

Collecting terms, the equations finally become

$$[n]A + \left[\sum_{i=1}^{n} \sin \frac{\pi}{10} x_i \right] B = \sum_{i=1}^{n} f(x_i)$$

$$\left[\sum_{i=1}^{n} \sin \frac{\pi}{10} x_i \right] A + \left[\sum_{i=1}^{n} \sin^2 \frac{\pi}{10} x_i \right] B = \sum_{i=1}^{n} f(x_i) \sin \frac{\pi}{10} x_i$$

For this particular problem, $n = 24$. Calculating the coefficients, we find

$$24A + 1.1328096B = -1.2999996$$

$$1.1328096A + 11.053666B = 47.515395$$

Using Gauss-Jordan elimination (double precision) yields

$$A = -0.25831225$$

$$B = 4.3250821$$

The approximating function is thus

$$g_2(x) = -0.25831225 + 4.3250821 \sin \frac{\pi}{10} x$$

Finally, we consider an approximating function of the form

$$g_3(x) = C \sin Dx$$

where C and D are to be determined. We again apply the least-squares error criterion, defining

$$E = \sum_{i=1}^{n} [C \sin Dx_i - f(x_i)]^2$$

which is minimized with respect to C and D by setting

$$\frac{\partial E}{\partial C} = 0 \qquad \text{and} \qquad \frac{\partial E}{\partial D} = 0$$

Inserting the expression for E,

$$\frac{\partial E}{\partial C} = 2 \sum_{i=1}^{n} [C \sin Dx_i - f(x_i)](\sin Dx_i) = 0$$

$$\frac{\partial E}{\partial D} = 2 \sum_{i=1}^{n} [C \sin Dx_i - f(x_i)](C \cos Dx_i)(x_i) = 0$$

Collecting terms, the two equations in C and D are

$$C \sum_{i=1}^{n} \sin Dx_i = \sum_{i=1}^{n} f(x_i) \sin Dx_i$$

$$C \sum_{i=1}^{n} x_i \sin Dx_i \cos Dx_i = \sum_{i=1}^{n} f(x_i) x_i \cos Dx_i$$

These two equations form a *nonlinear* set in the two unknowns C and D. There is no unique method for solving such problems. We will demonstrate one approach. Solving the first equation for C gives

$$C = \frac{\displaystyle\sum_{i=1}^{n} f(x_i) \sin Dx_i}{\displaystyle\sum_{i=1}^{n} \sin Dx_i}$$

Similarly, the second equation can be solved for C to yield

$$C = \frac{\displaystyle\sum_{i=1}^{n} f(x_i) x_i \cos Dx_i}{\displaystyle\sum_{i=1}^{n} x_i \sin Dx_i \cos Dx_i}$$

These two expressions for C can now be equated to give

$$\frac{\displaystyle\sum_{i=1}^{n} f(x_i) \sin Dx_i}{\displaystyle\sum_{i=1}^{n} \sin Dx_i} = \frac{\displaystyle\sum_{i=1}^{n} f(x_i) x_i \cos Dx_i}{\displaystyle\sum_{i=1}^{n} x_i \sin Dx_i \cos Dx_i}$$

If we denote the left side of this equation as $L(D)$ and the right side as $R(D)$, then

$$L(D) = R(D)$$

This problem can now be considered as a root-solving problem, since we are seeking the value of D for which this equation is satisfied. We can thus write

$$h(D) = L(D) - R(D)$$

and use a root-solving method, such as bisection, to find the zero of $h(D)$. We would expect D to be reasonably close to $\pi/10 = 0.31416$. Tabulation of $h(D)$ in the region $0.2 \leq D \leq 0.37$ shows changes in sign of $h(D)$ between $D = 0.26$ and $D = 0.27$ and between $D = 0.32$ and $D = 0.33$. Close examination of the region near $D = 0.26$ reveals very strange behavior of $h(D)$, apparently corresponding to the denominator of $R(D)$ approaching zero. This is unlikely to correspond to the desired root, and we temporarily ignore this region and turn to the other possible root. The function $h(D)$ behaves well in the region

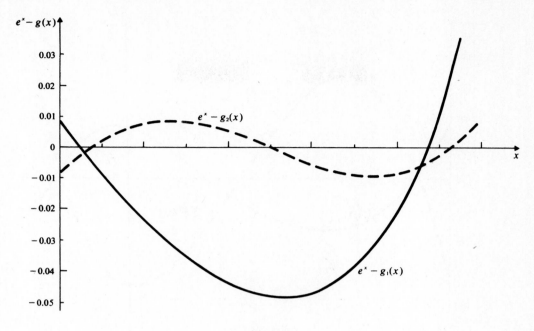

Fig. 7.7

The errors in each of the approximations are plotted in Fig. 7.7.

The errors in both approximations have nearly equal positive and negative peaks. However, the error in $g_2(x)$ is distributed much more uniformly over the interval. (The error in $g_1(x)$ is distributed quite uniformly over the interval $-1 \leq x \leq 1$ for which it was constructed, but $g_1(x)$ tends to overestimate e^x on much of $0 \leq x \leq 1$.) The magnitude of the maximum error of $g_1(x)$ is approximately 0.054, while that of $g_2(x)$ is approximately 0.0101, or only about 1/5 that of $g_1(x)$. It is almost inevitable that the quadratic $g_1(x)$ which must provide a good approximation over the interval $-1 \leq x \leq 1$ will have a larger maximum error than will an approximation of the same type $(g_2(x))$ which is constructed to serve as a good approximation over an interval only half as large $(0 \leq x \leq 1)$. It would be necessary to employ an economized approximation of higher degree than 2 in order to obtain the same accuracy on $-1 \leq x \leq 1$ that $g_2(x)$ provides on $0 \leq x \leq 1$. It should be apparent that the simplest, most effective approximations can be obtained by restricting the interval of approximation to the absolute minimum size required.

7.6 The following rational function approximation to $f(x) = e^x$ is given by Meinardus[8]:

$$r(x) = \frac{0.995705 + 0.668203x}{1 - 0.388848x}, \qquad 0 \leq x \leq 1$$

Evaluate the error in this approximation and compare the maximum error with the maximum error of the Chebyshev economized polynomial $g_2(x)$ from the preceding problem. Why is it reasonable to compare these two approximations?

The error in the rational function $r(x)$ is plotted in Fig. 7.8.

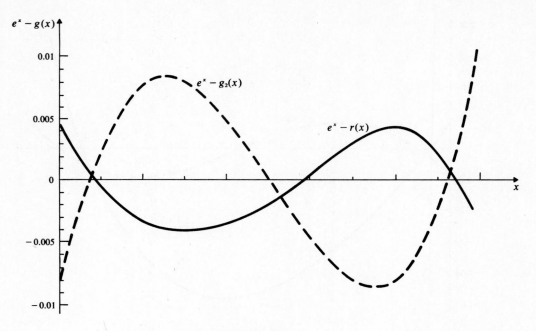

Fig. 7.8

The error is distributed quite well over the interval $0 \leq x \leq 1$ with a maximum magnitude of about 0.0043. This is less than one-half of the maximum error of $g_2(x)$ from the preceding problem. The comparison of $r(x)$ with $g_2(x)$ is legitimate in the sense that each of these approximating functions has three parameters (constants) which characterize the approximation. For the same number of parameters, the best rational function approximation is generally superior to the best polynomial approximation.

7.7 A typical rational function approximation is of the form

$$r(x) = \frac{a_0 + a_1 x + a_2 x^2 + a_3 x^3 + a_4 x^4}{b_0 + b_1 x + b_2 x^2 + b_3 x^3 + b_4 x^4}$$

Evaluate the number of each of the basic arithmetic operations (addition, multiplication, and division) necessary to evaluate this function for a given value of x.

We are of course interested in the minimum possible number of operations. The most efficient way of evaluating $r(x)$ is to group the operations as follows:

$$r(x) = \frac{a_0 + x(a_1 + x(a_2 + x(a_3 + x(a_4))))}{b_0 + x(b_1 + x(b_2 + x(b_3 + x(b_4))))}$$

The evaluation of the numerator thus requires 4 multiplications and 4 additions, with the same number of operations required to evaluate the denominator. Finally, a single division is necessary. The number of operations is thus

Additions	Multiplications	Divisions	Total
8	8	1	17

7.8   Acton[12] gives an algorithm for converting the rational function of the preceding problem into the following algebraically equivalent continued fraction:

$$c(x) = e_0 + \cfrac{e_1}{x + e_2 + \cfrac{e_3}{x + e_4 + \cfrac{e_5}{x + e_6 + \cfrac{e_7}{x + e_8}}}}$$

Evaluate the number of each of the basic arithmetic operations necessary to evaluate this continued fraction.   Next, given the following execution times and assuming all other factors are the same, decide which function, $r(x)$ or $c(x)$, should be used if the function is to be evaluated many times:

UNIVAC 1108 Execution Times
(floating point single precision arithmetic)

Add	Multiply	Divide
1.750 μsec	2.625 μsec	8.250 μsec

The number of basic arithmetic operations needed to evaluate $c(x)$ can be found by simply counting the number of divide and add operations in the expression as given:

Additions	Multiplications	Divisions	Total
8	0	4	12

The total time needed to perform the arithmetic operations can now be computed.   For $r(x)$,

$$t_r = \underset{(add.)}{8(1.750 \ \mu\text{sec})} + \underset{(mult.)}{8(2.625 \ \mu\text{sec})} + \underset{(div.)}{1(8.250 \ \mu\text{sec})} = 43.25 \ \mu\text{sec}$$

For $c(x)$,

$$t_c = \underset{(add.)}{8(1.750 \ \mu\text{sec})} + \underset{(mult.)}{0(2.625 \ \mu\text{sec})} + \underset{(div.)}{4(8.250 \ \mu\text{sec})} = 47.00 \ \mu\text{sec}$$

The rational function $r(x)$ is slightly faster, and we would probably choose it for this application.   For machines which have more nearly equal execution times for the different arithmetic operations, the continued fraction approximation would probably be preferable.

Problems

7.9 Given the following data, fit a straight line to the data using the least-squares criterion:

(a)

x	1.1	2.9	4.3	6.2
f(x)	50	43	28	25

*(b)

x	2.1	4.2	4.8	6.0	7.1	7.9	10.0	10.2	11.2
f(x)	63	68	57	66	53	62	67	59	48
x	13.8	15.0	16.8	17.0	19.9	20.1	21.3	23.0	24.3
f(x)	61	52	41	47	48	36	42	29	33

*7.10 Given the following data, choose and fit a suitable low order polynomial by least squares:

x	1.4	2.5	3.1	3.9	5.0	7.1	9.5	11.9	14.1	15.0	16.5	17.2
f(x)	3.8	2.6	4.1	5.2	6.2	6.9	7.2	6.7	5.8	3.8	3.8	2.8

*7.11 Given the following data:

x	1.2	2.8	4.3	5.4	6.8	7.9
f(x)	2.1	11.5	28.1	41.9	72.3	91.4

Using the least-squares criterion, fit a function of the form $g(x) = Ax^B$ to this data (i.e. determine A and B).

*7.12 Given the following data:

x	0	0.50	1.25	2.00	2.70	3.00	3.50	3.90	4.75	5.25
f(x)	1.37	1.48	2.09	2.77	3.60	4.10	4.88	6.01	7.95	9.90

Fit a function of the form Ae^{Bx} to this data using the least-squares criterion.

7.13 Find a three-term approximate expression for $\sin x$ on $-1 \leq x \leq 1$ by Chebyshev economization of the Taylor series. Truncate the original series after four terms. Evaluate the maximum error in the three-term approximation and compare this with the maximum error which could result if the first three terms of the Taylor series were used.

7.14   Find a quadratic approximation to

$$f(y) = y^4 - 2y^3 + y - 6$$

on the interval $-1 \leq y \leq 2$ by using Chebyshev economization.   Give a bound for the error of this approximation.   If a computer is available, plot the error as a function of y over the interval of interest.

7.15   Consider the function arctan x.   The Taylor series expansion of this function is

$$\arctan x = x - \frac{x^3}{3} + \frac{x^5}{5} - \frac{x^7}{7} + \frac{x^9}{9} - \cdots, \qquad |x| \leq 1$$

A continued fraction representation is

$$\arctan x = \frac{x}{1+} \frac{x^2}{3+} \frac{4x^2}{5+} \frac{9x^2}{7+} \frac{16x^2}{9+} \frac{25x^2}{11+} \cdots$$

Compute arctan x for $x = 1$ by using the continued fraction representation and terminating the continued fraction after $25x^2/11+$.   (This is called termination at the *sixth convergent* of the continued fraction.)   Compare this computed value with the exact value and compute the error.   Finally, determine the number of terms of the Taylor series expansion which would be needed to guarantee an error no greater than the error in the terminated continued fraction.

7.16   Using the table of arithmetic computation times for the UNIVAC 1108 given in Problem 7.8, compare the total arithmetic computation time required to evaluate the rational function approximation (7.21) of $(\sin x)/x$ with that required to evaluate the truncated Taylor series which would guarantee comparable accuracy on the same interval.   Consider only arithmetic operations and ignore all other factors.

Chapter 8

Numerical Integration

8.0 INTRODUCTION

The primary purpose of *numerical integration* (also called *quadrature*) is the evaluation of integrals which are either impossible or else very difficult to evaluate analytically. Analytical closed form expressions for integrals have many advantages over numerical evaluations, so numerical techniques should not be employed without first making a serious effort at analytical evaluation (including a search of available integral tables). The advantages of an analytical expression include its exactness (there is always concern about error in numerical integration), its generality (numbers need not be inserted for any parameters involved in the integral), and the possibility of evaluating the physical effects of varying any parameters involved. Nevertheless, numerical integration is indispensable in many cases, since it can mean the difference between getting an accurate answer and having no answer at all.*

Numerical integration is also essential in the evaluation of integrals of functions available only at discrete points. Such functions often result from the numerical solution of differential equations or from experimental data taken at discrete intervals.

We will now formulate and evaluate a variety of techniques for numerical integration.

8.1 THE TRAPEZOIDAL RULE

Consider an integrable function $f(x)$ on the interval $a \leq x \leq b$. We wish to evaluate the integral

$$I = \int_a^b f(x) \, dx \tag{8.1}$$

We divide the interval $a \leq x \leq b$ into n equal subintervals each of width Δx, where

$$\Delta x = \frac{b - a}{n} \tag{8.2}$$

---

*The reader should be aware that a middle ground exists between the exact analytical evaluation of an integral and a pure numerical approach. This middle ground includes various approximate techniques and series expansions. Such methods can be very useful at times as an adjunct to numerical techniques, but no attempt will be made to discuss them in general.

Subtracting (8.24) from (8.23) yields

$$I(x_{j+1}) - I(x_{j-1}) = 2(\Delta x)f(x_j) + \frac{(\Delta x)^3}{3}f''(x_j) + \frac{(\Delta x)^5}{60}f^{iv}(x_j) + \mathcal{O}(\Delta x)^7 \qquad (8.25)$$

We now replace $f''(x_j)$ by a central difference representation, including the error term. This representation is

$$f''(x_j) = \frac{f(x_{j+1}) - 2f(x_j) + f(x_{j-1})}{(\Delta x)^2} - \frac{(\Delta x)^2}{12}f^{iv}(x_j) + \mathcal{O}(\Delta x)^4 \qquad (8.26)$$

Inserting (8.26) into (8.25) and collecting terms, we obtain

$$I(x_{j+1}) - I(x_{j-1}) = \frac{\Delta x}{3}[f(x_{j-1}) + 4f(x_j) + f(x_{j+1})] - \frac{(\Delta x)^5}{90}f^{iv}(x_j) + \mathcal{O}(\Delta x)^7 \qquad (8.27)$$

But $I(x_{j+1}) - I(x_{j-1})$ constitutes the area of the two panels between x_{j-1} and x_{j+1}. Equation (8.27) is called *Simpson's rule* for two panels.

In order to obtain the integral over the interval $a \leq x \leq b$, it is necessary to add the results of (8.27) for all *pairs* of panels. Thus if

$$D_j = I(x_{j+1}) - I(x_{j-1})$$

then

$$I = \sum_{\substack{j=1 \\ j\ odd}}^{n-1} D_j = D_1 + D_3 + \cdots + D_{n-3} + D_{n-1} \qquad (8.28)$$

Note that this requires that the number of panels n must be even. Summing (8.27) for all pairs of panels yields

$$I = \frac{\Delta x}{3}[f(a) + 4f(a + \Delta x) + 2f(a + 2\Delta x) + 4f(a + 3\Delta x) + \cdots + 2f(b - 2\Delta x)$$

$$+ 4f(b - \Delta x) + f(b)] - \frac{(\Delta x)^5}{90}\sum_{\substack{j=1 \\ j\ odd}}^{n-1} f^{iv}(x_j) + \frac{n}{2}\mathcal{O}(\Delta x)^7 \qquad (8.29)$$

The dominant error term in (8.29) can be treated by the same method as was used for the dominant error term in the trapezoidal rule. Thus

$$-\frac{(\Delta x)^5}{90}\sum_{\substack{j=1 \\ j\ odd}}^{n-1} f^{iv}(x_j) = -\frac{(\Delta x)^4}{180}(b - a)f^{iv}(\bar{x})$$

We also note that

$$\frac{n}{2}\mathcal{O}(\Delta x)^7 = \frac{b - a}{2(\Delta x)}\mathcal{O}(\Delta x)^7 = \mathcal{O}(\Delta x)^6$$

Making these substitutions, (8.29) becomes

$$I = \frac{\Delta x}{3}\left(f_o + f_n + 4\sum_{\substack{j=1 \\ j\ odd}}^{n-1} f_j + 2\sum_{\substack{j=2 \\ j\ even}}^{n-2} f_j\right) - \frac{(\Delta x)^4}{180}(b - a)f^{iv}(\bar{x}) + \mathcal{O}(\Delta x)^6 \qquad (8.30)$$

Equation (8.30) is Simpson's rule* for the entire interval. It is a *fourth order* method. Recalling that the geometric interpretation of this method involves the use of

---

*The term "Simpson's one-third rule" is sometimes used for this method to distinguish it from a similar formula involving a factor of $3\Delta x/8$ instead of $\Delta x/3$.

parabolic arcs to approximate $f(x)$, it is interesting to note that since all terms involving $f'''(x)$ have cancelled out of (8.30), the technique is exact for cubics.

Since the dominant error term in (8.30) involves such a high order derivative, it is impractical for various reasons to attempt to provide error correction by approximating this term. Instead, a very accurate formula involving end correction can be found by assuming that the derivatives of $f(x)$ are known at the end points of each double panel. Since $f(x)$ is known at three points in the double panel, this is equivalent to approximating $f(x)$ with a fourth degree interpolating polynomial over the two panels. When the integral is evaluated by summing all pairs of panels, the derivatives at all interior points vanish, and the approximation to the integral becomes

$$I \approx \frac{\Delta x}{15}\left[14\left[\frac{1}{2}f(a)+f(a+2\Delta x)+f(a+4\Delta x)+\cdots+f(b-2\Delta x)+\frac{1}{2}f(b)\right]\right.$$
$$+16[f(a+\Delta x)+f(a+3\Delta x)+\cdots+f(b-3\Delta x)$$
$$\left.+f(b-\Delta x)]+\Delta x[f'(a)-f'(b)]\right] \tag{8.31}$$

or, in subscript notation,

$$I \approx \frac{\Delta x}{15}\left[14\left[\frac{1}{2}(f_0+f_n)+\sum_{\substack{j=2 \\ j\text{ even}}}^{n-2}f_j\right]+16\sum_{\substack{j=1 \\ j\text{ odd}}}^{n-1}f_j+\Delta x[f'(a)-f'(b)]\right] \tag{8.32}$$

Equation (8.32) is called *Simpson's rule with end correction*. The formula is sixth order. As with the regular Simpson's rule, n must be even.

The standard Simpson's rule (8.30) can also be used to integrate a function known only at discrete evenly spaced intervals *if* the number of panels is even. The use of Simpson's rule with end correction (8.32) for such a function requires the approximation of the derivatives by difference representations. The resulting answer may well be more accurate than that obtained by using the standard Simpson's rule, but the error is dependent on the type of difference representations employed.

Still more accurate numerical integration formulas than the trapezoidal rule and Simpson's rule can be obtained by replacing more derivatives in the Taylor series with difference expressions. A general family of numerical integration formulas called the *Newton-Cotes formulas* can be obtained in this way for equally spaced points. The higher order formulas are seldom employed in digital computation. They are unwieldy, and the high order formulas have poor roundoff error characteristics. More important, when very accurate integration techniques are needed, such methods as Romberg integration and Gauss quadrature (to be discussed in succeeding sections) are more efficient and better suited to digital computation.

8.3 ROMBERG INTEGRATION

This powerful and efficient numerical integration technique is based on the use of the trapezoidal rule combined with *Richardson extrapolation*. In order to apply this extrapolation, it is necessary to know the general form of the error terms for the trapezoidal rule. In the course of the derivation of the trapezoidal rule in Sec. 8.1, we did not consider the error terms beyond the dominant $\mathcal{O}(\Delta x)^2$ term. The derivation of these terms is lengthy and will not be given here. The details are given by Ralston[3]. The result is that the trapezoidal rule may be written as

$$I = \frac{\Delta x}{2}\left[f(a)+f(b)+2\sum_{j=1}^{n-1} f(a+j\Delta x)\right] + C(\Delta x)^2 + D(\Delta x)^4 + E(\Delta x)^6 + \cdots$$

$$(8.33)$$

where C, D, E, etc. are functions of $f(x)$ and its derivatives, but are not functions of Δx. The terms involving the odd powers of Δx have vanished from the error.

Let

$$\bar{I} = \frac{\Delta x}{2}\left[f(a)+f(b)+2\sum_{j=1}^{n-1} f(a+j\Delta x)\right]$$

$$(8.34)$$

Equation (8.33) may then be rearranged in the form

$$\bar{I} = I - C(\Delta x)^2 - D(\Delta x)^4 - E(\Delta x)^6 - \cdots$$

$$(8.35)$$

Consider now the use of two different mesh sizes, Δx_1 and Δx_2. If we denote the values of $\bar{I}$ corresponding to Δx_1 and Δx_2 as $\bar{I}_1$ and $\bar{I}_2$ respectively, then from (8.35),

$$\bar{I}_1 = I - C(\Delta x_1)^2 - D(\Delta x_1)^4 - E(\Delta x_1)^6 - \cdots$$

$$(8.36)$$

$$\bar{I}_2 = I - C(\Delta x_2)^2 - D(\Delta x_2)^4 - E(\Delta x_2)^6 - \cdots$$

$$(8.37)$$

Now suppose $\Delta x_1 = 2\Delta x_2$. Then (8.36) becomes, in terms of Δx_2,

$$\bar{I}_1 = I - 4C(\Delta x_2)^2 - 16D(\Delta x_2)^4 - 64E(\Delta x_2)^6 - \cdots$$

$$(8.38)$$

Now multiply equation (8.37) by 4, subtract (8.38), and divide by 3:

$$\frac{4\bar{I}_2 - \bar{I}_1}{3} = I + 4D(\Delta x_2)^4 + 20E(\Delta x_2)^6 + \cdots$$

$$(8.39)$$

The error term involving $(\Delta x)^2$ has vanished and (8.39) thus furnishes an approximation to the integral which is of $\mathcal{O}(\Delta x_2)^4$. Extrapolation of this type is termed Richardson extrapolation. (By inserting the expressions for $\bar{I}_1$ and $\bar{I}_2$ into (8.39), we also find that we have rediscovered Simpson's rule!) If we now evaluate $\bar{I}_3$, where $\Delta x_3 = \Delta x_2/2$, and extrapolate $\bar{I}_2$ and $\bar{I}_3$, we obtain

$$\frac{4\bar{I}_3 - \bar{I}_2}{3} = I + 4D(\Delta x_3)^4 + 20E(\Delta x_3)^6 + \cdots$$

$$(8.40)$$

Between (8.39) and (8.40), the term in $(\Delta x)^4$ may be eliminated to furnish an estimate to I which is accurate to $\mathcal{O}(\Delta x)^6$. Thus for each new evaluation of an $\bar{I}$, one more term in the error can be eliminated by extrapolation. This systematic procedure is called *Romberg integration*.

In order to describe the algorithm in detail, we adopt a new notation. The trapezoidal rule estimates of the integral will be denoted as

$$T_{1,k} = \frac{\Delta x}{2}\left[f(a)+f(b)+2\sum_{j=1}^{l} f(a+j\Delta x)\right]$$

$$(8.41)$$

where $\Delta x = (b-a)/2^{k-1}$ and $l = 2^{k-1} - 1$. The number of panels involved in $T_{1,k}$ is 2^{k-1}. Thus

$$T_{1,1} = \frac{b-a}{2}[f(a)+f(b)]$$

$$T_{1,2} = \frac{b-a}{4}\left[f(a)+f(b)+2f\left(a+\frac{b-a}{2}\right)\right]$$

$$T_{1,3} = \frac{b-a}{8}\left[f(a)+f(b)+2f\left(a+\frac{b-a}{4}\right)+2f\left(a+\frac{b-a}{2}\right)+2f\left(a+\frac{3(b-a)}{4}\right)\right]$$

etc.

Note that

$$T_{1,2} = \frac{T_{1,1}}{2}+\frac{b-a}{2}\left[f\left(a+\frac{b-a}{2}\right)\right]$$

$$T_{1,3} = \frac{T_{1,2}}{2}+\frac{b-a}{4}\left[f\left(a+\frac{b-a}{4}\right)+f\left(a+\frac{3(b-a)}{4}\right)\right]$$

etc.

This means that each succeeding trapezoidal rule approximation can be obtained from the preceding approximation without having to recompute $f(x)$ at any of the points where it has already been computed.

The extrapolation is carried out according to

$$T_{l,k} = \frac{1}{4^{l-1}-1}(4^{l-1}T_{l-1,k+1}-T_{l-1,k}) \tag{8.42}$$

For example, for $l = 2$,

$$T_{2,1} = \frac{1}{3}(4T_{1,2}-T_{1,1})$$

$$T_{2,2} = \frac{1}{3}(4T_{1,3}-T_{1,2})$$

(These extrapolations each eliminate the $\mathcal{O}(\Delta x)^2$ error term.)   Now for $l = 3$,

$$T_{3,1} = \frac{1}{15}(16T_{2,2}-T_{2,1})$$

(This extrapolation eliminates the $\mathcal{O}(\Delta x)^4$ error term.)   These results can conveniently be arranged in tabular form:

$$
\begin{array}{c|ccccccc}
 & T_{1,1} & & & & & & \\
 & T_{1,2} & T_{2,1} & & & & & \\
 & T_{1,3} & T_{2,2} & T_{3,1} & & & & \\
 & T_{1,4} & T_{2,3} & T_{3,2} & T_{4,1} & & & \\
 & \vdots & & & & & & \\
 & T_{1,l} & T_{2,l-1} & T_{3,l-2} & \cdots & & T_{l-1,2} & T_{l,1}
\end{array}
\tag{8.43}
$$

(Increasingly accurate trapezoidal rule values — left column; Increasingly accurate extrapolated values — diagonal; $T_{l-1,1}$)

The extrapolated values along the diagonal will converge to the correct answer much more rapidly than the trapezoidal rule values in the first column.

As an example, consider the integral

$$I = \int_0^8 \left(\frac{5x^4}{8} - 4x^3 + 2x + 1 \right) dx$$

This polynomial can be easily integrated analytically to yield $I = 72$, and Romberg integration should yield this exact answer in only a few extrapolations (actually, the exact result will be obtained when the error term containing $f^{iv}(x)$ is eliminated). Now

$$f(x) = \frac{5x^4}{8} - 4x^3 + 2x + 1$$

so

$$f(0) = 1$$

$$f(8) = 2560 - 2048 + 16 + 1 = 529$$

and

$$b - a = 8 - 0 = 8$$

The trapezoidal rule approximations with one and two panels are

$$T_{1,1} = \frac{8}{2} [1 + 529] = 2120$$

$$T_{1,2} = \frac{2120}{2} + \frac{8}{2} f(4) = 1060 + 4(160 - 256 + 8 + 1) = 712$$

Extrapolating these two values to eliminate the $\mathcal{O}(\Delta x)^2$ error term yields

$$T_{2,1} = \frac{1}{3} [4(712) - 2120] = 242 \frac{2}{3}$$

The trapezoidal rule with four panels gives

$$T_{1,3} = \frac{712}{2} + \frac{8}{4} [f(2) + f(6)] = 356 + 2[(-17) + (-41)] = 240$$

Extrapolating $T_{1,2}$ and $T_{1,3}$ yields

$$T_{2,2} = \frac{1}{3} [4(240) - 712] = 82 \frac{2}{3}$$

By extrapolating $T_{2,1}$ and $T_{2,2}$ according to (8.42), the $\mathcal{O}(\Delta x)^4$ error term should be eliminated:

$$T_{3,1} = \frac{1}{15} (16(82\tfrac{2}{3}) - 242\tfrac{2}{3}) = 72$$

which is the exact answer. The Romberg table obtained so far is

```
2120
 712    242⅔
 240     82⅔     72
```

The best available trapezoidal rule value of 240 using four panels is still very far from correct, and the greatly accelerated convergence along the diagonal should be apparent. In general, of course, we would not know that the exact answer had been obtained, so another line of the table would have to be computed. After this computation, the table would be

$$
\begin{array}{llll}
2120 & & & \\
712 & 242\frac{2}{3} & & \\
240 & 82\frac{2}{3} & 72 & \\
128\frac{1}{2} & 72\frac{2}{3} & 72 & 72
\end{array}
$$

The criterion used to stop the Romberg integration procedure should clearly be based on a comparison between successive values along the diagonal of the table. Since two successive values agree exactly in the above table, there is no question that the method has converged and that $I = 72$ is the correct answer. In general, the criterion for convergence might be of the form

$$|T_{l,1} - T_{l-1,1}| < \epsilon \qquad (8.44)$$

If (8.44) is satisfied for some predetermined ϵ, then the procedure is stopped and $T_{l,1}$ considered to be the answer. As discussed in Chapter 6, a convergence criterion of the form (8.44) is termed an *absolute* convergence criterion, and is useful in the sense that the convergence decision is based on a change in a predetermined digit (for example, the third decimal place). For general use, a safer criterion is the *relative* convergence criterion

$$\left| \frac{T_{l,1} - T_{l-1,1}}{T_{l,1}} \right| < \epsilon \qquad (8.45)$$

since the algorithm may be used for many functions with widely different values for the integral. It is important to terminate the procedure by using a convergence criterion, since continuing the process far beyond the point where the correct answer is obtained can result in a significant drift away from the correct result due to roundoff error.

We are now in a position to present a detailed flow chart for Romberg integration (Fig. 8.3). This algorithm uses the relative convergence criterion (8.45). If desired, the absolute criterion (8.44) can be substituted.

8.4 GAUSS QUADRATURE

Gauss quadrature is a very powerful method of numerical integration which employs unequally spaced intervals. We have seen in previous chapters the effectiveness of orthogonal polynomials, such as Chebyshev polynomials, in the approximation of functions. If such polynomials can approximate functions so effectively, then numerical integration schemes based on orthogonal polynomials would seem to be a logical next step. (Remember that the trapezoidal rule and Simpson's rule are based respectively on approximating the original function by simple straight lines and parabolas.) The derivation of the quadrature formula is too long to present in detail here. The derivation begins along the lines used in developing Chebyshev interpolation in Chapter 4, including the normalization of the interval, the sampling of the function to be approximated at the (unequally spaced) zeros of the orthogonal polynomial, and the generation of the interpolating polynomial from the Lagrange formula. The quadrature formula is then developed by integrating the interpolating polynomial. See Lanczos[13] for the details.

Although we have referred to Chebyshev polynomials in this discussion because we have encountered them previously, in fact many different orthogonal polynomials can be employed to obtain Gauss-type quadrature formulas. The choice of the polynomial will depend on the type of function to be integrated and the limits of the integral. The most commonly employed polynomials in this context are actually the Legendre polynomials,

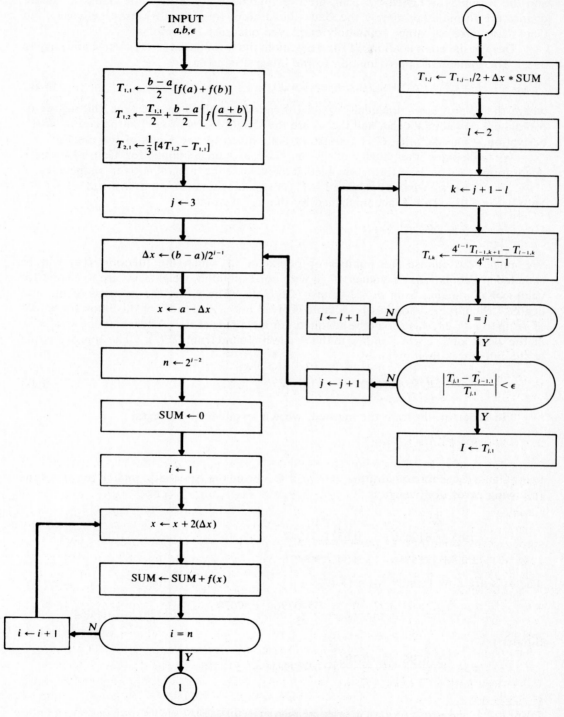

Fig. 8.3 Romberg integration.

and the formulas obtained by using these polynomials are termed the Gauss-Legendre quadrature formulas or simply the Gauss quadrature formulas. Gauss-Chebyshev and Gauss-Laguerre are other commonly employed quadrature formulas.

Despite the complications of the derivation, the formulas are very simple and easy to use. The numerical approximation to the integral is given by

$$\bar{I} = C[w_1 f(x_1) + w_2 f(x_2) + \cdots + w_m f(x_m)] \tag{8.46}$$

where the x_i are the m unequally spaced points determined by the type and degree of orthogonal polynomial used, and the w_i are the weight factors found in the course of the derivation. The quantity C is a constant determined by the limits of the integral.

We will show the details of the method and an example for Gauss-Legendre quadrature. All of the information needed to evaluate the integral is given on the interval $-1 \leqslant \xi \leqslant 1$, so if we wish to evaluate $I = \int_a^b f(x)\, dx$, the first task is to transform $-1 \leqslant \xi \leqslant 1$ onto $a \leqslant x \leqslant b$. This is accomplished by the transformation

$$x = \frac{b+a}{2} + \frac{b-a}{2}\xi \tag{8.47}$$

We must now choose the number of points m at which the function $f(x)$ will be sampled. Tabulations of values of ξ_k with corresponding weights w_k are available for values of m ranging from $m = 2$ to $m = 256$ [14]. (The ξ_k are the m zeros of the mth degree Legendre polynomials.) A table is given in the Appendix of this book for values of m up to $m = 24$; this should be adequate for most purposes. After selecting a value of m, the values of x_k corresponding to the ξ_k can be found from (8.47). The approximation to the integral is then given by

$$\bar{I} = \frac{b-a}{2} \sum_{k=1}^{m} w_k f(x_k) \tag{8.48}$$

In order to illustrate the method, we will evaluate the integral

$$I = \int_0^{\pi/2} x^2 \cos x \, dx$$

using Gauss-Legendre quadrature with $m = 4$. From the Appendix, we find for $m = 4$ the following zeros and weights:

ξ_k	w_k
± 0.3399810436	0.6521451549
± 0.8611363116	0.3478548451

The x_k's are now found* from (8.47):

$$x_1 = \frac{\pi/2 + 0}{2} + \frac{\pi/2 - 0}{2}\xi_1 = \frac{1.570796}{2} + \frac{1.570796}{2}(-0.861136) = 0.109064$$

Similarly

$$x_2 = \frac{1.570796}{2} + \frac{1.570796}{2}(-0.339981) = 0.518378$$

---

*These calculations were carried out in single precision on the IBM 360/67 and the results are rounded to six digits here for simplicity.

and

$$x_3 = 1.05242$$

$$x_4 = 1.46173$$

The corresponding values of $f(x) = x^2 \cos x$ are

$$f(x_1) = (0.109064)^2 \cos (0.109064) = 0.011824$$

$$f(x_2) = 0.233413$$

$$f(x_3) = 0.548777$$

$$f(x_4) = 0.232572$$

From (8.48), $\bar{I}$ is given by

$$\bar{I} = \frac{\pi/2 - 0}{2}[w_1 f(x_1) + w_2 f(x_2) + w_3 f(x_3) + w_4 f(x_4)]$$

$$= \frac{1.570796}{2}[(0.347855)(0.011824) + (0.652145)(0.233413)$$

$$+ (0.652145)(0.548777) + (0.347855)(0.232572)]$$

$$= 0.467402$$

The exact value of the integral is $I = 0.467401$.   The value $\bar{I}$ obtained from Gauss quadrature with only 4 points is remarkably accurate, even considering the fact that the function is smooth and well behaved.   For comparison with other methods, consider the following table:

Exact Value	Gauss Quadrature, $m = 4$	Trapezoidal Rule, 3 Panels	Simpson's Rule, 4 Panels
0.467401	0.467402	0.411411	0.466890

The Gauss quadrature and trapezoidal rule approximations to the integral each involve 4 evaluations of $f(x)$, while the Simpson's rule approximations involve 5 evaluations of $f(x)$ (since the number of panels must be even).

The dominant error term in Gauss quadrature involves very high order derivatives of $f(x)$ and since it is not generally useful in a practical sense, it will not be presented here.   The best method for evaluating the accuracy of an integral evaluated by Gauss quadrature is to compare the results for several significantly different values of m; a reasonably accurate assessment can then usually be made as to the number of decimal places which are correct in the answer.   In certain cases this comparison may result in a set of substantially different answers.   This is usually due to the presence of one or more singularities in $f(x)$ or to $f(x)$ being highly oscillatory in character.   These situations will be discussed further in Secs. 8.7 and 8.8.   Caution should be exercised if very large values of m are employed, since roundoff error can cause significant deterioration in the accuracy of the answer.   Actually all of the above comments regarding accuracy apply to any numerical integration scheme, and they are mentioned here only because the accuracy of Gauss quadrature for many functions can inspire such confidence that one may be tempted to do one evaluation with a single (perhaps large) value of m and to accept the answer blindly. Example problems in Sec. 8.7 and towards the end of the chapter will demonstrate the imprudence of this approach, particularly if singularities are present in the integrand and an accurate answer is required.

Some idea of the power of Gauss quadrature can be gained from the knowledge that the method essentially operates with an interpolating polynomial of degree $2m - 1$. Thus if $m = 10$, the interpolating polynomial is of degree 19. Because of this property, even poorly behaved functions can often be integrated reasonably accurately using relatively few points, while smooth functions can be integrated extremely accurately. Since the interpolating polynomial is of degree $2m - 1$, the method is exact for the integration of polynomials of degree $2m - 1$ or lower; but, of course, numerical methods are seldom used to integrate polynomials.

By proper choice of orthogonal polynomials and weighting functions, Gauss-type formulas can be derived which are very accurate for a wide variety of functions and integration limits. Some typical examples are

$$\int_0^1 x^k f(x)\, dx \qquad \text{(Jacobi polynomials)}$$

$$\int_a^b f(x)\sqrt{b - x}\, dx \qquad \text{(Legendre polynomials)}$$

$$\int_a^b \frac{f(x)}{\sqrt{b - x}}\, dx \qquad \text{(Legendre polynomials)}$$

$$\int_{-1}^1 \frac{f(x)}{\sqrt{1 - x^2}}\, dx \qquad \text{(Chebyshev polynomials)}$$

$$\int_a^b \frac{f(x)\, dx}{\sqrt{x - a}\sqrt{x - b}} \qquad \text{(Chebyshev polynomials)}$$

$$\int_0^\infty e^{-x} f(x)\, dx \qquad \text{(Laguerre polynomials)}$$

$$\int_{-\infty}^\infty e^{-x^2} f(x)\, dx \qquad \text{(Hermite polynomials)}$$

$$\int_0^1 f(x) \log_e(x)\, dx \qquad \text{(Special polynomials)}$$

The weights and zeros for these and other Gauss-type formulas are tabulated in Refs. 14 and 15. An example of the use of one of these special formulas is given in Problem 8.6.

Gauss-type quadrature formulas cannot in general be used with functions available only at discrete points since the functional evaluations must be made at the specified zeros of the proper polynomial. However, in some experimental situations, there is complete freedom in choosing the values of the independent variable at which data ($f(x)$) will be taken. If one of the main goals of the experiment is to evaluate $\int f(x)\, dx$, then it may be advantageous to consider the possibility of taking data on the zeros of the appropriate orthogonal polynomial (converted to the interval of interest) and then using the corresponding Gauss-type formula to perform the integration. Error bounds are virtually impossible to obtain for such cases, but if the data are relatively error free, then the effective use of a very high order interpolating polynomial may give a significantly more accurate integral than would a numerical integration with an equal number of points using equally spaced data.   If the data are noisy and smoothing would be required before carrying out the integration, then there would probably be no advantage to be gained by this procedure.

8.5   MULTIPLE INTEGRALS

We will illustrate the numerical approach to multiple integration by considering first a double integral.   The most general double integral is of the form

$$I = \int_a^b \int_{c(x)}^{d(x)} f(x,y)\, dy\, dx \tag{8.49}$$

For simplicity, we begin by assuming n equally spaced subintervals in x, each of width Δx.   We now evaluate the inner integrals:

$$g(a) = \int_{c(a)}^{d(a)} f(a,y)\, dy$$

$$g(a + \Delta x) = \int_{c(a+\Delta x)}^{d(a+\Delta x)} f(a + \Delta x, y)\, dy$$

$$\vdots \tag{8.50}$$

$$g(b - \Delta x) = \int_{c(b-\Delta x)}^{d(b-\Delta x)} f(b - \Delta x, y)\, dy$$

$$g(b) = \int_{c(b)}^{d(b)} f(b,y)\, dy$$

Since for each of these inner integrals the value of x is fixed, they become simple one dimensional integrals on y.   Each inner integral can be evaluated by any standard numerical technique, such as Simpson's rule or Gauss quadrature.   The outer integral can finally be evaluated using any method suitable for evenly spaced points.   For example, if n is even, Simpson's rule can be used to obtain

$$I \approx \frac{\Delta x}{3}\left[g(a) + g(b) + 4 \sum_{\substack{j=1 \\ j\ \text{odd}}}^{n-1} g(a + j\Delta x) + 2 \sum_{\substack{j=2 \\ j\ \text{even}}}^{n-2} g(a + j\Delta x) \right] \tag{8.51}$$

An example of a double integration by Simpson's rule is given in Problem 8.7.

There is, of course, no need to use evenly spaced subintervals in x.   If desired, both the inner and outer integrals can be evaluated by using Gauss quadrature.

We will not attempt to give an error analysis for double integration, since even if uniform spacing is used, the actual mesh sizes will in general vary for each of the inner integrals.   It should be apparent, however, that the errors for each of the inner integrals will accumulate when the outer integration is performed.   In addition, there will be inherent error due to the outer integration itself.   A further complicating factor is that considerable roundoff error can occur in multiple integration due to the large number of functional evaluations and additions which are inevitably involved.   For example, if 50 panels are used for both the inner and outer integrals of a double integral, then over 2500 evaluations of $f(x,y)$ will be required.   Gauss quadrature is a very desirable method to use for multiple integration because of the relatively small number of function evaluations and arithmetic operations required.

The extension of the general method to multidimensional integrals should be apparent. Accurate numerical evaluations of multidimensional integrals are sometimes difficult to obtain, however, since the effects of error can be overwhelming, even with Gauss quadrature. There is some evidence that Monte Carlo methods may be useful and practical for multidimensional integration, and the reader who is interested in learning about these fascinating techniques will find integration a suitable and relatively simple introduction [16].

8.6 INTEGRALS WITH INFINITE LIMITS

Suppose that it is necessary to numerically evaluate an integral of the form

$$\int_a^\infty f(x)\,dx \tag{8.52}$$

(sometimes called an improper integral of the first kind), and we have convinced ourselves that the integral exists and is finite. (The methods for proving these points can be found in almost any advanced calculus book.) We can deal with the infinite limit in several ways.

If the integral is finite and $f(x)$ is smooth, then $f(x)$ may approach zero in some kind of an asymptotic manner as $x \to \infty$. Often certain terms will dominate $f(x)$ as $x \to \infty$, so that the function can be integrated analytically for large x with negligible error. In this event, the integral (8.52) is broken up into two parts:

$$\int_a^\infty f(x)\,dx = \int_a^c f(x)\,dx + \int_c^\infty f(x)\,dx \tag{8.53}$$

The first integral is then evaluated by any suitable numerical technique, and the second integral by analytical means. The limit c must of course be chosen sufficiently large so that the asymptotic approximation to $f(x)$ is within the desired accuracy in the range $c \leq x < \infty$. An example of this approach is given in Problem 8.8.

If the integrand $f(x)$ is of a form for which Gauss-type integration tables of weights and zeros are available (see Sec. 8.4 and Refs. 14 and 15), then extremely accurate numerical evaluations of the integral can be made with relatively little effort.

If a suitable transformation can be found, one of the most effective methods of numerically evaluating an integral with an infinite limit is to change variables so that the infinite region is transformed into a finite region. Standard numerical techniques can then be used for the resulting integral or integrals. This approach can best be illustrated with an example. Consider the integral

$$I = \int_0^\infty x^2 e^{-x^2}\,dx$$

We first divide the integral into two parts:

$$I = \int_0^1 x^2 e^{-x^2}\,dx + \int_1^\infty x^2 e^{-x^2}\,dx$$

The second integral can be cast into a different form by the use of the transformation

$$y = \frac{1}{x^2}$$

so that

$$x^2 = y^{-1}$$

$$2x\, dx = -y^{-2}\, dy$$

$$dx = -\frac{1}{2y^{3/2}}\, dy$$

and since as $x \to \infty$, $y \to 0$ and at $x = 1$, $y = 1$, the second integral becomes

$$\int_1^\infty x^2 e^{-x^2}\, dx = -\frac{1}{2}\int_1^0 \frac{e^{-1/y}}{y^{5/2}}\, dy = \frac{1}{2}\int_0^1 \frac{e^{-1/y}}{y^{5/2}}\, dy$$

and so

$$I = \int_0^1 x^2 e^{-x^2}\, dx + \frac{1}{2}\int_0^1 \frac{e^{-1/y}}{y^{5/2}}\, dy = I_1 + I_2$$

These two finite integrals can now be integrated numerically using standard quadrature techniques. We arbitrarily choose Gauss quadrature. Considering first I_1, the following results are obtained for several different values of m:

m	$\bar{I}_1$
4	0.1894703
6	0.1894722
8	0.1894722

Based on these results, we can be reasonably confident of six decimal places in choosing $\bar{I}_1 = 0.189472$. Now consider the second integral,

$$I_2 = \frac{1}{2}\int_0^1 \frac{e^{-1/y}}{y^{5/2}}\, dy$$

This integral is slightly more troublesome than I_1. The integrand is indeterminate $(0/0)$ at $x = 0$, but this is easily resolved:

$$\frac{e^{-1/y}}{y^{5/2}} = \frac{1}{e^{1/y}y^{5/2}} = \frac{1}{y^{5/2}(1 + 1/y + 1/2y^2 + 1/6y^3 + 1/24y^4 + \cdots)}$$

$$= \frac{1}{y^{5/2} + y^{3/2} + y^{1/2}/2 + 1/6y^{1/2} + 1/24y^{3/2} + \cdots}$$

As $y \to 0$, the first three terms in the denominator vanish, and the remaining terms clearly become infinite, so that the entire integrand approaches zero. There remains a computational difficulty with $e^{-1/y}$ for small y. However for small ϵ,*

$$\int_0^\epsilon \frac{e^{-1/y}}{y^{5/2}}\, dy < \epsilon\left(\frac{e^{-1/\epsilon}}{\epsilon^{5/2}}\right) = \frac{e^{-1/\epsilon}}{\epsilon^{3/2}}$$

If we choose $\epsilon = 0.025$, then this integral is less than

$$\frac{e^{-1/0.025}}{(0.025)^{3/2}} = 1.075 \times 10^{-15}$$

---

*The reader can verify by taking the second derivative of the integrand that the integrand is concave upward for y less than about 0.1 and that this bound is thus correct for $\epsilon < 0.1$.

and can be ignored. Thus for our purposes

$$I_2 = \int_0^1 \frac{e^{-1/y}}{y^{5/2}} \, dy \approx \int_{0.025}^1 \frac{e^{-1/y}}{y^{5/2}} \, dy$$

but there is no problem in evaluating $e^{-1/0.025} = e^{-40}$ on most computers, so Gauss quadrature can now be applied directly. As might be expected, this integrand does not lend itself well to polynomial approximation, and more points are needed than were required to obtain I_1 accurately. The results for several values of m are

m	$\bar{I}_2$
10	0.2536942
16	0.2536414
24	0.2536407

We choose $\bar{I}_2 = 0.253641$ with reasonable confidence in the sixth decimal place. Then

$$\bar{I} = \bar{I}_1 + \bar{I}_2 = 0.189472 + 0.253641 = 0.443113$$

The exact answer is $I = \sqrt{\pi}/4 = 0.4431134$, so the numerical integration is exact to six decimal places.

Some transformations which may be useful in transforming integrals with infinite limits into integrals over finite regions include $y = e^{-x}$ and $y = 1/x^n$. Such transformations may in some cases result in the exchange of one problem for another, in that they may result in singularities at one of the limits. Whether or not the exchange is profitable will depend on the nature of the singularity and the means available to handle it. See Sec. 8.7.

If all else fails, then integrals with an infinite limit can be evaluated by standard numerical integration techniques simply carried out to very large values of x. See Problems 8.9 and 8.11 for examples of such an approach.

Some additional discussion of the numerical evaluation of integrals with infinite limits can be found in Davis and Rabinowitz[16] and Acton[12].

8.7 DEALING WITH SINGULARITIES

In this section we will discuss methods for the numerical evaluation of so-called improper integrals of the second kind. These are integrals with finite limits which have an integrand that is singular at one or both limits, but for which the integral exists and is finite. Typical simple examples of improper integrals of this type are

$$\int_0^1 \frac{1}{\sqrt{x}} \, dx \qquad\qquad\qquad (8.54)$$

and

$$\int_0^1 \frac{1}{\sqrt{1-x}} \, dx \qquad\qquad\qquad (8.55)$$

The best method for dealing with such singularities is to eliminate them if possible. Strategies to accomplish this are too varied and numerous to permit a general discussion, but they include integration by parts, "subtracting out" of the singularity, and a change of variables to eliminate the singularity.   An example is presented in Problem 8.12.   For some other interesting examples, see Davis and Rabinowitz[16] and Acton[12].

If $f(x)$ is of such a form that a Gauss-type formula is available, then the singularity will have been accounted for in the weighting function, and very accurate results can be obtained by using the tabulated weights and zeros.   See Problem 8.6 for an example of this type of integration.

If none of the above methods can be applied, then the singularity must be confronted directly with standard numerical integration techniques.   We will consider (8.54) as an example, since the exact solution is easily obtained for comparison:

$$\int_0^1 \frac{1}{\sqrt{x}}\, dx = 2x^{1/2}\Big|_0^1 = 2$$

The integrand $f(x) = 1/\sqrt{x}$ approaches infinity as $x \to 0$.   A sketch of the integrand is shown in Fig. 8.4.

A numerical integration technique based on equally spaced intervals, such as Simpson's rule, would involve $f(0)$ and thus cannot be used directly.   Alternatively, we might use such a technique to evaluate

$$\bar{I} = \int_\epsilon^1 \frac{1}{\sqrt{x}}\, dx \qquad\qquad\qquad (8.56)$$

where ϵ is a small number.   Hopefully, the result will be close to the correct answer.   But how should ϵ and the number of panels be chosen?   Some experimental calculations with Simpson's rule are shown in the following table:

ϵ	n	$\bar{I}$
0.01	4	2.17042
0.01	8	1.93027
0.01	16	1.83906
0.001	4	4.00065
0.001	8	2.86745
0.001	16	2.33792
0.001	100	1.96569
0.0001	100	2.20597
0.0001	500	2.00719
0.0001	1000	1.98882

Clearly, there are problems with this type of approach since even with the very small ϵ of 0.0001, and with 1000 panels, the result is still not very accurate.   This is because $\int_0^{0.0001} dx/\sqrt{x} = 0.02$ has been ignored.   Note that the value of $\bar{I}$ obtained for $\epsilon = 0.0001$, $n = 500$ appears to be reasonably accurate, but this is only an accident of the way in which $\bar{I}$ varies with n, and would be of little significance if we did not know the exact answer.   While for most functions a convergent strategy can be developed in which ϵ is systematically decreased as n is increased, a very large number of panels is necessary to obtain even a reasonably accurate answer[16].   The fundamental problem is that the

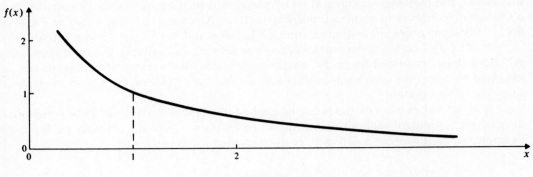

Fig. 8.4

closer the approach to the singularity, the finer the mesh size that is required in order that the interpolating polynomial (a parabola for Simpson's rule) be a reasonable approximation to the function. (Polynomials are of course very poor at functional approximation near a singularity.)

Gauss quadrature has some basic advantages in this situation. (We are referring here to basic Gauss-Legendre quadrature, not to any particular Gauss-type formula which is specially constructed to deal with the singularity.) The zeros of the Legendre polynomials are packed much more closely near the ends of the interval of interest than toward the center, and yet the values of $f(x)$ exactly at the ends of the interval are not required. This is exactly the type of behavior which should be most helpful with the present problem, and, in addition, the very high order interpolating polynomial which is implicit in Gauss quadrature can better approximate the function near the singularity. The following table shows the results of Gauss quadrature for $f(x) = 1/\sqrt{x}$ and various values of m:

m	$\bar{I}$
4	1.80634
8	1.89754
16	1.94722
24	1.96445

We are certainly getting more for our money in terms of the number of evaluations of $f(x)$ as compared with Simpson's rule (we have nearly matched with $m = 24$ the accuracy previously obtained with 100 panels and $\epsilon = 0.001$) but the result is still not very accurate. It should be noted, however, that one-half of the 24 points are concentrated in the interval $0.5 < x < 1.0$, where the function behaves very well and many of these points are essentially "wasted." The properties of Gauss quadrature can be much better exploited by doing the integration in two parts, with one of the integrals being carried out over a small region close to the singularity. Thus

$$I = \int_0^1 \frac{dx}{\sqrt{x}} = \int_0^{0.01} \frac{dx}{\sqrt{x}} + \int_{0.01}^1 \frac{dx}{\sqrt{x}} = I_A + I_B \tag{8.57}$$

Gauss quadrature with $m = 24$ for each integral produces the following result:

$$\bar{I}_A = 0.19644$$

$$\bar{I}_B = 1.79999$$

and so

$$\bar{I} = 1.99643$$

which is a quite satisfactory result for 48 functional evaluations. Procedures such as we have used for this example are sometimes said to "neglect the singularity" and are often considered somewhat dangerous. However, the Gauss quadrature approach employing several integrals, if used with care, can yield quite accurate results in most cases. This type of approach will *not* work if the function is oscillatory in the immediate region of the singularity.

Another possible approach to singularities is to interchange dependent and independent variables. A discussion of this approach is relegated to an example, Problem 8.10.

8.8 NUMERICAL INTEGRATION METHODS IN PERSPECTIVE

Now that we have examined a variety of numerical integration methods, we are in a position to review briefly these methods in terms of their suitability in any given situation.

For hand computation, it is very difficult indeed to find anything better than Gauss quadrature, since a minimum of functional evaluations and calculations are required for maximum accuracy. These same properties also make Gauss quadrature extremely desirable for machine computation, although the necessity for storing or computing large tables of weights and zeros can at times cause difficulties. Gauss quadrature can also deal effectively with singularities in many cases.

Romberg integration essentially allows any desired degree of accuracy in the evaluation of the integral to be selected as in input parameter. This feature, along with its high efficiency (relatively few functional evaluations), makes Romberg integration currently one of the most popular choices for machine computations with well behaved functions. Romberg integration does have certain disadvantages in the integration of periodic functions over an integer number of periods. (See Problem 8.5 for an example.)

If a program segment must be inserted in a larger program to perform the numerical integration of a well-behaved function, then Simpson's rule (if possible with end correction) furnishes a method which is both very simple to program and quite accurate. Simpson's rule remains probably the most widely used of all numerical integration methods. It is used for several of the illustrative problems in this chapter.

One particularly difficult class of functions to integrate numerically is those which are highly oscillatory. No attempt will be made here to discuss special approaches for such functions, but it should be noted that the trapezoidal rule has certain highly desirable properties for periodic functions, and other methods are available which are especially tailored to the integration of oscillatory functions. For details see Ref. 16.

For functions available at evenly spaced discrete points, Simpson's rule is probably the most effective technique (although the number of panels must be even). For an odd number of panels the trapezoidal rule can be used, or if desired, special formulas are available (such as Simpson's 3/8 rule) which allow the use of an odd number of panels with the error order of the standard Simpson's 1/3 rule (see Problem 8.14). Usually Simpson's 1/3 rule is used for most of the region, with the special formula used to evaluate the integral over the last few panels in the region. If a function is available only at discrete unevenly spaced points where the spacing is arbitrary, then the best procedure is usually to fit the data with a function (with or without smoothing as necessary) and integrate the resulting function (see Problem 8.15).

Illustrative Problems

8.1   Demonstrate in detail the use of the trapezoidal rule to evaluate

$$I = \int_0^\pi \sin x \, dx$$

and then include the end correction.   Use 3 panels.

The trapezoidal rule using 3 panels yields

$$\bar{I} = \frac{\pi/3}{2}[f(0) + 2f(\pi/3) + 2f(2\pi/3) + f(\pi)]$$

$$= \frac{\pi}{6}[\sin(0) + 2\sin(\pi/3) + 2\sin(2\pi/3) + \sin(\pi)]$$

$$= 0.523599[0 + 2(0.866025) + 2(0.866025) + 0]$$

$$= 1.813799$$

The correct answer is of course 2.
The end correction is

$$-\frac{(\Delta x)^2}{12}[f'(\pi) - f'(0)]$$

Now $\Delta x = \pi/3$ and $(d/dx)(\sin x) = \cos x$, so the end correction becomes

$$-\frac{(\pi/3)^2}{12}[\cos(\pi) - \cos(0)] = -\frac{(\pi/3)^2}{12}(-2) = +0.182770$$

Adding the end correction to the previously obtained trapezoidal rule value yields

$$\bar{I} = 1.813799 + 0.182770 = 1.996569$$

which is a very significant improvement and in error by only 0.003431.

8.2   Evaluate numerically using Simpson's rule the following function:

$$I = \int_0^\pi \log_e (5 - 4\cos x) \, dx$$

The following table gives the numerical value obtained by using Simpson's rule with different numbers of panels:

n	$\bar{I}$
4	4.384863
6	4.360494
8	4.356182
10	4.355369
12	4.355208
14	4.355170
16	4.355166
20	4.355163
30	4.355162
50	4.355161
100	4.355099
200	4.355081
500	4.355067
1,000	4.355023
5,000	4.353619
10,000	4.353477

But since all of the values of $\bar{I}$ are different, how do we know which one to choose as the best numerical approximation to I? For small values of n, the mesh size is too coarse for the parabola which is employed as the approximating function in Simpson's rule to give a good approximation to the integrand. This is apparent from the relatively large changes in $\bar{I}$ for different values of n ranging from 4 to about 10. For very large values of n, there is virtually no error due to mesh size; however, the calculation of $\bar{I}$ for large n involves a very large number of additions which can result in a significant amount of roundoff error. Also, each functional evaluation involves a certain amount of error, and this error accumulates as the many functional values are added. The net effect is most apparent for $n = 5000$ and 10,000. The value of $\bar{I}$ changes relatively little in the range from about $n = 14$ to $n = 50$. It is reasonable to assume that in this range the mesh size is sufficiently small to produce an excellent approximation, and that roundoff error has not yet become a serious problem. The variations in this range are in the seventh digit (sixth decimal place). Since the IBM 360/67 single precision word consists of essentially seven digits, this final digit is prone to several kinds of error including roundoff and thus there is no real reason to choose any of the values over any other. The conclusion then is that the best estimate of I is 4.35516 or 4.35517. The exact answer obtained by analytical methods is $I = 4.3551723$, which confirms our conclusion. A more accurate estimate of this answer could have been obtained by using double precision.

It is obviously not necessary in general to carry out and examine the results of a numerical integration for as many different values of n as we have done here. However, a smaller scale survey of the results for several "reasonable" values of n is usually advisable to obtain the best accuracy. One significant advantage of Romberg integration is that it essentially accomplishes this task automatically.

It is very important that no general conclusion be drawn from this problem concerning the number of panels necessary to obtain an accurate answer using Simpson's rule (or any other quadrature formula). The number of panels necessary for any given problem varies strongly with the functional form of the integrand and with the quadrature scheme chosen. The point at which roundoff error becomes significant depends primarily on the word size of the computer being used.

8.3   Evaluate numerically

$$I = \int_0^{\pi/2} \sin(2\cos x)\sin^2 x\, dx$$

using the trapezoidal rule and Simpson's rule with and without end correction. Compare the results for several different values of n.

The results are tabulated below, rounded to six places:

Method	n	$\bar{I}$	$I - \bar{I}$
Trapezoidal rule	4	0.481485	0.026482
	6	0.496396	0.011571
	10	0.503836	0.004131
Trapezoidal rule with end correction	4	0.507187	0.000780
	6	0.507819	0.000148
	10	0.507948	0.000019
Simpson's rule	4	0.512682	− 0.004715
	6	0.508646	− 0.000679
	10	0.508045	− 0.000078
Simpson's rule with end correction	4	0.508286	− 0.000319
	6	0.507984	− 0.000017
	10	0.507967	0.000000
Exact	—	0.507967	—

The results verify the theoretical predictions regarding the relative accuracy of the various methods.   The trapezoidal rule, which is a second order method, is significantly less accurate than any of the other methods.   The trapezoidal rule with end correction and Simpson's rule are both fourth order methods, and yield approximately the same degree of accuracy, where the trapezoidal rule with end correction is somewhat more accurate and on the low side while Simpson's rule is on the high side.   Simpson's rule with end correction is a sixth order method and yields the most accurate results in the table for any given value of n and the exact answer to six decimal places for $n = 10$.   As a matter of interest, Gauss quadrature with $m = 6$ yields $\bar{I} = 0.507968$.

8.4   Using Romberg integration with an absolute convergence criterion of $\epsilon = 1.0 \times 10^{-6}$, evaluate

$$I = \int_0^{0.8} e^{-x^2}\, dx$$

The Romberg algorithm yields the following table:

0.61092				
0.64632	0.65812			
0.65485	0.65770	0.65767		
0.65697	0.65767	0.65767	0.65767	
0.65749	0.65767	0.65767	0.65767	(0.65767)

This table has been rounded to 5 decimal places.   The encircled value is actually 0.6576691 as compared to the exact value, which can be found from tables of the error function to be 0.6576698.   Using 16 panels (17 functional evaluations), we have reproduced 6 digits (5 decimal places if rounded) of the exact answer.   Note that the best trapezoidal rule value (the bottom entry in the first column) is accurate to only three digits (2 decimal places if rounded).   This function is well behaved and well suited to Romberg integration.

8.5 Evaluate the following integral numerically using Romberg integration:

$$I = \int_0^{4\pi} \sin^2 x \, dx$$

Using an absolute convergence criterion of $\epsilon = 1.0 \times 10^{-5}$, the Romberg algorithm (Fig. 8.3) yields the following table (rounded to five decimal places):

0.00000
0.00000   0.00000
0.00000   0.00000   0.00000

and gives $\bar{I} = 1.812 \times 10^{-9}$.   Clearly something very strange has happened, since this integral can be easily evaluated analytically to yield $I = 2\pi = 6.283185$.

To find out why Romberg integration has yielded a totally incorrect answer, we sketch $f(x) = \sin^2 x$ on the interval $0 \leqslant x \leqslant 4\pi$ (Fig. 8.5).

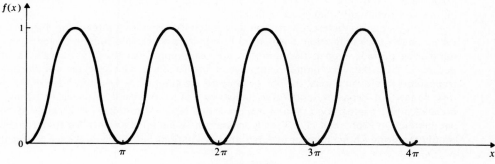

Fig. 8.5

The first single panel trapezoidal rule evaluation uses $f(0)$ and $f(4\pi)$, both of which are zero.   The estimate of the integral is thus zero.   Using two panels introduces $f(2\pi)$, but this is also zero so the estimate of the integral remains zero.   With four panels, $f(\pi)$ and $f(3\pi)$ are used, but these are also zero and the estimate of the integral does not change.   Since two successive evaluations (not counting the single panel evaluation which is not used for comparison) have yielded the same result (zero) without changing by more than 10^{-5}, the algorithm presumes convergence and yields an incorrect answer of zero (or more precisely 1.812×10^{-9}, due to roundoff error).   One more trapezoidal rule evaluation would have introduced nonzero values of $f(x)$ and the algorithm would have continued and produced the correct answer.

While in this case a clearly incorrect answer of zero was obtained, it is also possible to obtain a nonzero incorrect answer which might be more difficult to recognize as incorrect.   For example, suppose we were to use the Romberg algorithm (Fig. 8.3) to evaluate

$$\int_\delta^{4\pi+\delta} \sin^2 x \, dx$$

where $\delta < \pi/2$. The algorithm would produce $\bar{I} = 4\pi\delta$, which is clearly incorrect. (Why would this result be obtained?)

This rather alarming state of affairs can occur only for periodic functions, and the cure is simply to not use Romberg integration to integrate a periodic function over an integer number of periods greater than 1. Thus to evaluate

$$I = \int_0^{4\pi} \sin^2 x \, dx$$

we could simply split the integral into two parts so that neither integral is over an integer number of periods:

$$I = \int_0^1 \sin^2 x \, dx + \int_1^{4\pi} \sin^2 x \, dx$$

The standard Romberg algorithm will now yield the correct result for each of these integrals.

The question might arise as to what the effect would be of using a relative convergence criterion to begin with instead of an absolute one. In the case of $\int_0^{4\pi} \sin^2 x \, dx$, since the trapezoidal rule would produce zero for the first three evaluations, the convergence criterion would involve a division by zero and a possible computer halt. If roundoff error produces a nonzero result (which is likely), then the convergence criterion might not be satisfied and the algorithm might continue, eventually producing the correct result. This fortunate accident would probably not occur in the evaluation of $\int_\delta^{4\pi+\delta} \sin^2 x \, dx$ if δ is of a reasonable magnitude. (Why not?) In any event, splitting up the integral into two parts as discussed before will avoid any chance of difficulty.

In closing this discussion, it should be noted that Romberg integration may also give a false convergence indication if it is used to integrate a periodic function over a very large number of periods even if the limits do not correspond exactly to an integer number of periods. With the very limited sampling of the function which occurs for the first few trapezoidal rule evaluations, the points sampled are simply not representative of the oscillatory functional behavior, and false indications of convergence can easily occur. This makes Romberg integration in the form presented here not suitable for integrals of the type encountered in Problem 8.11. The algorithm can be modified to work for such functions by simply requiring a large number of functional evaluations before convergence testing begins.

8.6 Evaluate

$$I = \int_0^1 \frac{\log_e x}{x+1} \, dx$$

using the special Gauss quadrature formula for integrals of the form

$$\int_0^1 \log_e x \, f(x) \, dx$$

The integral has a logarithmic singularity at $x = 0$, but the Gauss-type quadrature scheme for which weights and zeros are given in the Appendix for $m = 2$, 3, and 4 automatically accounts for this singularity. In fact, the term $\log_e x$ is accounted for and *must not* be included in the "integrand." Thus

$$\bar{I} = \sum_{k=1}^m w_k(x_k) f(x_k)$$

where $f(x) = 1/(1 + x)$.   We will carry out the calculations for $m = 2$.   From the Appendix, we have

x_k	w_k
0.112009	-0.718539
0.602277	-0.281461

so

$$f(0.112009) = \frac{1}{1 + 0.112009} = 0.899273$$

$$f(0.602277) = \frac{1}{1 + 0.602277} = 0.624112$$

Now

$$\bar{I} = w_1 f(x_1) + w_2 f(x_2) = (-0.718539)(0.899273) + (-0.281461)(0.624112)$$
$$= -0.646163 - 0.175663$$

or

$$\bar{I} = -0.821826$$

The exact answer is $I = -\pi^2/12 = -0.822467$, so this answer is remarkably good with only two functional evaluations.   For comparison, we find that for $m = 3$,

$$\bar{I} = -0.822449$$

and for $m = 4$,

$$\bar{I} = -0.822466$$

The latter value is incorrect by only 1 in the sixth decimal place, which is remarkable considering that the weights and zeros were only given to six places.

The most important point about Gauss-type formulas which have been derived for the integration of functions of a certain form is that those parts of the function which have been included in the derivation of the weights must not be included in $f(x)$ when the quadrature formula of the type (8.46) is used.

8.7   Evaluate numerically

$$I = \int_2^3 \int_x^{2x^3} (x^2 + y) \, dy \, dx$$

This integral can be easily evaluated analytically to yield $I = 790.55$.   We will carry out the double integration numerically to illustrate the approach.   Simpson's rule will be used for simplicity, with 4 panels in each direction.   The integrand is

$$f(x,y) = x^2 + y$$

We denote the inner integral as

$$g(x) = \int_x^{2x^3} f(x,y) \, dy$$

Since 4 panels will be employed, we must find $\bar{g}(2)$, $\bar{g}(2.25)$, $\bar{g}(2.5)$, $\bar{g}(2.75)$, and $\bar{g}(3)$. ($\bar{g}$ denotes the numerical approximation to g.)

First we compute $\bar{g}(2)$.   The integral to be approximated is

$$g(2) = \int_2^{16} f(2,y) \, dy$$

For 4 panels, $\Delta y = (16 - 2)/4 = 3.5$. Thus from (8.30),

$$\bar{g}(2) = \frac{3.5}{3}[f(2,2) + 4f(2,5.5) + 2f(2,9) + 4f(2,12.5) + f(2,16)]$$

Now

$$f(2,2) = 2^2 + 2 = 6$$

$$f(2,5.5) = 2^2 + 5.5 = 9.5$$

$$f(2,9) = 2^2 + 9 = 13$$

$$f(2,12.5) = 2^2 + 12.5 = 16.5$$

$$f(2,16) = 2^2 + 16 = 20$$

so

$$\bar{g}(2) = \frac{3.5}{3}[6 + 4(9.5) + 2(13) + 4(16.5) + 20] = 182$$

Similarly,

$$\bar{g}(2.25) = 360.9009$$

$$\bar{g}(2.5) = 664.8438 \qquad (\Delta y \text{ is of course different for each}$$
$$\qquad\qquad\qquad\qquad\qquad\qquad\qquad \text{of these inner integrals.})$$

$$\bar{g}(2.75) = 1154.995$$

$$\bar{g}(3) = 1912.5$$

The outer integral is given by

$$I = \int_2^3 g(x)\, dx$$

so, using Simpson's rule,

$$\bar{I} = \frac{0.25}{3}[\bar{g}(2) + 4\bar{g}(2.25) + 2\bar{g}(2.5) + 4\bar{g}(2.75) + \bar{g}(3)]$$

$$= \frac{0.25}{3}[182 + 4(360.9009) + 2(664.8438) + 4(1154.995) + 1912.5]$$

$$= 790.6478$$

which is very close to the exact value of 790.55.

This accuracy is due largely to the favorable functional form of $f(x,y)$. The inner integrals are integrals of linear functions of y, for which Simpson's rule should yield exact results, while the outer integral has an integrand which is a sixth degree polynomial in x if the inner integral is evaluated exactly. While Simpson's rule will not evaluate a sixth degree polynomial exactly, it will be quite accurate if reasonable mesh sizes are used, as is apparent from the result.

8.8   Evaluate

$$I = \int_0^\infty \frac{dx}{e^x + e^{-x}}$$

We will take a numerical approach, but try to avoid the usual problems with the infinite limit. For large x, the negative exponent in the denominator can be ignored in comparison with the positive exponent. The resulting integral is $\int dx/e^x$, which is very easy to evaluate analytically. If we choose $x = 5$, then

$$e^5 = 148.413159, \qquad e^{-5} = 0.006738$$

and we should be able to ignore e^{-x} for this and all larger values of x. We rewrite the integral as

$$I = \int_0^5 \frac{dx}{e^x + e^{-x}} + \int_5^\infty \frac{dx}{e^x + e^{-x}} \approx \int_0^5 \frac{dx}{e^x + e^{-x}} + \int_5^\infty \frac{dx}{e^x}$$

Now

$$\int_5^\infty \frac{dx}{e^x} = -e^{-x}\Big|_5^\infty = e^{-5} = 0.006738$$

Using 20 panels with Simpson's rule for the first integral yields an apparently convergent result of 0.778659. Thus

$$\bar{I} = 0.778659 + 0.006738 = 0.785397$$

The exact result is $\pi/4 = 0.785398$.

8.9   Evaluate the following integral numerically without employing a transformation:

$$I = \int_0^\infty \frac{x\, dx}{e^x + 1}$$

Since this integral can be evaluated analytically, yielding $I = \pi^2/12 = 0.822467$, we have a basis for comparison. The integral is first split up into a sum of several integrals. We choose

$$\int_0^\infty f(x)\, dx = \int_0^4 f(x)\, dx + \int_4^{20} f(x)\, dx + \int_{20}^{50} f(x)\, dx + \int_{50}^\infty f(x)\, dx$$

Although there are undoubtedly various sophisticated ways of choosing the intervals of integration for each integral, we have used the following simple reasoning: as x becomes large, the function becomes small as does its slope. Far out on the "tail," integrals over large intervals of x with fairly coarse mesh sizes should still produce fairly accurate answers. In addition, the relative contribution of these integrals to the total will be small, so they need not be as accurate as those for smaller values of x. The limits of integration can thus be farther apart for each succeeding integral. We have chosen $x = 4$ as the upper limit for the first integral since $1/e^4 \approx 0.01$, so the integrand is only about 0.04 at this point, as compared with a maximum value of about $1/e$ or 0.37 at $x \approx 1$. The first integral should thus constitute by far the largest contribution to the total, but $f(x)$ does not become so small at the upper limit that we are "wasting" closely spaced points (needed for small x) by using them on the tail of the function. We have chosen $x = 50$ as the upper limit of the third integral since e^{50} is pushing the limits of the exponential subroutine on most computers. Hopefully, we will find $\int_{20}^{50} f(x)\, dx$ to be so small that $\int_{50}^\infty f(x)\, dx$ can be neglected without question. (This can strictly be justified only if $f(x)$ monotonically decreases for large x as it does in the present case.) If our guesses on interval size have been appropriate, then approximately the same number of panels should be sufficient for each integral.

We (arbitrarily) choose Simpson's rule and obtain the following results:

$$\int_0^4 \frac{x\, dx}{e^x + 1} \approx 0.731634 \qquad (n = 20)$$

$$\int_4^{20} \frac{x\, dx}{e^x + 1} \approx 0.090864 \qquad (n = 20)$$

$$\int_{20}^{50} \frac{x\, dx}{e^x + 1} \approx 0.5096 \times 10^{-7} \qquad (n = 20)$$

The latter integral is small enough that we can feel safe in neglecting $\int_{50}^{\infty} f(x)\,dx$. Summing these, we obtain

$$\int_0^{\infty} \frac{x\,dx}{e^x+1} \approx 0.822492$$

as compared to the exact value of 0.822467. This is accurate enough for most purposes. A few additional calculations confirm that 20 panels was a good choice for each of the integrals except the first, where $n = 10$ would suffice. It should be noted that the integral we have chosen was a favorable one since the exponential causes a rapid decay of $f(x)$. For a more difficult integral with an infinite limit, which requires a modified approach, see Problem 8.11.

8.10   Integrate numerically

$$\int_0^1 \frac{1}{\sqrt{x}}\,dx$$

Treat the singularity by interchanging the roles of the independent and dependent variables.

   The integral corresponds to the shaded area in the sketch shown in Fig. 8.6.

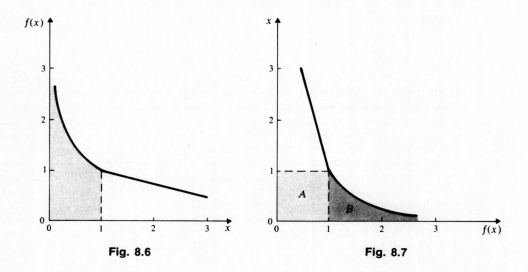

Fig. 8.6   Fig. 8.7

   We can write the integral as $I = \int_0^1 f(x)\,dx$, where $f(x) = 1/\sqrt{x}$. However, precisely the same area will be obtained if we evaluate the integral as

$$I = 1 + \int_1^{\infty} x\,df(x)$$

This can be seen more clearly if we turn Fig. 8.6 on its side (see Fig. 8.7).
   The area of the square region A is 1 and $\int_1^{\infty} x\,df(x)$ accounts for the area of region B. We have exchanged the problem of a singularity for the problem of an infinite limit which is hopefully easier (or at least different) to deal with. Now

$$f(x) = \frac{1}{\sqrt{x}}$$

$$f^2(x) = \frac{1}{x}$$

$$x = \frac{1}{f^2}$$

so the area of **B** is given by $\int_1^\infty df/f^2$. Although this integral could be easily evaluated analytically, we will use numerical techniques since we are attempting to describe a general numerical approach to dealing with singularities.

We split this integral up into several regions:

$$\int_1^\infty \frac{df}{f^2} = \int_1^{10} \frac{df}{f^2} + \int_{10}^{50} \frac{df}{f^2} + \int_{50}^{250} \frac{df}{f^2} + \int_{250}^{1000} \frac{df}{f^2} + \int_{1000}^\infty \frac{df}{f^2}$$

Applying Simpson's rule and neglecting the last integral, we obtain

$$\int_1^\infty \frac{df}{f^2} \approx \underset{(40)}{0.900292} + \underset{(20)}{0.080019} + \underset{(10)}{0.016046} + \underset{(10)}{0.003003}$$

The number in parenthesis under the numerical approximation to each integral is the number of panels used for that integral. This yields

$$\int_1^\infty \frac{df}{f^2} \approx 0.999360$$

Thus $\bar{I} = 1.999360$ as compared with the exact value of 2.000000. This is a better estimate of the integral than we were able to obtain by any of the direct numerical techniques for dealing with the singularity which were tried in Sec. 8.7. If numerical approximations to $\int_{1000}^\infty df/f^2$ were included, this would improve the accuracy.

8.11 Evaluate numerically

$$I = \int_0^\infty \frac{\sin^2 x}{x^2} \, dx$$

We arbitrarily subdivide the integral as follows:

$$I = \int_0^4 f(x) \, dx + \int_4^{20} f(x) \, dx + \int_{20}^{50} f(x) \, dx + \int_{50}^{200} f(x) \, dx$$
$$+ \int_{200}^{500} f(x) \, dx + \int_{500}^{1200} f(x) \, dx + \int_{1200}^\infty f(x) \, dx$$

These subdivisions are based to some extent on what we learned about $\int dx/x^2$ (actually it was $\int df/f^2$) in Problem 8.10, but more and smaller regions have been taken in this case because of the presence of $\sin^2 x$ in the numerator of the integrand. This oscillatory function makes it necessary that a much finer mesh spacing be used on the "tail" of the function than would be needed for a monotonic function. Each integral is now evaluated using Simpson's rule with various n, and a "sufficiently accurate" value chosen. The procedure used is essentially that employed in Problem 8.2 to find an accurate value of the integral, but for economy we select the first value which reproduces the first 4 decimal places reasonably well.

For example, consider $\int_{50}^{200} f(x)\, dx$.   The following results are obtained for various n:

n	$\bar{I}$
50	0.007718
100	0.007419
200	0.007451

The results for $n = 100$ and $n = 200$ are reasonably close, and we can expect the $n = 200$ value to be more accurate, so we select this value.   (The $n = 100$ value might have been acceptable, but we could not know this without finding the $n = 200$ value.)   Following this procedure for all the integrals, we find

$$\int_{0}^{4} f(x)\, dx \approx 1.430994 \qquad (20)$$

$$\int_{4}^{20} f(x)\, dx \approx 0.114335 \qquad (40)$$

$$\int_{20}^{50} f(x)\, dx \approx 0.015540 \qquad (60)$$

$$\int_{50}^{200} f(x)\, dx \approx 0.007451 \qquad (200)$$

$$\int_{200}^{500} f(x)\, dx \approx 0.001454 \qquad (200)$$

$$\int_{500}^{1200} f(x)\, dx \approx 0.000586 \qquad (500)$$

The number in parenthesis after each estimate is the number of panels employed for that integral.   Note that in contrast to previous problems with infinite limit which we have encountered, the number of panels must *increase* as the interval of integration becomes larger for large x.   This is simply due to the fact that $\sin^2 x$ has a period of π, and it is necessary to leave at least a few points in each period in order to adequately approximate this oscillatory function.   The approximate number of points per period used for each interval is

x	Points/Period
0–4	16
4–20	8
20–50	6
50–200	4
200–500	2
500–1200	2

The number of points per period can decrease for large x because the *relative* accuracy of these integrals need not be as great as is necessary for small x.   (Recall that we are attempting to maintain an approximately constant *absolute* accuracy of about 4 decimal places for each integral.)   The sum of these integrals yields

$$\bar{I} = 1.430994 + 0.114335 + 0.015540 + 0.007451 + 0.001454 + 0.000586$$
$$= 1.570360$$

This estimate of I could be improved by approximating $\int_{1200}^{\infty} f(x)\,dx$. We can bound the error made in neglecting this integral since

$$\int_{1200}^{\infty} \frac{\sin^2 x}{x^2}\,dx < \int_{1200}^{\infty} \frac{dx}{x^2} = \frac{1}{1200} = 0.000833$$

We have attempted to maintain 4-place accuracy in each integral and since the residual error in the neglected integral is less than 0.000833, we might reasonably expect the first three decimal places of $\bar{I}$ to be correct. This is confirmed by comparison of $\bar{I} = 1.570360$ with the exact value of $I = \pi/2 = 1.570796$.

We have taken a rather "brute force" approach requiring a large number of functional evaluations. For a more sophisticated approach to the treatment of oscillatory integrals over infinite limits see Ref. 16.

It should be noted that there is a small problem with this integral at $x = 0$ since the integrand is indeterminate and Simpson's rule uses $f(0)$. This can be easily dealt with by applying L'Hospital's rule twice to yield

$$\lim_{x \to 0} \frac{\sin^2 x}{x^2} = \lim_{x \to 0} \frac{\dfrac{d}{dx}\sin^2 x}{\dfrac{d}{dx}x^2} = \lim_{x \to 0} \frac{2 \sin x \cos x}{2x}$$

$$= \lim_{x \to 0} \frac{\dfrac{d}{dx}(\sin x \cos x)}{\dfrac{d}{dx}x} = \lim_{x \to 0} \frac{-\sin^2 x + \cos^2 x}{1} = 1$$

8.12   Eliminate the singularity at $x = 1$ in integrals of the form

$$I = \int_0^1 \frac{f(x)}{\sqrt{1 - x^2}}\,dx$$

by a transformation, so that the integration may be handled using standard numerical techniques.

We assume $f(x)$ has no singularities on $0 \leqslant x \leqslant 1$. If we let

$$x = \sin y$$

then

$$\sqrt{1 - x^2} = \sqrt{1 - \sin^2 y} = \cos y$$

and

$$dx = \cos y\,dy$$

To determine the limits, we confine y to the first quadrant, so that at $x = 0$, $\sin y = 0$ or $y = 0$. Similarly, at $x = 1$, $\sin y = 1$ so $y = \pi/2$. The integral now becomes

$$I = \int_0^1 \frac{f(x)}{\sqrt{1 - x^2}}\,dx = \int_0^{\pi/2} \frac{f \sin y}{\cos y} \cos y\,dy = \int_0^{\pi/2} f \sin y\,dy$$

which can be readily integrated numerically using any standard technique.

8.13 Using standard Gauss-Legendre quadrature and "ignoring the singularity," evaluate

$$I = \int_0^1 \frac{1}{x} \log_e \frac{1+x}{1-x} \, dx$$

The integrand is singular at $x = 1$ since $\log_e (2/0)$ is infinite. The value of the integrand at $x = 0$ is indeterminate since

$$\frac{\log_e (1)}{0} = \frac{0}{0}$$

It is important to determine whether there is a singularity at $x = 0$. We can apply L'Hospital's rule to the integrand to determine its limit as $x \to 0$:

$$\lim_{x \to 0} \frac{\log_e \frac{1+x}{1-x}}{x} = \lim_{x \to 0} \frac{\frac{d}{dx} \log_e \frac{1+x}{1-x}}{\frac{d}{dx} x} = \lim_{x \to 0} \frac{\left(\frac{1-x}{1+x}\right)[(1)(1-x)^{-1} + (1+x)(1-x)^{-2}]}{1} = 2$$

Thus there is no singularity in the integrand at $x = 0$. This does not necessarily mean that the integrand is free of computational difficulties at or near $x = 0$. Obviously there is trouble at $x = 0$, but Gauss quadrature never requires the evaluation of the integrand exactly at the end points of the interval of integration.

To determine whether there will be trouble near $x = 0$, consider the integrand at $x = 10^{-5}$:

$$\frac{\log_e \left(\frac{1.00001}{0.99999}\right)}{0.00001} = \frac{\log_e (1.00002)}{0.00001} = \frac{1.99998 \times 10^{-5}}{0.00001} = 1.99998$$

There appears to be no problem for values of x this small, so as long as the values of x needed for Gauss quadrature are greater than 10^{-5}, there should be no need for special precautions. Gauss quadrature yields the following results for various m:

m	$\bar{I}$
4	2.436538
6	2.452525
8	2.458681
10	2.461679
16	2.465076
24	2.466338

The value of $\bar{I}$ appears to be converging, but the singularity is obviously causing trouble. As discussed in Sec. 8.7, the situation can be improved by concentrating on the region near the singularity. We split the integral into two parts:

$$I = \int_0^{0.99} \frac{1}{x} \log \frac{1+x}{1-x} \, dx + \int_{0.99}^1 \frac{1}{x} \log \frac{1+x}{1-x} \, dx$$

Evaluating each of these integrals by using Gauss quadrature with $m = 24$, we obtain

$$\bar{I} = 2.404139 + 0.063239 = 2.467378$$

This is a reasonably accurate approximation to the exact answer, $I = \pi^2/4 = 2.467402$. More accurate results can be obtained in some similar situations by subdividing the original integral into still more subintegrals, although roundoff error can eventually become a problem.

The smallest value of x encountered in the above calculations is $x = 0.002382$ in evaluating $\int_0^{0.99} (1/x) \log [(1 + x)/(1 - x)] \, dx$ with $m = 24$. This presents no problem.

It should be noted that we have arbitrarily restricted m to an upper limit of 24 in these problems simply because this is as far as the tables in the Appendix are carried. Larger values of m can definitely produce more accurate integrals in some cases, but roundoff error becomes a distinct threat with large m.

8.14 Given the following function tabulated at evenly spaced intervals:

(x)	0	1	2	3	4	5	6	7	8	9
$f(x)$	0	0.5687	0.7909	0.5743	0.1350	-0.1852	-0.1802	0.0811	0.2917	0.3031

Evaluate $\int_0^9 f(x) \, dx$ using various suitable methods.

This oscillatory function tends to emphasize somewhat the differences in the results obtained from the various methods.

The trapezoidal rule gives

$$\bar{I}_A = \frac{1}{2}\left[f(0) + f(9) + 2 \sum_{j=1}^{8} f(j) \right] = 2.22785$$

Simpson's rule cannot be applied directly, since the number of panels (9) is odd. However, one might wonder what would happen if Simpson's rule were used for the first 8 panels and the trapezoidal rule for the last. This gives

$$\bar{I}_B = \frac{1}{3}\left[f(0) + f(8) + 4 \sum_{\substack{j=1 \\ j \text{ odd}}}^{7} f(j) + 2 \sum_{\substack{j=2 \\ j \text{ even}}}^{6} f(j) \right] + \frac{1}{2} [f(8) + f(9)]$$

$$= 1.97957 + 0.29740 = 2.27697$$

Presumably the most accurate results can be obtained by using a fourth order method throughout the region.

A formula which is of the same error order as the standard Simpson's rule, but which uses three panels, is often called Simpson's 3/8 rule and is given by

$$\int_{x_{j-2}}^{x_{j+1}} f(x) \, dx \approx \frac{3\Delta x}{8}[f(x_{j-2}) + 3f(x_{j-1}) + 3f(x_j) + f(x_{j+1})]$$

The integral over the entire interval can be evaluated by using Simpson's 1/3 rule for the first 6 panels and Simpson's 3/8 rule for the last 3 panels. This gives

$$\bar{I}_c = \frac{1}{3}\{f(0) + f(6) + 4[f(1) + f(3) + f(5)] + 2[f(2) + f(4)]\}$$

$$+ \frac{3}{8}[f(6) + 3f(7) + 3f(8) + f(9)]$$

$$= 1.83427 + 0.46548 = 2.29975$$

Accepting $\bar{I}_c$ as the most accurate value, we note that the trapezoidal rule value $\bar{I}_A$ is considerably different (and presumably less accurate). The value $\bar{I}_B$, which was obtained by using Simpson's rule over all but one panel, and the trapezoidal rule over that panel, appears to be reasonably accurate.   While this combination of methods with different error orders is not aesthetically pleasing, it will usually produce fairly good results, particularly for small mesh sizes and gently varying functions where the trapezoidal rule portion contributes relatively little to the total and/or is reasonably accurate.   However, since the combination of Simpson's 1/3 rule and 3/8 rule is as simple to compute as any other method, there would seldom be any reason to choose another technique.

8.15   Estimate

$$\int_0^{10} f(x)\, dx$$

from the following experimental data:

(x)	0.99	2.10	3.22	4.40	5.70	7.12	8.01	8.37	9.32	9.98
$f(x)$	4.90	5.70	4.20	7.04	8.31	7.82	5.97	7.01	6.68	4.79

The data are plotted in Fig. 8.8.

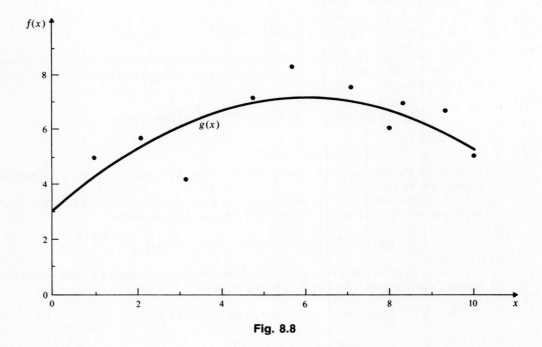

Fig. 8.8

Since the data are obviously noisy, we choose to smooth the data by a least-squares polynomial fit.   There appears to be some curvature to the data so we select a quadratic fit.   Applying the method discussed in Sec. 7.1 gives

$$g(x) = 2.92278 + 1.43472x - 0.117903x^2$$

This function is shown as the solid line in Fig. 8.8.   This polynomial can be easily integrated analytically to yield

$$\int_0^{10} g(x)\,dx = \left(2.92278x + \frac{1.43472x^2}{2} - \frac{0.117903x^3}{3}\right)\Bigg|_0^{10} = 61.6628$$

and we assume

$$\int_0^{10} f(x)\,dx \approx \int_0^{10} g(x)\,dx$$

Problems

All of the integrals given here are to be evaluated numerically (except as noted), even though many of these integrals could be evaluated analytically. The purpose, of course, is not to discourage analytical evaluation, but rather to provide experience in numerical integration.   Many of the integrals are to be evaluated "as accurately as possible."   No absolute standards are specified since the accuracy which can be practically obtained is dependent on whether or not a computer is available, and if a computer is used, is dependent on the word size of that computer and any time and/or money restrictions which might be imposed.   Accuracy standards which are compatible with the facilities available can be imposed if desired.

Any numerical integration will be considerably easier if a digital computer is available; however, a significant number of representative problems are included here that can be reasonably accurately evaluated by hand if necessary.   The problems for which the use of a computer is highly desirable have been marked with an asterisk.   For these problems, the complexity of the integrand and the number of evaluations of the integrand necessary in order to obtain reasonable accuracy make hand computation impractical.

*8.16 Write computer programs to evaluate an integral using the following methods:
   (*a*) The trapezoidal rule.
   (*b*) The trapezoidal rule with end correction.
   (*c*) Simpson's rule.
   (*d*) Simpson's rule with end correction.

Input data to each program should include the limits of integration and the number of panels to be used.   The function to be integrated and its derivative (if needed) should be assumed to be available as function subprograms.

*8.17 Write a computer program to carry out Romberg integration using the algorithm (Fig. 8.3) with an absolute convergence criterion.   The input data should include the limits of integration and the convergence criterion.   The function to be integrated should be assumed to be available as a function subprogram.

*8.18 Write a computer program to evaluate an integral by Gauss quadrature.   Input data should include the limits of the integral and the number of points at which the function is to be evaluated, as well as the set of weights and zeros corresponding to this number of points.   Allow for a maximum of 24 points.

*8.19 Write a computer program to evaluate a double integral by using Simpson's rule. Input data should include the limits of the outer integral and the number of panels to be used for the inner integral and for the outer integral. The function to be integrated and both limits of the inner integral should be assumed to be available as function subprograms.

8.20 The following integrals have integrands which are well behaved and have no singularities or indeterminacies. Evaluate the integrals numerically, using the indicated method or methods and the indicated number of panels. If the number of panels is not indicated, evaluate the integrals as accurately as possible.

(a) $\displaystyle\int_0^{\pi/2} \frac{\sin x}{\sqrt{1 - 0.25 \sin^2 x}}\, dx$

Method: Compare the trapezoidal rule with and without end correction to Simpson's rule. Use $n = 4$.

(b) $\displaystyle\int_{-1.1\pi}^{1.1\pi} \cos^2 x\, dx$

Method: Compare Simpson's rule to Simpson's rule with end correction. Use $n = 10$.

(c) $\displaystyle\int_0^{\pi/4} \frac{x}{\cos^2 x}\, dx$

Method: Compare Simpson's rule to Simpson's rule with end correction. Use $n = 4$.

(d) $\displaystyle\int_0^{\pi/2} \frac{dx}{(1 + \sin x)^2}$

Method: Simpson's rule.

(e) $\displaystyle\int_0^1 \frac{e^x}{1 + e^x}\, dx$

Method: Trapezoidal rule with end correction.

8.21 Evaluate the following integral analytically:

$$\int_{-1}^2 (x^7 + 2x^3 - 1)\, dx$$

What is the minimum number of points at which the integrand would have to be evaluated in order to obtain the exact value of this integral by using Gauss quadrature? Carry out this numerical integration.

8.22 Evaluate the integral given in Problem 8.21 by using Romberg integration by hand. The algorithm should converge to the exact answer.

*8.23 Evaluate the following integrals by using Romberg integration. If possible, use an absolute convergence criterion of $\epsilon = 1 \times 10^{-5}$. Some indeterminacies may have to be disposed of.

(a) $\displaystyle\int_1^{10} \sin(\log_e x)\, dx$

(b) $\displaystyle\int_0^2 \frac{\cos x - 1}{x}\, dx$

(c) $\displaystyle\int_0^{1.127} \frac{12.127 + \log_e\left(e^{\frac{2.4386}{x}} - 1\right)}{x^4\left(e^{\frac{2.4386}{x}} - 1\right)}\, dx$

8.24   Evaluate as accurately as possible using Gauss quadrature:

(a) $\displaystyle\int_0^{\pi/4} \log_e (1 + \tan x)\, dx$

*(b) $\displaystyle\int_0^{0.8} \frac{\sinh x}{x}\, dx$

8.25   Evaluate the following integrals numerically as accurately as possible:

(a) $\displaystyle\int_0^{\infty} \frac{dx}{e^x + e^{-x}}$

> Method: Find a transformation which changes this integral into an integral with finite limits, and evaluate this integral by any suitable numerical method.   (This integral was attacked by a different approach in Problem 8.8.)

*(b) $\displaystyle\int_0^{\infty} \frac{\cos x}{1 + x^2}\, dx$

> Method: Evaluate the integral by using Simpson's rule directly without any transformation.

*(c) $\displaystyle\int_0^{\infty} e^{2(1-\cosh x)} \cosh x\, dx$

> Method: Same as (b).

*8.26   The integrands of the following integrals have singularities at one or both limits.   Evaluate these integrals numerically as accurately as possible.

(a) $\displaystyle\int_0^1 \left(\log_e \frac{1}{x}\right)^{1/2} dx$

(b) $\displaystyle\int_0^{\pi/2} x \log_e (\sin x)\, dx$

(c) $\displaystyle\int_0^1 \frac{\log_e x}{x^2 - 1}\, dx$

> Note: The special Gauss-type formula for the integration of functions of the form $f(x) \log_e x$ is not very accurate for this integral.   Why not?

8.27   Evaluate the following double integrals numerically as accurately as possible:

(a) $\displaystyle\int_0^1 \int_0^x xy e^{-y^2}\, dy\, dx$

*(b) $\displaystyle\int_0^{1.2} \int_0^{e^{-x}} (x^2 + y^2)^{3/2}\, e^{-y^2}\, dy\, dx$

*(c) $\displaystyle\int_0^{\pi/2} \int_0^{2\sin\theta} r^3 \sinh (r \sin \theta)\, dr\, d\theta$

8.28   Choose the most suitable technique and evaluate the following integrals numerically as accurately as possible:

*(a) $\displaystyle \int_0^\infty \frac{dx}{x^{1/2}(1+x)}$

*(b) $\displaystyle \int_0^\infty \log_e \frac{e^x+1}{e^x-1}\, dx$

*(c) $\displaystyle \int_0^{\pi/4} x \tan x\, dx$

(d) $\displaystyle \int_0^1 \frac{\log_e x}{\sqrt{1+x^3}}\, dx$

*(e) $\displaystyle \int_0^\infty e^{-x} \log_e x\, dx$

*(f) $\displaystyle \int_0^\infty x^3 e^{-x}\, dx$

8.29   Given the following data at equally spaced intervals:

x	0	0.1	0.2	0.3	0.4	0.5	0.6	0.7	0.8	0.9	1.0	1.1
$f(x)$	93	87	68	55	42	37	35	39	48	53	51	39

The data is felt to be relatively error-free.   Evaluate as accurately as possible the integral

$$\int_0^{1.1} f(x)\, dx$$

Chapter 9

The Numerical Solution of Ordinary Differential Equations

9.0 INTRODUCTION

The numerical approach to the solution of ordinary differential equations is remarkable in the sense that any one of the enormous variety of techniques available can be applied (with varying degrees of success and effectiveness) to virtually any differential equation. Nonlinearities in the differential equations and the boundary conditions or initial conditions seldom require any modifications in the numerical techniques. That the numerical technique can often be chosen virtually without regard for the differential equation to be solved is, of course, in marked contrast to the problem of trying to find an exact analytical solution to a differential equation. Even linear problems can sometimes present monumental obstacles to finding a suitable analytical technique, and some linear and most nonlinear differential equations are virtually impossible to solve using exact analytical methods. It is often possible to find approximate solutions for such problems, but the accuracy of approximate solutions can seldom be properly evaluated.

While numerical techniques for ordinary differential equations are very powerful and can be applied to a wide variety of problems, it should be kept in mind that such numerical methods can have inherent difficulties of their own, as we shall see in this chapter. In addition, since numerical techniques are such powerful and flexible tools, it is natural that they will be applied to extremely complex and possibly poorly-behaved differential equations. In such circumstances, it is entirely reasonable to expect the inherent difficulties of the problem to be manifested in some undesirable way in the application of the numerical method. Numerical techniques for ordinary differential equations should thus never be considered as foolproof, and their results should not be accepted as correct without the careful scrutiny which is deserved by any problem of importance.

We will now identify two broad categories into which all problems involving ordinary differential equations must fall. These are the categories of *initial value problems* and *boundary value problems*. Despite our earlier statements of the broad range of applicability of numerical techniques for ordinary differential equations, somewhat different numerical approaches are required for problems in these two categories. However, as we shall presently see, the differences are not as great as they might at first appear.

Initial value problems are those for which conditions are specified at only *one* value of the independent variable. These conditions are termed *initial conditions* whether or not they are specified at the point where the independent variable is actually equal to zero (we will usually use zero for simplicity). A typical initial value problem might be of the form

$$A\frac{d^2y}{dt^2} + B\frac{dy}{dt} + Cy = g(t), \qquad y(0) = y_0, \qquad \frac{dy}{dt}(0) = V_0$$

This problem could describe the forced response of a simple harmonic oscillator with time. Both conditions have been specified at $t = 0$. It is important to note that such problems are termed initial value problems whether or not the independent variable represents time. In many cases, for example, the independent variable may represent a spatial coordinate, but as long as the conditions are specified at a single value of the independent variable, the problem is an initial value problem.

Boundary value problems are those for which conditions are specified at *two* values of the independent variable.* A typical boundary value problem might be of the form

$$\frac{d^2y}{dx^2} + D\frac{dy}{dx} + Ey = h(x), \qquad y(0) = y_0, \qquad y(L) = y_l$$

This problem could describe the steady-state temperature distribution in a one-dimensional heat transfer problem with temperatures y_0 at $x = 0$ and y_l at $x = L$. These are called the *boundary conditions* whether or not the points $x = 0$ and $x = L$ represent actual physical boundaries. The problem is a boundary value problem if *any* conditions are specified at two different values of the independent variable. Thus

$$\frac{d^4y}{dx^4} + Ay = f(x)$$

$$y(0) = y_0, \qquad \frac{dy}{dx}(0) = w_0, \qquad \frac{d^2y}{dx^2}(0) = v_0, \qquad y(L) = y_l$$

is a boundary value problem.

We will now turn to a detailed discussion of initial value problems. In fact, much of the emphasis of this chapter will be on such problems. This is not to imply that initial value problems are more important or more frequently encountered in practice than boundary value problems. The reason is simply that virtually all of the capability which will be developed for solving initial value problems can be directly and efficiently applied to the solution of boundary value problems, as we shall see in Sec. 9.9.

9.1 THE GENERAL INITIAL VALUE PROBLEM

Any initial value problem can be represented as a set of one or more coupled first-order ordinary differential equations, each with an initial condition. For example, the simple harmonic oscillator described by

$$A\frac{d^2y}{dt^2} + B\frac{dy}{dt} + C = g(t) \tag{9.1}$$

---

*Although it is conceivable that boundary conditions might be specified at more than two points, this situation is so specialized that we will not consider it here.

$$y(0) = y_0 \tag{9.2}$$

$$\frac{dy}{dt}(0) = V_0 \tag{9.3}$$

can be restated by making the substitution

$$z = \frac{dy}{dt} \tag{9.4}$$

The differential equation (9.1) can now be written as

$$A\frac{dz}{dt} + Bz + Cy = g(t) \tag{9.5}$$

With some rearrangement, the problem represented by equations (9.1)–(9.3) can now be written as

$$\frac{dy}{dt} = z \tag{9.6}$$

$$\frac{dz}{dt} = -\frac{B}{A}z - \frac{C}{A}y \tag{9.7}$$

with initial conditions

$$y(0) = y_0 \tag{9.8}$$

$$z(0) = V_0 \tag{9.9}$$

Any nth order differential equation can similarly be reduced to a system of n first-order differential equations, and coupled sets of any order can be reduced to a coupled set of first order equations. (See, for example, Problems 9.2 and 9.3.)

The general form of any initial value problem can thus be stated as

$$\frac{dy_1}{dt} = f_1(y_1, y_2, \ldots, y_n, t)$$

$$\frac{dy_2}{dt} = f_2(y_1, y_2, \ldots, y_n, t) \tag{9.10}$$

$$\vdots$$

$$\frac{dy_n}{dt} = f_n(y_1, y_2, \ldots, y_n, t)$$

subject to the initial conditions

$$y_1(0) = y_{10}$$

$$y_2(0) = y_{20} \tag{9.11}$$

$$\vdots$$

$$y_n(0) = y_{n0}$$

Since any initial value problem can be expressed as a set of first-order ordinary differential equations, our primary concern in this chapter will be to develop and assess numerical methods for the solution of first-order differential equations. In fact, we will deal primarily with an initial value problem consisting of a single first-order differential equation and its associated initial condition. The extension to coupled sets of first order equations is straightforward, as we shall show in Sec. 9.8. A number of numerical techniques have been developed to deal with higher order differential equations directly, without reduction to a first order set. However, these methods must be developed specifically for a given order equation (usually second order) or for an equation of a particular form. Although such methods may be advantageous in some cases, they are not of sufficient generality for us to consider here. The interested reader can find examples of such methods in Refs. 3 and 17.

We thus can consider the general initial value problem by examining an initial value problem of the form

$$\frac{dy}{dt} = f(y,t) \tag{9.12}$$

$$y(0) = y_0 \tag{9.13}$$

The next logical question is whether a solution to this problem exists, and if so, whether the solution is unique. Fortunately, existence and uniqueness can be proven under rather weak (unrestrictive) conditions on the behavior of $f(y,t)$. For example, if $f(y,t)$ is defined and continuous over the region of interest (in both y and t) and has a continuous partial derivative with respect to y which is bounded in this region, this is sufficient to prove existence and uniqueness. These conditions are actually stronger than necessary; see Henrici[17] for a statement of weaker sufficient conditions and a detailed proof.

We will now briefly outline the overall concepts involved in obtaining numerical solutions to initial value problems. These concepts can best be illustrated by assuming that the solution to the differential equation (9.12) subject to the initial condition (9.13) is known on the interval $0 \leq t \leq t_j$. Our objective will be to advance the solution to $t_{j+1} = t_j + \Delta t$ (see Fig. 9.1). No matter what specific method is chosen, the underlying principle will clearly be extrapolation.

We will be concerned with two classes of methods. The first of these consists of formulas of the *Runge-Kutta* type. In these formulas, the desired solution y_{j+1} is obtained in terms of y_j, $f(y_j, t_j)$, and $f(y,t)$ evaluated for various estimated values of y between t_j and t_{j+1}. Since the solution is carried directly from t_j to t_{j+1} without requiring values of y or $f(y,t)$ for $t < t_j$, these methods are self-starting. That is, if $t_j = 0$, and hence $y_j = y(0)$, which is the initial condition, these methods can be used to find $y_{j+1} = y(0 + \Delta t) = y(\Delta t)$ and as many succeeding values of y as desired.

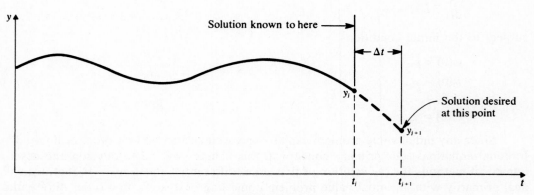

Fig. 9.1

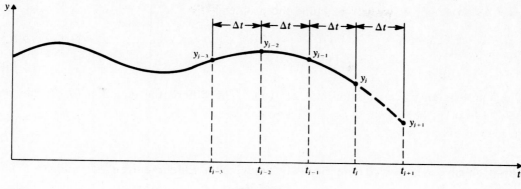

Fig. 9.2

A second class of methods which we will consider consists of formulas of the *multistep* type. These formulas, in general, require information for $t < t_j$. Consider Fig. 9.2.

In a typical accurate multistep formula, the solution for y_{j+1} might require the value of y_j and values of $f(y,t)$ at each of the points t_j, t_{j-1}, t_{j-2}, and t_{j-3}. Except in the simplest cases (those which do not involve values of y and $f(y,t)$ for $t < t_j$) these multistep formulas are obviously not self-starting, and other methods must be used to obtain the solution for the first few steps beyond the initial condition.

We will begin our detailed discussion of numerical methods for ordinary differential equations by considering the simplest of all such methods.

9.2 THE EULER METHOD

Consider again the first-order initial value problem

$$\frac{dy}{dt} = f(y,t) \qquad (9.14)$$

$$y(0) = y_0 \qquad (9.15)$$

One straightforward approach to obtaining a numerical solution to this problem is to replace dy/dt by a simple forward difference representation. Thus (9.14) can be approximated by

$$\frac{y_{j+1} - y_j}{\Delta t} = f(y_j, t_j) \qquad (9.16)$$

(We leave the error analysis to the next section.) Solving (9.16) for y_{j+1} yields

$$y_{j+1} = y_j + (\Delta t)f(y_j, t_j) \qquad (9.17)$$

Given the initial condition (9.15), it is now possible to "march" forward in t from $t = 0$, using (9.17) to obtain a value of y at each new value of t. We shall see in later sections that the Euler formula is a member of the set of multistep formulas of the Adams type. Since the solution can be carried out from $t = 0$, the method is self-starting.

As an example, we will examine the problem

$$\frac{dy}{dt} + y^2 = 0 \qquad (9.18)$$

$$y(0) = 1 \qquad (9.19)$$

which has as an exact solution $y = 1/(1 + t)$. The differential equation (9.18) can be written as

$$\frac{dy}{dt} = -y^2 \qquad (9.20)$$

This problem can be solved numerically by applying the Euler recurrence formula (9.17):

$$y_{j+1} = y_j + \Delta t(-y_j^2) \qquad (9.21)$$

Starting at $t = 0$ $(j = 0)$ and using $\Delta t = 0.1$, we can find y at $t = 0.1$:

$$y_1 = 1 + (0.1)(-1^2) = 0.9$$

The exact solution at this point is

$$y_{\text{exact}}(0.1) = \frac{1}{1 + 0.1} = 0.9090909$$

Next, at $t = 0.2$,

$$y_2 = 0.9 + (0.1)(-(0.9)^2) = 0.819$$

The exact solution is

$$y_{\text{exact}}(0.2) = \frac{1}{1 + 0.2} = 0.8333333$$

After 10 steps of $\Delta t = 0.1$, we find

$$y_{10} = 0.4627810$$

$$y_{\text{exact}}(1.0) = \frac{1}{1 + 1} = 0.5$$

Although this numerical technique is very simple, it is obviously not extremely accurate for the value of Δt used here. In fact, the Euler method is so inaccurate that it is virtually never used in practice. However, because the method is so simple, it is convenient to use as an introduction to numerical techniques for ordinary differential equations. The error analysis for this method is also much simpler than for more complex methods, and we will consider this topic next.

9.3 TRUNCATION ERROR

In order to illustrate the concepts of truncation error, we will examine the Euler method. Starting from t_j with a known y_j, the solution can be advanced an amount Δt to t_{j+1} using the Euler formula:

$$y_{j+1} = y_j + \Delta t\, f(y_j, t_j) \qquad (9.22)$$

Now, for the moment, assume that there is no roundoff error involved in any of the calculations. (Roundoff error will, of course, always be present, but we must neglect it here to gain a clear picture of truncation error.)   In order to distinguish between the finite difference solution and the exact solution to the differential equation, we will denote the exact solution as Y.   Now suppose that (9.22) is used to take a step from t_j to t_{j+1}, and that the exact solution to the differential equation is known at t_j and is used in the formula.   Thus

$$y_{j+1} = Y_j + \Delta t\, f(Y_j, t_j) \tag{9.23}$$

Assuming that the exact solution to the differential is analytic near t_j, we can also find this exact solution at t_{j+1} by a Taylor series expansion:

$$Y_{j+1} = Y_j + \Delta t \frac{dY}{dt}\bigg|_{t_j} + \frac{(\Delta t)^2}{2}\frac{d^2 Y}{dt^2}\bigg|_{t_j} + \frac{(\Delta t)^3}{3!}\frac{d^3 Y}{dt^3}\bigg|_{t_j} + \cdots \tag{9.24}$$

But $\dfrac{dY}{dt}\bigg|_{t_j} = f(Y_j, t_j)$, $\dfrac{d^2 Y}{dt^2}\bigg|_{t_j} = f'(Y_j, t_j)$, etc.   Thus (9.24) can be written as

$$Y_{j+1} = Y_j + \Delta t\, f(Y_j, t_j) + \frac{(\Delta t)^2}{2} f'(Y_j, t_j) + \frac{(\Delta t)^3}{3!} f''(Y_j, t_j) + \cdots \tag{9.25}$$

Subtracting (9.25) from (9.23) yields

$$y_{j+1} - Y_{j+1} = E_{j+1} = -\frac{(\Delta t)^2}{2} f'(Y_j, t_j) + \mathcal{O}(\Delta t)^3 \tag{9.26}$$

But $y_{j+1} - Y_{j+1}$ is exactly the error made by using a finite difference method to take the step from t_j to t_{j+1} starting with the exact solution at t_j.   We will term E_{j+1} the *truncation error of the formula (9.17) per step*.   Thus we see that the truncation error per step of the Euler formula is $\mathcal{O}(\Delta t)^2$.   This is by far the easiest form of truncation error to evaluate.   However, this error is obviously not the total solution error at t_{j+1} due to the use of the finite difference method, except for the first step where $y_j = y(0)$ is the initial condition and is presumably exact.   For any other step, the value of y_j will involve error accumulated in previous steps.

We will now estimate the total solution error due to truncation for the Euler method.   Subtracting (9.25) from (9.22), we obtain

$$y_{j+1} - Y_{j+1} = y_j - Y_j + \Delta t[f(y_j, t_j) - f(Y_j, t_j)] - \frac{(\Delta t)^2}{2} f'(Y_j, t_j) + \mathcal{O}(\Delta t)^3$$

$$= y_j - Y_j + \Delta t[f(y_j, t_j) - f(Y_j, t_j)] + E_{j+1} \tag{9.27}$$

Since we no longer require that the finite difference solution start from an exact value at t_j, then y_j will include error propagated from earlier values of t.   If we assume that the finite difference solution was started from the initial condition, then $y_{j+1} - Y_{j+1}$ represents the total solution error due to truncation at t_{j+1}.   We denote this as ϵ_{j+1}.   Then (9.27) can be written as

$$\epsilon_{j+1} = \epsilon_j + \Delta t[f(y_j, t_j) - f(Y_j, t_j)] + E_{j+1} \tag{9.28}$$

Following Crandall[18], we note that

$$\frac{f(y_j, t_j) - f(Y_j, t_j)}{y_j - Y_j} = \frac{\partial f}{\partial y}(\xi_j, t_j) \tag{9.29}$$

if f has a continuous partial derivative with respect to y, and ξ_j is somewhere between y_j and Y_j.   (One of the mean value theorems of calculus states that under certain conditions on f, such a difference expression will always be equal to the derivative evaluated somewhere between the end points used in forming the difference expression.) Using (9.29) and denoting $\frac{\partial f}{\partial y}(\xi_j, t_j)$ as p_j, equation (9.28) becomes

$$\epsilon_{j+1} = \epsilon_j + \Delta t[\epsilon_j p_j] + E_{j+1} = \epsilon_j[1 + (\Delta t)p_j] + E_{j+1} \tag{9.30}$$

Even for such a simple method as the Euler method, (9.30) is not practical to evaluate, since p and E would have to be evaluated at each step. However, we can gain an estimate of ϵ_{j+1} by assuming that p and E are constant over the interval of interest. Then (9.30) becomes

$$\epsilon_{j+1} = \epsilon_j[1 + (\Delta t)p] + E \tag{9.31}$$

Now, starting from the initial condition $j = 0$, $y_0 = y(0) = Y(0)$ so

$$\epsilon_0 = 0$$

$$\epsilon_1 = E$$

$$\epsilon_2 = E[1 + (\Delta t)p] + E = 2E + E(\Delta t)p$$

$$\epsilon_3 = E[2 + (\Delta t)p][1 + (\Delta t)p] + E = 3E + E(\Delta t)^2 p^2 + 3E(\Delta t)p$$

$$\epsilon_4 = E[2 + (\Delta t)p][1 + (\Delta t)p]^2 + E[1 + (\Delta t)p] + E = 4E + \mathcal{O}(\Delta t)^3$$

$$\vdots$$

$$\epsilon_{j+1} = (j + 1)E + \mathcal{O}(\Delta t)^j$$

Recall that $E = \mathcal{O}(\Delta t)^2$, and note that $t_{j+1} = (j + 1)\Delta t$. Then ϵ_{j+1} can be written as

$$\epsilon_{j+1} \approx \frac{t_{j+1}}{\Delta t} E \approx \frac{t_{j+1}}{\Delta t} \mathcal{O}(\Delta t)^2 = \mathcal{O}(\Delta t) \tag{9.32}$$

Thus we find that the total error in the numerical solution due to truncation is $\mathcal{O}(\Delta t)$ for Euler's method or one order less than the truncation error of the formula per step. Since it is the total error due to truncation which is of primary concern in practice, it is this error order which is used to characterize the method. Thus the Euler method is termed a *first order method*.

A similar relationship between truncation error per step and total solution error due to truncation holds for the higher order methods to be discussed later in this chapter. Thus a method which has a truncation error per step of $\mathcal{O}(\Delta t)^5$ is termed a fourth order method, since this is the order of the total solution error due to truncation.

9.4 CONVERGENCE AND STABILITY

In this section the basic concepts of convergence and stability and the practical implications of these properties will be discussed, but we will avoid a detailed mathematical approach for reasons which will be indicated later. The interested reader will find an abundance of mathematical detail in Henrici[17] and Ralston[3].

A numerical method applied to a given differential equation* is termed convergent if, assuming there is no roundoff error, the numerical solution approaches the exact solution

---

*For convenience, we refer to a single differential equation. Except as noted, the discussion applies also to sets of differential equations.

to the differential equation as the step size Δt approaches zero.   This is generally not a problem of practical concern, since all standard numerical techniques are convergent when applied to virtually any differential equation.   This does *not* mean that in practice the numerical solution will always approach the exact solution to the differential equation as $\Delta t \rightarrow 0$, since roundoff error will inevitably be present in any real computation.

The stability of the numerical method used to solve a given differential equation is a matter of considerable practical importance.   We should first emphasize that the property of stability (or instability) is actually a joint property of the method and the differential equations and not of either one alone.   (The term "stability" is also widely used to describe a certain behavior of the exact solution to a differential equation.   The two concepts of stability are not directly related, although as we shall presently see, it is sometimes difficult to distinguish between their effects.)

The ideas behind the stability of numerical methods for ordinary differential equations can best be illustrated by considering multistep methods.   These methods involve values of $f(y,t)$ at several points along the t axis.   The multistep formulas are, of course, nothing more than difference representations of the original differential equation.   These difference equations can, in theory, be solved analytically, although actual analytical solutions can usually only be obtained for extremely simple cases.   Nevertheless, the general form of the analytical solutions is such that the presence of the multiple values of $f(y,t)$ along the t axis results in multiple solutions to the difference equation.   If the method is convergent for the problem being considered, one of these solutions to the difference equation (called the *fundamental solution*) will approximate the exact solution to the differential equation, and will approach this exact solution arbitrarily closely as $\Delta t \rightarrow 0$ (except for roundoff error).   The remaining solutions to the difference equation are termed *parasitic solutions*, and it is the behavior of these solutions which determines whether or not the numerical solution is stable.

These parasitic solutions acquire their name from the fact that they feed on errors in the numerical solution (such errors will always be present, due to truncation and roundoff).   Instability is the result of a feedback process in which the parasitic solutions grow as each succeeding step is taken in obtaining the solution, and the resulting increased error causes an increased growth rate in these solutions.   The growth of the parasitic solution is usually exponential (of the form Ae^{ct}) and is often oscillatory.   The fundamental solution is soon overpowered, and the resulting numerical solution no longer bears any resemblance to the exact solution of the differential equation.

Having discussed instability, we can now see that a stable numerical solution is one in which the parasitic solutions remain small relative to the fundamental solution of the difference equation, and that the fundamental solution thus remains a reasonably good approximation to the exact solution of the differential equation (as long as Δt is sufficiently small).   This does not mean that there cannot be cumulative growth of both truncation and roundoff error.   As was mentioned earlier, the marching-type solution to an initial value problem corresponds in many ways to an extrapolation, and it is entirely reasonable to expect cumulative error as an extrapolation is extended farther and farther.   However, any errors will at worst grow at a nearly constant rate in a stable solution, but will be strongly amplified in an unstable one, due to the growth of the parasitic solutions.

In almost all situations, it is easy to distinguish an unstable numerical solution from a stable one, due to the exponential growth of the error in an unstable solution.   However, if the exact solution of the differential equation grows strongly with time (which in some contexts is also called an instability), it may be difficult to distinguish between the two effects. However, the unstable numerical effects are dependent on step size (Δt). Thus, if numerical solutions are obtained with two significantly different (and reasonably small) step sizes and show significant differences, it is reasonable to assume that a numerical instability is present. If the two solutions are essentially the same, then the numerical solution is probably stable and is reproducing the solution to the differential equation reasonably well.

We have foregone a formal mathematical presentation of stability, simply because it is not practical to perform a formal stability analysis on any real problem. In practice, the procedure is to choose a suitable method, and to assume that there will not be any difficulty with stability. If instability is encountered, then it may be worthwhile to try the same method with a reduced step size in hopes of curing the problem. If the problem persists, the alternative is to change to a different method, and this strategy will usually have the desired result.

9.5 RUNGE-KUTTA TYPE FORMULAS

Formulas of the Runge-Kutta type are among the most widely used formulas for the numerical solution of ordinary differential equations. We will begin our discussion of these somewhat controversial methods by listing the positive and negative aspects of their use. Their advantages include:

1. They are easy to program.
2. They have good stability characteristics.
3. The step size can be changed as desired without any complications.
4. They are self-starting. (This is perhaps the most important advantage of these methods, but it cannot be appreciated until we discuss the methods which are not self-starting.)

Their primary disadvantages are:

1. They require significantly more computer time than other methods of comparable accuracy.
2. Local error estimates are somewhat difficult to obtain.

It is probably a fair summary of the current attitude toward these formulas to state that numerical analysts feel that they are only worth using to start more efficient methods (such as the predictor-corrector methods discussed in Sec. 9.7). However, Runge-Kutta methods are widely used to solve complete problems by those users who are less theoretically inclined, and who need a simple, easy-to-program method which yields reasonably accurate results.

The author is inclined to sympathize with these users, as long as the problem is one which will be run a relatively small number of times with a small expenditure of computer time (or money) per run. In fact, many of the small example problems at the end of this chapter have been solved using Runge-Kutta methods. However, if a substantial computing investment is involved (as in production codes), then the user would be wise to consider one of the more efficient methods to be discussed later in this chapter. At the end of the present section, we will explore ways of ensuring that the results obtained from Runge-Kutta type methods are reasonably accurate.

We are now ready to discuss the methods themselves. It is beyond the scope of this text to give the theoretical background and derivation of these formulas. The ignorance of their origins in no way impairs their usefulness. The curious can find the details of their derivation in Ralston[3].

One of the simplest of the Runge-Kutta type formulas is

$$y_{j+1} = y_j + \Delta t \, f(y^*_{j+1/2}, t_{j+1/2})$$

(9.33)

where

$$y^*_{j+1/2} = y_j + \frac{\Delta t}{2} f(y_j, t_j)$$

and

$$t_{j+1/2} = t_j + \frac{\Delta t}{2}$$

This is a second order formula. Note that the formula is not a multistep formula in the usual sense (no values of y earlier than y_j are required) and hence the formula is self-starting. However, $f(y,t)$ is evaluated more than once (twice in the present case). One evaluation is at (y_j, t_j). Then $y^*_{j+1/2}$ is obtained, which is a simple Euler estimate of y at $t_{j+1/2} = t_j + \Delta t/2$. Next $f(y^*_{j+1/2}, t_{j+1/2})$ is evaluated, and used in finding y_{j+1}. This multiple evaluation of f for different values of y and t provides additional information about the behavior of f and hence serves to increase the accuracy.

The most widely used formula of the Runge-Kutta type is the fourth order formula, which is usually referred to as *the* Runge-Kutta formula:

$$y_{j+1} = y_j + \Delta t \left[\frac{1}{6} f(y_j, t_j) + \frac{1}{3} f(y^*_{j+1/2}, t_{j+1/2}) \right.$$

$$\left. + \frac{1}{3} f(y^{**}_{j+1/2}, t_{j+1/2}) + \frac{1}{6} f(y^*_{j+1}, t_{j+1}) \right]$$

(9.34)

where

$$y^*_{j+1/2} = y_j + \frac{\Delta t}{2} f(y_j, t_j)$$

$$y^{**}_{j+1/2} = y_j + \frac{\Delta t}{2} f(y^*_{j+1/2}, t_{j+1/2})$$

$$y^*_{j+1} = y_j + \Delta t \, f(y^{**}_{j+1/2}, t_{j+1/2})$$

The intermediate values $y^*_{j+1/2}$, $y^{**}_{j+1/2}$, and y^*_{j+1} must be computed in the order given since they are interdependent. This formula requires four evaluations of f, which for complicated functions can be quite time consuming.

Another fourth order formula of the Runge-Kutta type uses different coefficients in order to minimize truncation error. See Ralston[3] for details. Runge-Kutta formulas of sixth order[19] and eighth order[20] are also available but are much less commonly employed.

It is essential (as with all methods) to verify that the step size is sufficiently small to give accurate answers. This can be done on a qualitative basis by running the problem with two different step sizes (the most common procedure is to halve the step size after the first run and then rerun the problem). If the answers agree "well enough," perhaps to 4 or 5 digits, then they can usually be considered reasonably accurate (see Problem 9.7).

A more quantitative estimate of the truncation error per step (not the total solution error) can be found by using a variation of the same interval halving approach mentioned above.   Starting from t_j, one step is taken using a given value of Δt.   Now, again starting from t_j, two steps of $\Delta t/2$ are used to arrive at the same point $(t + \Delta t)$ as with the coarser step.   If the value obtained using one step of Δt is denoted as y_{j+1}, and that using two steps of $\Delta t/2$ is denoted as $\hat{y}_{j+1}$, then an estimate of the truncation error incurred between t_j and t_{j+1} is obtained by the expression

$$E_{j+1} \approx \frac{\hat{y}_{j+1} - y_{j+1}}{2^{-k} - 1} \tag{9.35}$$

where k is the order of the method ($k = 4$ for the usual Runge-Kutta formula (9.34)).   The step size can be adjusted as desired to keep this error estimate below some predetermined tolerance.

We should note that Runge-Kutta formulas are sometimes also called "single-step" formulas since the solution is carried directly from t_j to t_{j+1}, without requiring values of y or f for $t < t_j$.

9.6   THE ADAMS FORMULAS—A CLASS OF MULTISTEP FORMULAS

The Adams multistep formulas are particularly easy to derive, yet these formulas or variations of them are used in some of the most efficient modern packaged computer sub-routines for the solution of ordinary differential equations.   Multistep formulas in general, and the Adams formulas in particular, fall into two general categories: open formulas and closed formulas.   Each of these categories has its own place in the numerical solution of ordinary differential equations, and we will first examine them separately.

The Adams Open Formulas (Adams-Bashforth Formulas)

Consider once again the initial value problem

$$\frac{dy}{dt} = f(y,t) \tag{9.36}$$

$$y(0) = y_0 \tag{9.37}$$

We begin the derivation of the open formulas by performing a forward Taylor series expansion about an arbitrary value of t:

$$y(t + \Delta t) = y(t) + \Delta t\, y'(t) + \frac{(\Delta t)^2}{2!} y''(t) + \frac{(\Delta t)^3}{3!} y'''(t) + \cdots \tag{9.38}$$

Denoting t as t_j and employing the usual subscript notation yields

$$y_{j+1} = y_j + \Delta t\, y_j' + \frac{(\Delta t)^2}{2} y_j'' + \frac{(\Delta t)^3}{3!} y_j''' + \cdots \tag{9.39}$$

But $y_j' = f_j$, $y_j'' = f_j'$, etc. and (9.39) may be written as

$$y_{j+1} = y_j + \Delta t \left[f_j + \frac{\Delta t}{2} f_j' + \frac{(\Delta t)^2}{3!} f_j'' + \cdots \right] \tag{9.40}$$

If (9.40) is truncated after the first term in the bracket (f_j), the Euler formula (9.17) is reproduced, and this can be considered to be the first of the open Adams formulas as well.   More accurate formulas can be obtained by replacing the derivatives in (9.40) by backward differences.   For example,

$$f'_j = \frac{f_j - f_{j-1}}{\Delta t} + \frac{\Delta t}{2} f''_j + \mathcal{O}(\Delta t)^2 \tag{9.41}$$

Substituting (9.41) into (9.40) yields

$$y_{i+1} = y_i + \Delta t \left\{ f_j + \frac{\Delta t}{2} \left[\frac{f_j - f_{j-1}}{\Delta t} + \frac{\Delta t}{2} f''_j + \mathcal{O}(\Delta t)^2 \right] + \frac{(\Delta t)^2}{3!} f''_j + \cdots \right\} \tag{9.42}$$

or, collecting terms,

$$y_{i+1} = y_i + \Delta t \left[\frac{3}{2} f_j - \frac{1}{2} f_{j-1} \right] + \frac{5}{12} (\Delta t)^3 f''_j + \mathcal{O}(\Delta t)^4 \tag{9.43}$$

Thus

$$y_{i+1} = y_i + \Delta t \left[\frac{3}{2} f_j - \frac{1}{2} f_{j-1} \right] + \mathcal{O}(\Delta t)^3 \tag{9.44}$$

is the second open Adams formula, and is of second order. These formulas are called *open* formulas since y_{i+1} can be solved for explicitly in terms of values of y_i, f_j, f_{j-1}, etc., which are assumed known. However, at the initial condition ($t = 0$), the only known quantities are one value of y (the initial value y_0) and the corresponding value of f. Therefore, the formula (9.44), which requires two values of f (f_i and f_{j-1}) in order to solve for each new y, cannot be started from $t = 0$. The formula (9.44) and all higher order open Adams formulas are thus not self-starting. In order to start such a formula, the most common practice is to employ a formula of the Runge-Kutta type which is of the same error order as the formula to be started. Thus the second-order Runge-Kutta formula (9.33) could be used to start (9.44).

The next higher order formula can be found from (9.40) by substituting the backward difference expression for f''_j:

$$f''_j = \frac{f_j - 2f_{j-1} + f_{j-2}}{(\Delta t)^2} + \mathcal{O}(\Delta t) \tag{9.45}$$

Substituting this expression into (9.40) and collecting terms yields

$$y_{i+1} = y_i + \Delta t \left[\frac{23}{12} f_j - \frac{16}{12} f_{j-1} + \frac{5}{12} f_{j-2} \right] + \mathcal{O}(\Delta t)^4 \tag{9.46}$$

which is of third order. To obtain more accurate formulas, the correct error terms would have to be included for (9.45) as well as for the difference representations of higher order derivatives. The derivations will not be carried out here. The open Adams formulas

Table 9.1   Coefficients β_{nk} of the Open Adams Formulas

n \ k	0	1	2	3	4	5	Order of Method
0	1						1
1	3/2	−1/2					2
2	23/12	−16/12	5/12				3
3	55/24	−59/24	37/24	−9/24			4
4	1901/720	−2774/720	2616/720	−1274/720	251/720		5
5	4277/1440	−7923/1440	9982/1440	−7298/1440	2877/1440	−475/1440	6

may be written in general as

$$y_{j+1} = y_j + \Delta t \sum_{k=0}^{n} \beta_{nk} f_{j-k} + \mathcal{O}(\Delta t)^{n+2} \tag{9.47}$$

where the order of the method is one less than the order of the truncation error per step indicated in (9.47). The coefficients β_{nk} are given in Henrici[17] and are shown in Table 9.1 for values of n up to $n = 5$.

The Adams Closed Formulas (Adams-Moulton Formulas)

The method of derivation for the closed formulas is very similar to that employed for the open formulas. However, for the closed formulas, a backward Taylor series expansion is used to yield

$$y(t) = y(t + \Delta t) - (\Delta t)y'(t + \Delta t) + \frac{(\Delta t)^2}{2} y''(t + \Delta t) - \frac{(\Delta t)^3}{3!} y'''(t + \Delta t) + \cdots \tag{9.48}$$

Employing the subscript notation and noting that $y' = f$, $y'' = f'$, etc., (9.48) becomes

$$y_j = y_{j+1} - (\Delta t)f_{j+1} + \frac{(\Delta t)^2}{2} f'_{j+1} - \frac{(\Delta t)^3}{3!} f''_{j+1} + \cdots \tag{9.49}$$

Solving for y_{j+1} yields

$$y_{j+1} = y_j + \Delta t \left[f_{j+1} - \frac{(\Delta t)}{2} f'_{j+1} + \frac{(\Delta t)^2}{3!} f''_{j+1} + \cdots \right] \tag{9.50}$$

The first Adams closed formula is found by truncating the expression in the bracket after f_{j+1} to yield

$$y_{j+1} = y_j + (\Delta t)f_{j+1} + \mathcal{O}(\Delta t)^2 \tag{9.51}$$

This formula is termed *closed* since the expression for y_{j+1} involves f_{j+1}, which in turn will, in general, involve y_{j+1}. An iterative method will thus be required in order to solve for y_{j+1}. This iteration will consist of estimating y_{j+1}, evaluating f_{j+1}, then obtaining a new estimate of y_{j+1} by using (9.51), and repeating the process until it converges to any desired accuracy.

The higher order formulas are obtained by replacing the derivatives of f in (9.50) with backward difference representations. For example,

$$f'_{j+1} = \frac{f_{j+1} - f_j}{\Delta t} + \mathcal{O}(\Delta t) \tag{9.52}$$

Substituting this representation into (9.50) and collecting terms yields the second order method

$$y_{j+1} = y_j + \Delta t \left[\frac{1}{2} f_{j+1} + \frac{1}{2} f_j \right] + \mathcal{O}(\Delta t)^3 \tag{9.53}$$

(The observant reader will note that we have rediscovered the trapezoidal rule!) This formula happens to be self-starting since no points behind t_j are involved. However, all of the closed Adams formulas of order higher than 2 are not self-starting.

We will not carry out the derivation of the higher order formulas. The closed Adams formulas may be written as

$$y_{j+1} = y_j + \Delta t \sum_{k=0}^{n} \beta_{nk}^* f_{j+1-k} + \mathcal{O}(\Delta t)^{n+2} \qquad (9.54)$$

The coefficients β_{nk}^* are given in Ref. 17 and are shown in Table 9.2 for values of n up to $n = 5$.

Table 9.2   The Coefficients β_{nk}^* of the Closed Adams Formulas

k n	0	1	2	3	4	5	Order of Method
0	1						1
1	1/2	1/2					2
2	5/12	8/12	−1/12				3
3	9/24	19/24	−5/24	1/24			4
4	251/720	646/720	−264/720	106/720	−19/720		5
5	475/1440	1427/1440	−798/1440	482/1440	−173/1440	27/1440	6

One could reasonably ask at this point why the closed Adams formulas should even be considered, since the iterative solution required for the closed formulas is obviously more time consuming than the explicit solution which can be obtained for the open Adams formulas.   The answer is simply that the *actual* error of a closed formula of a given order is considerably less than that of an open formula of the same order.   (This assumes that the closed formula is iterated an infinite number of times.   This relationship between the accuracies of the two types of formulas usually still holds, even if the closed formula is iterated a relatively small number of times, if the initial guess supplied to the closed formula is reasonably accurate.)

There are many types of open and closed formulas other than the Adams type, but we will not consider them here.   See Refs. 17 and 18 for descriptions of some of these other formulas.

We have discussed the open and closed Adams formulas at some length.   We must admit at this point that these formulas (or any other open or closed formulas) are seldom used by themselves in practice.   However, a combination of open and closed formulas provides a very powerful tool which we will discuss in the next section.

9.7 PREDICTOR-CORRECTOR METHODS

The primary advantage of closed formulas is their accuracy, and the primary disadvantage is the time consuming iterative procedure necessary for their solution.   Thus it would seem that the most effective procedures involving closed formulas would be those which would also include an accurate method of providing a first estimate of the solution at each step in order to minimize the number of iterations necessary to converge the closed formula.   The logical choice to provide this first estimate is an open formula of at least the error order of the closed formula.   Thus, for example, we might choose as a "predictor" the fourth-order open Adams formula

$$y_{j+1}^{(0)} = y_j + \Delta t \left[\frac{55}{24} f_j - \frac{59}{24} f_{j-1} + \frac{37}{24} f_{j-2} - \frac{9}{24} f_{j-3} \right] \qquad (9.55)$$

and as a "corrector" the fourth-order closed Adams formula

$$y_{j+1}^{(l+1)} = y_j + \Delta t \left[\frac{9}{24} f_{j+1}^{(l)} + \frac{19}{24} f_j - \frac{5}{24} f_{j-1} + \frac{1}{24} f_{j-2} \right] \tag{9.56}$$

The calculational procedure could then be to first use a fourth-order (or higher) Runge-Kutta type formula to obtain the values of y and f for the first three steps of Δt beyond the initial condition. With these starting values, the predictor (9.55) can be used to estimate the next value of y, denoted as $y_{j+1}^{(0)}$. With this value as a first estimate, the corrector (9.56) can be iterated until the desired degree of convergence is obtained. As many steps as needed can now be taken, beginning with the predictor, and finishing with the corrector, until the desired maximum value of t is reached. The predicted value of y_{j+1} can be considerably improved by combining the error series for the predictor and corrector to provide an estimate of the error in the predictor. The error correction is carried out by the use of the following modifier after the predictor:

$$\tilde{y}_{j+1}^{(0)} = y_{j+1}^{(0)} - \frac{251}{270} (y_j - y_j^{(0)}) \tag{9.57}$$

where $y_j^{(0)}$ is the unmodified predicted value from the last step. The procedure is thus to apply the predictor (9.55), the modifier (9.57), and then iterate the corrector (9.56) as desired. The use of the modifier will in general reduce the number of iterations required of the corrector. The modifier is not used for the first step (after the starting values have been obtained) since no predicted value from the preceding step is available.

Another widely used and effective predictor-corrector scheme is termed Hamming's method[3]. This method consists of the following:

Predictor:

$$y_{j+1}^{(0)} = y_{j-3} + \frac{4}{3} (\Delta t)(2f_j - f_{j-1} + 2f_{j-2}) \tag{9.58}$$

Modifier:

$$\tilde{y}_{j+1}^{(0)} = y_{j+1}^{(0)} + \frac{112}{121} (y_j - y_j^{(0)}) \tag{9.59}$$

Corrector:

$$y_{j+1}^{(l+1)} = \frac{1}{8} (9y_j - y_{j-2}) + \frac{3}{8} (\Delta t)(f_{j+1}^{(l)} + 2f_j - f_{j-1}) \tag{9.60}$$

One of the most valuable aspects of the use of predictor-corrector methods is the ability to estimate the truncation error of the formula (E_{j+1}) at each step. The availability of both a predicted value and a converged corrected value makes it possible to eliminate terms between the error series for both the predictor and the corrector, and thus to estimate E_{j+1}. (Note that this is *not* the total solution error.) We will not show the details here, but will give the truncation error estimates for the two predictor-corrector schemes we have mentioned:

Adams fourth order:

$$E_{j+1} \approx \frac{19}{270} [y_{j+1} - y_{j+1}^{(0)}] \tag{9.61}$$

Hamming:

$$E_{j+1} \approx \frac{9}{121}[y_{j+1} - y_{j+1}^{(0)}] \tag{9.62}$$

The calculation of the truncation error estimate (*9.62*) for Hamming's method is illustrated in Problem 9.5.

With this truncation error estimate in hand, we can determine whether it might be necessary to reduce the step size or possibly to allow it to be increased.

The changing of step size (Δt) in the course of a solution is somewhat awkward when predictor-corrector methods are used. This is due to the evenly spaced values of f that are required for the open and closed multistep formulas used in predictor-corrector methods. However, certain strategies can be employed to allow step size changes. One approach is to simply restart the entire procedure, using the last obtained value of y as an initial condition, and continuing with the new step size. This approach requires the use of a starting method (probably Runge-Kutta) and hence may also require that several steps (perhaps 3 or 4) be taken with the new step size before consideration can be given to again changing the step size. A more efficient strategy is to interpolate (and, if necessary, extrapolate) for the required values of f with the new spacing. Thus if an error analysis or other consideration indicates a reduction in step size, the procedure might be as shown in Fig. 9.3.

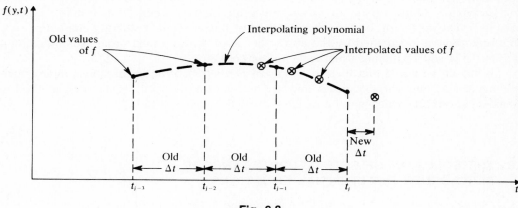

Fig. 9.3

A polynomial can be passed through the stored values of $f(y,t)$ with the old step size spacing, and values which have the desired new step size spacing can be obtained by interpolation on this polynomial. After one step with the new step size, the step size can be changed again if desired, and the same procedure followed.

The efficiency of predictor-corrector methods is one of the primary reasons for their current popularity. For many problems, the most time consuming (and hence expensive) part of the numerical solution is the evaluation of the derivative $f(y,t)$. Recall that the fourth-order Runge-Kutta formula (*9.34*) required four evaluations of f at each step. A typical predictor-corrector method (regardless of order) requires one evaluation of

f (at t_j) for the predictor (all of the other values of f will have been previously computed and stored) and one evaluation of f (at t_{j+1}) for each iteration of the corrector. Thus three iterations could be performed on the corrector before the total number of evaluations of f would equal that required by the Runge-Kutta formula. In practice, one or two iterations of the corrector will usually be sufficient to meet most reasonable convergence criteria, although three or more iterations may occasionally be necessary. For most problems, predictor-corrector methods can thus be considered as using less computer time than Runge-Kutta formulas of the same order. (Many factors other than the number of evaluations of f must be included in order to assess accurately the relative efficiencies of different techniques; detailed discussion is beyond the scope of this text, but some very interesting comparisons can be found in Ref. 21.)

Some sources recommend that the corrector should be iterated only once, regardless of whether or not any convergence criterion is satisfied. However, this can occasionally be dangerous, particularly if the step sizes are fairly coarse. Henrici[17] does give a proof that at least the error *order* is preserved if the predictor and the corrector are of the same order and the corrector is iterated only once. In the author's opinion, the best approach is usually to iterate the corrector as many times as necessary to meet a reasonable convergence criterion, although it is also usually desirable to set some upper limit on the number of iterations. This number might be approximately 3 for efficiency, more for ensured accuracy. If this limit is exceeded, the result can be flagged and/or the program terminated if desired.

We have not yet considered the problem of stability for predictor-corrector methods. The stability of the predictor is not of concern since it is only used to provide a first estimate. Many commonly used predictors have rather poor stability characteristics. The corrector, on the other hand, must have excellent stability characteristics. This requirement is satisfied by the correctors used in the fourth order Adams method (9.55)–(9.57) and Hamming's method (9.58)–(9.60).

It should be noted that the most modern predictor-corrector methods employ variable mesh size and variable order and are self-starting as well. One such method is Gear's method[22], which will be discussed briefly in Sec. 9.10.

9.8 THE SOLUTION OF SETS OF SIMULTANEOUS FIRST-ORDER DIFFERENTIAL EQUATIONS

As we have seen in Sec. 9.1, any differential equation (or set of differential equations) of any order can be written as a coupled set of first-order differential equations of the form

$$\frac{dy_1}{dt} = f_1(y_1, y_2, y_3, \ldots, y_n, t)$$

$$\frac{dy_2}{dt} = f_2(y_1, y_2, y_3, \ldots, y_n, t)$$

$$\frac{dy_3}{dt} = f_3(y_1, y_2, y_3, \ldots, y_n, t) \qquad (9.63)$$

$$\vdots$$

$$\frac{dy_n}{dt} = f_n(y_1, y_2, y_3, \ldots, y_n, t)$$

or

$$\frac{d\bar{y}}{dt} = \bar{f}(\bar{y}, t) \tag{9.64}$$

where $d\bar{y}/dt$, $\bar{f}$, and $\bar{y}$ are n-dimensional vectors. This is a particularly convenient form to use on a computer, since the vectors $\bar{f}$ and $\bar{y}$ can be stored and manipulated as arrays.

The Runge-Kutta formulas require the calculation of several intermediate values of f between t_j and t_{j+1}. Before each of these values of f can be calculated, a corresponding value of y must be found. For a coupled set of equations, f and y become the vectors $\bar{f}$ and $\bar{y}$ as indicated in (9.64). Thus the complete vectors $\bar{y}$ and then $\bar{f}$ must be calculated at each intermediate point before moving to the next intermediate calculation. In the notation used for the fourth-order Runge-Kutta formula (9.34), the computations must be carried by first finding $\bar{f}(\bar{y}_j, t_j)$, then $\bar{y}_{j+1/2}^*$, then $\bar{f}(\bar{y}_{j+1/2}^*, t_{j+1/2})$, then $\bar{y}_{j+1/2}^{**}$, etc. Since there is cross-coupling between the equations for these vectors, it is necessary to update *all* components of each vector before moving on to the next vector. The method is illustrated in detail in Problem 9.2.

For all multistep formulas, it is necessary to store sets of vectors $\bar{f}(\bar{y}_{j-1}, t_{j-1})$, $\bar{f}(\bar{y}_{j-2}, t_{j-2})$, etc. at as many points as required by the formula, and any vectors $\bar{y}$ which may be needed. For the open formulas, it is only necessary to calculate the vector $\bar{f}(\bar{y}_j, t_j)$ and then the vector $\bar{y}_{j+1}$. For a predictor-corrector scheme, the predicted vector $\bar{y}_{j+1}^{(0)}$ is first calculated ($\bar{f}(\bar{y}_j, t_j)$ is available from the preceding step), then a modifier is applied if desired to find $\bar{y}_{j+1}^{(0)}$, and finally the corrector is iterated as many times as desired, calculating $\bar{f}(\bar{y}_{j+1}, t_{j+1})$ and $\bar{y}_{j+1}$ in order until the specified convergence level is attained on *all* components of $\bar{y}_{j+1}$.

9.9   BOUNDARY VALUE PROBLEMS

Two-point boundary value problems were defined at the beginning of this chapter as consisting of a set of one or more ordinary differential equations, with associated boundary conditions which are specified at two different values of the independent variable. The numerical approach to the solution of boundary value problems can best be illustrated by use of an example. We choose as an example the following boundary value problem:

$$\frac{d^2y}{dx^2} + Ay = B$$

$$y(0) = 0, \quad y(L) = 0 \tag{9.65}$$

We can now consider the two principal classes of methods used for solving this (or any other) boundary value problem.

Matrix Methods

We will consider, by means of an example, one possible approach to second-order boundary value problems which results in a matrix formulation. Other approaches are given by Keller[23].

For the example problem (9.65), the region $0 \leq x \leq L$ is first divided into $n + 1$ equally spaced intervals of length Δx as shown in Fig. 9.4.

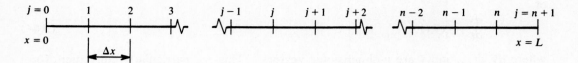

Fig. 9.4 Finite difference grid for boundary value problem.

The differential equation can now be represented at the point j by

$$\frac{y_{j+1} - 2y_j + y_{j-1}}{(\Delta x)^2} + Ay_j = B \qquad (9.66)$$

The derivative d^2y/dx^2 has been replaced by a central difference representation of $\mathcal{O}(\Delta x)^2$. There are n equations of the form (9.66), one for each interior point of the region shown in Fig. 9.4. There is also one unknown value of y for each interior point of the region. Thus we have n simultaneous linear equations in the n unknowns $y_1, y_2, \ldots, y_n$. After multiplying through each equation by $(\Delta x)^2$, this set of equations can be written as

$$y_2 - 2y_1 + (0) + A(\Delta x)^2 y_1 = B(\Delta x)^2$$

$$y_3 - 2y_2 + y_1 + A(\Delta x)^2 y_2 = B(\Delta x)^2$$

$$\vdots \qquad\qquad (9.67)$$

$$y_n - 2y_{n-1} + y_{n-2} + A(\Delta x)^2 y_{n-1} = B(\Delta x)^2$$

$$(0) - 2y_n + y_{n-1} + A(\Delta x)^2 y_n = B(\Delta x)^2$$

Collecting coefficients of the unknowns, and writing the set (9.67) in matrix form yields

$$\begin{bmatrix} \alpha & 1 & & & & & \\ 1 & \alpha & 1 & & & & \\ & 1 & \alpha & 1 & & & \\ & - & - & - & & & \\ & & - & - & - & & \\ & & & 1 & \alpha & 1 \\ & & & & 1 & \alpha \end{bmatrix} \begin{bmatrix} y_1 \\ y_2 \\ y_3 \\ - \\ - \\ y_{n-1} \\ y_n \end{bmatrix} = \begin{bmatrix} B(\Delta x)^2 \\ B(\Delta x)^2 \\ B(\Delta x)^2 \\ - \\ - \\ B(\Delta x)^2 \\ B(\Delta x)^2 \end{bmatrix} \qquad (9.68)$$

where $\alpha = -2 + A(\Delta x)^2$. The coefficient matrix of this set of equations is tridiagonal, and, as we have seen in Chapter 6, such sets can be solved quite easily and rapidly even if n is very large. The error analysis of the numerical solution of boundary value problems is beyond the scope of this text, but the method being discussed is essentially second order. This error can be made fourth order without increasing the bandwidth of the matrix by using a method discussed by Henrici[17] and Keller[23]. The error order can also be increased by using higher order difference representations for the derivative, but only at the expense of increased bandwidth of the coefficient matrix and some awkward computational problems near the ends of the interval. The easiest method for ensuring accuracy is simply to obtain solutions for several values of Δx, with each value one-half of the preceding value. This procedure can be stopped when the results indicate adequate convergence. Richardson extrapolation can be employed if desired.

Boundary conditions on derivatives (such as on dy/dx in this example) can result in a coefficient matrix with elements off of the tridiagonal band; however, some simple row manipulations of the Gauss elimination type will restore the banded form.

Equations of higher order than two and sets of coupled ordinary differential equations will still result in tridiagonal coefficient matrices if the problem is reformulated as a set of differential equations, each of order no higher than two, and if central difference representations of $\mathcal{O}(\Delta x)^2$ are used for the derivatives.

The main advantage of the matrix approach is its simplicity. The most serious drawback to this technique is the difficulty encountered in dealing with nonlinear differential equations. Consider, for example, a nonlinear differential equation of the form

$$\frac{d^2y}{dx^2} + Dy^2 = E \tag{9.69}$$

Using the same central difference approach as we previously employed for equation (9.65), we obtain

$$\frac{y_{j+1} - 2y_j + y_{j-1}}{(\Delta x)^2} + Dy_j^2 = E \tag{9.70}$$

If this equation is written at each of the interior points of the region of interest, a set of nonlinear algebraic equations results. Iterative techniques must be employed, and difficulties can be encountered in obtaining a solution. This type of problem is discussed in detail in Ref. 17.

In the author's opinion, nonlinear problems can be handled in the most straightforward way by using the initial-value-based methods which we will discuss next.

Shooting Methods

We now take the approach of attempting to convert a boundary value problem into an equivalent initial value problem. This would permit the use of the powerful and accurate techniques developed in preceding sections for initial value problems.

To illustrate the approach, we turn again to the example used earlier:

$$\frac{d^2y}{dx^2} + Ay = B$$
$$y(0) = 0, \quad y(L) = 0 \tag{9.71}$$

This problem can be recast as the following initial value problem:

$$\frac{d^2y}{dx^2} + Ay = B$$
$$y(0) = 0, \quad \frac{dy}{dx}(0) = U \tag{9.72}$$

where U is unknown, and must be chosen such that $y(L) = 0$ and thus the boundary value problem (9.71) is reproduced. If we arbitrarily choose a value for U, and solve the initial value problem (9.72) by any standard numerical method, the solution might appear graphically as shown in Fig. 9.5. (We will assume that the step size is sufficiently small that truncation error is negligible, and we will neglect roundoff error.) Since $y(L)$ is not zero, we have not reproduced the boundary value problem (9.71). (Since $y(L)$ is clearly a

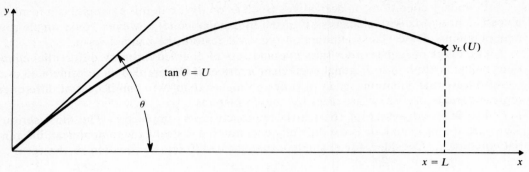

Fig. 9.5

function of U, we have denoted $y(L)$ as $y_L(U)$.)   In order to bring $y_L(U)$ closer to zero, the strategy should apparently be to reduce U.   (The similarity to a ballistics problem is of course the motivation for the term "shooting method.")   Seeking the appropriate value of U in order to satisfy the boundary condition at $x = L$ can be stated as searching for U such that

$$y_L(U) = y(L) = 0 \qquad\qquad (9.73)$$

This is a root solving problem, and we can employ any of the standard methods which do not utilize explicitly the derivative of the function.   Thus bisection or the secant method are likely candidates in this situation.   Since the secant method is more rapidly convergent for well-behaved functions with simple roots, it will usually be the first choice for the present application.

We have only to provide two estimates of the root of (9.73); call them U_{00} and U_0.   Now two solutions of the initial value problem (9.72) are carried out, yielding $y_L(U_{00})$ and $y_L(U_0)$.   A new estimate of U can then be obtained, given by

$$U_1 = U_0 - \frac{y_L(U_0)}{[y_L(U_0) - y_L(U_{00})]/(U_0 - U_{00})} \qquad\qquad (9.74)$$

The process is continued to convergence, with each functional evaluation of $y_L(U)$ requiring a numerical solution of the initial value problem (9.72).   Examples are given in Problems 9.11 and 9.14.

Since iteration to convergence may require from three to ten or more iterations, depending on many factors, it makes good economic sense in many cases to use a reasonably efficient method to solve the initial value problem.   One of the predictor-corrector schemes such as the fourth-order Adams method or Hamming's method would seem suitable.   However, since the solution must be obtained precisely at $x = L$, the use of a method which makes automated step size changes is probably not desirable.   Instead, it may be best to use a fixed step size or a series of predetermined step sizes which together arrive exactly at $x = L$.   (If the end point is not hit exactly, the value of y at this point can be found by interpolation, but this is just another complicating factor and adds to the possibility of error.)

Strategies can be evolved to solve a wide variety of boundary value problems by the shooting approach.   An example of the solution of a boundary value problem involving a third-order differential equation is given in Problem 9.14.

Shooting and Superposition for Linear Equations

There are a wide variety of boundary value problems involving linear ordinary differential equations for which analytical solutions cannot readily be obtained.   Linear differential equations with nonconstant coefficients are often particularly difficult to handle analytically.   The linearity of the differential equation(s) allows the application of a simplified variation of the shooting method to be applied.   Consider once more the (linear) boundary value problem (9.71) which we have seen can be reformulated as the initial value problem (9.72), where U is to be determined such that $y(L) = 0$.   Now consider two different estimates of U; call them U_C and U_D.   Corresponding to each of these estimates, we can obtain, by the usual numerical techniques, a solution to the initial value problem (9.72) which we will assume to have negligible error of any kind.   Call these solutions $y_C(x)$ and $y_D(x)$.   Since the differential equation in (9.72) is linear, and both $y_C(x)$ and $y_D(x)$ are solutions of the differential equation, then so is the sum of these solutions, or in fact any linear combination of these solutions.   Thus

$$y(x) = C_1 y_C(x) + C_2 y_D(x) \tag{9.75}$$

is a solution, where C_1 and C_2 are constants.   This solution automatically satisfies the condition that $y(0) = 0$.   The condition that $y(L) = 0$ yields

$$y(L) = 0 = C_1 y_C(L) + C_2 y_D(L) \tag{9.76}$$

This is one equation in the two unknowns C_1 and C_2.   The additional relation between C_1 and C_2 can in this case be obtained from the differential equation since the differential equation is not homogeneous.   (There must be an inhomogeneity in either the boundary conditions or the differential equation(s) in order to produce a nontrivial solution.) Substituting (9.75) into the differential equation, we find

$$C_1\left(\frac{d^2 y_C}{dx^2} + A y_C\right) + C_2\left(\frac{d^2 y_D}{dx^2} + A y_D\right) = B \tag{9.77}$$

but since $y_C(x)$ and $y_D(x)$ each separately satisfy the differential equation, we find

$$\frac{d^2 y_C}{dx^2} + A y_C = \frac{d^2 y_D}{dx^2} + A y_D = B \tag{9.78}$$

Thus (9.77) becomes

$$C_1 B + C_2 B = B$$

or

$$C_1 + C_2 = 1 \tag{9.79}$$

and from (9.76)

$$C_1 = - C_2 \frac{y_D(L)}{y_C(L)}$$

so

$$C_2 \left[1 - \frac{y_D(L)}{y_C(L)}\right] = 1$$

or

$$C_2 = \frac{1}{[1 - y_D(L)/y_C(L)]} \tag{9.80}$$

and

$$C_1 = 1 - C_2 \tag{9.81}$$

The solution (9.75), with C_2 and C_1 given by (9.80) and (9.81) respectively, now satisfies both the differential equation and the boundary conditions. The uniqueness of the solution to a boundary value problem is ensured if essentially the same weak conditions required for initial value problems are satisfied as specified at the beginning of the chapter. This can be easily demonstrated for the present case and thus (9.75) is *the* solution to the boundary value problem. Therefore, only two solutions to an initial value problem are required to solve a linear boundary value problem. An example of the method is given in Problem 9.12.

9.10   THE STATE OF THE ART

As of this writing, the most effective and efficient numerical techniques available for the solution of ordinary differential equations appear to be either modifications of the well-known predictor-corrector methods, or the relatively new methods based on Richardson extrapolation.

An extremely efficient method based on the Adams predictor-corrector formulas has been presented by Gear[22]. This algorithm adjusts both the order (up to seven) and the mesh size to produce the desired local truncation error level, and is self-starting as well. The algorithm also includes a special approach for dealing with "stiff" differential equations. (See Problem 9.9 for an example of such a differential equation.)

The method of Bulirsch and Stoer[24] is based on the Richardson extrapolation techniques, which we have already seen to be so powerful when employed in Romberg integration. This method has been shown to be capable of producing accuracy comparable to other methods while using step sizes which are much larger than those required by the conventional methods.

Complete descriptions of the algorithms for Gear's method and the method of Bulirsch and Stoer are given in the cited references (as ALGOL procedures) and both methods have been made available by at least one software vendor as packaged subroutines in FORTRAN.

The efficiency of these and other modern methods have been compared in a recent paper[21] which gives an excellent picture of the current state of the art.

Illustrative Problems

A simple fourth-order Runge-Kutta method has been used for some of these problems where the purist might insist on a more efficient method.   This has been done in the interest of simplicity and is not meant to demean the value of the more efficient methods where economics (and ease of evaluation of local truncation error) are of prime concern.

9.1   Using the fourth-order Runge-Kutta formula (*9.34*), page 195, take one step of $\Delta t = 0.1$ for the following initial value problem:

$$\frac{dy}{dt} = \frac{4t}{y} - ty, \qquad y(0) = 3$$

Show the details of the computation.

For this problem,

$$f(y,t) = \frac{4t}{y} - ty$$

We start from $t = t_0 = 0$, $y(0) = y_0 = 3$:

$$f(y_0,t_0) = \frac{4(0)}{3} - (0)3 = 0$$

$$y_{1/2}^* = y_0 + \frac{(\Delta t)}{2} f(y_0,0) = 3 + \frac{0.1}{2}(0) = 3$$

$$f(y_{1/2}^*,t_{1/2}) = \frac{4(0.1/2)}{3} - \left(\frac{0.1}{2}\right)(3) = -0.083333$$

$$y_{1/2}^{**} = y_0 + \frac{(\Delta t)}{2} f(y_{1/2}^*,t_{1/2}) = 3 + \frac{0.1}{2}(-0.083333) = 2.995833$$

$$f(y_{1/2}^{**},t_{1/2}) = \frac{4(0.1/2)}{2.995833} - \frac{0.1}{2}(2.995833) = -0.083033$$

$$y_1^* = y_0 + (\Delta t)f(y_{1/2}^{**},t_{1/2}) = 3 + 0.1(-0.083033) = 2.991697$$

$$f(y_1^*,t_1) = \frac{4(0.1)}{2.991697} - 0.1(2.991697) = -0.165466$$

Now

$$y_1 = y_0 + \Delta t \left[\frac{1}{6} f(y_0,t_0) + \frac{1}{3} f(y_{1/2}^*,t_{1/2}) + \frac{1}{3} f(y_{1/2}^{**},t_{1/2}) + \frac{1}{6} f(y_1^*,t_1)\right]$$

$$= 3 + 0.1 \left[\frac{1}{6}(0) + \frac{1}{3}(-0.083333) + \frac{1}{3}(-0.083033) + \frac{1}{6}(-0.165466)\right]$$

$$= 2.991697$$

9.2   Show one step of the fourth-order Runge-Kutta solution of the following initial value problem:

$$\frac{d^2y}{dt^2} = \frac{y}{e^t + 1}, \qquad y(0) = 1, \qquad \frac{dy}{dt}(0) = 0$$

Use $\Delta t = 0.1$.

We first transform the problem into a set of two first order equations. Let

$$z = \frac{dy}{dt}$$

Then

$$\frac{dz}{dt} = \frac{y}{e^t + 1}, \qquad z(0) = 0$$

and

$$\frac{dy}{dt} = z, \qquad y(0) = 1$$

are the coupled equations which we will solve. For the first step, $y_0 = 1$ and $z_0 = 0$, and we wish to find y_1 and z_1. As discussed in Sec. 9.8, the dependent variables and their derivatives must be dealt with as vectors, and each component of each vector must be calculated before proceeding. Thus

$$f_1(y,z,t) = \frac{y}{e^t + 1}, \qquad f_2(y,z,t) = z$$

are the components of the derivative vector $\bar{f}$. Now

$$f_1(y_0,z_0,t_0) = \frac{1}{e^0 + 1} = 0.5, \qquad f_2(y_0,z_0,t_0) = 0$$

and

$$z_{1/2}^* = z_0 + \frac{(\Delta t)}{2} f_1(y_0,z_0,t_0) = 0 + \frac{0.1}{2}(0.5) = 0.025$$

$$y_{1/2}^* = y_0 + \frac{(\Delta t)}{2} f_2(y_0,z_0,t_0) = 1 + \frac{0.1}{2}(0) = 1$$

We next return to the derivatives

$$f_1(y_{1/2}^*,z_{1/2}^*,t_{1/2}) = \frac{1}{e^{0.05} + 1} = \bar{0}.487503$$

$$f_2(y_{1/2}^*,z_{1/2}^*,t_{1/2}) = 0.025$$

and then calculate again the dependent variables and continue this cyclic process:

$$z_{1/2}^{**} = z_0 + \frac{\Delta t}{2} f_1(y_{1/2}^*,z_{1/2}^*,t_{1/2}) = 0 + \frac{0.1}{2}(0.487503) = 0.024375$$

$$y_{1/2}^{**} = y_0 + \frac{\Delta t}{2} f_2(y_{1/2}^*,z_{1/2}^*,t_{1/2}) = 1 + \frac{0.1}{2}(0.025) = 1.001250$$

$$f_1(y_{1/2}^{**},z_{1/2}^{**},t_{1/2}) = \frac{1.001250}{e^{0.05} + 1} = 0.488112$$

$$f_2(y_{1/2}^{**},z_{1/2}^{**},t_{1/2}) = 0.024375$$

$$z_1^* = z_0 + \Delta t\, f_1(y_{1/2}^{**},z_{1/2}^{**},t_{1/2}) = 0 + 0.1(0.488112) = 0.048811$$

$$y_1^* = y_0 + \Delta t\, f_2(y_{1/2}^{**},z_{1/2}^{**},t_{1/2}) = 1 + 0.1(0.024375) = 1.002438$$

$$f_1(y_1^*,z_1^*,t_1) = \frac{1.002438}{e^{0.1} + 1} = 0.476179$$

$$f_2(y_1^*,z_1^*,t_1) = 0.048811$$

The first step can now be completed:

$$z_1 = z_0 + \Delta t \left[\frac{1}{6} f_1(y_0, z_0, t_0) + \frac{1}{3} f_1(y_{1/2}^*, z_{1/2}^*, t_{1/2}) + \frac{1}{3} f_1(y_{1/2}^{**}, z_{1/2}^{**}, t_{1/2}) + \frac{1}{6} f_1(y_1^*, z_1^*, t_1) \right]$$

$$= 0 + 0.1 \left[\frac{1}{6}(0.5) + \frac{1}{3}(0.487503) + \frac{1}{3}(0.488112) + \frac{1}{6}(0.476179) \right] = 0.048790$$

and

$$y_1 = 1 + 0.1 \left[\frac{1}{6}(0) + \frac{1}{3}(0.025) + \frac{1}{3}(0.024375) + \frac{1}{6}(0.048811) \right] = 1.002459$$

9.3 Given the initial value problem

$$\frac{d^2 y}{dt^2} + 2\frac{dy}{dt} + 4y = 0$$

$$y(0) = 2, \quad \frac{dy}{dt}(0) = 0$$

Compare numerical solutions obtained by Euler and Runge-Kutta methods in the range $0 \le t \le 5$.

The problem is first converted to the first order system

$$\frac{dz}{dt} = -2z - 4y$$

$$z(0) = 0, \quad \frac{dy}{dt} = z, \quad y(0) = 2$$

Numerical solutions to this system by the Euler method for a variety of step sizes and by Runge-Kutta with $\Delta t = 0.1$ are given in Table 9.3 along with the exact solution $y(t) = 2e^{-t}[\cos \sqrt{3}\, x + (1/\sqrt{3}) \sin x]$.

One purpose of this exercise is to illustrate the difficulty of attempting to obtain accurate solutions with a low order method. Using a relatively coarse mesh size of $\Delta t = 0.1$, the fourth-order Runge-Kutta formula yields answers which are in error by no more than 2×10^{-5} at any point shown. In addition, since a relatively small number of steps (50) is required to

Table 9.3

| | Euler | | | | Runge-Kutta | |
| | $\Delta t = 0.1$ | $\Delta t = 0.01$ | $\Delta t = 0.001$ | $\Delta t = 0.0001$ | $\Delta t = 0.1$ | Exact |
t						
0	2.00000	2.00000	2.00000	2.00000	2.00000	2.00000
0.5	1.35936	1.32204	1.31950	1.31784	1.31941	1.31940
1	0.185381	0.290310	0.300021	0.300537	0.301137	0.301149
1.5	−0.429152	−0.264378	−0.250157	−0.247868	−0.248730	−0.248709
2	−0.400114	−0.314608	−0.306954	−0.305134	−0.306259	−0.306245
2.5	−0.121281	−0.147718	−0.148984	−0.148551	−0.149182	−0.149181
3	+0.076168	+0.001436	−0.003992	−0.004495	−0.004572	−0.004579
3.5	0.107975	0.056026	0.051721	+0.051052	+0.051289	+0.051282
4	0.049308	0.043271	0.042095	0.041759	0.041989	0.041987
4.5	−0.008092	0.013009	0.014018	0.014032	0.014131	0.014132
5	−0.026704	−0.005912	−0.004490	−0.004335	−0.004342	−0.004340

cover the region of interest, it is reasonable to expect that the accuracy of these answers could be considerably improved by reducing the step size. However, the first-order Euler method cannot match this accuracy even with $\Delta t = 0.0001$ (50,000 steps to cover the range of interest). At some points in the interval $0 \le t \le 5$, an error of at least 1×10^{-3} is encountered for even the best Euler solutions, those for $\Delta t = 0.001$ and $\Delta t = 0.0001$. No results are given for smaller step sizes since the number of steps is already absurdly large compared to the number required for the fourth-order Runge-Kutta solution. We should note that the form of the differential equation is very simple, otherwise it is likely that roundoff error would be a serious problem for the small step size Euler solutions due to the enormous number of evaluations of $f(y,t)$ involved.

It is reasonable to conclude from this example that the Euler method is simply too inaccurate to employ in practice.

9.4 Solve the initial value problem posed in Problem 9.3 by using the second-order Adams open and closed formulas with $\Delta t = 0.1$ and compare the results.

The second-order Adams open and closed formulas are given in the second line of Tables 9.1 and 9.2, respectively. The open formula is solved in a straightforward way and needs no explanation. For the closed formula, an iterative solution is necessary. Since efficiency is of no concern, the Euler method (first order) is used as a simple predictor. An absolute convergence criterion of 10^{-6} is used to ensure convergence of the closed formula. The number of iterations of the closed formula necessary to attain convergence varies from 6 near $t = 0$ to 4 near $t = 6.0$. The results for $y(t)$ are shown in Table 9.4.

Table 9.4

t	Adams 2nd Order Open	Adams 2nd Order Closed	Exact Solution
0	2.00000	2.00000	2.00000
0.5	1.29784	1.32380	1.31940
1.0	0.288870	0.303185	0.301149
1.5	− 0.237923	− 0.251177	− 0.248709
2.0	− 0.285847	− 0.310339	− 0.306245
2.5	− 0.135850	− 0.151691	− 0.149181
3.0	− 0.003256	− 0.004684	− 0.004579
3.5	+ 0.045696	+ 0.052483	+ 0.051282
4.0	0.036369	0.043119	0.041987
4.5	0.011811	0.014564	0.014132
5.0	− 0.003803	− 0.004484	− 0.004340
5.5	− 0.007122	− 0.008929	− 0.008610
6.0	− 0.004139	− 0.005380	− 0.005170

The increased accuracy of the closed formula is obvious. The error in the solution obtained with the closed formula ranges from about 1% near the beginning of the interval to about 4% near the end of the interval where $y(t)$ becomes quite small. The error in the solution obtained with the open formula ranges from about 4% near the beginning of the interval to over 17% near the end. The motivation for the use of closed formulas to obtain final answers should be apparent, while open formulas of the same order are usually relegated to use as predictors for the closed formulas.

9.5 Illustrate in detail the use of Hamming's method for the following initial value problem:

$$\frac{dy}{dt} = (y + t)^2, \quad y(0) = -1$$

We arbitrarily choose $\Delta t = 0.1$. Some idea of whether this step size is adequate can be obtained by the local error estimates which are possible with a predictor-corrector scheme. For Hamming's method, it is necessary to obtain 3 starting values in addition to the initial condition. We obtain these values with the fourth-order Runge-Kutta formula (*9.34*), and find

$$y(0) = -1 \qquad\qquad \frac{dy}{dt}(0) = 1$$

$$y(0.1) = -0.917628 \qquad \frac{dy}{dt}(0.1) = 0.668516$$

$$y(0.2) = -0.862910 \qquad \frac{dy}{dt}(0.2) = 0.439450$$

$$y(0.3) = -0.827490 \qquad \frac{dy}{dt}(0.3) = 0.278246$$

The value of $y(0.4)$ can now be found using Hamming's method. The predictor (*9.58*), page 200, yields

$$y_4^{(0)} = -1 + \frac{4(0.1)}{3}[2(0.278246) - 0.439450 + 2(0.668516)] = -0.806124$$

Since we have no predicted value from the last step, we cannot use the modifier (*9.59*) and we turn directly to the corrector (*9.60*), page 200:

$$y_4^{(1)} = \frac{1}{8}[9(-0.827490) - (-0.917628)]$$

$$+ \frac{3(0.1)}{8}[(-0.806124 + 0.4)^2 + 2(0.278246) - (0.439450)]$$

$$= -0.805649$$

The expression $(-0.806124 + 0.4)^2$ is the derivative $f(y_4^{(0)}, 0.4)$. The corrected value -0.805649 differs from the predicted value by 0.000475. This is fairly large, so we will iterate the corrector again:

$$y_4^{(2)} = \frac{1}{8}[9(-0.827490) - (-0.917628)]$$

$$+ \frac{3(0.1)}{8}[(-0.805649 + 0.4)^2 + 2(0.278246) - (0.439450)]$$

$$= -0.805663$$

This varies from the last corrected value by 1.4×10^{-5}. A reasonable convergence criterion for the present problem might be an absolute criterion of 1×10^{-5}. If this were used for the present problem, we would be forced to iterate the corrector once more. This yields

$$y_4^{(3)} = -0.805663$$

which is unchanged from the previous value and obviously satisfies the convergence criterion; thus we set

$$y(0.4) = y_4^{(3)} = -0.805663$$

That $y_4^{(3)}$ is, in fact, quite close to $y_4^{(1)}$ raises once again the question of whether it is ever really advantageous to iterate the corrector more than once. We will deal with this question in the next problem. It is of interest at this point to examine the estimate of the local truncation error of the method for this step. This estimate is given by (9.62), page 201, as

$$E_4 = \frac{9}{121}(y_4^{(0)} - y_4) = \frac{9}{121}[-0.806124 - (-0.805663)] = 3.42 \times 10^{-5}$$

It takes some experience to develop a feeling as to what levels of error are acceptable to provide a reasonably accurate solution. If we assume that 20 steps of Δt are required to cover the desired range of t for the present problem, and that the total solution error can be estimated as the sum of local truncation errors per step, then 20 errors of the size of E_4 would mean that the third decimal place of the value of y at the end of the interval could be in error by 1 digit. If this is unacceptable, then the step size should be reduced.

   To illustrate the use of the modifier, we will take one more step. The predicted value is

$$y_5^{(0)} = -0.793658$$

The modifier yields

$$\bar{y}_5^{(0)} = y_5^{(0)} + \frac{112}{121}[y_4 - y_4^{(0)}]$$

$$= -0.793658 + \frac{112}{121}[-0.805663 - (-0.806124)] = -0.793231$$

Two iterations with the corrector yield

$$y_5^{(1)} = -0.793374, \qquad y_5^{(2)} = -0.793371$$

which can be considered as converged. The modifier obviously provides a much better estimate of the final converged value than does the predictor alone.

9.6   Consider once again the initial value problem

$$\frac{d^2y}{dt^2} + 2\frac{dy}{dt} + 4y = 0$$

$$y(0) = 2, \quad \frac{dy}{dt}(0) = 0$$

and solve this problem by Hamming's method, comparing the results obtained when the corrector is iterated to convergence and when the corrector is iterated only once.

   The results are compared in Table 9.5 for two step sizes, $\Delta t = 0.1$ and $\Delta t = 0.25$. The converged values have been iterated until there is no change in any digit of the solution.

   Both the fully converged and the single iteration values are reasonably accurate for $\Delta t = 0.1$. Although the fully converged values are very slightly more accurate than the single iteration values (the variations between the two solutions are in the fifth decimal place), the differences are probably not sufficient to warrant the extra time required for the additional iterations. The answers for $\Delta t = 0.25$ are, of course, considerably less accurate than those for $\Delta t = 0.1$. The single iteration values are significantly less accurate than the fully converged values, and it would appear that the accuracy gains obtained by iterating to convergence are worth the extra time involved for this case. (In fairness, we should note

Table 9.5

t	Converged $\Delta t = 0.1$	1 Iteration $\Delta t = 0.1$	Converged $\Delta t = 0.25$	1 Iteration $\Delta t = 0.25$	Exact
0	2.00000	2.00000	2.00000	2.00000	2.00000
0.5	1.31940	1.31938	1.31986	1.31986	1.31940
1	0.301178	0.301175	0.301129	0.298918	0.301149
1.5	-0.248641	-0.248624	-0.247692	-0.247534	-0.248709
2	-0.306194	-0.306181	-0.304866	-0.302352	-0.306245
2.5	-0.149175	-0.149175	-0.148651	-0.146498	-0.149181
3	-0.004604	-0.004612	-0.005056	-0.005071	-0.004579
3.5	$+0.051256$	$+0.051249$	$+0.050467$	$+0.048917$	$+0.051282$
4	0.041975	0.041973	0.041471	0.039962	0.041987
4.5	0.014134	0.014136	0.014075	0.013527	0.014132
5	-0.004333	-0.004330	-0.004138	-0.003839	-0.004340

that the time involved to iterate the corrector to convergence for the $\Delta t = 0.25$ case is probably greater than that required to obtain the single iteration solution for $\Delta t = 0.1$ which is more accurate.)

We might generalize these results by stating that if care is taken to ensure that the step size is "sufficiently" small, then a single iteration of the corrector will usually be sufficient.   If, on the other hand, there is a chance that the step size will be excessively large, even in a local region, then multiple iterations of the corrector will ensure better accuracy.   As previously mentioned, some idea of whether the step size is sufficiently small can be obtained by using the estimate of the truncation error per step [equation (9.62)].   For the single iteration case, this first corrected value replaces the fully converged value in (9.62), with some additional uncertainty introduced into the local error estimate.

9.7   Consider the problem of choosing the proper uniform step size for a fourth-order Runge-Kutta solution of the initial value problem

$$\frac{d^2y}{dt^2} + ty = 0$$

$$y(0) = 1, \quad \frac{dy}{dt}(0) = 0$$

We will consider the range $0 \le t \le 4$.   Fourth-order Runge-Kutta solutions are shown in Table 9.6 for step sizes ranging from $\Delta t = 0.8$ to $\Delta t = 0.05$.

Table 9.6

t	$\Delta t = 0.8$	$\Delta t = 0.4$	$\Delta t = 0.2$	$\Delta t = 0.1$	$\Delta t = 0.05$
0	1.00000	1.00000	1.00000	1.00000	1.00000
0.8	0.914667	0.916055	0.916110	0.916113	0.916113
1.6	0.403740	0.405445	0.405407	0.405401	0.405400
2.4	-0.414102	-0.425276	-0.426101	-0.426148	-0.426151
3.2	-0.606459	-0.631307	-0.631750	-0.631739	-0.631736
4.0	$+0.173902$	$+0.215231$	$+0.219653$	$+0.219934$	$+0.219953$

The solutions become more accurate and change less with decreasing step size. However, the point to be emphasized is that it is impossible to assess the accuracy of a solution for any given step size without another solution for a different step size to compare with. Thus if we had only the solution for $\Delta t = 0.8$, it would be impossible to determine how accurate the solution was. The solution for $\Delta t = 0.4$ shows large variations from that for $\Delta t = 0.8$, particularly for larger values of t. The only conclusion that we can draw from this is that the solution for $\Delta t = 0.8$ is probably inaccurate. We cannot conclude anything about the accuracy of the $\Delta t = 0.4$ solution. However, comparison with the $\Delta t = 0.2$ solution shows much smaller differences, and it is apparent that we are approaching a reasonably accurate solution. The comparison between the $\Delta t = 0.2$ and $\Delta t = 0.1$ solutions is sufficiently good to indicate that we can probably have confidence in the third decimal place of the $\Delta t = 0.1$ solution, and the $\Delta t = 0.05$ solution verifies this.

We should note that the estimate of local truncation error [equation (*9.35*), page 196] for the fourth-order Runge-Kutta method is not useful in the present context. The purpose of this error estimate is to serve as a local error control on the step size and is only meant to be used to provide a means of adjusting the step size in the middle of the solution. For the estimate to be meaningful, the two solutions $\hat{y}_{j+1}$ and y_{j+1} must be based on the same solution at t_j. This information is not available in the present problem. In any event, this error estimate is for local truncation error, not total solution error. A sophisticated Runge-Kutta routine could be written which adjusts the step size to keep the local truncation error below some predetermined level, but this is one step beyond the simple uniform step approach we have examined here.

9.8 Solve the initial value problem

$$\frac{d^2y}{dt^2} + 9y = 0$$

$$y(0) = 1, \quad \frac{dy}{dt}(0) = 0$$

by using the Euler method with $\Delta t = 0.1$.

The mechanics of obtaining the numerical solution are straightforward and will not be discussed here. However, the results are interesting. The numerical solution is shown in Fig. 9.6 along with the exact solution $y = \cos 3t$. The growth of the error in the numerical solution is characteristic of an unstable solution. Since the Euler method uses no values of the derivative other than the one at t_j, it would seem at first glance that the Euler method could not be unstable since no parasitic solutions could arise. However, in solving a second order system as a set of two first order differential equations, there are two derivatives evaluated at t_j (one for each equation), and thus a spurious solution to the difference equation can be introduced. It might be noted that a smaller step size slows down the rate of error growth but does not appear to prevent the eventual instability. On the other hand, a fourth-order Runge-Kutta method with $\Delta t = 0.1$ provides a stable, accurate solution.

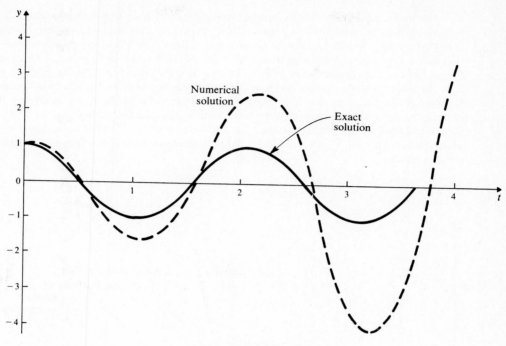

Fig. 9.6

9.9   Solve the initial value problem

$$\frac{dy}{dt} = 5(y - t^2), \quad y(0) = 0.08$$

numerically over the range $0 \leq t \leq 5$.

This innocent-appearing differential equation has been discussed in Ref. 25 and belongs to a class of differential equations which have the property of "stiffness." This property can best be explained by considering the exact solution to the differential equation, which is of the form

$$y = Ae^{5t} + t^2 + 0.4t + 0.08$$

where the term Ae^{5t} is the homogeneous solution and the remainder is the particular solution. If the initial condition is $y(0) = 0.08$, then $A = 0$, and the exact solution is

$$y = t^2 + 0.4t + 0.08$$

The exponential term lurks in the background, however, ready to explode if our numerical solution strays even slightly from the exact solution. One way to visualize this situation is to think of each new step along the t axis as solving a new initial value problem. If the solution at the last step is slightly different from the particular solution, then for the next step, A is not quite zero. The positive exponent amplifies the error, and for the next step A is larger in magnitude. The practical consequences can be seen from Fig. 9.7. If we carry out a fourth-order Runge-Kutta solution using $\Delta t = 0.1$, the numerical solution follows the exact solution nicely up to about $t = 1.7$ (the numerical solution is slightly below the exact solution up to this point, but not enough to show on the graph). The numerical solution then turns abruptly downward and disappears from the graph in an exponential manner. This behavior could be considered as corresponding to A acquiring negative values. Reducing the step size to $\Delta t = 0.01$ reduces the error in the numerical solution, and the numerical solution follows the exact solution up to about $t = 2.7$ and then behaves as before. Once again, the numerical solution lies very slightly below the exact solution over the range $0 \leqslant t \leqslant 2.7$. In order to overcome this problem, we might be tempted to modify the initial condition slightly so that the numerical solution would lie slightly above the exact solution. If we choose $y(0) = 0.080001$, which is a very small modification indeed, we find that the numerical solution is now slightly above the analytical solution for $0 \leqslant t \leqslant 2.4$, but then abruptly turns exponentially upward. This situation could be considered as corresponding to A attaining positive values.

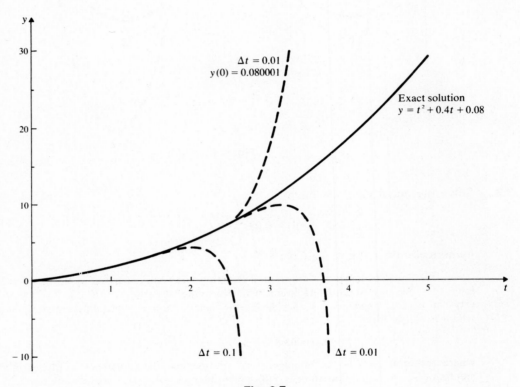

Fig. 9.7

It is important to distinguish this behavior from that which we usually term instability. Here we have what amounts to a parasitic solution to the differential equation (as opposed to a parasitic solution to the difference equation which is usually considered as the cause of instability). There is no easy approach to the problem of "stiff" equations which can be discussed within the scope of this book. However, there are effective numerical techniques for handling this problem, and we once again refer the reader to the method of Gear[22], which includes provisions for solving stiff equations.

9.10 Solve the boundary value problem

$$\frac{d^2y}{dx^2} + \frac{1}{4}y = 8$$

$$y(0) = 0, \quad y(10) = 0$$

by the matrix method discussed in Sec. 9.9, page 203.

We arbitrarily chose $\Delta x = 1$ (10 intervals from $x = 0$ to $x = 10$). Then, following the notation of Sec. 9.9, $\alpha = -2 + \frac{1}{4}(1)^2 = -1.75$ and the elements of the right-hand side vector are $8(1)^2 = 8$. The matrix formulation is

$$\begin{bmatrix} -1.75 & 1 & & & & & \\ 1 & -1.75 & 1 & & & & \\ & 1 & -1.75 & & & & \\ & & & - & - & - & \\ & & & & - & - & \\ & & & & 1 & -1.75 & 1 \\ & & & & & 1 & -1.75 \end{bmatrix} \begin{bmatrix} y_1 \\ y_2 \\ y_3 \\ - \\ - \\ y_8 \\ y_9 \end{bmatrix} = \begin{bmatrix} 8 \\ 8 \\ 8 \\ - \\ - \\ 8 \\ 8 \end{bmatrix}$$

The solution to this set, along with the exact solution given by

$$y = 32\left[\frac{(\cos(5) - 1)}{\sin(5)} \sin(x/2) - \cos(x/2) + 1\right]$$

is shown in Table 9.7. The solution is symmetric about $x = 5$ and we have only shown half of the region.

Table 9.7

x	Matrix Method	Exact
0	0	0
1	14.9384	15.3779
2	34.1422	34.8254
3	52.8105	53.5812
4	66.2761	67.0532
5	71.1173	71.9429

The accuracy of the solution can, of course, be improved by reducing Δx.

We could have taken advantage of the symmetry to reduce the number of unknowns. Since the solution is symmetric about $x = 5$, we could write

$$\frac{dy}{dx}(5) = 0$$

Using a backward difference representation of error order $(\Delta x)^2$ (to be consistent with the central difference representations which are also of error order $(\Delta x)^2$), this derivative can be represented as

$$\frac{3y_5 - 4y_4 + y_3}{2(1)} = 0$$

The difference representation of the differential equation written at $x = 1, 2, 3,$ and 4 now provides 4 equations in the 5 unknowns y_1, y_2, y_3, y_4, and y_5. The additional equation is the difference representation of the derivative at $x = 5$ which can be rewritten as

$$(1)y_3 + (-4)y_4 + (3)y_5 = 0$$

The matrix formulation now becomes

$$\begin{bmatrix} -1.75 & 1 & & & \\ 1 & -1.75 & 1 & & \\ & 1 & -1.75 & 1 & \\ & & 1 & -1.75 & 1 \\ & & 1 & -4 & 3 \end{bmatrix} \begin{bmatrix} y_1 \\ y_2 \\ y_3 \\ y_4 \\ y_5 \end{bmatrix} = \begin{bmatrix} 8 \\ 8 \\ 8 \\ 8 \\ 0 \end{bmatrix}$$

Since this set is so small, there is no real necessity to make the set tridiagonal. However, if we were striving for accuracy, the set would be much larger, and the advantages of having a tridiagonal coefficient matrix could be very significant. The matrix can be made tridiagonal by simply subtracting the fourth equation from the fifth equation. Thus the new matrix formulation becomes

$$\begin{bmatrix} -1.75 & 1 & & & \\ 1 & -1.75 & 1 & & \\ & 1 & -1.75 & 1 & \\ & & 1 & -1.75 & 1 \\ & & & -2.25 & 2 \end{bmatrix} \begin{bmatrix} y_1 \\ y_2 \\ y_3 \\ y_4 \\ y_5 \end{bmatrix} = \begin{bmatrix} 8 \\ 8 \\ 8 \\ 8 \\ -8 \end{bmatrix}$$

A similar method can be applied to any problem involving a gradient boundary condition, with the end result being a tridiagonal set.

9.11 By using the shooting method described in Sec. 9.9, page 205, solve the boundary value problem posed in Problem 9.10.

We first transform the boundary value problem to an equivalent initial value problem:

$$\frac{dy}{dx} = z, \quad y(0) = 0$$

$$\frac{dz}{dx} = 8 - \frac{1}{4}y, \quad z(0) = U$$

where U is unknown and must be determined such that $y(10) = 0$. We choose $U = 10$ for our first attempt. (From the preceding problem a reasonable estimate can be obtained for this slope; in many cases the initial guess will be farther off, but the method will usually still work unless the initial estimate is *very* far from the correct value.) Using a fourth-order Runge-Kutta method with $\Delta x = 0.1$, we find $y(10) = 3.74517$. A second solution must be obtained before the root solving approach discussed in Sec. 9.9 can be employed. If $U = 11$ is used, then the numerical solution of the initial value problem yields $y(10) = 1.82730$. This is (perhaps surprisingly) closer to the desired value of zero than the solution for $U = 10$. (One would be tempted to reduce the slope if $y(10)$ is too high for the first estimate of U. However, this is by no means always the proper approach. The secant method will eventually converge to the correct value in any case.) Enough information is now available to determine the next estimate of U based on the secant method given by (9.74), page 206. We let $U_{00} = 10$ and $U_0 = 11$. Then $y_L(U_{00}) = 3.74517$ and $y_L(U_0) = 1.82730$. Equation (9.74) then yields

$$U_1 = 11 - \frac{1.82730}{(1.82730 - 3.74517)/(11 - 10)} = 11.95277$$

The solution to the initial value problem with this as $z(0)$ gives $y(10) = 5.72205 \times 10^{-5}$. This is remarkably small, and we will accept this solution, which is

$y(0) = 0$	$y(6) = 67.0530$
$y(1) = 15.3783$	$y(7) = 53.5809$
$y(2) = 34.8260$	$y(8) = 34.8250$
$y(3) = 53.5817$	$y(9) = 15.3776$
$y(4) = 67.0535$	$y(10) = 0.000057$
$y(5) = 71.9429$	

Comparison with Table 9.7 shows that these values differ from the exact solution by less than 1 digit in the third decimal place. Only three solutions of the initial value problem were necessary to obtain this solution. More iterations would be required if poorer initial estimates of U were made.

9.12 The boundary value problem considered in Problems 9.10 and 9.11 involves a linear differential equation. Solve this boundary value problem by forming a linear combination of two initial value problems.

Consider two initial value problems of the form posed in Problem 9.11. We postulate two initial conditions on $z(0)$: $U_C = 10$ and $U_D = 20$. We denote the solution corresponding to U_C as $y_C(x)$, and that corresponding to U_D as $y_D(x)$. Then from equations (9.75), (9.80), and (9.81),

$$y(x) = C_1 y_C(x) + C_2 y_D(x)$$

where

$$C_2 = \frac{1}{1 - y_D(10)/y_C(10)}$$

and

$$C_1 = 1 - C_2$$

Carrying out the initial value problems using a fourth-order Runge-Kutta method with $\Delta x = 0.1$, we find

$$y_C(10) = 3.74517, \qquad y_D(10) = -15.4331$$

Thus

$$C_2 = \frac{1}{1 - (-15.4331/3.74517)} = 0.195282$$

and

$$C_1 = 1 - C_2 = 0.804718$$

The solutions to the two initial value problems and the linear combination of the two which satisfies both boundary conditions and hence is the solution to the boundary value problem, are all shown in Table 9.8.

Comparison of the tabulated values of $y(x)$ with the exact solution given in Table 9.7, page 219, shows that the present solution is quite accurate, off by no more than one digit in the third decimal place.

Table 9.8

x	$y_C(x)$	$y_D(x)$	$y(x)$
0	0	0	0
1	13.5058	23.0943	15.3783
2	31.5396	48.3689	34.8261
3	49.6860	69.6358	53.5818
4	63.5022	81.6881	67.0536
5	69.6056	81.5750	71.9430
6	66.5018	69.3243	67.0530
7	54.9508	47.9354	53.5808
8	37.7807	22.6450	34.8250
9	19.1954	-0.354892	15.3776
10	3.74517	-15.4331	0

9.13 Solve numerically the boundary value problem

$$\frac{d^2y}{dx^2} + 2x\frac{dy}{dx} = 0$$

$$y(0) = 1, \quad y(\infty) = 0$$

The unusual aspect of this problem is the presence of the boundary condition at infinity. The procedure employed for such problems is to choose some finite value of x and to assume that this value can effectively be considered as infinity. Then the boundary value problem is solved by any suitable method. One or more additional solutions are then carried out with other values of x representing infinity, and comparison of the various solutions will determine which solution best corresponds to a boundary condition at infinity.

We first assume that $x = 1.5$ will effectively represent infinity. Then the second boundary condition becomes $y(1.5) = 0$. We solve this boundary value problem by the shooting method illustrated in Problem 9.11 using a fourth-order Runge-Kutta method with $\Delta x = 0.05$. Five iterations yield $y(1.5) = 0.271 \times 10^{-6}$ and we consider the method to have converged. Some sample points are shown in Table 9.9.

Table 9.9

x	y
0	1.00000
0.4	0.556578
0.8	0.231863
1.0	0.127734
1.2	0.057749
1.4	0.014305
1.5	0.0000002

Although it is not clear whether we have made a good choice for an "effective infinity," it would seem that we at least have the proper order of magnitude, since $y(x)$ seems to approach $x = 1.5$ with a reasonably small slope. (It should be apparent that the correct $y(x)$ should approach zero asymptotically for large x.) If we had chosen the value of x which represents infinity much too small, then $y(x)$ would approach this effective infinity with a rather large slope. On the other hand, if this value of x were chosen much too large, then the solution $y(x)$ would be virtually zero over the bulk of the range of x considered. Solutions with effective values of infinity of $x_\infty = 2, 2.5,$ and 3 and with $\Delta x = 0.05$ are shown in Table 9.10 along with the solution for $x_\infty = 1.5$ at selected points.

Table 9.10

x	$x_\infty = 1.5$ y	$x_\infty = 2$ y	$x_\infty = 2.5$ y	$x_\infty = 3$ y
0	1.00000	1.00000	1.00000	1.00000
0.4	0.556578	0.569595	0.571443	0.571599
0.8	0.231863	0.254412	0.257597	0.257884
1.0	0.127734	0.153340	0.156956	0.157282
1.2	0.057749	0.085409	0.089316	0.089667
1.4	0.014305	0.043240	0.047328	0.047695
2.0	—	4.42×10^{-6}	0.004273	0.004657
2.5	—	—	-1.44×10^{-6}	0.000386

The solution for $x_\infty = 2$ yields results which differ significantly from those for $x_\infty = 1.5$, so it would seem that the latter was not sufficiently large. (We assume in all of this discussion that Δx is kept sufficiently small to ensure minimal truncation error.) For $x_\infty = 2.5$, the variations from the $x_\infty = 2$ solution are much smaller and it is apparent that we approach a sufficiently large x to result in a reasonably accurate solution to the original problem. The $x_\infty = 3$ solution shows still smaller variations and would appear to be an acceptable solution for our purposes.

9.14 Develop a shooting method for solving the boundary value problem

$$\frac{d^3y}{dx^3} + 2y\frac{d^2y}{dx^2} - \left(\frac{dy}{dx}\right)^2 + 1 = 0$$

$$y(0) = 0, \quad \frac{dy}{dx}(0) = 0, \quad \frac{dy}{dx}(4.4) = 1$$

We let $w = dy/dx$ and $z = dw/dx$. Then the boundary value problem can be reformulated as the initial value problem

$$\frac{dy}{dx} = w, \quad y(0) = 0$$

$$\frac{dw}{dx} = z, \quad w(0) = 0 = \frac{dy}{dx}(0)$$

$$\frac{dz}{dx} = -2yz + (w)^2 - 1, \quad z(0) = U$$

where U must be determined such that $w(4.4) = 1$. Note that the original differential equation is nonlinear, so the method of superposition of two solutions to the initial value problem is not applicable. The standard shooting method can be employed by considering the search for U to be a root solving problem such that $w(4.4)$, which we will denote as $w_L(U)$, becomes equal to 1. Thus we are searching for the value of U such that

$$f(U) = w_L(U) - 1 = 0$$

Starting with two initial estimates of U, the secant method can now be applied after each solution of the initial value problem to provide a better estimate of the correct value of U. The method is virtually the same as that discussed in Sec. 9.9, except that $f(U)$ replaces $y_L(U)$. The actual solution is left as a problem for the reader (Problem 9.31).

Problems

In contrast to our practice in preceding chapters, we will not attempt to indicate which of the following problems are suitable for hand computation and which require a computer. In all honesty, hand calculation of the numerical solutions to ordinary differential equations is a laborious, time consuming, and often boring task. By far the most benefit can be gained from these problems if a computer is available. However, if hand calculations are necessary, they will usually have to be restricted to Euler solutions of the simpler problems, or to only a few steps using the more accurate methods.

For many problems no step size is indicated, and the choice of a proper step size (or sizes) to produce accurate results is considered to be part of the problem. The incorporation of an automatically adjusted step size feature in the computer programs is probably not worthwhile in terms of understanding the basic methods, so no such sophistication is asked of the reader. For most problems, the method is not specified, and any suitable method can be employed.

9.15   Write a computer program to solve an arbitrary initial value problem consisting of a set of coupled first-order differential equations with their associated initial conditions. Use a fourth-order Runge-Kutta method with a constant step size. The program should accommodate up to four coupled differential equations. Input variables should include the number of equations, the step size, the vector of initial conditions and the initial value of the independent variable, and the value of the independent variable at which the solution is to be terminated. An external subroutine should supply the details of the specific set of differential equations to be solved by evaluating the derivative vector $\bar{f}(\bar{y},t)$ when called with the vector of dependent variables $\bar{y}$ and the value of the independent variable t as input parameters.

9.16   Write a program to accomplish the task described in Problem 9.15 but use Hamming's method to solve the differential equations. Use a fourth-order Runge-Kutta formula to provide the necessary starting values. Additional input variables should include a convergence criterion for the corrector and the maximum number of iterations permissible on the corrector. In addition to the solution, the program should provide an estimate of truncation error for each step.

9.17   Write a similar program to that described in the previous problem but use the fourth-order Adams predictor-corrector method described in Sec. 9.7, page 199.

9.18 $\dfrac{dy}{dt} + y^2 = 1, \quad y(0) = 0$

Range: $0 \le t \le 2.5$
Step size: $\Delta t = 0.1$
Method: fourth-order Runge-Kutta

9.19 $(e^t + 1)\dfrac{d^2 y}{dt^2} = y, \quad y(0) = 1, \quad \dfrac{dy}{dt}(0) = 0$

Range: $0 \le t \le 4$
Step size: $\Delta t = 0.1$
Method: fourth-order Runge-Kutta

(This problem was also considered in Problem 9.2.)

9.20 $\dfrac{dy}{dt} = \dfrac{4t}{y} - yt, \quad y(0) = 3$

Range: $0 \le t \le 1.8$
Step size: $\Delta t = 0.1$
Method: Hamming's method

(This problem was also considered in Problem 9.1.)

9.21 $\dfrac{d^2 y}{dt^2} + \dfrac{dy}{dt} - y^2 = 0, \quad y(0) = 1, \quad \dfrac{dy}{dt}(0) = 0$

Range: $0 \le t \le 3.5$
Method: Hamming's method

(Watch for trouble near the upper limit.)

9.22 $\dfrac{d^3 y}{dt^3} + 2\dfrac{d^2 y}{dt^2} - \left(\dfrac{dy}{dt}\right)^2 + 3y = 10 \sin 6t$

$y(0) = 0, \quad \dfrac{dy}{dt}(0) = 0, \quad \dfrac{d^2 y}{dt^2}(0) = 0$

Range: $0 \le t \le 4$

9.23 $\dfrac{dy}{dt} + |y|^{3/2} = \cos t, \quad y(0) = 1$

Range: $0 \le t \le 4$

9.24 $\dfrac{d^2 y}{dt^2} + \sin y = 0, \quad y(0) = 1, \quad \dfrac{dy}{dt}(0) = 0$

Range: $0 \le t \le 4$

9.25 $\dfrac{dy}{dt} = -10^{10}(y^4 - 10^{12}), \quad y(0) = 530$

Range: $0 \le t \le 1.5$

9.26 $\dfrac{d^2y}{dt^2} = 16y,$ $y(0) = 1,$ $\dfrac{dy}{dt}(0) = -4$

Range: $0 \leqslant t \leqslant 4$

If possible, use $\Delta t = 0.05$. Compare your results with the exact solution and attempt to explain any discrepancies.

9.27 Solve by using a matrix method:

$$x^2\frac{d^2y}{dx^2} + x\frac{dy}{dx} + x^2y = 0$$

$$y(1) = 1, \quad y(8) = 0$$

9.28 Solve the preceding problem by using a shooting method. Take advantage of the linearity of the differential equation. Use any fourth order method with $\Delta x = 0.1$.

9.29 Solve by using a shooting method:

$$\frac{d^3y}{dx^3} + y\frac{d^2y}{dx^2} = 0$$

$$y(0) = 0, \quad \frac{dy}{dx}(0) = 0, \quad \frac{dy}{dx}(\infty) = 2$$

9.30 Solve the second-order linear boundary value problem discussed in Problem 9.13 by using a matrix method.

9.31 Carry out the solution to the third-order nonlinear boundary value problem posed in Problem 9.14.

Chapter 10

Matrix Eigenvalue Problems

10.0 INTRODUCTION

Matrix eigenvalue problems arise from a wide variety of physical and mathematical situations, ranging from the determination of the natural frequencies of vibration of a structure to problems in quantum physics.   We will examine a number of solution techniques, since no single technique can be said to be optimal in all situations.   We begin with some definitions and a discussion of the properties of matrix eigenvalue problems.

10.1 THE GENERAL PROBLEM

The matrix eigenvalue problem can be stated in the form

$$HX = \lambda X \tag{10.1}$$

where H is a known square matrix, X is an unknown column vector with the same row dimension as H, and λ is an unknown constant.   The solution of the eigenvalue problem involves finding those vectors X and constants λ which satisfy (10.1).   Clearly the vectors X can only be determined to within a multiplicative constant, since if any vector X_i satisfies (10.1), then so will cX_i, where c is a constant.

If H is of dimension n, then there will in general be n different vectors X_j $(j = 1,2,\ldots,n)$ which satisfy (10.1).   These vectors are called the *eigenvectors* of H. Associated with each eigenvector is a constant λ_j which is termed an *eigenvalue.* These eigenvalues will in general each be different, but it is entirely possible to have repeated (multiple) eigenvalues in a given problem.

We can obtain a formal solution for the eigenvalues by writing (10.1) in the form

$$(H - \lambda I)X = 0 \tag{10.2}$$

Since this represents a set of homogeneous linear algebraic equations, it should be apparent from Cramer's rule that the only way in which a nontrivial vector X can satisfy (10.2) is if

$$\det (H - \lambda I) = 0 \tag{10.3}$$

or

$$\det \begin{bmatrix} h_{11}-\lambda & h_{12} & h_{13} & - & h_{1n} \\ h_{21} & h_{22}-\lambda & h_{23} & - & h_{2n} \\ h_{31} & h_{32} & h_{33}-\lambda & - & - \\ - & - & - & - & - \\ h_{n1} & h_{n2} & h_{n3} & - & h_{nn}-\lambda \end{bmatrix} = 0 \qquad (10.4)$$

Expansion of the determinant in (10.4) produces a polynomial of degree n in λ. This polynomial is called the *characteristic polynomial* of H, and its roots are the desired eigenvalues. Using a root solving procedure is not a computationally practical approach to obtaining the eigenvalues except in special circumstances or for sparse or very small matrices. However, it should be apparent that some of the same difficulties which arise in root solving can also affect the various methods which we will use for finding eigenvalues. In particular, special attention must often be given to closely spaced and multiple eigenvalues. It also becomes clear that since a polynomial with all real coefficients can have complex roots, a matrix composed of all real elements can have complex eigenvalues.

A great many physical problems result in a real symmetric form for the matrix H. We will restrict the remainder of this section and, in fact, much of this chapter, to eigenvalue problems involving real symmetric matrices. The complications of unsymmetric matrices are very severe, and we will defer discussion of eigenvalue problems involving such matrices until Sec. 10.10.

If H is symmetric and V is an arbitrary column vector, then

$$HV = W \qquad (10.5)$$

and

$$V^T H = W^T \qquad (10.6)$$

where W is a column vector. This can be easily verified by noting that the jth element of the column vector HV is given by

$$(HV)_j = \sum_{k=1}^{n} h_{jk} v_k \qquad (10.7)$$

and the jth element of the row vector $V^T H$ is given by

$$(V^T H)_j = \sum_{k=1}^{n} v_k h_{kj} \qquad (10.8)$$

but since $h_{jk} = h_{kj}$, the column vector $(V^T H)^T$ is the same as HV. Now consider another arbitrary column vector Y and note that

$$Y^T W = W^T Y \qquad (10.9)$$

since both sides of (10.9) represent simply the scalar result of the dot product of the vectors Y and W. Substituting (10.5) and (10.6) into (10.9) yields

$$Y^T H V = V^T H Y \qquad (10.10)$$

Now let $Y = X_a$ and $V = X_b$, two different eigenvectors of H. Then

$$X_a^T H X_b = X_b^T H X_a \qquad (10.11)$$

but

$$HX_a = \lambda_a X_a \tag{10.12}$$

and

$$HX_b = \lambda_b X_b \tag{10.13}$$

thus

$$\lambda_b X_a^T X_b = \lambda_a X_b^T X_a \tag{10.14}$$

But since $X_a^T X_b = X_b^T X_a$, it would seem that (10.14) implies $\lambda_a = \lambda_b$. Since this cannot be true in general, then it must be true that

$$X_a^T X_b = 0 \tag{10.15}$$

The eigenvectors are thus said to be *orthogonal*. A set of n orthogonal vectors, each of dimension n, are said to span the n-dimensional vector space. Thus any arbitrary vector V of dimension n can be expressed as a linear combination of the eigenvectors:

$$V = c_1 X_1 + c_2 X_2 + \cdots + c_n X_n \tag{10.16}$$

Not only are the eigenvectors of a symmetric matrix orthogonal, it can also be shown that all of the eigenvalues are real, which considerably simplifies the computational details.

Before continuing with the details of the various approaches to eigenvalue problems, we should mention some of the available references on the subject. It is widely accepted that the most authoritative work on the subject is that of Wilkinson[26], who has also been deeply involved in the effort to make many of the best methods available as efficiently coded ALGOL procedures (see Sec. 10.11). Of the available general numerical analysis texts, Ralston[3] and Acton[12] have extensive treatments. Crandall[18] presents a physical as well as a mathematical picture, although the mathematical methods discussed are those which were available in the middle 1950's.

10.2   REDUCTION OF THE PROBLEM $AX = \lambda BX$ TO $HX = \lambda X$: THE CHOLESKI DECOMPOSITION

For many real situations, the eigenvalue problem does not arise in the standard form $HX = \lambda X$ which we considered in Sec. 10.1, but rather in the form

$$AX = \lambda BX \tag{10.17}$$

where A and B are symmetric square matrices of the same size. Often B occurs as a diagonal matrix (Crandall[18] terms this a *special* eigenvalue problem). While it might be possible to deal with problems of the form (10.17) directly, it is much more convenient if (10.17) can be converted to the standard form $HX = \lambda X$ which we will consider throughout this chapter. It is apparent that (10.17) can be converted to the desired form simply by premultiplying by B^{-1}. Thus

$$B^{-1}AX = \lambda X \tag{10.18}$$

or

$$HX = \lambda X \tag{10.19}$$

However, even if A and B are both symmetric, $B^{-1}A$ will not in general be symmetric. ($B^{-1}A$ is not symmetric even if B is diagonal, except for the trivial case $B = I$.) Since, as we have seen, it is highly desirable that H be symmetric, we will have to consider another approach.

If B is *positive definite*, then B can be written as the product of a lower triangular matrix with its transpose, or

$$B = LL^T \qquad (10.20)$$

While the term *positive definite* can be defined in several ways, it will be adequate for our purposes to state that if all eigenvalues of B are positive, this is sufficient to ensure that the matrix is positive definite. We might also note that it is *necessary* that all diagonal elements be positive.

Now, assuming that the decomposition (10.20) can be accomplished, we premultiply (10.17) by L^{-1}:

$$L^{-1}AX = \lambda L^{-1}BX = \lambda L^{-1}(LL^T)X = \lambda L^T X \qquad (10.21)$$

We note without proof that

$$(L^{-1})^T = (L^T)^{-1} \qquad (10.22)$$

And we define $(L^{-1})^T$ as L^{-T} for convenience. Now since $L^{-T}L^T = I$, then $A(L^{-T}L^T) = AI = A$. Thus we can write the left side of (10.21) as

$$L^{-1}AX = L^{-1}A(L^{-T}L^T)X \qquad (10.23)$$

Combining (10.23) and (10.21), we obtain

$$(L^{-1}AL^{-T})(L^T X) = \lambda(L^T X) \qquad (10.24)$$

The matrix $(L^{-1}AL^{-T})$ obviously has the same eigenvalues as the original problem (10.17), and if A is symmetric, then it can be shown that $(L^{-1}AL^{-T})$ is also symmetric. Since we can write (10.24) as

$$HZ = \lambda Z \qquad (10.25)$$

where H is symmetric and $Z = L^T X$, we have accomplished the desired objective. The eigenvalues are the same as the original problem, and the eigenvectors Z are related to the eigenvectors of the original problem by

$$X = L^{-T}Z \qquad (10.26)$$

We should also note that if B is not positive definite but A is, then the problem (10.17) can be rewritten as

$$BX = \frac{1}{\lambda}AX = \lambda'AX \qquad (10.27)$$

where the λ' are the reciprocals of the original eigenvalues. We can now proceed as before, simply interchanging the roles of A and B.

In order to obtain the form of (10.24), starting from the form $AX = \lambda BX$, we must be able to decompose the matrix B into the product LL^T and then to obtain L^{-1}.

The decomposition of B can be obtained by the *Choleski decomposition*. We denote the elements of B as b_{ij} and those of L as l_{ij}. The algorithm is

$$l_{11} = (a_{11})^{1/2}$$

$$l_{ij} = \left(b_{ij} - \sum_{k=1}^{i-1} l_{ik}l_{jk} \right) \bigg/ l_{jj}, \quad j = 1, 2, \ldots, i-1$$

$$l_{ii} = \sqrt{b_{ii} - \sum_{k=1}^{i-1} l_{ik}^2} \qquad\qquad\qquad\qquad \right\} \quad i = 2, 3, \ldots, n \qquad (10.28)$$

$$l_{i-1,j} = 0, \quad j = i, i+1, \ldots, n$$

We have employed the usual summation convention in which the sum is taken to be zero if the upper limit is less than the lower limit. Thus $\Sigma_{k=1}^{0} l_{ik}l_{jk} = 0$. (This point requires special computer programming if a FORTRAN DO loop is employed since such a loop is always executed once before the index is checked to determine if the upper limit has been reached. Many ALGOL based languages check the index against the upper limit before executing the loop the first time, and the indicated summation would never be performed and would thus automatically be taken as zero.) If the matrix B is not positive definite, then the argument of the square root in (10.28) will be negative at some point in the algorithm, and computation must, of course, be discontinued.

We must now consider the inversion of the lower triangular matrix L. By taking advantage of the special form, considerable savings in computational effort can be made. It can readily be shown that the inverse of a lower triangular matrix is also lower triangular. In order to evaluate L^{-1}, we then simply write

$$L^{-1}L = I \qquad (10.29)$$

or, denoting the elements of L^{-1} as l_{ij}^{-1},

$$l_{ii}^{-1}l_{ii} = 1, \quad i = 1, 2, \ldots, n \qquad (10.30)$$

$$\sum_{k=j}^{i} l_{ik}^{-1}l_{kj} = 0, \quad \begin{cases} i = 2, 3, \ldots, n \\ j = k-1, k-2, \ldots, 1 \end{cases} \qquad (10.31)$$

from which we can directly deduce the inversion algorithm:

$$l_{11}^{-1} = 1/l_{11}$$

$$l_{ii}^{-1} = 1/l_{ii}$$

$$l_{ij}^{-1} = \frac{-\sum_{k=j+1}^{i} l_{ik}^{-1}l_{kj}}{l_{jj}}, \quad j = i-1, i-2, \ldots, 1 \quad \right\} \quad i = 2, 3, \ldots, n \qquad (10.32)$$

All of the necessary tools are now available to transform the problem $AX = \lambda BX$ into the form $HX = \lambda X$. See Problems 10.1–10.3 for examples of the method.

10.3 THE POWER METHOD

We have seen that for a symmetric $n \times n$ matrix H, the eigenvectors span the space, i.e. any n-dimensional vector V can be written as

$$V = c_1 X_1 + c_2 X_2 + c_3 X_3 + \cdots + c_n X_n \qquad (10.33)$$

Note that if V is a good estimate of one of the eigenvectors X_i, then the constant c_i

associated with that eigenvector will be considerably larger in magnitude than the other c's. Now suppose we form the product HV. From (10.33) we obtain

$$HV = c_1 HX_1 + c_2 HX_2 + c_3 HX_3 + \cdots + c_n HX_n \qquad (10.34)$$

but $HX_1 = \lambda_1 X_1$, $HX_2 = \lambda_2 X_2$, etc. Thus (10.34) can be written as

$$HV = c_1 \lambda_1 X_1 + c_2 \lambda_2 X_2 + c_3 \lambda_3 X_3 + \cdots + c_n \lambda_n X_n \qquad (10.35)$$

If we again premultiply by H, (10.35) becomes

$$H(HV) = c_1 \lambda_1^2 X_1 + c_2 \lambda_2^2 X_2 + c_3 \lambda_3^2 X_3 + \cdots + c_n \lambda_n^2 X_n \qquad (10.36)$$

Each succeeding multiplication by H increases by one the power to which the eigenvalues are raised, and it should be apparent that the term involving the eigenvalue which is largest in magnitude will eventually dominate the right side of the equation. This is the principle behind the power method. If the largest eigenvalue in magnitude (called the dominant eigenvalue) is denoted as λ_1 and the next largest as λ_2, then the ratio

$$r = \frac{|\lambda_2|}{|\lambda_1|} \qquad (10.37)$$

defined as the *dominance ratio*, is clearly of fundamental importance in how rapidly the term involving λ_1 overwhelms all other terms. If V is a good estimate of the eigenvector associated with λ_1, then this will also accelerate the process, since the corresponding value of c will be large in magnitude compared with the other c's.

In practice, the power method is usually applied as follows. Denote the first estimate of the eigenvector as V_0. (All elements of V_0 are usually taken as 1 unless there is a better estimate available.) Then calculate

$$HV_0 = V_1 \qquad (10.38)$$

Now normalize the vector V_1 by making one of its elements equal to 1. This is done by dividing each of its elements by any one element (usually chosen as the largest in magnitude to ensure best accuracy). Thus

$$V_1 = p_1 V_1' \qquad (10.39)$$

where p_1 is a constant equal to the element which has been normalized to 1, and V_1' is the normalized vector found by dividing each element of V_1 by p_1. We now form the product

$$HV_1' = V_2 = p_2 V_2' \qquad (10.40)$$

and continue this process as many times as desired. As the number of iterations increases, p approaches the largest eigenvalue (in magnitude of H, and V' approaches its associated eigenvector.

The method can best be illustrated with an example. Consider the eigenvalue problem

$$\begin{bmatrix} 3 & 7 & 9 \\ 7 & 4 & 3 \\ 9 & 3 & 8 \end{bmatrix} \begin{bmatrix} x_1 \\ x_2 \\ x_3 \end{bmatrix} = \lambda \begin{bmatrix} x_1 \\ x_2 \\ x_3 \end{bmatrix}$$

As a first guess, we choose

$$X = \begin{bmatrix} 1 \\ 1 \\ 1 \end{bmatrix}$$

Now compute

$$\begin{bmatrix} 3 & 7 & 9 \\ 7 & 4 & 3 \\ 9 & 3 & 8 \end{bmatrix} \begin{bmatrix} 1 \\ 1 \\ 1 \end{bmatrix} = \begin{bmatrix} 19 \\ 14 \\ 20 \end{bmatrix} = 20 \begin{bmatrix} 0.95 \\ 0.70 \\ 1 \end{bmatrix}$$

(We have normalized the vector by dividing through by its largest element.) The next iteration yields

$$\begin{bmatrix} 3 & 7 & 9 \\ 7 & 4 & 3 \\ 9 & 3 & 8 \end{bmatrix} \begin{bmatrix} 0.95 \\ 0.70 \\ 1 \end{bmatrix} = 18.65 \begin{bmatrix} 0.898123 \\ 0.667560 \\ 1 \end{bmatrix}$$

After 13 iterations, the estimate of the eigenvector differs by less than 10^{-6} from that obtained on the 12th iteration, and we accept the following answer which is correct (for the eigenvalue) to five decimal places:

$$\lambda = 18.10138, \qquad X = \begin{bmatrix} 0.902178 \\ 0.660591 \\ 1 \end{bmatrix}$$

Note that even the 2nd iteration yielded a reasonably accurate estimate of the eigenvalue and eigenvector for this case.

Acceleration of the Power Method

The convergence rate of the power method can be accelerated by various strategies. The simplest of these is a shift of all of the eigenvalues by a constant value. Under certain conditions, this shift can result in a beneficial decrease in the dominance ratio. For example, if the two largest eigenvalues in magnitude are $+25$ and -20, the dominance ratio is close to 1 and convergence will be relatively slow. However, adding 10 to each eigenvalue changes them to $+35$ and -10 respectively, yielding a dominance ratio of $1/3.5$ with a resultant increase in the convergence rate. Such shifts of all eigenvalues by a constant can be simply accomplished by adding this constant to each main diagonal element of the matrix. Since, of course, the benefit of such a shift cannot be determined beforehand because the eigenvalues are not known, this is largely a "cut and try" approach. Care is required or the shift may cause the power method to produce a different eigenvalue than the one which was originally dominant. Thus a shift of -10 in the case discussed above would cause the eigenvalue which was originally -20 to become dominant.

Another approach to acceleration of the power method is to apply over- or under-relaxation in a manner analogous to that used for the solution of sets of linear algebraic equations. Thus if after $l + 1$ iterations the power method yields a normalized vector V'_{l+1}, then the vector which is stored is not V'_{l+1}, but a modified value given by

$$(V'_{l+1})_{\text{stored}} \longleftarrow (V'_l)_{\text{stored}} + \omega[V'_{l+1} - (V'_l)_{\text{stored}}] \qquad (10.41)$$

where ω is a relaxation parameter between 0 and 2. An optimum value of ω cannot be chosen beforehand. However, some idea of the approximate value of ω to employ can be obtained by examining the results of a few iterations with the straight power method ($\omega = 1$). If the estimates of the dominant eigenvalue tend to decrease or increase in a monotonic fashion with succeeding iterations, then overrelaxation ($1 < \omega < 2$) will usually accelerate the convergence. If there is a tendency of the estimates of the eigenvalues to oscillate, then underrelaxation ($0 < \omega < 1$) will usually result in an accelerated convergence rate.

Examples of acceleration of the power method by shifting and relaxation are given in Problems 10.4 and 10.5.

A "once only" acceleration technique known as the Rayleigh quotient can be used to find an accurate estimate of an eigenvalue based on a relatively inaccurate estimate of its associated eigenvector. Let V be an arbitrary vector. Then

$$\lambda_R = \frac{V^T H V}{V^T V} \tag{10.42}$$

is defined as the Rayleigh quotient. If $V = X_a$, then $\lambda_R = \lambda_a$. If V is an estimate of X_a, then λ_R is a much better estimate of λ_a than V is of X_a. Although this method was once widely used in hand computation, its primary value in machine computation would seem to be in conjunction with the use of the power method for very large matrices. In this situation, each iteration of the power method is very expensive and one must sometimes settle for an eigenvector estimate which is not fully converged. Equation (10.42) can then yield an estimate of the eigenvalue which is more accurate than that which would be obtained by a rather large number of additional iterations of the power method. See Ref. 18 for a description of the theory behind the Rayleigh quotient. The method is illustrated in Problem 10.6.

Ralston[3] gives several other acceleration techniques for the power method.

Subdominant Eigenvalues

The power method can also be employed directly to find the smallest eigenvalue in absolute magnitude. The standard eigenvalue problem is stated in the form

$$HX = \lambda X \tag{10.43}$$

If we premultiply by H^{-1}, (10.43) becomes

$$H^{-1}HX = \lambda H^{-1}X \tag{10.44}$$

but $H^{-1}H = I$, so (10.44) can be written as

$$X = \lambda H^{-1}X \tag{10.45}$$

and if we denote H^{-1} as G and divide through (10.45) by λ, we obtain

$$GX = \frac{1}{\lambda} X \tag{10.46}$$

The power method applied to G will then yield the largest value in magnitude of $1/\lambda$ and its associated eigenvector. But this largest value of $1/\lambda$ corresponds to the smallest value in magnitude of λ. This approach will not be practical for large matrices due to the large amount of computation necessary to find H^{-1}.

There are a number of strategies for employing the power method to find intermediate eigenvalues between the smallest and largest.   These methods are too computationally inefficient and generally too numerically inaccurate to be used for finding more than a few of the largest (or smallest) eigenvalues if the matrix is large.   However, these few eigenvalues are often the most important in a real physical problem, and it is thus worthwhile for us to consider at least one of these methods.

Suppose that the dominant eigenvalue λ_1 and its corresponding eigenvector X_1 of a matrix H have been found by the power method.   Then form

$$D_1 = H - \frac{\lambda_1(X_1 X_1^T)}{X_1^T X_1} \tag{10.47}$$

Note that $X_1^T X$ is a scalar, while $X_1 X_1^T$ is a square matrix of the same dimension as H and can be easily seen to be symmetric.   Now D_1 can be shown to have the same eigenvalues and eigenvectors as H, except that λ_1 is replaced by zero.   Thus the power method applied to D_1 will converge to the second largest eigenvalue λ_2 and its associated eigenvector.   Next we can calculate

$$D_2 = D_1 - \frac{\lambda_2(X_2 X_2^T)}{X_2^T X_2} \tag{10.48}$$

which has λ_1 and λ_2 replaced by zero and will converge to λ_3.   This method can be carried as far as desired (or until roundoff error overwhelms it).   The method is called *Hotelling's deflation*.   It should be noted that at each stage of the process, the effective dominance ratio is the ratio of the eigenvalue currently being sought to the next smallest in magnitude.   Thus the power method could converge extremely rapidly for a few eigenvalues, then suddenly slow down drastically if two succeeding eigenvalues are encountered which are nearly equal in magnitude.   Acceleration procedures of the type discussed earlier in this section can of course be applied at any stage of the process.   An example of Hotelling's deflation is given in Problem 10.7.

Deflation techniques are also available which result in a reduction in size of the matrix by one row and one column each time a new eigenvalue is found[3].   These techniques are more economical if many eigenvalues are to be found.   However, as we have already noted, the power method approach in general is not the best approach to take if many eigenvalues of a large matrix are required.

10.4 SIMILARITY AND ORTHOGONAL TRANSFORMATIONS

The efficient methods for finding all of the eigenvalues of matrices are based on similarity transformations and orthogonal transformations.

Consider a square matrix H (which for our purposes we can consider to be the matrix of an eigenvalue problem) and a general nonsingular matrix S of the same size.   Then a similarity transformation of H into C is defined by

$$C = S^{-1}HS \tag{10.49}$$

(SHS^{-1} is also a similarity transformation, but in general is a different one.)   Now consider the eigenvalue problem

$$HX = \lambda X \tag{10.50}$$

and premultiply by S^{-1}:

$$S^{-1}HX = \lambda S^{-1}X \tag{10.51}$$

The quantity $S^{-1}X$ is a vector which we will call Z. Then since $X = SZ$, (10.51) can be written as

$$(S^{-1}HS)Z = \lambda Z \tag{10.52}$$

or

$$CZ = \lambda Z \tag{10.53}$$

This is a new eigenvalue problem, but note that λ has come through the manipulations untouched and hence the eigenvalues of the problem (10.53) are the same as those of the problem (10.50). Thus a similarity transformation *preserves eigenvalues* (but does not preserve eigenvectors).

Now suppose that $S^{-1} = S^T$, i.e. that S is orthogonal. Then

$$S^{-1}HS = S^THS \tag{10.54}$$

In order to distinguish this special case, we will use the symbol Q instead of S and term the transformation

$$D = Q^THQ \tag{10.55}$$

an *orthogonal** transformation. (QHQ^T is also an orthogonal transformation.) This special form of similarity transformation preserves symmetry as well as the eigenvalues, i.e. if H is symmetric, then D is symmetric also. We will find orthogonal transformations particularly useful.

10.5 THE JACOBI METHOD

The Jacobi method for finding all of the eigenvalues and eigenvectors of a symmetric matrix is based on relatively simple orthogonal transformations. The method is not competitive in terms of computer time with the more efficient methods for finding all of the eigenvalues which will be discussed in succeeding sections. (All commonly used methods for finding all of the eigenvalues of a symmetric matrix require on the order of n^3 basic arithmetic operations, but the Jacobi method may require about 10 times as many operations as the most efficient method.) However, the Jacobi method is safe and sure in all situations and has the considerable advantage of being capable of producing the eigenvectors along with the eigenvalues. (The more efficient methods for finding the eigenvalues generally require a separate procedure for calculating the eigenvectors.) In addition, if only one subprogram for finding eigenvalues and eigenvectors is available in a computer library, it will almost invariably be based on the Jacobi method. Since the method is widely used in practice, and does have some advantages, we will discuss it in detail.

The objective of the Jacobi method is, through a series of orthogonal transformations, to convert the matrix H to diagonal form. Since the eigenvalues must be preserved through these orthogonal transformations, the elements of the final diagonal matrix must be the eigenvalues of H. The form of the matrices involved in the orthogonal transformation is particularly simple, since we seek only the limited objective of reducing one

---

*In the numerical analysis literature, the reader may encounter the term *unitary transformation*. For real matrices, unitary and orthogonal mean the same thing.

off-diagonal element in the upper half of H to zero at each step. (In the full symmetric matrix this means that two symmetrically placed off-diagonal elements will be reduced to zero.)

If we denote the orthogonal matrices at each step as U, then we wish to find U such that the transformation $U^T H U$ reduces the element in the pth row and the qth column of H to zero. (The element in the qth row and pth column will also automatically be reduced to zero.) This can be accomplished if U is of the form

$$U = \begin{matrix} & & p & & q & \\ & \begin{bmatrix} 1 & & & & & \\ & \diagdown & & & & \\ & & \diagdown & & & \\ p & & & c & & s & \\ & & & & 1 & \\ & & & \diagdown & & \\ q & & & -s & & c & \\ & & & & & \diagdown & \\ & & & & & & \diagdown \\ & & & & & & & 1 \end{bmatrix} \end{matrix} \qquad (10.56)$$

where c and s are constants which depend on the elements of H, and all off-diagonal elements of U are zero except for u_{pq} and u_{qp}, which are s and $-s$ respectively. All diagonal elements of U are 1 except for u_{pp} and u_{qq}, which are c.

The reader can readily verify that premultiplication of H by U^T and postmultiplication by U affect only the pth and qth rows and pth and qth columns of the resulting matrix. In order to determine how to choose c and s, we need only examine the modifications which h_{pp}, h_{qq}, h_{pq}, and h_{qp} undergo in this transformation. The following multiplication of submatrices results in the proper modifications to these elements of H:

$$\begin{bmatrix} c & -s \\ s & c \end{bmatrix} \begin{bmatrix} h_{pp} & h_{pq} \\ h_{qp} & h_{qq} \end{bmatrix} \begin{bmatrix} c & s \\ -s & c \end{bmatrix} = \begin{bmatrix} h'_{pp} & h'_{pq} \\ h'_{qp} & h'_{qq} \end{bmatrix} \qquad (10.57)$$

(The other elements of the matrices involved do not affect the elements of H which are of interest here.) Equation (10.57) yields

$$h'_{pp} = c^2 h_{pp} + s^2 h_{qq} - 2cs h_{pq} \qquad (10.58)$$

$$h'_{qq} = c^2 h_{qq} + s^2 h_{pp} + 2cs h_{pq} \qquad (10.59)$$

$$h'_{pq} = h'_{qp} = (c^2 - s^2) h_{pq} + cs(h_{pp} - h_{qq}) \qquad (10.60)$$

We now can determine c and s. First note that for the transformation to be orthogonal, $U^T = U^{-1}$. In order for $U^T U$ to be equal to I, it is necessary that

$$c^2 + s^2 = 1 \qquad (10.61)$$

One additional relationship is necessary to determine c and s, and it can be found from (10.60) by requiring that $h'_{pq} = h'_{qp} = 0$, which eliminates the desired element. It is convenient (and consistent with (10.61)) to set

$$c = \cos \theta \tag{10.62}$$

$$s = \sin \theta \tag{10.63}$$

and to determine θ such that $h'_{pq} = 0$. From (10.60),

$$(\cos^2 \theta - \sin^2 \theta)h_{pq} + \sin \theta \cos \theta (h_{pp} - h_{qq}) = 0 \tag{10.64}$$

but

$$\cos^2 \theta - \sin^2 \theta = \cos 2\theta$$

and

$$\sin \theta \cos \theta = \frac{1}{2} \sin 2\theta$$

Using these trigonometric identities, (10.64) becomes

$$(\cos 2\theta)h_{pq} + \frac{1}{2}(\sin 2\theta)(h_{pp} - h_{qq}) = 0$$

or

$$\frac{\sin 2\theta}{\cos 2\theta} = \tan 2\theta = \frac{h_{pq}}{\frac{1}{2}(h_{pp} - h_{qq})} \tag{10.65}$$

Rather than to find θ from (10.65) and then compute $\sin \theta$ and $\cos \theta$, it is more accurate to compute $\sin \theta$ and $\cos \theta$ directly using trigonometric relationships. After some manipulation, we find

$$c = \cos \theta = \left(\frac{1}{2} + \frac{|\alpha|}{2\beta}\right)^{1/2} \tag{10.66}$$

and

$$s = \sin \theta = \frac{\alpha(-h_{pq})}{2\beta|\alpha| \cos \theta} \tag{10.67}$$

where $\alpha = \frac{1}{2}(h_{pp} - h_{qq})$ and $\beta = (h^2_{pq} + \alpha^2)^{1/2}$. It is now necessary to know the effect of the orthogonal transformation on all other elements in the pth and qth rows and pth and qth columns of H. We will not show the details, but these elements become:

pth row and qth row ($j \neq p$ or q)

$$h'_{pj} = ch_{pj} - sh_{qj} \tag{10.68}$$

$$h'_{qj} = sh_{pj} + ch_{qj} \tag{10.69}$$

pth column and qth column ($i \neq p$ or q)

$$h'_{ip} = ch_{ip} - sh_{iq} \tag{10.70}$$

$$h'_{iq} = sh_{ip} + ch_{iq} \tag{10.71}$$

All other elements of H remain unchanged.

The computational procedure now consists of choosing the element h_{pq} which it is desired to make zero (we will discuss the strategy for this choice shortly), then calculate c and s from (10.66) and (10.67). The new values h'_{pp} and h'_{qq} can then be found from (10.58) and (10.59) and h_{pq} and h_{qp} are set to zero. Finally (10.68)–(10.71) provide the remaining modifications to H.

The procedure is now repeated with a new choice of p and q. Unfortunately, in zeroing the new off-diagonal element, the previously zeroed element will, in general, become nonzero.   However, for any logical strategy of zeroing off-diagonal elements, the matrix eventually tends toward diagonal form.   Since the process is an infinite one, some decision must be made as to when the off-diagonal elements have become sufficiently small.

An effective and efficient strategy for choosing the elements to annihilate, as well as for determining when the procedure can be considered to have converged, is termed the *threshold method* and will now be briefly described[3].

The sum of the squares of the off-diagonal elements is given by

$$v = \sum_{\substack{i=1 \\ i \neq j}}^{n} \sum_{j=1}^{n} (h_{ij})^2 \qquad (10.72)$$

Compute v for the original untransformed matrix H (call this value v_0) and then compute

$$\mu_1 = \sqrt{v_0}/n \qquad (10.73)$$

The value μ_1 is now considered to be a threshold value, and all off-diagonal elements greater than or equal to μ_1 are annihilated on a single sweep through the matrix.   Then a new threshold is calculated by

$$\mu_2 = \mu_1/n \qquad (10.74)$$

and the sweep through the matrix is repeated, annihilating any off-diagonal element greater than or equal to μ_2.   The procedure is repeated as many times as necessary, stopping when

$$\mu_i \leq \epsilon \mu_1 \qquad (10.75)$$

where ϵ can be chosen as desired.   This will ensure that the final sum of the squares of the off-diagonal elements is less than $\epsilon^2 v_0$.   (Typically ϵ might be chosen as 10^{-6} or smaller.)

If it is desired to compute the eigenvectors along with the eigenvalues, this can be accomplished by initializing the matrix R as I, and then modifying R along with the modifications to H in the following way:

pth column
$$r_{ip} = cr_{ip} - sr_{iq} \qquad (10.76)$$

qth column

$$r_{iq} = sr_{ip} + cr_{iq} \qquad (10.77)$$

All other columns remain unchanged.   When the eigenvalue problem has converged, the columns of R become the eigenvectors of the original matrix.   Each eigenvector corresponds to the eigenvalue in the same column of the final diagonal form of H.

A flow chart for the Jacobi method, incorporating the threshold strategy and eigenvector computation, is shown in Fig. 10.1.   This flow chart has been condensed somewhat by putting the obvious computation of v_0 in a single block and by using the block with the heavy left border (note A) to denote the matrix operation of setting the matrix R (which has components r_{ij}) to the identity matrix I.

The method can be made more computationally efficient and will require less storage if only the upper half of the matrix is considered.   The algorithm is, however, made somewhat more complicated by this approach.

A detailed example of the Jacobi method is presented in Problem 10.8.

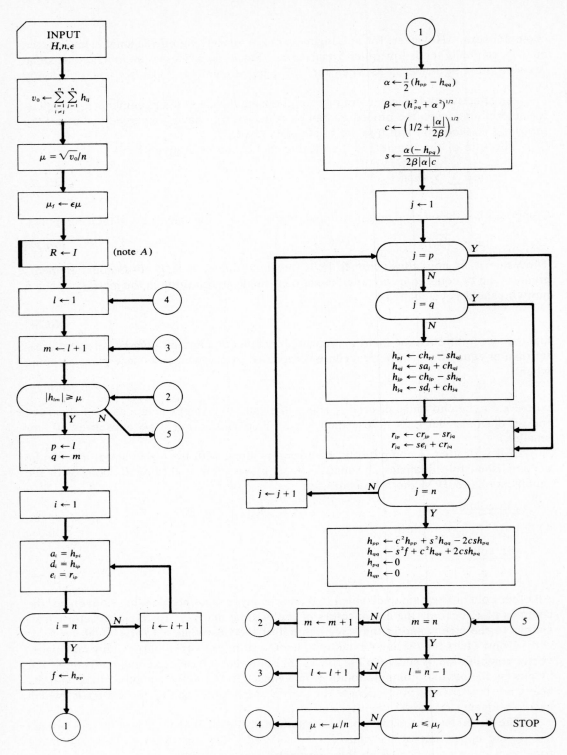

Fig. 10.1 The threshold Jacobi method.

10.6 HOUSEHOLDER'S METHOD

We have just seen that each of the orthogonal transformations in the Jacobi method produces one off-diagonal zero element in the upper half of the matrix (two symmetric zeros in the full matrix) but that this zero is destroyed in subsequent operations.   We will now consider a method for which each orthogonal transformation produces a large number of zeros in a given row (and column).   Furthermore, any zeros produced will remain zero under all subsequent transformations.   This highly efficient technique is known as Householder's method.

Consider once again the $n \times n$ symmetric matrix H which we illustrate as a 4×4 matrix:

$$H = \begin{bmatrix} h_{11} & h_{12} & h_{13} & h_{14} \\ h_{21} & h_{22} & h_{23} & h_{24} \\ h_{31} & h_{32} & h_{33} & h_{34} \\ h_{41} & h_{42} & h_{43} & h_{44} \end{bmatrix} \tag{10.78}$$

We will now construct a symmetric orthogonal matrix T_1 such that

$$T_1 H T_1^T = \begin{bmatrix} h'_{11} & h'_{12} & 0 & 0 \\ h'_{21} & h'_{22} & h'_{23} & h'_{24} \\ 0 & h'_{32} & h'_{33} & h'_{34} \\ 0 & h'_{42} & h'_{43} & h'_{44} \end{bmatrix} \tag{10.79}$$

where the product $T_1 H$ will produce the zeros in the first column, and the postmultiplication by T_1^T (which is also T_1 due to the symmetry of T_1) will produce the zeros in the first row.   The general form of T_1 for this first application of the orthogonal transformation is

$$T_1 = \begin{bmatrix} 1 & 0 & 0 & 0 \\ 0 & & & \\ 0 & & P & \\ 0 & & & \end{bmatrix} \tag{10.80}$$

where P is a symmetric orthogonal submatrix chosen to produce the desired zeros in the first column of H.   Consider the product $T_1 H$:

$$T_1 H = \begin{bmatrix} 1 & 0 & 0 & 0 \\ 0 & & & \\ 0 & & P & \\ 0 & & & \end{bmatrix} \begin{bmatrix} h_{11} & h_{12} & h_{13} & h_{14} \\ h_{21} & h_{22} & h_{23} & h_{24} \\ h_{31} & h_{32} & h_{33} & h_{34} \\ h_{41} & h_{42} & h_{43} & h_{44} \end{bmatrix}$$

The first row of H is clearly not affected by this premultiplication by T_1.   The matrix P thus acts on the lower $n-1$ rows of H (the lower 3 rows in our example).   The effect of P on the first column of H is that of a matrix times a vector, or

$$\begin{bmatrix} & P & \end{bmatrix} \begin{bmatrix} h_{21} \\ h_{31} \\ h_{41} \end{bmatrix}$$

As indicated in (10.79), we wish this product to produce zeros in the last two elements of the vector.   Thus

$$\begin{bmatrix} & P & \end{bmatrix}\begin{bmatrix} h_{21} \\ h_{31} \\ h_{41} \end{bmatrix} = \begin{bmatrix} h'_{21} \\ 0 \\ 0 \end{bmatrix} = h'_{21}\begin{bmatrix} 1 \\ 0 \\ 0 \end{bmatrix} \qquad (10.81)$$

Since P is orthogonal, the length of the original vector is preserved in this product, so

$$h'_{21} = \sqrt{h_{21}^2 + h_{31}^2 + h_{41}^2} = S \qquad (10.82)$$

A suitable matrix P to accomplish the desired result is given by

$$P = I - \frac{UU^T}{S^2 \pm h_{21}S} \qquad (10.83)$$

where U is a vector defined as

$$U = \begin{bmatrix} h_{21} \pm S \\ h_{31} \\ h_{41} \end{bmatrix} \qquad (10.84)$$

and where the sign to be used in both (10.83) and (10.84) is the sign which *maximizes* $|h_{21} \pm S|$. As we have noted earlier in this chapter, a matrix formed as the product of a vector times its transpose is symmetric. Thus $UU^T/(S^2 \pm h_{21}S)$ is symmetric, and since I is symmetric, P must be symmetric. We now have the tools to construct T_1 as given by (10.80). Forming the product T_1H produces the desired zeros in the first column of H. We noted earlier that the product T_1H left the first row of H unchanged. In an entirely similar way, postmultiplying T_1H by T_1 leaves the first column of T_1H unchanged. Since the transformation is orthogonal, T_1HT_1 must be symmetric, and the zeros from the first column of T_1H also appear in the first row of T_1HT_1. We thus have a matrix of the form shown in (10.79).

The next step is to create zeros in the second row and second column of the matrix. This can be accomplished by use of the orthogonal matrix

$$T_2 = \begin{bmatrix} 1 & 0 & 0 & 0 \\ 0 & 1 & 0 & 0 \\ 0 & 0 & \multicolumn{2}{c}{} \\ 0 & 0 & \multicolumn{2}{c}{P} \end{bmatrix} \qquad (10.85)$$

The submatrix P is constructed exactly as before, except that the vector U is constructed from the second column of (10.79) with the top 2 elements omitted. If we denote the original matrix H as H_1, and the matrix (10.79) as H_2, then

$$T_2H_2T_2 = \begin{bmatrix} h'_{11} & h'_{12} & 0 & 0 \\ h'_{21} & h''_{22} & h''_{23} & 0 \\ 0 & h''_{32} & h''_{33} & h''_{34} \\ 0 & 0 & h''_{43} & h''_{44} \end{bmatrix} \qquad (10.86)$$

For the 4×4 example, this is as far as the method can be carried. The matrix (10.86) is tridiagonal and symmetric. It is apparent that if the same method is applied to a symmetric matrix of arbitrary size, a symmetric tridiagonal matrix will result.

We have not yet obtained the eigenvalues of the original matrix, but we have reduced the original full matrix to a specialized form which is much easier to deal with. We are

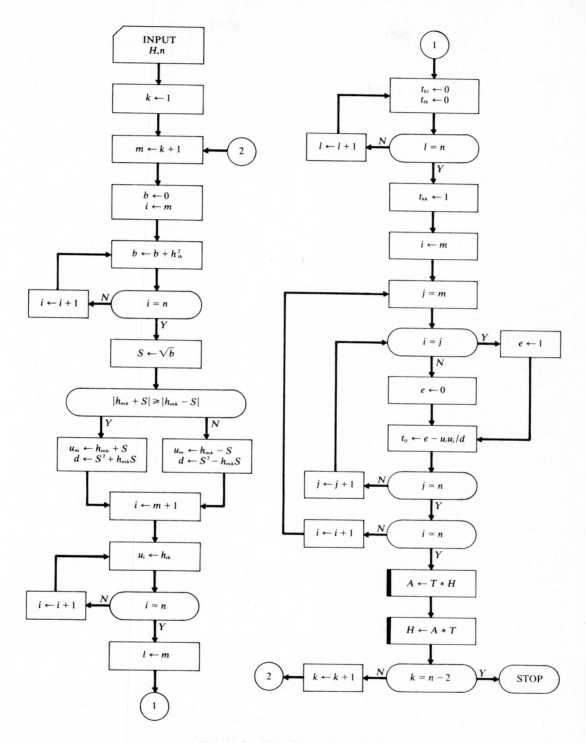

Fig. 10.2 Householder's method.

now in a position to present a flow chart of Householder's method. The flow chart is shown in Fig. 10.2. As in the previous section, the boxes with the heavy left borders in Fig. 10.2 represent operations on complete matrices, i.e. the multiplication of T times H and storage in the temporary matrix A, and then the postmultiplication of (TH) by T. If desired, only those parts of the matrices which affect the final result need be multiplied (the lower $n - m + 1$ rows and columns of each matrix) and the remaining elements can be ignored or filled in with the expected zeros, etc. The details are obvious and are not shown, so as to simplify the flow chart.

This algorithm can be made more efficient and will use less storage space by taking full advantage of symmetry and operating with only the upper halves of matrices.

A detailed example of Householder's method is presented in Problem 10.9.

A number of methods can be employed to find the eigenvalues of the symmetric tridiagonal matrix which results from Householder's method. The most efficient and effective techniques are based on the LR and QR transformations. In the next section we will consider these transformations in general, and then in the following section a specific method for tridiagonal matrices will be discussed in detail.

10.7 THE *LR* AND *QR* ALGORITHMS

The LR algorithm was originated by Rutishauser[27] in 1958, while the QR algorithm is due to Francis[28] and first appeared in 1961. The letter L refers to a lower triangular matrix (its original meaning was *L*eft), while R refers to an upper triangular matrix (*R*ight). The letter Q denotes an orthogonal matrix.

The LR algorithm is based on the fact that virtually any matrix can be decomposed into a product of lower triangular and upper triangular matrices. Thus if we denote the original matrix H as H_1, we can write

$$H_1 = L_1 R_1 \tag{10.87}$$

and the upper triangular matrix R_1 can be expressed as

$$R_1 = L_1^{-1} H_1 \tag{10.88}$$

If we now multiply the lower and upper triangular matrices of (10.87) in reverse order, we find

$$R_1 L_1 = (L_1^{-1} H_1) L_1 \tag{10.89}$$

In other words, the reverse multiplication $R_1 L_1$ is a similarity transformation of H_1 and thus preserves the eigenvalues of H_1. Now let

$$H_2 = R_1 L_1 \tag{10.90}$$

and decompose H_2 as was done with H_1:

$$H_2 = L_2 R_2 \tag{10.91}$$

and then compute

$$H_3 = R_2 L_2 \tag{10.92}$$

Under certain conditions on the original matrix H, as $k \to \infty$ the matrix H_k will approach a lower triangular matrix with the eigenvalues in decreasing order of magnitude on the main diagonal. If H is symmetric and positive definite, then the method will converge, and the decomposition into lower and upper triangular matrices can be accomplished very efficiently by the Choleski decomposition discussed in Sec. 10.2. (See Problem 10.11.) If H is symmetric but not positive definite, then the method tends to be unstable due to roundoff error. This can be overcome by performing the decomposition by a method which is essentially Gauss elimination with maximization of pivot elements by means of row interchanges [26]. We will reserve the discussion of unsymmetric H for Sec. 10.10.

The QR algorithm is similar to the LR algorithm except that H is decomposed into the product of an orthogonal matrix and an upper triangular matrix. That is,

$$H_1 = Q_1 R_1 \tag{10.93}$$

Now, interchanging the order of multiplication, we find

$$H_2 = R_1 Q_1 = (Q_1^{-1} H_1) Q_1 \tag{10.94}$$

The transformation of H_1 into H_2 is orthogonal (since Q_1 is orthogonal) and thus preserves not only the eigenvalues of H_1 but also symmetry (assuming that H_1 is symmetric). In addition, algorithms based on orthogonal transformations tend to be stable, so that the instability which can afflict the LR algorithm is not a problem with QR. When the QR algorithm is convergent (which it is for most matrices), H_k ($k \rightarrow \infty$) is upper triangular (diagonal if the original matrix is symmetric) with the eigenvalues of the original matrix on the main diagonal in decreasing order of magnitude. It is beyond the scope of this text to give the details of the decomposition into Q and R in general. However, in the next section we will discuss in detail a version of the QR algorithm which is tailored specifically to symmetric tridiagonal matrices.

Both the LR and QR algorithms converge at essentially the same rate, although the QR algorithm requires considerably more computation per step and is thus less efficient than LR. The rate of convergence of both methods is, in fact, usually too slow to be practical for large matrices unless some acceleration scheme is employed. Consider the QR algorithm for the case where the eigenvalues are real and there are no multiple eigenvalues. Recall that H_k is the matrix after k iterations. Denote the eigenvalues as $\lambda_1, \lambda_2, \ldots, \lambda_n$ in decreasing order of magnitude. Then an element below the main diagonal of H_k, say $h_{ij}^{(k)}$, converges to zero like $(|\lambda_i|/|\lambda_j|)^k$. (Since $h_{ij}^{(k)}$ is below the main diagonal, $i > j$ and thus the ratio $|\lambda_i|/|\lambda_j|$ is less than one.) Another way of looking at this convergence rate is that the difference between the bottom diagonal element $h_{nn}^{(k)}$, and the smallest eigenvalue in magnitude, λ_n, is decreased by a factor of approximately λ_n/λ_{n-1} on each iteration. This factor can be considerably decreased by a shifting strategy which shows a certain family resemblance to the shifting approach used for accelerating the power method. If we have an estimate of λ_n, say η_n, and instead of decomposing H_k, we let

$$H_k - \eta_n I = Q_k R_k \tag{10.95}$$

and then shift back on the reverse multiplication:

$$H_{k+1} = R_k Q_k + \eta_k I \tag{10.96}$$

the resulting transformation is still orthogonal and converges considerably faster. In fact, if we choose η_k as the eigenvalue of the 2×2 submatrix at the bottom right corner of the matrix which is closest to $h_{nn}^{(k)}$, then $h_{nn}^{(k)} - \lambda_n$ will be decreased by a factor of approximately $(n/\lambda_{n-1})^2$ at each iteration. When λ_n is found sufficiently accurately (i.e.

does not change by more than a predetermined value on a given iteration), then the matrix can be deflated by dropping the last row and column and continuing the iterative process. Thus not only is the convergence accelerated, but the matrix becomes successively smaller as each new eigenvalue is found, further reducing the labor. An entirely analogous acceleration method can be employed with the *LR* algorithm for symmetric positive definite matrices, although the shift at each stage must be adjusted so that the positive definite character of the matrix is retained.

Finally, and perhaps most importantly, we note that the *LR* and *QR* algorithms, even in accelerated form, are not efficient enough for general use in obtaining all of the eigenvalues of a full symmetric matrix.* However, they are highly useful in obtaining the eigenvalues from the symmetric tridiagonal form which results from Householder's method. If the matrix is positive definite (or if one is willing to make it positive definite by adding an unknown constant to all main diagonal elements), then the accelerated *LR* algorithm using the Choleski decomposition is the most efficient known method. Some special strategy will usually be required to deal with multiple eigenvalues. A safer approach, which works whether or not the matrix is positive definite, is the accelerated *QR* algorithm or a modification thereof. In the following section we will consider a modification of the *QR* algorithm, called the *QL* algorithm, which is very well suited for general use and is quite efficient.

10.8 THE *QL* ALGORITHM

The *QL* algorithm is based on a minor modification of the *QR* algorithm and is intended specifically for finding the eigenvalues of symmetric tridiagonal matrices such as those produced by Householder's method. The algorithm as described here is that of Bowdler, Martin, Reinsch, and Wilkinson[29]. As its name implies, the algorithm is based on the decomposition of the matrix into the product of an orthogonal matrix and a lower triangular matrix:

$$H_1 = Q_1 L_1 \tag{10.97}$$

This decomposition is followed by the reverse multiplication of these two matrices:

$$H_2 = L_1 Q_1 = Q_1^{-1} H Q_1 = Q_1^T H_1 Q_1 \tag{10.98}$$

which is an orthogonal transformation of H_1. The eigenvalues and symmetry of H_1 are thus preserved. The decomposition and reverse multiplication could be carried out as many times as desired, eventually resulting in a diagonal matrix with the eigenvalues on the diagonal. However, the method can be considerably accelerated by using a variation of the shift technique discussed in the last section. This modified procedure yields H_{j+1} from H_j through the operations

$$H_j - \eta_j I = Q_j L_j \tag{10.99}$$

$$H_{j+1} = L_j Q_j \tag{10.100}$$

where η_j is a constant which changes at each stage of the process. Note that the shift η_j is not added back on during the remultiplication (10.100). This is accommodated by

---

*Or, for that matter, in finding the eigenvalues of a full unsymmetric matrix. They are invaluable as *a part* of the overall strategy for unsymmetric matrices, but we defer this discussion until Sec. 10.10.

accumulating the shift and adding it back to each newly computed eigenvalue before it is finally stored.   The orthogonal matrix Q_i is constructed as the product of a set of $n - 1$ simple orthogonal matrices, each of which is chosen such that it eliminates one of the off-diagonal elements of the tridiagonal matrix.   We will not go through the details of the derivation here.   We do note that symmetry is preserved due to the orthogonal transformations, and that no nonzero elements appear outside of the tridiagonal band.   The notation for the elements of the tridiagonal matrix is given by

$$
H_i = \begin{bmatrix}
d_1^{(j)} & e_1^{(j)} & & & & \\
e_1^{(j)} & d_2^{(j)} & e_2^{(j)} & & & \\
& - & - & - & & \\
& & - & - & - & \\
& & & e_{n-2}^{(j)} & d_{n-1}^{(j)} & e_{n-1}^{(j)} \\
& & & & e_{n-1}^{(j)} & d_n^{(j)}
\end{bmatrix}
\qquad (10.101)
$$

Due to the symmetry, we need deal only with the diagonal elements $d_1^{(j)}, d_2^{(j)}, \ldots, d_n^{(j)}$ and the superdiagonal elements $e_1^{(j)}, e_2^{(j)}, \ldots, e_{n-1}^{(j)}$.   One complete iteration through (10.99) and (10.100) results in the following modifications to the d and e arrays:

$$
d_i^{(j)} = d_i^{(j)} - \eta_j, \quad i = 1, 2, \ldots, n
$$

$$
p_n = d_n^{(j)}
$$

$$
c_n = 1
$$

$$
s_n = 0
$$

$$
\left.
\begin{aligned}
r_{i+1} &= (p_{i+1}^2 + (e_i^{(j)})^2)^{1/2} \\
g_{i+1} &= c_{i+1} e_i^{(j)} \\
h_{i+1} &= c_{i+1} p_{i+1} \\
\rightarrow e_{i+1}^{(j+1)} &= s_{i+1} r_{i+1} \\
c_i &= p_{i+1}/r_{i+1} \\
s_i &= e_i^{(j)}/r_{i+1} \\
p_i &= c_i d_i^{(j)} - s_i g_{i+1} \\
\rightarrow d_{i+1}^{(j+1)} &= h_{i+1} + s_i(c_i g_{i+1} + s_i d_i^{(j)})
\end{aligned}
\right\} \quad i = n-1, n-2, \ldots, 1 \qquad (10.102)
$$

$$
\rightarrow e_1^{(j+1)} = s_1 p_1
$$

$$
\rightarrow d_1^{(j+1)} = c_1 p_1
$$

The shift η_j is first chosen in such a way that an eigenvalue tends to appear at the upper left corner of the matrix in the position of d_1 as e_1 tends to zero.   Once this eigenvalue has been isolated, the first row and column of the matrix can be eliminated from consideration, and the algorithm carried out on a submatrix consisting of the remaining $n - 1$ rows and columns.   This time the shift is chosen such that an eigenvalue will tend to appear in the position of d_2 as e_2 tends to zero, etc.   This is continued until all eigenvalues have been found.   The resulting eigenvalues are not arranged in any specific order on the diagonal.

The choice of the shift η_j to produce the desired behavior can now be described. Suppose that at some stage we are dealing with the submatrix starting with $d_q^{(j)}$. Then the shift is given by the eigenvalue of the 2×2 matrix

$$\begin{bmatrix} d_q^{(j)} & e_q^{(j)} \\ e_q^{(j)} & d_{q+1}^{(j)} \end{bmatrix}$$

which is closest to $d_q^{(j)}$. The shift η_j is thus chosen as one of the two values of η_j obtained from

$$\det \begin{bmatrix} d_q^{(j)} - \eta_j & e_q^{(j)} \\ e_q^{(j)} & e_q^{(j)} - \eta_j \end{bmatrix} = 0 \qquad\qquad (10.103)$$

Now suppose that we are about to iterate for the eigenvalue which will appear in the position d_q. Then compute

$$t_q = \epsilon(|d_q^{(j)}| + |e_q^{(j)}|) \qquad\qquad (10.104)$$

where ϵ is a very small number, on the order of the smallest number which can be represented on the particular computer being used. Next choose

$$b_q = \max_{i=1,2,\ldots,q} t_i \qquad\qquad (10.105)$$

At the current stage, any off-diagonal element $e_i^{(j)}$ such that

$$|e_i^{(j)}| < b_q \qquad\qquad (10.106)$$

is assumed to be zero. In particular, when $|e_q^{(j)}| < b_q$, then $d_q^{(j)}$ (plus the accumulated shift) is the desired eigenvalue.

If there are multiple or very close eigenvalues, then some off-diagonal element farther down in the matrix may also satisfy (10.106). If so, then the matrix splits at that point into two independent tridiagonal matrices. The part of the matrix which is below the negligible off-diagonal can then be ignored in determining the eigenvalues which appear in the diagonal positions above that point. This can result in significant savings in computer time in some cases.

A flow chart of the algorithm is shown in Fig. 10.3. Not all of the sophistication of the original algorithm has been included, but the essentials are present. Reference 29 also includes a slightly modified form of the algorithm which produces the eigenvectors along with the eigenvalues. The algorithm is remarkably efficient (often only 2 or 3 iterations per eigenvalue are required) and will work accurately for almost all tridiagonal symmetric matrices. See the original paper for some possible difficulties involving elements of widely differing magnitudes. (The algorithm is designed to be most accurate with matrices which have the largest elements in magnitude in the lower right corner. This is the reason for the use of the QL strategy rather than QR.) An example of QL is given in Problem 10.10.

A different version of the QL algorithm with better roundoff error properties has been given by Martin and Wilkinson[30].

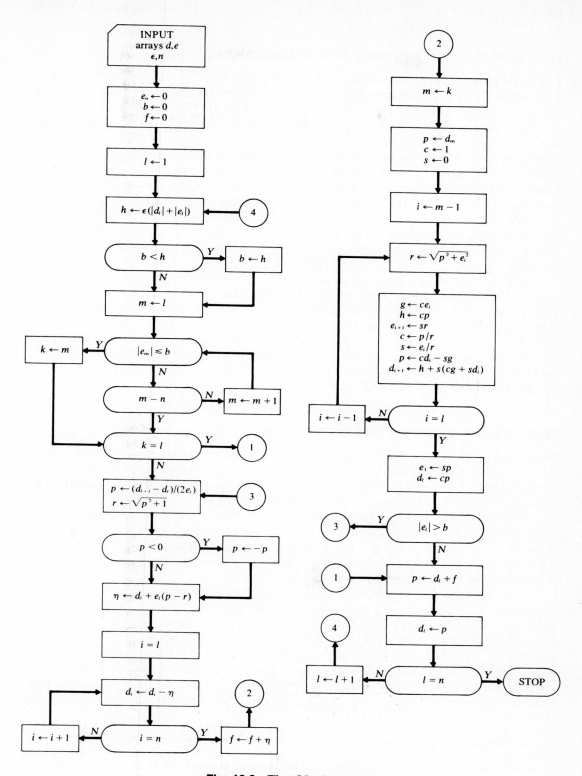

Fig. 10.3 The QL algorithm.

10.9 A REVIEW OF METHODS FOR SYMMETRIC MATRICES

For single problems involving small and moderate-sized matrices (say $n \leq 40$),* efficiency is of relatively little importance, and it is entirely reasonable and safe to use the Jacobi method to obtain all of the eigenvalues, and, if desired, the eigenvectors as well.

If it is necessary to find all of the eigenvalues of large matrices (n ranging up to several hundred), then efficiency becomes a prime consideration.   In this event, the best combination of efficiency and safety probably consists of Householder's method to produce a tridiagonal form, followed by the QL algorithm to obtain the final eigenvalues.   Variations of the LR algorithm which involve the Choleski decomposition can be more efficient than QL if it is known that the tridiagonal matrix is positive definite.

We should note that some rather effective techniques are also available for finding the eigenvalues from a form of the characteristic polynomial of the tridiagonal matrix which results from Householder's method.   See Wilkinson[26] for a discussion of these methods.

For matrices of any size, the power method, including acceleration procedures as needed, can be effectively used to find the dominant eigenvalue and its associated eigenvector.   For very large matrices (size limited only by hardware and economic considerations) this is often the only possible approach.   Deflation techniques can subsequently be used for matrices of any size to find at least the first few subdominant eigenvalues.   However, this approach may eventually stall due to the slow convergence which results from closely spaced eigenvalues, or for large matrices will eventually fail due to accumulation of roundoff error.

10.10 EIGENVALUES OF UNSYMMETRIC MATRICES

Unlike real symmetric matrices, real *unsymmetric* matrices can have complex eigenvalues.   In addition, the eigenvectors are not in general orthogonal, but do possess the weaker property of *biorthogonality*.   This means that the eigenvectors of the matrix are orthogonal to the eigenvectors of the transposed matrix.

While the procedures for such problems will necessarily be somewhat different from those employed for symmetric matrices, the tools which we have acquired from previous sections are still useful.   We will not go into the details of the various methods here, but we will give a brief overall view of the possible approaches, and indicate where detailed descriptions of the effective methods can be found.

It was determined in preceding sections that the most efficient approach to solving eigenvalue problems involving symmetric matrices began with the use of Householder's method to reduce the matrix to tridiagonal form.   The eigenvalues could then be obtained from the tridiagonal form through the use of various modifications of the LR or QR algorithms.   A somewhat analogous approach is used for unsymmetric matrices.   However, the special matrix form which can most readily be obtained for unsymmetric matrices is not tridiagonal, but instead consists of an upper triangular form with an addition band of elements adjacent to the main diagonal.   This form is known as an *upper*

---

*As we observed in Chapter 6, when matrix problems are involved, the meaning of "large" and "small" is determined entirely by the available computer hardware (and money).   The numbers we quote in this section are purely for discussion purposes, and the reader should determine the various break-even points in the context of the available computing environment.

Hessenberg (or simply *Hessenberg*) form and is shown in Fig. 10.4.   (This form is also called "almost triangular.")

$$\begin{bmatrix} h_{11} & h_{12} & — & — & — & — & h_{1n} \\ h_{21} & h_{22} & — & — & — & — & h_{2n} \\ & h_{32} & — & — & — & — & — \\ & & — & — & — & — & — \\ & & & — & — & — & — \\ & & & & — & — & — \\ & & & & & h_{n,n-1} & h_{nn} \end{bmatrix}$$

Fig. 10.4   A matrix in Hessenberg form.

If Householder's method is applied to an unsymmetric matrix, then the result is, in fact, a Hessenberg matrix and not a tridiagonal one.   However, Householder's method is not the most efficient method for obtaining such a form.   A version of Gauss elimination, slightly modified to ensure that it is a similarity transformation, and including maximization of pivot elements to provide stability against roundoff error, also yields a Hessenberg form.   This approach requires only about half the number of basic operations required by Householder's method.   This method as well as other effective approaches for accomplishing the same objective is described by Martin and Wilkinson[31] and presented in the form of ALGOL procedures.

For obtaining the eigenvalues from the upper Hessenberg form, a variety of approaches are possible, including the *LR* and *QR* algorithms.   The best approach would appear to be the stable *QR* algorithm in the efficient form presented by Martin, Peters, and Wilkinson[32].

If the dominant eigenvalue of the matrix is real, then the power method can be employed exactly as discussed in Sec. 10.3 and will yield this dominant eigenvalue.   However, if the dominant eigenvalue is complex, the standard power method is not convergent and some modifications will be required[26].   Hotelling's deflation (Sec. 10.3) is best suited to symmetric matrices, and other deflation techniques are suggested for unsymmetric matrices.   See Ralston[3] for some discussion of the use of the power method and deflation for unsymmetric matrices with possibly complex eigenvalues.

10.11 ALGORITHMS AVAILABLE AS ALGOL PROCEDURES

Many of the most effective algorithms for finding the eigenvalues (and in some cases the eigenvectors) of matrices are available in the form of ALGOL procedures (the ALGOL equivalent of a FORTRAN subroutine).   These algorithms have been, for the most part, very efficiently coded, and the conversion from ALGOL to any other language is surprisingly simple once one has mastered the rudiments of ALGOL.   In this connection, McCracken[33] can be very helpful.   As we have noted previously, familiarity with any algebraic language makes the understanding of virtually any other algebraic language quite simple.

All of these algorithms have appeared in the journal *Numerische Mathematik* (these articles are in English), mostly in the Handbook Series Linear Algebra.   The algorithms and the volume number, year, and page are given below for easy reference.   The complete titles and authors can be found in the list of references at the back of this book.

1. Choleski decomposition of a positive definite matrix. v 7, 1965, p. 362. [34]
2. Reduction of $AX = \lambda BX$ to $HX = \lambda X$. v 7, 1968, p. 99. [35]
3. Householder's method (real matrices). v 11, 1968, p. 181. [36]
4. The QL algorithm (also includes eigenvectors). v 11, 1968, p. 293. [29]
5. The implicit QL algorithm (has better roundoff properties than the original QL algorithms; also includes eigenvectors). v 12, 1969, p. 377. [30]
6. The LR algorithm (real symmetric matrices). v 5, 1963, p. 273. [37]
7. The QR algorithm (real symmetric tridiagonal matrices—particularly suited to calculation of a few of the largest or smallest eigenvalues). v 11, 1968, p. 264. [38]
8. Balancing a matrix for calculation of eigenvalues and eigenvectors (preprocessing of matrices with this algorithm will give best accuracy when the other algorithms quoted here are employed). v 13, 1969, p. 293. [39]
9. Similarity reduction of a general matrix to Hessenberg form (a variety of approaches applicable to complex as well as real matrices). v 12, 1969, p. 349. [31]
10. The QR algorithm (real Hessenberg matrices). v 14, 1969, p. 219. [32]

Illustrative Problems

10.1 Put the following special eigenvalue problem in the standard form $HX = \lambda X$ where H is symmetric:

$$\begin{bmatrix} 4 & 7 & 3 \\ 7 & 8 & 2 \\ 3 & 2 & 1 \end{bmatrix} \begin{bmatrix} x_1 \\ x_2 \\ x_3 \end{bmatrix} = \lambda \begin{bmatrix} 9 & 0 & 0 \\ 0 & 4 & 0 \\ 0 & 0 & 2 \end{bmatrix} \begin{bmatrix} x_1 \\ x_2 \\ x_3 \end{bmatrix}$$

The matrix on the right-hand side is particularly easy to decompose.   (It is obviously positive definite, since the diagonal elements, which are the eigenvalues, are positive.)   The Choleski decomposition (*10.28*) of this matrix involves simply taking the square root of the diagonal elements.   Thus

$$L = \begin{bmatrix} \sqrt{9} & 0 & 0 \\ 0 & \sqrt{4} & 0 \\ 0 & 0 & \sqrt{2} \end{bmatrix} = L^T$$

and

$$L^{-1} = \begin{bmatrix} \dfrac{1}{\sqrt{9}} & 0 & 0 \\ 0 & \dfrac{1}{\sqrt{4}} & 0 \\ 0 & 0 & \dfrac{1}{\sqrt{2}} \end{bmatrix} = L^{-T}$$

Using (10.24), the original problem can now be written as

$$
\begin{bmatrix} \dfrac{1}{\sqrt{9}} & 0 & 0 \\[2mm] 0 & \dfrac{1}{\sqrt{4}} & 0 \\[2mm] 0 & 0 & \dfrac{1}{\sqrt{2}} \end{bmatrix}
\begin{bmatrix} 4 & 7 & 3 \\ 7 & 8 & 2 \\ 3 & 2 & 1 \end{bmatrix}
\begin{bmatrix} \dfrac{1}{\sqrt{9}} & 0 & 0 \\[2mm] 0 & \dfrac{1}{\sqrt{4}} & 0 \\[2mm] 0 & 0 & \dfrac{1}{\sqrt{2}} \end{bmatrix}
\begin{bmatrix} z_1 \\ z_2 \\ z_3 \end{bmatrix} = \lambda \begin{bmatrix} z_1 \\ z_2 \\ z_3 \end{bmatrix}
$$

or

$$
\begin{bmatrix} \dfrac{2}{3} & \dfrac{7}{6} & \dfrac{1}{\sqrt{2}} \\[2mm] \dfrac{7}{6} & 2 & \dfrac{1}{\sqrt{2}} \\[2mm] \dfrac{1}{\sqrt{2}} & \dfrac{1}{\sqrt{2}} & \dfrac{1}{2} \end{bmatrix}
\begin{bmatrix} z_1 \\ z_2 \\ z_3 \end{bmatrix} = \lambda \begin{bmatrix} z_1 \\ z_2 \\ z_3 \end{bmatrix}
$$

where $Z = L^T X$. This is the desired form.

10.2 Illustrate the Choleski decomposition of

$$
B = \begin{bmatrix} 8 & 1 & 3 \\ 1 & 6 & 4 \\ 3 & 4 & 4 \end{bmatrix}
$$

Following the Choleski decomposition algorithm (10.28), we find

$$l_{11} = (b_{11})^{1/2} = (8)^{1/2} = 2.828427$$

$$l_{21} = \left(b_{21} - \sum_{k=1}^{0} l_{2k}l_{1k}\right)/l_{11} = b_{21}/l_{11} = 1/2.828427 = 0.3535534$$

$$l_{22} = \sqrt{b_{22} - \sum_{k=1}^{1} l_{2k}^2} = \sqrt{b_{22} - l_{21}^2} = \sqrt{6 - (0.3535534)^2}$$
$$= 2.423840$$

$$l_{31} = \left(b_{31} - \sum_{k=1}^{0} l_{3k}l_{1k}\right)\Big/ l_{11} = b_{31}/l_{11} = 3/2.828427 = 1.060660$$

$$l_{32} = \left(b_{32} - \sum_{k=1}^{1} l_{3k}l_{2k}\right)\Big/ l_{22} = (b_{32} - l_{31}l_{21})/l_{22}$$
$$= (4 - (1.060660)(0.3535534))/2.423840 = 1.495561$$

$$l_{33} = \sqrt{b_{33} - \sum_{k=1}^{2} l_{3k}^2} = \sqrt{b_{33} - l_{31}^2 - l_{32}^2}$$
$$= \sqrt{4 - (1.060660)^2 - (1.495561)^2} = 0.7989374$$

Thus

$$
L = \begin{bmatrix} 2.828427 & 0 & 0 \\ 0.3535534 & 2.423840 & 0 \\ 1.060660 & 1.495561 & 0.7989374 \end{bmatrix}
$$

This is the required Choleski decomposition such that $LL^T = B$.

10.3 Convert the eigenvalue problem

$$\begin{bmatrix} 7 & 4 & 3 \\ 4 & 8 & 2 \\ 3 & 2 & 6 \end{bmatrix} \begin{bmatrix} x_1 \\ x_2 \\ x_3 \end{bmatrix} = \lambda \begin{bmatrix} 8 & 1 & 3 \\ 1 & 6 & 4 \\ 3 & 4 & 4 \end{bmatrix} \begin{bmatrix} x_1 \\ x_2 \\ x_3 \end{bmatrix}$$

into the standard symmetric form $HX = \lambda X$.

In the previous problem, we performed the Choleski decomposition of the matrix on the right-hand side of the equation into the product LL^T. The next step is to find L^{-1}. Using the algorithm (10.32) to invert the lower triangular matrix, we find

$$l_{11}^{-1} = 1/l_{11} = 1/2.828427 = 0.3535534$$

$$l_{22}^{-1} = 1/l_{22} = 1/2.423840 = 0.4125684$$

$$l_{21}^{-1} = \frac{-\sum_{k=2}^{2} l_{2k}^{-1} l_{k1}}{l_{11}} = \frac{-l_{22}^{-1} l_{21}}{l_{11}} = \frac{-(0.4125684)(0.3535534)}{2.828427} = -0.0515710$$

$$l_{33}^{-1} = 1/l_{33} = 1/0.7989374 = 1.251663$$

$$l_{32}^{-1} = \frac{-\sum_{k=3}^{3} l_{3k}^{-1} l_{k2}}{l_{22}} = \frac{-l_{33}^{-1} l_{32}}{l_{22}} = \frac{-(1.251663)(1.495561)}{2.423840} = -0.7723027$$

$$l_{31}^{-1} = \frac{-\sum_{k=2}^{3} l_{3k}^{-1} l_{k1}}{l_{11}} = \frac{-l_{32}^{-1} l_{21} - l_{33}^{-1} l_{31}}{l_{11}}$$

$$= \frac{-(-0.7723027)(0.3535534) - (1.251663)(1.060660)}{2.828427} = -0.3728357$$

Thus

$$L^{-1} = \begin{bmatrix} 0.3535534 & 0 & 0 \\ -0.0515710 & 0.4125684 & 0 \\ -0.3728357 & -0.7723027 & 1.251663 \end{bmatrix}$$

and $L^{-T} = (L^{-1})^T$. Now if we let

$$A = \begin{bmatrix} 7 & 4 & 3 \\ 4 & 8 & 2 \\ 3 & 2 & 6 \end{bmatrix}$$

and then form $H = L^{-1} A L^{-T}$, we find

$$H = \begin{bmatrix} 0.874995 & 0.4558279 & -0.6873331 \\ 0.4558280 & 1.210105 & -2.031250 \\ -0.6873331 & -2.031250 & 10.78151 \end{bmatrix}$$

The desired eigenvalue problem is now given by

$$HZ = \lambda Z$$

where $Z = L^T X$, and X represents the eigenvectors of the original problem.

The eigenvalues and eigenvectors of H can be determined by any standard method and are

$$\lambda_1 = 11.25110, \qquad \lambda_2 = 1.116762, \qquad \lambda_3 = 0.4987418$$

and

$$Z_1 = \begin{bmatrix} -0.0735353 \\ -0.2009482 \\ 0.9768379 \end{bmatrix}, \qquad Z_2 = \begin{bmatrix} 0.7174467 \\ 0.6696962 \\ 0.1917738 \end{bmatrix}, \qquad Z_3 = \begin{bmatrix} -0.6927215 \\ 0.7149313 \\ 0.0949232 \end{bmatrix}$$

The eigenvalues are those of the original problem, and the original eigenvectors can be determined from $X = L^{-T}Z$. For example,

$$X_1 = L^{-T}Z_1 = \begin{bmatrix} 0.3535534 & -0.0515710 & -0.3728357 \\ 0 & 0.4125684 & -0.7723027 \\ 0 & 0 & 1.251663 \end{bmatrix} \begin{bmatrix} -0.0735353 \\ -0.2009482 \\ 0.9768379 \end{bmatrix}$$

$$= \begin{bmatrix} -0.3798356 \\ -0.8373193 \\ 1.222672 \end{bmatrix}$$

10.4 Find the dominant eigenvalue and corresponding eigenvector of

$$\begin{bmatrix} -3 & 8 & 9 \\ 8 & -2 & 4 \\ 9 & 4 & 2 \end{bmatrix}$$

Use the power method, and show the effects of shifting to increase the convergence rate.

The straight power method, without relaxation, and with an initial guess of

$$V = \begin{bmatrix} 1 \\ 1 \\ 1 \end{bmatrix}$$

and an absolute convergence criterion of 10^{-5} on the eigenvalue, requires 124 iterations to produce the following results:

$$\lambda_1 = 13.25761, \qquad X_1 = \begin{bmatrix} 0.9199474 \\ 0.7445194 \\ 1 \end{bmatrix}$$

From the large number of iterations required, it should be apparent that $|\lambda_1| \approx |\lambda_2|$, or in other words that the dominance ratio is close to unity. As we have mentioned in this chapter, a strategy of shifting all of the eigenvalues by a constant may be helpful in this situation, particularly if λ_1 and λ_2 have opposite signs. Simply by adding a constant to the main diagonal elements of the matrix, the eigenvalues are all shifted by this constant. We will attempt to accelerate the slow convergence in the present problem by adding 5 to each main diagonal element. The resulting matrix is

$$\begin{bmatrix} 2 & 8 & 9 \\ 8 & 3 & 4 \\ 9 & 4 & 7 \end{bmatrix}$$

Again using an initial estimate of all 1's for the eigenvector, the power method applied to this matrix with the same convergence criterion as before requires only 14 iterations to yield

$$\lambda_1 = 18.25760, \qquad X_1 = \begin{bmatrix} 0.9199485 \\ 0.7445199 \\ 1 \end{bmatrix}$$

Subtracting 5 from λ_1 yields a value of 13.25760 which is virtually identical to that obtained before the shift with 124 iterations. The eigenvectors are also in good agreement.

The enormous increase in convergence rate which we have observed in this case cannot be expected in general when applying shifting. (The exact values of the first two eigenvalues of the original matrix are 13.25761 and -12.70709. The shift makes these eigenvalues 18.25761 and -7.70709 respectively. The dominance ratio thus changes from 0.95848 to 0.42213, which is obviously extremely beneficial to the power method.) However, shifting is certainly worth trying if slow convergence of the power method is encountered, and shifting strategies for such other methods as the LR and QR algorithms are almost indispensible.

10.5 Show the effects of relaxation on accelerating the power method for the matrix of the preceding problem.

We have noted in the previous problem that for an initial guess of all 1's for the eigenvector, and with an absolute convergence criterion of 10^{-5}, 124 iterations of the power method were necessary to produce the dominant eigenvalue $\lambda_1 = 13.25761$. It is instructive to examine the first few estimates of the eigenvalue which are obtained using the power method:

Iteration	Estimate of Eigenvalue
1	15.00000
2	13.06667
3	13.04592
4	13.57802
5	12.93436
6	13.57171
7	12.97441

The estimates of the eigenvalue appear to be oscillating but slowly converging. Each iteration apparently overshoots the desired value in one direction and the next iteration overshoots in the opposite direction. This tendency can be overcome by underrelaxation (using $0 < \lambda < 1$). For the present case we will arbitrarily choose $\lambda = 0.5$. Using the relaxation approach given by (10.41) and the same convergence criterion as before, we find that 14 iterations yield

$$\lambda_1 = 13.25761, \qquad X_1 = \begin{bmatrix} 0.9199480 \\ 0.7445192 \\ 1 \end{bmatrix}$$

The chosen relaxation factor would appear to be extremely effective. A little further experimentation shows that the same results can be obtained in only 10 iterations with $\lambda = 0.6$.

10.6 Demonstrate the use of the Rayleigh quotient in the acceleration of the power method for finding the dominant eigenvalue of the matrix

$$\begin{bmatrix} 3 & 7 & 9 \\ 7 & 4 & 3 \\ 9 & 3 & 8 \end{bmatrix}$$

This is the example considered to illustrate the power method in Sec. 10.3. Consider the result of the 3rd iteration of the power method. The eigenvector and eigenvalue estimates are

$$V = \begin{bmatrix} 0.9049802 \\ 0.6611325 \\ 1 \end{bmatrix}, \qquad \lambda_{est} = 18.08579$$

The Rayleigh quotient is given by

$$\lambda_R = \frac{V^T H V}{V^T V}$$

Now

$$HV = \begin{bmatrix} 3 & 7 & 9 \\ 7 & 4 & 3 \\ 9 & 3 & 8 \end{bmatrix}\begin{bmatrix} 0.9049802 \\ 0.6611325 \\ 1 \end{bmatrix} = \begin{bmatrix} 16.34286 \\ 11.97939 \\ 18.12822 \end{bmatrix}$$

and thus

$$\lambda_R = \frac{[0.9049802 \quad 0.6611325 \quad 1]\begin{bmatrix} 16.34286 \\ 11.97939 \\ 18.12822 \end{bmatrix}}{[0.9049802 \quad 0.6611326 \quad 1]\begin{bmatrix} 0.9049802 \\ 0.6611325 \\ 1 \end{bmatrix}}$$

$$= \frac{40.83815}{2.256085} = 18.10133$$

The exact eigenvalue is 18.10138. This accuracy is not attained with the straight power method until the 9th iteration. Since the present answer was obtained using only 3 iterations (actually 4, since the quantity HV in the numerator of the Rayleigh quotient is equivalent to one additional iteration), the accelerative effects of the Rayleigh quotient should be apparent.

10.7 Illustrate the use of Hotelling's deflation to find the second largest eigenvalue of the matrix considered in the previous problem.

In Sec. 10.3, we found that the dominant eigenvalue and corresponding eigenvector of the matrix are

$$\lambda_1 = 18.10138, \qquad X_1 = \begin{bmatrix} 0.9021784 \\ 0.6605912 \\ 1 \end{bmatrix}$$

Now if we calculate

$$D_1 = H - \frac{\lambda_1 (X_1 X_1^T)}{X_1^T X}$$

this matrix should have the same eigenvalues and eigenvectors as H, except that λ_1 is replaced by zero. Next we find

$$X_1^T X = [0.9021784 \quad 0.6605912 \quad 1] \begin{bmatrix} 0.9021784 \\ 0.6605912 \\ 1 \end{bmatrix} = 2.250307$$

and

$$X_1 X_1^T = \begin{bmatrix} 0.9021784 \\ 0.6605912 \\ 1 \end{bmatrix} [0.9021784 \quad 0.6605912 \quad 1]$$

$$= \begin{bmatrix} 0.8139258 & 0.5959711 & 0.9021784 \\ 0.5959711 & 0.4363807 & 0.6605912 \\ 0.9021784 & 0.6605912 & 1 \end{bmatrix}$$

Then

$$\frac{\lambda_1 X_1 X_1^T}{X_1^T X_1} = \begin{bmatrix} 6.547187 & 4.793968 & 7.257087 \\ 4.793968 & 3.510229 & 5.313769 \\ 7.257087 & 5.313769 & 8.043960 \end{bmatrix}$$

and

$$H - \frac{\lambda_1 X_1 X_1^T}{X_1^T X_1} = \begin{bmatrix} -3.547187 & 2.206032 & 1.742913 \\ 2.206032 & 0.489771 & 2.313769 \\ 1.742913 & 2.313769 & 0.043960 \end{bmatrix}$$

Applying the power method to this matrix with an initial guess of

$$V = \begin{bmatrix} 1 \\ 1 \\ 1 \end{bmatrix}$$

produces after 24 iterations an eigenvalue and eigenvector of

$$\lambda_2 = -5.70586, \qquad X_2 = \begin{bmatrix} -1.869206 \\ 1.039006 \\ 1 \end{bmatrix}$$

The eigenvalue differs from the exact answer of -5.70585 by only one digit in the fifth decimal place.

One useful check is to determine if the eigenvectors X_1 and X_2 are orthogonal, as they should be. We compute

$$X_1^T X_2 = [0.9021784 \quad 0.6605912 \quad 1] \begin{bmatrix} -1.869206 \\ 1.039006 \\ 1 \end{bmatrix} = 0.0000010$$

which is certainly zero to within any reasonable accuracy. Thus X_1 and X_2 are orthogonal.

10.8 Illustrate the use of the Jacobi method in finding the eigenvalues and eigenvectors of the matrix

$$H = \begin{bmatrix} 4 & 2 & 3 & 7 \\ 2 & 8 & 5 & 1 \\ 3 & 5 & 12 & 9 \\ 7 & 1 & 9 & 7 \end{bmatrix}$$

The procedure is much too long to reveal all of its details, but we will show as much of one iteration as possible, and will demonstrate the threshold strategy.   We begin by calculating

$$v_0 = \sum_{\substack{i=1 \\ i \neq j}}^{4} \sum_{j=1}^{4} h_{ij}^2 = 338$$

and

$$\mu_1 = \sqrt{v_0}/4 = \sqrt{338}/4 = 4.596194$$

This is the initial threshold value; that is, on the first sweep through the matrix we will only zero those elements which are greater than 4.596194 in magnitude.   We also choose the final threshold value at this point as $\mu_f = \epsilon\mu_1 = 10^{-6} \times \mu_1 = 4.596194 \times 10^{-6}$.   When all off-diagonal elements are smaller than μ_1 in magnitude, we will consider the solution to be converged.   Using μ_1 as the threshold value, we now sweep through the rows of the matrix, searching for an off-diagonal element larger in magnitude than μ_1.   The first such element is $h_{14} = 7$, and we will now zero this element, using the notation $p = 1$, $q = 4$.   Remember that only elements in the 1st and 4th rows and 1st and 4th columns will be affected by these calculations.   The values of c and s are first determined:

$$\alpha = \frac{1}{2}(h_{11} - h_{44}) = \frac{1}{2}(4 - 7) = -1.5$$

$$\beta = (h_{14}^2 + \alpha^2)^{1/2} = (7^2 + (-1.5)^2)^{1/2} = 7.158911$$

and then

$$c = \left(\frac{1}{2} + \frac{|\alpha|}{2\beta}\right)^{1/2} = \left(\frac{1}{2} + \frac{1.5}{2(7.158911)}\right)^{1/2} = 0.7776661$$

$$s = \frac{\alpha(-h_{14})}{2\beta|\alpha|C} = \frac{(-1.5)(-7)}{2(7.158911)(1.5)(0.7776661)} = 0.6286775$$

We can now modify the elements of the matrix:

$$h'_{11} = c^2 h_{11} + s^2 h_{44} - 2csh_{14}$$
$$= (0.7776661)^2(4) + (0.6286775)^2(7) - 2(0.7776661)(0.6286775)(7) = -1.658911$$

$$h'_{44} = c^2 h_{44} + s^2 h_{11} + 2csh_{14}$$
$$= (0.7776661)^2(7) + (0.6286775)^2(4) + 2(0.7776661)(0.6286775)(7) = 12.65891$$

$$h'_{12} = ch_{12} - sh_{42} = (0.7776661)(2) - (0.6286775)(1) = 0.9266547 = h'_{21}$$

$$h'_{13} = ch_{13} - sh_{43} = (0.7776661)(3) - (0.6286775)(9) = -3.325099 = h'_{31}$$

$$h'_{42} = sh_{12} + ch_{42} = (0.6286775)(2) + (0.7776661)(1) = 2.035021 = h'_{24}$$

$$h'_{43} = sh_{13} + ch_{43} = (0.6286775)(3) + (0.7776661)(9) = 8.885027 = h'_{34}$$

The matrix now has the form

$$\begin{bmatrix} -1.658911 & 0.9266547 & -3.325099 & 0 \\ 0.9266547 & 8 & 5 & 2.035021 \\ -3.325099 & 5 & 12 & 8.885027 \\ 0 & 2.035021 & 8.885027 & 12.65891 \end{bmatrix}$$

If it is also desired to find the eigenvectors, then the R matrix, which is initialized as the unit matrix, is modified as follows:

$$r'_{11} = cr_{11} - sr_{14} = (0.7776661)(1) - (0.6286775)(0) = 0.7776661$$

$$r'_{21} = cr_{21} - sr_{24} = c(0) - s(0) = 0$$

$$r'_{31} = cr_{31} - sr_{34} = c(0) - s(0) = 0$$

$$r'_{41} = cr_{41} - sr_{44} = c(0) - (0.6286775)(1) = -0.6286775$$

$$r'_{14} = sr_{11} + cr_{14} = (0.6286775)(1) + c(0) = 0.6286775$$

$$r'_{24} = sr_{21} + cr_{24} = s(0) + c(0) = 0$$

$$r'_{34} = sr_{31} + cr_{34} = s(0) + c(0) = 0$$

$$r'_{44} = sr_{41} + cr_{44} = s(0) + (0.7776661)(1) = 0.7776661$$

Thus the modified R matrix is

$$\begin{bmatrix} 0.7776661 & 0 & 0 & 0.6286775 \\ 0 & 1 & 0 & 0 \\ 0 & 0 & 1 & 0 \\ -0.6286775 & 0 & 0 & 0.7776661 \end{bmatrix}$$

We now continue the sweep, searching for elements in H which exceed the threshold value. The next such element is 5, in the $p = 2$, $q = 3$ position, and we repeat the entire process, this time affecting only the 2nd and 3rd rows and 2nd and 3rd columns. The process continues until the bottom right corner of the matrix is reached. We now modify the threshold value to

$$\mu_2 = \mu_1/4 = 1.1399048$$

and begin the sweep again. (We are guaranteed that each time the threshold constant is changed, there will be at least one off-diagonal element of the matrix which will be greater in magnitude than the new threshold constant.) When $\mu < \mu_f$, the process is considered to have converged, and we stop. For this problem, the final forms of the H and R matrices are

$$H = \begin{bmatrix} -3.233881 & 4.89 \times 10^{-9} & -6.06 \times 10^{-15} & 1.72 \times 10^{-5} \\ 4.89 \times 10^{-9} & 3.739112 & 0 & -3.78 \times 10^{-10} \\ -6.06 \times 10^{-15} & 0 & 23.04466 & 5.14 \times 10^{-6} \\ 1.72 \times 10^{-5} & -3.78 \times 10^{-10} & 5.14 \times 10^{-6} & 7.450091 \end{bmatrix}$$

$$R = \begin{bmatrix} 0.5807812 & 0.6787282 & 0.3456577 & 0.2872997 \\ -0.2037415 & 0.3749573 & 0.3117012 & -0.8489628 \\ 0.3651426 & -0.6174604 & 0.6883553 & -0.1076074 \\ -0.6984646 & 0.1321995 & 0.5563532 & 0.4302800 \end{bmatrix}$$

The eigenvalues of the original matrix are on the diagonal of the final version of H.

10.9 Using Householder's method, put the following matrix in tridiagonal form:

$$H_1 = \begin{bmatrix} 6 & 2 & 3 & 1 \\ 2 & 5 & 4 & 8 \\ 3 & 4 & 9 & 1 \\ 1 & 8 & 1 & 7 \end{bmatrix}$$

We first wish to find an orthogonal symmetric matrix T_1 such that premultiplication of the above matrix by T_1 eliminates the last two elements of the first column. The matrix T_1 is of the form

$$T_1 = \begin{bmatrix} 1 & 0 & 0 & 0 \\ 0 & & & \\ 0 & & P & \\ 0 & & & \end{bmatrix}$$

In order to construct P, we need

$$S = \sqrt{h_{21}^2 + h_{31}^2 + h_{41}^2} = \sqrt{2^2 + 3^2 + 1^2} = \sqrt{14} = 3.741658$$

Now form the vector

$$U = \begin{bmatrix} 2 \pm 3.741658 \\ 3 \\ 1 \end{bmatrix} = \begin{bmatrix} 5.741658 \\ 3 \\ 1 \end{bmatrix}$$

(We have chosen the sign which maximizes the first element.)   Now form the matrix

$$UU^T = \begin{bmatrix} 5.741658 \\ 3 \\ 1 \end{bmatrix} [5.741658 \quad 3 \quad 1]$$

$$= \begin{bmatrix} 32.96664 & 17.22497 & 5.741658 \\ 17.22497 & 9 & 3 \\ 5.741658 & 3 & 1 \end{bmatrix}$$

which we note is symmetric.   Now the submatrix P is given by

$$P = I - \frac{UU^T}{S^2 \pm h_{21}S}$$

where the sign is the same as that chosen before.   Therefore, we choose the + sign and find

$$S^2 + h_{21}S = 14 + 2(3.741658) = 21.48332$$

and thus

$$P = \begin{bmatrix} 1 & 0 & 0 \\ 0 & 1 & 0 \\ 0 & 0 & 1 \end{bmatrix} - \frac{1}{21.48332} \begin{bmatrix} 32.96664 & 17.22497 & 5.741658 \\ 17.22497 & 9 & 3 \\ 5.741658 & 3 & 1 \end{bmatrix}$$

$$= \begin{bmatrix} -0.534523 & -0.801783 & -0.267261 \\ -0.801783 & 0.581070 & -0.139643 \\ -0.267261 & -0.139643 & 0.953452 \end{bmatrix}$$

The matrix T_1 is now completely determined.   Premultiplication of H_1 by T_1 zeros the desired elements, and postmultiplication by T_1 restores symmetry and zeros the third and fourth elements in the first row.   The details of the matrix multiplication are straightforward and will not be shown here.   The result is

$$T_1 H_1 T_1 = \begin{bmatrix} 6.000000 & 3.741657 & 0 & 0 \\ 3.741657 & 13.85713 & 1.808209 & -3.138917 \\ 0 & 1.808209 & 4.291560 & -6.007794 \\ 0 & -3.138917 & -6.007794 & 2.851295 \end{bmatrix}$$

We denote this matrix as H_2.   Our objective now is to zero the last element in the second column.   This can be accomplished by premultiplying H_2 by T_2 where

$$T_2 = \begin{bmatrix} 1 & 0 & 0 & 0 \\ 0 & 1 & 0 & 0 \\ 0 & 0 & \vdots & P \\ 0 & 0 & \vdots & \end{bmatrix}$$

Now

$$S = \sqrt{h_{32}^2 + h_{42}^2} = \sqrt{(1.808209)^2 + (-3.138917)^2} = 3.622487$$

and

$$U = \begin{bmatrix} 1.808209 \pm 3.622487 \\ -3.138917 \end{bmatrix} = \begin{bmatrix} 5.430696 \\ -3.138917 \end{bmatrix}$$

Once again we have chosen the + sign.   Now we form

$$UU^T = \begin{bmatrix} 5.430696 \\ -3.138917 \end{bmatrix} [5.430696 \quad -3.138917] = \begin{bmatrix} 29.49246 & -17.04650 \\ -17.04650 & 9.852800 \end{bmatrix}$$

and finally

$$S^2 + h_{32}S = 13.12242 + (1.808209)(3.622487) = 19.67263$$

The submatrix P is now given by

$$P = \begin{bmatrix} 1 & 0 \\ 0 & 1 \end{bmatrix} - \frac{1}{19.67263}\begin{bmatrix} 29.49246 & -17.04650 \\ -17.04650 & 9.852800 \end{bmatrix}$$

$$= \begin{bmatrix} -0.499163 & 0.866509 \\ 0.866509 & 0.499162 \end{bmatrix}$$

The matrix T_2 is now completely determined.   The product $T_2 H_2 T_2$ is

$$T_2 H_2 T_2 = \begin{bmatrix} 6.000000 & 3.741657 & 0 & 0 \\ 3.741657 & 13.85713 & 3.622490 & 0 \\ 0 & 3.622490 & 8.407250 & 3.636920 \\ 0 & 0 & 3.636920 & -1.264370 \end{bmatrix}$$

which is the desired tridiagonal form.

10.10 Demonstrate the use of the QL algorithm to find the eigenvalues of the tridiagonal matrix which resulted from the preceding problem.

   The diagonal elements of the tridiagonal matrix are denoted as d_1 through d_4, and the superdiagonal elements as e_1 through e_3.   We cannot go into great detail in the illustration of the algorithm, but we will attempt to show as much of one complete iteration as possible.   The initial shift η_1 is chosen as the eigenvalue of the 2×2 submatrix in the upper left corner which is closest to d_1.   Thus η_1 is one of the roots of

$$\det \begin{bmatrix} 6 - \eta_1 & 3.741657 \\ 3.741657 & 13.85713 - \eta_1 \end{bmatrix} = 0$$

Expanding the quadratic and solving for the roots gives

$$\eta_1 = 15.353841, \quad 4.503289$$

We choose $\eta_1 = 4.503289$ as being closest to 6.   The diagonal elements d_1 through d_4 then become

$$d_1 = 6 - 4.503289 = 1.496711$$

$$d_2 = 13.85713 - 4.503289 = 9.353841$$

$$d_3 = 8.407250 - 4.503289 = 3.903961$$

$$d_4 = -1.264370 - 4.503289 = -5.767659$$

Now, following the algorithm (10.102),

$$p_4 = d_4 = -5.767659$$

$$c_4 = 1$$

$$s_4 = 0$$

and for $i = 3$,

$$r_4 = (p_4^2 + (e_3)^2)^{1/2} = ((-5.767659)^2 + (3.636920)^2)^{1/2} = 6.818583$$

$$g_4 = c_4 e_4 = (1)(3.636920) = 3.636920$$

$$h_4 = c_4 p_4 = (1)(-5.767659) = -5.767659$$

$$\rightarrow e_4 = s_4 r_4 = (0)(6.818583) = 0$$

$$c_3 = p_4/r_4 = -5.767659/6.818583 = -0.8458735$$

$$s_3 = e_3/r_4 = 3.636920/6.818583 = 0.5333835$$

$$p_3 = c_3 d_3 - s_3 g_4 = (-0.8458735)(3.903961) - (0.5333835)(3.636920)$$
$$= -5.242130$$

$$\rightarrow d_4 = h_4 + s_3(c_3 g_4 + s_3 d_3)$$
$$= -5.767659 + (0.5333835)((-0.8458735)(3.636920) + (0.5333835)(3.903961))$$
$$= -6.297877$$

(The arrows indicate the actual matrix element modifications.)   In a similar fashion, for $i = 2$,

$$e_3 = 3.398715, \qquad d_3 = 8.890384$$

and for $i = 1$,

$$e_2 = 3.997386, \qquad d_2 = 6.708286$$

A separate set of calculations yields

$$e_1 = 0.1973130, \qquad d_1 = -0.3139396$$

This completes one iteration.   Note that e_1 is considerably smaller than before.   This trend continues on succeeding iterations until on the fourth iteration, the following values are obtained:

$$d_1 = -1.387560 \times 10^{-28} \qquad\qquad e_1 = 2.474652 \times 10^{-43}$$

$$d_2 = 4.362420 \qquad\qquad e_2 = 0.3344836$$

$$d_3 = 2.992812 \qquad\qquad e_3 = 9.705934$$

$$d_4 = 2.915200$$

with an accumulated shift of 4.182390.   The value of e_1 is so small that we can consider d_1 to have been isolated as an eigenvalue.   In order to finally compute the eigenvalue, we must add the accumulated shift.   Thus

$$\lambda_1 = -1.38 \times 10^{-28} + 4.182390 = 4.182390$$

We can now discard d_1 and e_1 and work only with d_2 through d_4 and e_2 through e_3. Three more iterations yield

$$\lambda_2 = 8.543056$$

and four more iterations yield

$$\lambda_3 = 16.84915, \qquad \lambda_4 = -2.574616$$

(The fourth and final eigenvalue appears along with λ_3, since $e_4 = 0$.)

10.11 Find the eigenvalues of the matrix

$$H_1 = \begin{bmatrix} 7 & 3 & 1 \\ 3 & 4 & 2 \\ 1 & 2 & 3 \end{bmatrix}$$

by using the *LR* method.

We try the Choleski decomposition, hoping that the matrix is positive definite and that we can express H_1 as $L_1 L_1^T$. The Choleski decomposition yields

$$L_1 = \begin{bmatrix} 2.645751 & 0 & 0 \\ 1.133893 & 1.647510 & 0 \\ 0.3779645 & 9.9538204 & 1.395481 \end{bmatrix}$$

Since the Choleski decomposition was successful, the matrix must be positive definite. We now form

$$L_1^T L_1 = \begin{bmatrix} 8.428568 & 2.228609 & 0.5274423 \\ 2.228609 & 3.624061 & 1.331038 \\ 0.5274423 & 1.331038 & 1.947367 \end{bmatrix} = H_2$$

Since this matrix is a similarity transformation of H_1, which was positive definite, this matrix is also positive definite (why?) and can also be Choleski decomposed. Ten more decompositions and reverse multiplications yield

$$H_{12} = \begin{bmatrix} 9.433488 & 0.0160184 & 0.0000184 \\ 0.0160184 & 3.419430 & 0.0062214 \\ 0.0000184 & 0.0062214 & 1.147035 \end{bmatrix}$$

The process is clearly converging and will yield the eigenvalues in order of decreasing magnitude on the main diagonal. These eigenvalues have in fact already been determined fairly accurately at this point, since the exact eigenvalues are 9.433551, 3.419421, and 1.147028.

10.12 Consider the following boundary value problem involving an ordinary differential equation:

$$\frac{d^2 y}{dx^2} + \nu^2 y = 0$$

$$y(-\pi) = 0, \quad y(\pi) = 0$$

where ν^2 is an unknown constant. Determine the smallest value of ν^2 which satisfies this problem.

This problem would appear to be out of place in the present chapter, since in its present form it is certainly not a matrix eigenvalue problem. It is, however, termed an eigenvalue problem, and similar problems are commonly encountered in dynamics, structural analysis, and even nuclear reactor calculations. The present problem can be solved analytically to yield

$$y = A \cos \nu x$$

and the smallest value of ν which satisfies the boundary conditions is clearly $\nu = 1/2$. More complex problems of this type often cannot be solved analytically, and we will examine a numerical technique which results in a matrix eigenvalue problem of the type which we have been considering in this chapter.

We first write the differential equation in central difference form:

$$\frac{y_{j+1} - 2y_j + y_{j-1}}{(\Delta x)^2} + \nu^2 y_j = 0$$

Taking the term involving ν^2 to the right-hand side and multiplying through the equation by $(\Delta x)^2$, we obtain

$$-y_{j-1} + 2y_j - y_{j+1} = \nu^2 (\Delta x)^2 y_j$$

If $\Delta x = 2\pi/n$ (n equally spaced intervals from $x = -\pi$ to $x = \pi$), then there are $n - 1$ such equations, which can be written in matrix form (incorporating the boundary conditions) as

$$
\begin{bmatrix}
2 & -1 & & & & & \\
-1 & 2 & -1 & & & & \\
& -1 & 2 & -1 & & & \\
& - & - & - & & & \\
& & - & - & - & & \\
& & & -1 & 2 & -1 \\
& & & & -1 & 2
\end{bmatrix}
\begin{bmatrix}
y_1 \\ y_2 \\ y_3 \\ - \\ - \\ y_{n-2} \\ y_{n-1}
\end{bmatrix}
= \nu^2 (\Delta x)^2
\begin{bmatrix}
y_1 \\ y_2 \\ y_3 \\ - \\ - \\ y_{n-2} \\ y_{n-1}
\end{bmatrix}
$$

This is an eigenvalue problem of the form we have considered in this chapter, with the quantity $\nu^2(\Delta x)^2$ representing the eigenvalue. Any of the standard techniques discussed in this chapter can be used to find the eigenvalues, although since the matrix is already in tridiagonal form, the QL algorithm would seem particularly well suited.

Carrying out the calculations with $n = 10$ ($\Delta x = \pi/5$), we find that the smallest eigenvalue is $\nu^2(\Delta x)^2 = 0.09788697$, or $\nu = (5/\pi)(0.09788697)^{1/2} = 0.4979464$ as compared to the exact value of $1/2$. The accuracy could be improved by using a larger value of n.

Problems

Although the use of a computer is virtually mandatory for eigenvalue problems of any size, some useful experience can be gained by the hand solution of small problems with certain methods. Therefore, with these problems we resume the practice of indicating with an asterisk those problems for which the use of a computer is highly desirable. For the remaining problems, hand calculations can yield meaningful results if no computer is available.

*10.13 Write a computer subprogram to use the Choleski algorithm to decompose an arbitrary positive definite symmetric matrix into a product of lower triangular and upper triangular matrices.

*10.14 Write a computer subprogram to invert a lower triangular matrix of arbitrary size using the algorithm discussed in Sec. 10.2.

*10.15 Write a computer program to convert a problem of the form $AX = \lambda BX$ where B is positive definite into the form $HX = \lambda X$ where H is symmetric. Use the subprograms written for Problems 10.13 and 10.14 as needed.

*10.16 Write a computer program to find the dominant eigenvalue and corresponding eigenvector of a matrix by the power method. The program should include the use of a relaxation factor which can be set to 1 if the standard power method is desired. Input parameters should include this relaxation factor and a convergence criterion on the eigenvalue. (This criterion can be absolute or relative, as desired.)

*10.17 Write a computer program to find an arbitrary number of the largest eigenvalues (in magnitude) and the corresponding eigenvectors of a symmetric matrix by using Hotelling's deflation. Input parameters should include a convergence criterion, and an integer representing the maximum number of iterations which are permitted to find each eigenvalue before the method is considered to have failed. (If this safety feature is not included, the program may run a very long time indeed in attempting to find one of two closely spaced eigenvalues.)

*10.18 Write a computer program to find the eigenvalues and eigenvectors of an arbitrary symmetric matrix using the Jacobi method with the threshold strategy. Use $\epsilon = 10^{-6}$ or smaller if possible.

*10.19 Write a computer program to use Householder's method to reduce an arbitrary symmetric matrix to tridiagonal form.

*10.20 Write a computer program to use the QL algorithm to obtain the eigenvalues of an arbitrary tridiagonal symmetric matrix. Use $\epsilon = 10^{-25}$ if possible.

*10.21 Write a computer program to find the eigenvalues of an arbitrary symmetric positive definite matrix using the LR algorithm (acceleration need not be included). Use the subprogram written for Problem 10.13 to do the decomposition.

10.22 Using the algorithm discussed in Sec. 10.2, invert the lower triangular matrix

$$\begin{bmatrix} 4 & 0 & 0 \\ 9 & 3 & 0 \\ 1 & 2 & 7 \end{bmatrix}$$

10.23 Convert the following matrix into a product of lower triangular and upper triangular matrices using the Choleski decomposition:

$$\begin{bmatrix} 5 & 4 & 2 & 3 \\ 4 & 8 & 3 & 2 \\ 2 & 3 & 10 & 1 \\ 3 & 2 & 1 & 13 \end{bmatrix}$$

10.24 Using the power method, find the dominant eigenvalue and corresponding eigenvector of the following matrices:

(a) $\begin{bmatrix} 2 & 3 & 8 \\ 3 & 9 & 4 \\ 8 & 4 & 1 \end{bmatrix}$

*(b) $\begin{bmatrix} 4 & -2 & 7 & 3 & -1 & 8 \\ -2 & 5 & 1 & 1 & 4 & 7 \\ 7 & 1 & 7 & 2 & 3 & 5 \\ 3 & 1 & 2 & 6 & 5 & 1 \\ -1 & 4 & 3 & 5 & 3 & 2 \\ 8 & 7 & 5 & 1 & 2 & 4 \end{bmatrix}$

10.25 By inverting the matrix and applying the power method, find the smallest eigenvalue (in magnitude) of

(a) the matrix of Problem 10.24(a),
*(b) the matrix of Problem 10.24(b).

*10.26 Perform a few iterations on the following matrix using the power method. Then, based on the results, choose a suitable relaxation factor and carry the iterative process to convergence.

$$\begin{bmatrix} 1 & 3 & 2 \\ 3 & -1 & 1 \\ 2 & 1 & -2 \end{bmatrix}$$

*10.27 Using Hotelling's deflation, find all of the eigenvalues and eigenvectors of:

(a) the matrix of Problem 10.24(a),

(b) $\begin{bmatrix} 11 & 2 & 3 & 1 & 4 & 2 \\ 2 & 9 & 3 & 5 & 2 & 1 \\ 3 & 3 & 15 & 4 & 3 & 2 \\ 1 & 5 & 4 & 12 & 4 & 3 \\ 4 & 2 & 3 & 4 & 17 & 5 \\ 2 & 1 & 2 & 3 & 5 & 8 \end{bmatrix}$

*10.28 Using the Jacobi method (preferably with the threshold strategy), find the eigenvalues and eigenvectors of

$$\begin{bmatrix} 9 & 2 & 7 & 3 & 4 \\ 2 & 10 & 4 & 1 & 2 \\ 7 & 4 & 7 & 5 & 1 \\ 3 & 1 & 5 & 8 & 3 \\ 4 & 2 & 1 & 3 & 6 \end{bmatrix}$$

10.29 Using Householder's method, bring the following matrices to tridiagonal form:

$$(a) \begin{bmatrix} 5 & 2 & 3 \\ 2 & 8 & 1 \\ 3 & 1 & 7 \end{bmatrix}$$

$$*(b) \begin{bmatrix} 7 & 4 & 3 & 5 & 2 & 1 \\ 4 & 5 & 2 & 4 & 3 & 4 \\ 3 & 2 & 9 & 4 & 1 & 8 \\ 5 & 4 & 4 & 3 & 2 & 5 \\ 2 & 3 & 1 & 2 & 11 & 3 \\ 1 & 4 & 8 & 5 & 3 & 10 \end{bmatrix}$$

10.30 Using the QL algorithm, find all of the eigenvalues of these tridiagonal matrices:

$$(a) \begin{bmatrix} 2 & -1 & 0 \\ -1 & 2 & -1 \\ 0 & -1 & 2 \end{bmatrix}$$

$$*(b) \begin{bmatrix} 7 & 3 & 0 & 0 & 0 \\ 3 & 4 & 8 & 0 & 0 \\ 0 & 8 & 5 & 2 & 0 \\ 0 & 0 & 2 & 9 & 6 \\ 0 & 0 & 0 & 6 & 8 \end{bmatrix}$$

(c) the result of Problem 10.29(a),
*(d) the result of Problem 10.29(b).

*10.31 Find the eigenvalues of the tridiagonal form resulting from Problem 10.29(a) by expanding the characteristic polynomial and using a root solving approach.

*10.32 Given the matrices A and B for an eigenvalue problem of the form $AX = \lambda BX$, convert the problem into the standard symmetric form $HX = \lambda X$ and find the eigenvalues of the original problem.   The matrices A and B are:

$$(a) \quad A = \begin{bmatrix} 14 & 10 & 8 & 3 \\ 10 & 7 & 4 & 2 \\ 8 & 4 & 8 & 1 \\ 3 & 2 & 1 & 3 \end{bmatrix}, \quad B = \begin{bmatrix} 10 & 2 & 3 & 5 \\ 2 & 7 & 4 & 1 \\ 3 & 4 & 8 & 2 \\ 5 & 1 & 2 & 5 \end{bmatrix}$$

$$(b) \quad A = \begin{bmatrix} 8 & 1 & 1 & 3 \\ 1 & 7 & 2 & 1 \\ 1 & 2 & 4 & 3 \\ 3 & 1 & 3 & 5 \end{bmatrix}, \quad B = \begin{bmatrix} 2 & 3 & 4 & 7 \\ 3 & 1 & 5 & 6 \\ 4 & 5 & 3 & 2 \\ 7 & 6 & 2 & 1 \end{bmatrix}$$

*10.33 Using the LR method, find the eigenvalues of these matrices:

$$(a) \begin{bmatrix} 6 & 2 & 1 \\ 2 & 8 & 2 \\ 1 & 2 & 9 \end{bmatrix}$$

$$(b) \begin{bmatrix} 5 & 4 & 2 & 3 \\ 4 & 8 & 3 & 2 \\ 2 & 3 & 10 & 1 \\ 3 & 2 & 1 & 13 \end{bmatrix}$$

Chapter 11

Introduction to Partial Differential Equations

11.0 INTRODUCTION

It is the purpose of this chapter to introduce the reader to some of the most widely used techniques for the numerical solution of partial differential equations. The techniques and problems actually considered in detail are quite simple. However, these should serve to present the concepts and terminology which are essential for the study of more advanced techniques and complex problems. Suitable references for the study of the more advanced techniques are suggested at appropriate points throughout the chapter.

For simplicity, we will deal throughout the chapter with second-order partial differential equations involving two independent variables. The extensions to higher order differential equations and to equations in three or more independent variables are usually surprisingly straightforward. Details can be found in what has come to be considered as the standard reference work on the subject of the numerical solution of partial differential equations, Forsythe and Wasow[6].

11.1 CLASSIFICATION OF SECOND-ORDER PARTIAL DIFFERENTIAL EQUATIONS

There are three basic classes of second-order partial differential equations involving two independent variables, and a different numerical approach is required for each of the three classes. Each class bears the name of one of the conic sections; for our present purposes it will not be necessary to describe in detail the reason for the names. We should note, however, that the names are derived from the form of a family of curves, called the *characteristics*, which are associated with each class.

Partial differential equations belonging to each class can be put into a simple form (a change of variables may be required) called the *canonical form* for that class. These forms and their corresponding classifications are

$$\frac{\partial^2 u}{\partial x^2} = \Phi \qquad \text{(parabolic)} \qquad (11.1)$$

$$\frac{\partial^2 u}{\partial x^2} + \frac{\partial^2 u}{\partial y^2} = \Phi \qquad \text{(elliptic)} \qquad (11.2)$$

$$\frac{\partial^2 u}{\partial x^2} - \frac{\partial^2 u}{\partial y^2} = \Phi \qquad \text{(hyperbolic)} \qquad (11.3)$$

269

where $\Phi = \Phi(x, y, u, \partial u/\partial x, \partial u/\partial y)$. Note that the classification depends only on the manner in which the highest (2nd order) derivative appears.

The most commonly encountered parabolic equation is of the form

$$\alpha \frac{\partial^2 u}{\partial x^2} = \frac{\partial u}{\partial y} \qquad (\alpha \text{ constant}) \qquad (11.4)$$

This equation is called the one-dimensional transient diffusion equation (with y often representing time), or (primarily by mathematicians) the heat equation.

Commonly encountered elliptic equations are

$$\frac{\partial^2 u}{\partial x^2} + \frac{\partial^2 u}{\partial y^2} = 0 \qquad (11.5)$$

and

$$\frac{\partial^2 u}{\partial x^2} + \frac{\partial^2 u}{\partial y^2} = \text{constant} \qquad (11.6)$$

Equation (11.5) is called Laplace's equation, while (11.6) is called Poisson's equation.

Hyperbolic equations often occur in the form

$$\frac{\partial^2 u}{\partial x^2} = \beta \frac{\partial^2 u}{\partial y^2} \qquad (\beta \text{ constant}) \qquad (11.7)$$

This is called the wave equation.

In this chapter we will examine the most commonly used numerical techniques for the solution of parabolic and elliptic equations. However, the efficient numerical solution of hyperbolic equations requires a rather different approach from that for the other two classes of partial differential equations, and we will limit our treatment of this subject to a short qualitative discussion in Sec. 11.4.

11.2 NUMERICAL METHODS FOR THE SOLUTION OF PARABOLIC EQUATIONS

We will present the methods for parabolic equations by dealing with the specific example of the one-dimensional transient diffusion equation, (11.4). However, the extension of these methods to problems involving other parabolic equations is quite straightforward.

Consider the following problem:

$$\alpha \frac{\partial^2 u}{\partial x^2} = \frac{\partial u}{\partial y} \qquad (11.8)$$

$$u(a,y) = u_a \qquad (11.9)$$

$$u(b,y) = u_b \qquad (11.10)$$

$$u(x,0) = u_0 \qquad (11.11)$$

Conditions (11.9) and (11.10) are termed boundary conditions (the problem is boundary valued in x), while condition (11.11) is termed an initial condition (the problem is initial valued in y). We wish to find $u(x,y)$. It is useful to examine the (x,y) domain as shown in Fig. 11.1.

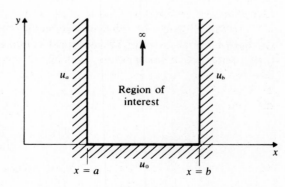

Fig. 11.1

The region of interest is bounded by the x axis and the lines $x = a$ and $x = b$, and extends to infinity in the $+ y$ direction.   Values of u are specified on the three boundaries of this region as shown.

We now superimpose a finite difference grid on the region of interest and adopt the notation shown in Fig. 11.2.

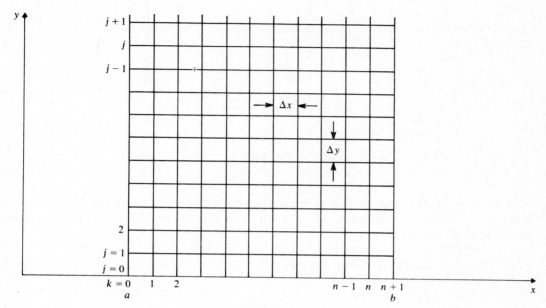

Fig. 11.2

For the present discussion, it will be assumed that Δx and Δy are each constant (but in general are not equal, and in fact may have different units).   Instead of referring to a point on the grid by its coordinates y and x, we can now use the indices j and k.   Thus we denote u at a point (j,k) as $u_{j,k}$.   The initial condition is $u_{0,k} = u_0$ $(k = 0, 1, \ldots, n + 1)$ and the boundary conditions are $u_{j,0} = u_a$ and $u_{j,n+1} = u_b$ $(j = 1, 2, \ldots)$.

Qualitatively, the task of solving the problem numerically consists of starting from the initial condition, and advancing the solution along the y direction in somewhat the same way as for an initial value problem involving an ordinary differential equation.   However, for each step taken in the y direction, it is necessary to solve what amounts to a boundary value problem in x.

Suppose now that the solution has been obtained up to y_j and that we wish to advance it to y_{j+1}.   First, the differential equation (11.8) must be written in a finite difference form.   There are many possible choices for this difference form.   For example, starting from the point (j,k), the derivative with respect to x can be represented by a central difference expression, and the derivative with respect to y by a simple forward difference expression.   This approach yields the difference equation

$$\frac{u_{j,k+1} - 2u_{j,k} + u_{j,k-1}}{(\Delta x)^2} = \frac{1}{\alpha}\left(\frac{u_{j+1,k} - u_{j,k}}{\Delta y}\right) \tag{11.12}$$

The finite difference "molecule," which shows the points involved in this representation, is illustrated in Fig. 11.3.

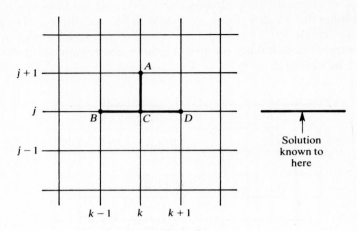

Fig. 11.3

Since all of those values of u with subscript j are assumed known, the only unknown value in (11.12) is $u_{j+1,k}$ (represented by point A in Fig. 11.3). Equation (11.12) can be solved directly for $u_{j+1,k}$ to yield

$$u_{j+1,k} = u_{j,k} + \frac{\alpha(\Delta y)}{(\Delta x)^2}(u_{j,k+1} - 2u_{j,k} + u_{j,k-1}) \qquad (11.13)$$

or

$$u_{j+1,k} = \left[\frac{\alpha(\Delta y)}{(\Delta x)^2}\right]u_{j,k-1} + \left[1 - \frac{2\alpha(\Delta y)}{(\Delta x)^2}\right]u_{j,k} + \left[\frac{\alpha(\Delta y)}{(\Delta x)^2}\right]u_{j,k+1} \qquad (11.14)$$

The unknowns $u_{j+1,k}$ $(k = 1, 2, \ldots, n)$ can be determined from (11.14) in any order desired. Once all of the unknowns have been found, another step can be taken in the y direction by repeating the process, with the newly determined values now appearing on the right-hand side of (11.14) and assuming the subscript j. This same procedure can obviously be used to take the first step after the initial conditions (simply set $j = 0$ in (11.14)). Thus (11.14) furnishes a complete method which can be used to "march" the solution outward along the y direction, starting from the initial condition and continuing to as large a value of y as desired.

Since the unknowns can be explicitly determined from (11.14), this method is termed *explicit*, and the difference representation (11.12) is called an explicit representation.

The primary disadvantage of the explicit method is one of instability. Instability in the numerical solution of partial differential equations is similar to that encountered in solving ordinary differential equations in the sense that it results from an amplification of errors (of both the truncation and roundoff variety). It is beyond the scope of this chapter to explore this instability problem in mathematical detail. The interested reader is referred to the classic paper by O'Brien, Hyman, and Kaplan[40] for a quite readable introduction to this subject.

We will simply state without proof that the explicit difference solution (11.14) becomes unstable when

$$\frac{\alpha(\Delta y)}{(\Delta x)^2} > \frac{1}{2} \qquad (11.15)$$

It is not accidental that when the inequality (11.15) is satisfied, the coefficient of $u_{j,k}$ in (11.14) is negative.   However, we will not pursue this point further.   It is probably most useful to think of the stability criterion (11.15) as setting a maximum permissible step size Δy when Δx and α are fixed.   Thus for a problem where α is predetermined, and where Δx is set such that truncation error of the difference representation of $\partial^2 u/\partial x^2$ is not excessive, it is necessary that

$$\Delta y \leqslant \frac{(\Delta x)^2}{2\alpha} \tag{11.16}$$

for stability.   The crucial question is whether the condition (11.16) forces a smaller value of Δy to be used than would be necessary to hold truncation error down to a reasonable level.   Much computational experience indicates that the answer is unfortunately in the affirmative in most cases.   It would thus appear to be worthwhile to search for other approaches which are less restrictive on the matter of step size.

Consider a new difference representation of the original differential equation (11.8) which is based at the point ($j + 1, k$).   If the derivative $\partial^2 u/\partial x^2$ is represented by a central difference expression, and the derivative $\partial u/\partial y$ by a simple backward difference expression, then the resulting difference equation is

$$\frac{u_{j+1,k+1} - 2u_{j+1,k} + u_{j+1,k-1}}{(\Delta x)^2} = \frac{1}{\alpha} \left(\frac{u_{j+1,k} - u_{j,k}}{\Delta y} \right) \tag{11.17}$$

The finite difference molecule depicting the points involved in (11.17) is shown in Fig. 11.4.

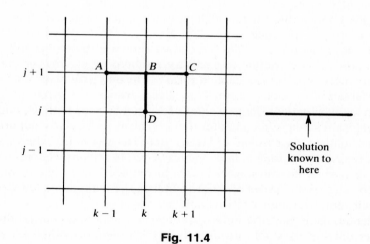

Fig. 11.4

Note that the values of u at the points A, B, and C are all unknown.   Obviously, (11.17) cannot be solved explicitly for the unknowns.   However, if (11.17) is written for all of the points $k = 1, 2, \ldots, n$, then we have a set of n linear algebraic equations in the n unknowns $u_{j+1,k}$.   Since the unknowns are implicit in this set of equations, the difference representation (11.17) is termed an *implicit* representation.

A logical first impression would be that we have exchanged the simplicity of the explicit representation for a much more time-consuming approach. However, each of the equations (*11.17*) can be written in the form

$$[1]u_{j+1,k-1} + \left[-2 - \frac{(\Delta x)^2}{\alpha(\Delta y)} \right] u_{j+1,k} + [1]u_{j+1,k+1} = \left[-\frac{(\Delta x)^2}{\alpha(\Delta y)} \right] u_{j,k} \qquad (11.18)$$

and the complete set of equations expressed in matrix form is given by

$$
\begin{bmatrix}
\beta & 1 & & & & & \\
1 & \beta & 1 & & & & \\
& 1 & \beta & 1 & & & \\
& - & - & - & & & \\
& & - & - & - & & \\
& & & 1 & \beta & 1 \\
& & & & 1 & \beta
\end{bmatrix}
\begin{bmatrix}
u_{j+1,1} \\
u_{j+1,2} \\
u_{j+1,3} \\
- \\
- \\
u_{j+1,n-1} \\
u_{j+1,n}
\end{bmatrix}
=
\begin{bmatrix}
\Omega u_{j,1} - u_a \\
\Omega u_{j,2} \\
\Omega u_{j,3} \\
- \\
- \\
\Omega u_{j,n-1} \\
\Omega u_{j,n} - u_b
\end{bmatrix}
\qquad (11.19)
$$

where

$$\beta = -2 - \frac{(\Delta x)^2}{\alpha(\Delta y)}, \qquad \Omega = -\frac{(\Delta x)^2}{\alpha(\Delta y)}$$

Since the coefficient matrix of (*11.19*) is in the highly desirable tridiagonal form, the number of basic arithmetic operations necessary to solve the set (and thus to take one step of Δy) is only of $\mathcal{O}(n)$. But this is of the same order as the number of basic arithmetic operations which are necessary to take one step in the y direction using the explicit formula. It might then be expected that the computer time required to take one step would be roughly comparable for the explicit and implicit representations, and this has been found to be true in practice.

However, the implicit representation can be shown to be universally stable for all mesh sizes, and thus the restriction to small Δy required by (*11.16*) for the explicit representation is not necessary for the implicit form. The only size restriction on Δy for the implicit representation is that required to keep truncation error at a reasonable level. Thus in many situations, larger values of Δy can be used with the implicit method, resulting in significant savings in computer time. This is particularly important for those cases where the solution approaches a "steady state" as $y \to \infty$, i.e. where $u(x,y)$ eventually becomes a function of x only at large values of y. In regions where the solution does vary slowly with y, accurate solutions can often be obtained by using the implicit representation with step sizes on the order of 10 to 100 times the maximum step size permissible with the explicit representation due to stability restrictions.

Due to the advantages of the implicit representation, the author recommends it (or one of its other universally stable variations) as the standard method for solving (*11.8*) numerically on a digital computer. However, there are still some cases where the explicit method can be used, at least for a few steps, to advantage. This is primarily due to the slightly different error characteristics of the implicit and explicit representations.

The truncation error of the explicit and implicit representations would not seem to be appreciably different, since a central difference expression of error order $(\Delta x)^2$ has been used for the second derivative in both cases, and the difference expressions for the first derivative (forward for explicit, backward for implicit) are both of error order Δy. However, as we have seen before, two methods with the same error order do not necessarily have the same actual error. Thus in certain situations, one of the methods may be more accurate than the other. Some sophisticated general programs, such as those for solving heat conduction problems, allow a choice of an implicit or explicit method at each step, and may even make this choice automatically. We cannot discuss this situation in detail, but mention it here primarily to indicate some motivation for the continued existence and use of the explicit method.

In our discussion heretofore, we have omitted a rather widely used, universally stable variation of the implicit form called the *Crank-Nicholson representation*. The Crank-Nicholson representation of (11.8) is

$$\frac{\alpha}{2}\left[\frac{u_{j+1,k+1} - 2u_{j+1,k} + u_{j+1,k-1}}{(\Delta x)^2} + \frac{u_{j,k+1} - 2u_{j,k} + u_{j,k-1}}{(\Delta x)^2}\right] = \frac{u_{j+1,k} - u_{j,k}}{\Delta y} \qquad (11.20)$$

The left side of this equation is simply an average of the central difference expressions for $\alpha(\partial^2 u/\partial y^2)$ at the points $(j+1,k)$ and (j,k). The right side is the same difference expression as used in the explicit and implicit representations, but now it is no longer clear whether it is a forward or backward difference expression. This can be partially clarified by examining the finite difference molecule shown in Fig. 11.5.

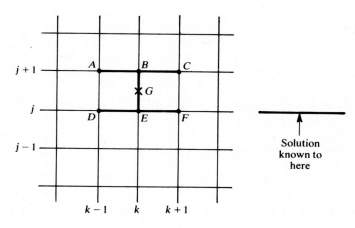

Fig. 11.5

Since the central difference expressions at $(j+1,k)$ and (j,k) are equally weighted, their average can be thought of as an estimate of the second derivative at the point G (or if you prefer, $(j+1/2,k)$). The right side of (11.20) can in a similar fashion be considered as a sort of central difference representation of $\partial u/\partial y$ at the point G.

The advantage of the Crank-Nicholson representation is that for given values of Δx and Δy, the resulting solution has somewhat less truncation error in the term involving Δy than do the standard explicit and implicit representations. This reduction in error is gained with very little expense in additional computation over the standard implicit representation. The matrix form of (11.20) for the problem given by (11.8)–(11.11) is

$$
\begin{bmatrix}
\gamma & 1 & & & & & \\
1 & \gamma & 1 & & & & \\
& 1 & \gamma & 1 & & & \\
& & — & — & — & & \\
& & & — & — & — & \\
& & & & 1 & \gamma & 1 \\
& & & & & 1 & \gamma
\end{bmatrix}
\begin{bmatrix}
u_{j+1,1} \\
u_{j+1,2} \\
u_{j+1,3} \\
— \\
— \\
u_{j+1,n-1} \\
u_{j+1,n}
\end{bmatrix}
=
\begin{bmatrix}
\phi_1 - u_a \\
\phi_2 \\
\phi_3 \\
— \\
— \\
\phi_{n-1} \\
\phi_n - u_b
\end{bmatrix}
\qquad (11.21)
$$

where

$$
\gamma = -2 - \frac{2(\Delta x)^2}{\alpha(\Delta y)}, \qquad \phi_k = \left[2 - \frac{2(\Delta x)^2}{\alpha(\Delta y)}\right] u_{j,k} - u_{j,k-1} - u_{j,k+1}
$$

Other than the slight additional computation necessary for the calculation of the ϕ_k in the right-hand side column vector, the solution to the set (11.21) proceeds in exactly the same manner as for the tridiagonal set (11.19) which resulted from the implicit formulation.

We should note that the Crank-Nicholson representation is a special case of the more general formula

$$
\alpha\left[\theta \frac{u_{j+1,k+1} - 2u_{j+1,k} + u_{j+1,k-1}}{(\Delta x)^2} + (1-\theta)\frac{u_{j,k+1} - 2u_{j,k} + u_{j,k-1}}{(\Delta x)^2}\right] = \frac{u_{j+1,k} - u_{j,k}}{\Delta y}
$$
$$(11.22)$$

where θ is termed the "degree of implicitness." Setting $\theta = 1$ in (11.22) yields the implicit representation, $\theta = 1/2$ gives the Crank-Nicholson representation, and $\theta = 0$ the explicit form. The representation (11.22) is universally stable for $\theta \geq 1/2$, but is only conditionally stable for $\theta < 1/2$. This representation is an example of the concept called "theta differencing" by some applied numerical analysts.

Problems 11.1–11.3 at the end of this chapter are concerned with parabolic differential equations. These problems include some discussion of boundary conditions other than the simple ones included in the present section. Some of the approaches for solving parabolic equations more complex than (11.8) are presented briefly in Problem 11.3.

11.3 NUMERICAL METHODS FOR THE SOLUTION OF ELLIPTIC EQUATIONS

In order to discuss most effectively the numerical techniques for elliptic partial differential equations, we once again turn to an example problem. Nearly all of the methods we discuss here will, however, be directly applicable to elliptic problems in general. Consider the rectangular region R shown in Fig. 11.6.

Suppose that the partial differential equation

$$
\frac{\partial^2 u}{\partial x^2} + \frac{\partial^2 u}{\partial y^2} = 0 \qquad (11.23)
$$

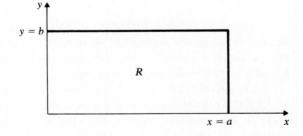

Fig. 11.6

holds over the entire region R, and that u is completely specified on the boundaries of R. We wish to find $u(x,y)$ on the interior of R. This is called a *Dirichlet* problem. We now impose a finite difference grid on the region R as shown in Fig. 11.7.

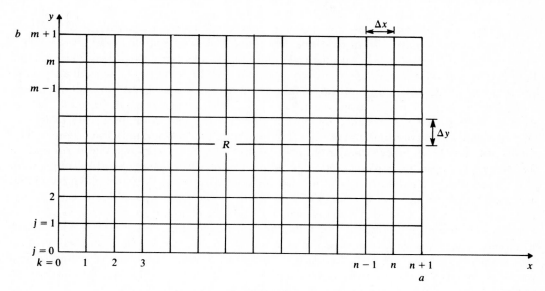

Fig. 11.7

For simplicity, we divide the length a in the x direction into $n + 1$ equal spaces given by

$$\Delta x = \frac{a}{n + 1} \qquad (11.24)$$

and the length b in the y direction into $m + 1$ equal spaces given by

$$\Delta y = \frac{b}{m + 1} \qquad (11.25)$$

The differential equation (*11.23*) can now be written in central difference form at a point (j,k) as

$$\frac{u_{j,k+1} - 2u_{j,k} + u_{j,k-1}}{(\Delta x)^2} + \frac{u_{j+1,k} - 2u_{j,k} + u_{j-1,k}}{(\Delta y)^2} = 0 \qquad (11.26)$$

The dependent variable u is unknown at the mn interior points of R. The equation (*11.26*) can be written at each of the interior points of R, and we thus have mn simultaneous linear equations in the mn unknowns $u_{j,k}$.

The product mn can become very large if an accurate solution is required (that is, if Δx and Δy must be small). If the set of equations is written in matrix form, the matrix of coefficients is sparse, but is not banded in quite the same way as we have come to expect of sparse matrices. Instead, the matrix is "striped," with the familiar tridiagonal band along the main diagonal, but with two additional bands, each one element wide, displaced from the main diagonal by a considerable amount. One of these stripes is above the tridiagonal band, and the other is below.*

For general use, iterative techniques probably represent the best approach to the solution of such sets of equations and we will deal with these techniques in some detail later in this section. However, direct (noniterative) solution of such sets is practical if the number of equations is not too large, and there appears to be a trend toward solving larger and larger sets by direct methods, particularly among specialists in certain fields involving elliptic equations. Although we will not discuss the details of direct methods here (some useful information has already been presented in Chapter 6), we will attempt to present briefly the advantages, disadvantages, and range of practicality of such methods.

The primary consideration is the available fast access storage capacity of the machine being used. If we denote the number of rows and columns in the matrix as N ($N = mn$ for the particular problem which we have just formulated), then there will be approximately $5N$ nonzero elements in the matrix ($3N$ for the tridiagonal band and an additional $2N$ for the off-diagonal stripes). In our discussion of the solution to tridiagonal sets in Chapter 6, we found that the zero elements off of the tridiagonal band never became nonzero in the course of the solution, and thus no additional storage was required beyond that needed for the original nonzero elements of the matrix. In the present case we are not so fortunate, and many of the elements of the matrix which were originally zero will become nonzero in the course of the computation, and will require storage space. Thus although there are only about $5N$ nonzero elements in the original matrix, there is a need for many more storage locations in the course of obtaining a solution. The width of the band containing nonzero elements is given by $2r - 1$, where $r_{max} = N^{1/2} + 1$, and we should note that it often involves a prohibitive amount of book-keeping to take advantage of the elements which remain zero in this band.

The most effective methods of direct solution require a number of storage locations equal to only about one-half the total number of elements in the band, or about $2N^{3/2}$ locations. Thus for $N = 900$ (a very coarse mesh for most purposes), the bandwidth will be about 59, and approximately 54,000 storage locations will be required. This number of locations is pushing the high speed storage limitations of many large machines. If $N = 4900$ (not at all unreasonable), then about 646,000 storage locations are required, which means a large amount of time-consuming shuffling of data to and from secondary storage (disc, tape, drum, low speed core, etc.).

Hopefully, the reader has now gained some perspective as to when direct methods for elliptic problems are practical for whatever specific computer hardware might be available. (We should note that the picture is considerably darker for three-dimensional problems, and that direct methods are very seldom used.) If direct methods can be employed, their advantages over iterative methods include:

1. Less computer time is usually required to obtain a solution of comparable accuracy (unless an excellent first guess is available for the iterative method). This advantage is lost if excessive data shuffling to and from secondary storage is necessary.
2. Under certain circumstances (although not for Laplace's equation), the iterative methods may simply not converge, while the direct method will yield answers in any case.

---

*For problems involving irregularly shaped regions and different boundary conditions, the matrix will not have exactly the form described here. The off-diagonal stripes may be of various lengths and in scattered locations. However, all of the nonzero elements will still fall within a band whose width is considerably smaller than the dimension of the matrix.

The direct methods ,a of course, suffer from roundoff error, which is not a significant problem with iterative methods. Interchanges (e.g. maximization of pivot elements) in an attempt to overcome roundoff problems will usually increase the number of storage locations required for the direct methods.

While Gauss elimination can be used for the direct solution of sets of equations of the type considered here, the most effective direct methods, particularly in terms of minimizing storage space, are those based on block partitioning and decomposition of the matrix into lower and upper triangular forms. The details are beyond the scope of this introductory discussion and the reader is referred to Fox[41] and Forsythe and Wasow[6] for the mechanics of the methods.

It is the author's feeling that direct methods should be carefully explored by anyone who intends to become deeply involved in solving many elliptic problems. For general use, iterative methods are preferable since they are easier to program, use much less storage space, and are applicable to sets of equations of any size.

The simplest iterative method—and one of the most effective—is successive overrelaxation by points (SOR). This is precisely the relaxation method discussed in Chapter 6, and involves a simple modification of Gauss-Siedel iteration. We first multiply (11.26) by $(\Delta x)^2$ and collect coefficients of the various unknowns:

$$[1]u_{j,k+1} + [1]u_{j,k-1} + \left[-2 - 2\frac{(\Delta x)^2}{(\Delta y)^2}\right]u_{j,k} + \left[\frac{(\Delta x)^2}{(\Delta y)^2}\right]u_{j+1,k} + \left[\frac{(\Delta x)^2}{(\Delta y)^2}\right]u_{j-1,k} = 0$$

$$(11.27)$$

The coefficient of $u_{j,k}$ is obviously the largest in magnitude, and since there is one equation of the form (11.27) for each $u_{j,k}$, the set of equations can clearly be arranged in the diagonally dominant form which is essential for the convergence of a Gauss-Siedel type method. Solving (11.27) for $u_{j,k}$ yields

$$u_{j,k} = \frac{u_{j,k+1} + u_{j,k-1} + [(\Delta x)^2/(\Delta y)^2](u_{j+1,k} + u_{j-1,k})}{2 + 2(\Delta x)^2/(\Delta y)^2}$$

$$(11.28)$$

Often it is desirable to set $\Delta x = \Delta y$, and in this case (11.28) becomes

$$u_{j,k} = \frac{1}{4}(u_{j,k+1} + u_{j,k-1} + u_{j+1,k} + u_{j-1,k})$$

$$(11.29)$$

By sweeping through all of the interior points of R in any orderly fashion, and solving for $u_{j,k}$ from (11.28) (or (11.29)) at each point, one complete Gauss-Siedel iteration is carried out. This can be repeated until convergence is attained. For the particular problem under consideration, this iterative process will *always* converge. However, as we indicated at the beginning of this discussion, it is much more effective to employ overrelaxation rather than straight Gauss-Siedel iteration. This overrelaxation can be accomplished by using (6.51) to modify each value of $u_{j,k}$ after it has been computed using Gauss-Siedel iteration. Equation (6.51) written in terms of the variable $u_{j,k}$ is

$$u_{j,k}^{(l+1)} = u_{j,k}^{(l)} + \lambda(u_{j,k}^{(l+1)*} - u_{j,k}^{(l)})$$

$$(11.30)$$

where the number of the iteration is denoted by the superscript, and the asterisk indicates the Gauss-Siedel value. Since we have mentioned overrelaxation, obviously we will be interested in values of λ between 1 and 2.

In Chapter 6, we noted that while an optimum value of λ exists for any problem, it is often difficult to find this optimum value. Fortunately, a great deal of information is available on estimating optimum relaxation factors for the sets of equations which result from the application of finite difference methods to elliptic problems. The relatively straightforward method which we will present here is from Forsythe and Wasow [6]. Much additional information on the choice of relaxation factors can also be found in the same reference and in Varga [42] and Fox [41].

The optimum overrelaxation factor for the problem considered here can be estimated by

$$\lambda_{opt} = \frac{2}{1 + (1 - \omega^2)^{1/2}} \tag{11.31}$$

where ω^2 is determined as follows. Let

$$Y_{j,k}^{(l+1)} = u_{j,k}^{(l+1)} - u_{j,k}^{(l)} \tag{11.32}$$

A norm of $Y^{(l+1)}$ is given by

$$\| Y^{(l+1)} \| = \sum_{j=1}^{n} \sum_{k=1}^{n} | Y_{j,k}^{(l+1)} | \tag{11.33}$$

Now

$$\frac{\| Y^{(l+1)} \|}{\| Y^{(l)} \|} \to \omega^2 \quad \text{as } l \to \infty \tag{11.34}$$

Generally, this estimation of λ_{opt} is carried out using Gauss-Siedel iteration ($\lambda = 1$ in (11.30)). As each value of $u_{j,k}^{(l+1)}$ is computed on a sweep through the matrix, the value of $Y_{j,k}^{(l+1)}$ can be calculated from (11.32) just before the newly computed value $u_{j,k}^{(l+1)}$ replaces the old value $u_{j,k}^{(l)}$ in memory. This $Y_{j,k}^{(l+1)}$ can then be added to a running sum which eventually becomes $\| Y^{(l+1)} \|$ through (11.33). In this way no significant additional amount of storage space is required over that necessary for the Gauss-Siedel iteration. The use of (11.34) to estimate ω^2 presents something of a dilemma. Obviously if we wait until l becomes very large (many iterations) then we will have an accurate estimate of ω^2, but it will not be needed since we will have already solved the problem using Gauss-Siedel iteration! If, on the other hand, l is too small, then we will obtain a poor estimate of ω^2 and hence of λ_{opt}. (For the first few iterations, it is entirely possible that $\| Y^{(l+1)} \| / \| Y^{(l)} \|$ may be greater than 1. This would obviously cause disaster if it were used as an estimate of ω^2 in (11.31).)

One effective procedure is to simply take enough iterations to ensure that the estimate of ω^2 has settled down to a reasonably constant level less than 1, and then use (11.31) to estimate λ_{opt}. This may require from ten to several hundred Gauss-Siedel iterations, depending on the problem and mesh sizes involved. The estimate of λ_{opt} is then used in (11.30) and the problem iterated to convergence using this relaxation factor. Even if the estimate of λ_{opt} is fairly crude, the convergence rate will still be far better than with Gauss-Siedel iteration alone. (We might note that in terms of convergence rate it is generally better to overestimate λ_{opt} than to underestimate it.)

We now turn to a brief qualitative discussion of the most efficient class of iterative methods for elliptic problems, the alternating direction implicit (ADI) methods. Denoting the current iteration by the superscript $(l + 1)$, and the preceding iteration by (l), we rewrite the difference equation (11.26) in the form

$$\frac{u_{j,k+1}^{(l)} - 2u_{j,k}^{(l)} + u_{j,k-1}^{(l)}}{(\Delta x)^2} + \frac{u_{j+1,k}^{(l+1)} - 2u_{j,k}^{(l+1)} + u_{j-1,k}^{(l+1)}}{(\Delta y)^2} = 0 \tag{11.35}$$

Note that the difference representation of $\partial^2 u / \partial y^2$ involves unknown values of u from the current iteration, but the representation of $\partial^2 u / \partial x^2$ involves only known values of u from the preceding iteration. If (11.35) is written for every value of j along a vertical line in Fig. 11.2, then we obtain a set of simultaneous equations involving *only* the values of u along that line. Moreover, the matrix of coefficients of that set is tridiagonal. A similar tridiagonal set can be formed for every vertical line. These tridiagonal sets can be solved independently, resulting in new u values over the interior of R. Now we reverse the process, representing the horizontal (x) derivative with unknown values from the current iteration, and the vertical (y) derivative with known values from the preceding iteration. This results in a tridiagonal set of simultaneous equations for each horizontal line, and the solution of these sets again gives a new u value for every interior point of the region R. It is usual to consider one complete iteration as consisting of the solution along the vertical lines followed by the solution along the horizontal lines (or vice versa). This iteration can be repeated as many times as necessary until convergence is attained. In practice, an acceleration parameter, analogous to the relaxation factor used in (11.30), is used to modify the computation for each "half" of the iteration. If a single optimum value of this acceleration parameter is used, then the convergence rate of the ADI method is essentially the same as that of SOR with an optimum value of λ. If, however, a series of properly chosen different acceleration parameters are employed in cyclic order, then vastly superior acceleration rates can be attained. The reader is referred to Forsythe and Wasow[6], Varga[42], and Westlake[43] for detailed treatments.

It should be noted that ADI methods also represent a most efficient direct (noniterative) method of solving equations of the form

$$\alpha\left(\frac{\partial^2 u}{\partial x^2} + \frac{\partial^2 u}{\partial y^2}\right) = \frac{\partial u}{\partial t}$$

See Forsythe and Wasow[6].

We have confined our discussion in this section to simple rectangular regions and Dirichlet boundary conditions. Many of the most difficult problems to deal with in the solution of elliptic equations arise from the irregularly shaped regions and unusual boundary conditions which are typical of real physical problems. Forsythe and Wasow[6] and Allen[44] provide much useful information in these areas. See also Problem 11.6 for an example involving boundary conditions which are not of the Dirichlet type.

Examples of numerical solutions to elliptic equations can be found in Problems 11.4–11.6.

11.4 NUMERICAL METHODS FOR THE SOLUTION OF HYPERBOLIC EQUATIONS

It is possible to formulate straightforward finite difference methods for the solution of hyperbolic equations. In particular, for the wave equation (11.7), the methods are very similar to those which were developed for parabolic equations in Sec. 11.2, and include a conditionally stable explicit formulation and a universally stable implicit method. See Fox[41] for the details of these methods and see also Problem 11.7.

However, the most effective numerical techniques for hyperbolic equations are based on the *method of characteristics*. It is beyond the scope of this book to discuss this approach, and the reader is referred to the book by Abbott[45], and to the extensive treatment of the subject which can be found in the literature of the compressible fluid flow and plasticity fields. The most notable advantage of the method of characteristics is that discontinuities in the solution, which are quite common with hyperbolic problems, can be accurately represented and maintained as the solution is carried out. With the usual finite difference methods, such discontinuities tend to "diffuse" or smear out.

11.5 FINITE ELEMENT METHODS

We should not close this chapter without at least a brief introduction to finite element methods as applied to problems involving partial differential equations. The finite element approach is a relatively recent development which has its origins in the field of solid mechanics (elasticity, plasticity, and structural analysis). As of this writing, finite element methods have replaced finite difference methods in many areas of solid mechanics and are making inroads into fluid mechanics, heat transfer, and other fields. However, in fields other than solid mechanics, much of the emphasis is still on the development of the finite element approach itself, rather than on the solution of problems. For the solution of problems of practical importance, finite difference methods are employed in the majority of cases, and the methods discussed earlier in this chapter are most relevant. In any case, the potential of finite element methods in all fields involving partial differential equations appears sufficiently great to warrant some introductory discussion.

With the finite element approach, the partial differential equations describing the desired quantity (such as displacement) in the continuum often are not dealt with directly.* Instead, the continuum is divided into a number of "finite elements," which are assumed to be joined at a discrete number of points along their boundaries. A functional form is then chosen to represent the variation of the desired quantity over each element in terms of the values of this quantity at the discrete boundary points of the element. By using the physical properties of the continuum and the appropriate physical laws (usually involving some sort of minimization principle), a set of simultaneous equations in the unknown quantities at the element boundary points can be obtained. This set of equations is in general quite large, but the matrix is banded.

For those situations where the finite element technology has been developed, there are three primary advantages of the finite element approach over finite difference methods. These are:

1. Irregularly shaped regions can be handled easily, without the special treatment usually required by finite difference methods.
2. The size of the finite elements can easily be varied over the region, permitting the use of small elements where strong variations occur and large elements where only gentle variations are expected. With finite difference methods, at least in their conventional form, the use of many such mesh size variations can cause bookkeeping difficulty.
3. For comparable accuracy, the finite elements can usually be considerably larger than the mesh elements of a finite difference grid. As a result, when elliptic problems are involved the band matrix referred to earlier is usually small enough to be solved directly without recourse to the iterative methods which are usually necessary with finite difference methods.

Required reading for anyone interested in the subject of finite elements is the book by Zienkiewicz[46], which deals not only with solid mechanics but also with extensions of the method into other areas of engineering and science.

---

*It should be noted, however, that a significant amount of work has also been done on the development of finite element methods directly from the differential equations. This approach has been found to be particularly useful in fields other than solid mechanics. See Ref. 46.

Illustrative Problems

11.1   Solve the problem

$$\frac{\partial^2 u}{\partial x^2} = \frac{\partial u}{\partial y}$$

$$u(0,y) = 200, \quad u(1,y) = 200, \quad u(x,0) = 0$$

by using an explicit numerical technique with $\Delta x = 0.2$. Show results for two different values of Δy: 0.04 and 0.015.

   The explicit stability criterion for this problem requires that

$$\Delta y \le \frac{(\Delta x)^2}{2} = \frac{(0.2)^2}{2} = 0.02$$

Since $\Delta y = 0.04$ exceeds this value, we would expect instability, while $\Delta y = 0.015$ should provide a stable solution. Solutions for the two values of Δy at $x = 0.4$ are shown in Fig. 11.8 as a function of y. The solution for $\Delta y = 0.015$ is smooth and stable, and approaches the correct "steady state" value of 200. (A more accurate solution for small y could be obtained by using smaller values of Δy in this region.) The solution for $\Delta y = 0.04$ is clearly unstable, as would have been expected from the stability criterion. (No attempt has been made to draw a smooth curve for this solution; the solution points were simply connected with straight lines.)

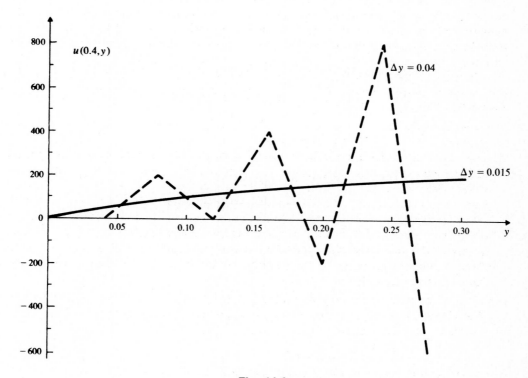

Fig. 11.8

11.2   Formulate an implicit numerical solution to the problem

$$\frac{\partial^2 u}{\partial x^2} = \frac{\partial u}{\partial y}$$

$$u(0,y) = 10, \quad \frac{\partial u}{\partial x}(1,y) = 7, \quad u(x,0) = 0$$

Using the notation of Sec. 11.2, the gradient condition on $(\partial u / \partial x)(1,y)$ can be expressed in backward difference form as

$$\frac{\partial u}{\partial x}(1,y) \approx \frac{3u_{j+1,n+1} - 4u_{j+1,n} + u_{j+1,n-1}}{2(\Delta x)} = 7$$

Note that we have used a difference representation which is of error order $(\Delta x)^2$ to be consistent with the truncation error of the central difference representation of $\partial^2 u / \partial x^2$ used in Sec. 11.2.   The quantity $u_{j+1,n+1}$ is unknown for this problem, and the finite difference form of the boundary condition furnishes the necessary additional equation.   If we write this equation in the form

$$[1]u_{j+1,n-1} + [-4]u_{j+1,n} + [3]u_{j+1,n+1} = 14(\Delta x)$$

then the matrix formulation (*11.19*) can be written for the present problem as

$$\begin{bmatrix} \beta & 1 & & & & \\ 1 & \beta & 1 & & & \\ & 1 & \beta & 1 & & \\ & & - & - & - & \\ & & & - & - & - \\ & & & 1 & \beta & 1 \\ & & & & 1 & -4 & 3 \end{bmatrix} \begin{bmatrix} u_{j+1,1} \\ u_{j+1,2} \\ u_{j+1,3} \\ - \\ - \\ u_{j+1,n} \\ u_{j+1,n+1} \end{bmatrix} = \begin{bmatrix} \Omega u_{j,1} - 10 \\ \Omega u_{j,2} \\ \Omega u_{j,3} \\ - \\ - \\ \Omega u_{j,n} \\ 14(\Delta x) \end{bmatrix}$$

This set is no longer tridiagonal, but it can be simply converted to tridiagonal form.   This is left as an exercise (Problem 11.10).

An alternative formulation is often used to handle the gradient boundary condition. Consider Fig. 11.9.

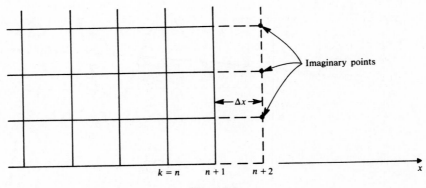

Fig. 11.9

We have added a column of "imaginary" points at a distance Δx from the true right-hand boundary.   We assume that the differential equation also applies to this added region, and hence we can write the difference equation (*11.17*) at $k = n + 1$, yielding

$$\frac{u_{j+1,n+2} - 2u_{j+1,n+1} + u_{j+1,n}}{(\Delta x)^2} = \frac{u_{j+1,n+1} - u_{j,n+1}}{\Delta t}$$

The gradient boundary condition can be expressed in central difference form as

$$\frac{u_{j+1,n+2} - u_{j+1,n}}{2(\Delta x)} = 7$$

These two equations are sufficient to complete the set. Note that we have added the additional unknown $u_{j+1,n+2}$ at the imaginary point and hence require one more equation than in the previous formulation. The entire set in matrix form can be written as

$$\begin{bmatrix} \beta & 1 & & & & & \\ 1 & \beta & 1 & & & & \\ & 1 & \beta & 1 & & & \\ & & - & - & - & & \\ & & & - & - & - & \\ & & & & 1 & \beta & 1 \\ & & & & & -1 & 0 & 1 \end{bmatrix} \begin{bmatrix} u_{j+1,1} \\ u_{j+1,2} \\ u_{j+1,3} \\ - \\ - \\ u_{j+1,n+1} \\ u_{j+1,n+2} \end{bmatrix} = \begin{bmatrix} \Omega u_{j,1} - 10 \\ \Omega u_{j,2} \\ \Omega u_{j,3} \\ - \\ - \\ \Omega u_{j,n+1} \\ 14(\Delta x) \end{bmatrix}$$

This form can also readily be made tridiagonal. Once again the details are left to Problem 11.10.

11.3 Devise a finite difference method for solving the nonlinear parabolic equation

$$\frac{\partial^2 u}{\partial x^2} = u \frac{\partial u}{\partial y}$$

There are many possible approaches to this problem. We will limit our discussion to two implicit methods, both of which are universally stable. Using the notation of Sec. 11.2, one possible difference form for the differential equation is

$$\frac{u_{j+1,k+1} - 2u_{j+1,k} + u_{j+1,k-1}}{(\Delta x)^2} = u_{j,k} \left[\frac{u_{j+1,k} - u_{j,k}}{\Delta y} \right]$$

This form is very similar to the implicit form (11.17) employed for the one-dimensional transient diffusion equation, except that the nonlinearity on the right side of the equation has been accommodated by using the known value $u_{j,k}$ to multiply the difference representation of $\partial u / \partial y$. (Recall that those quantities with subscript $j+1$ are unknown, and those with subscript j are known.) The resulting equation is linear in the unknown values of u, and the solution procedure is virtually identical to that for (11.17). The only modification necessary is a slight change in the diagonal elements of the tridiagonal matrix and in the right-hand side column vector of (11.17) to include $u_{j,k}$.

We briefly note that another possible difference representation is

$$\frac{u_{j+1,k+1} - 2u_{j+1,k} + u_{j+1,k-1}}{(\Delta x)^2} = u_{j+1,k} \left[\frac{u_{j+1,k} - u_{j,k}}{\Delta y} \right]$$

Since the unknown $u_{j+1,k}$ has been used to multiply the difference representation of $\partial u / \partial y$, this difference form involves $(u_{j+1,k})^2$ and hence is nonlinear in $u_{j+1,k}$. The set of simultaneous algebraic equations which results when the difference equation is written for each point in the x direction is thus nonlinear in the unknown values of u, and must be solved iteratively. This additional complication can, under certain circumstances, be balanced by the increased accuracy which usually can be obtained from the nonlinear difference form.

11.4 Solve Laplace's equation on the interior of the region shown in Fig. 11.10 using the indicated boundary conditions with Gauss-Siedel iteration.

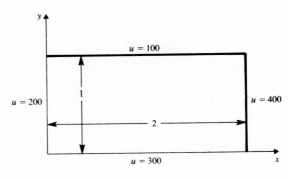

Fig. 11.10

We arbitrarily choose the reasonably coarse mesh of $\Delta x = \Delta y = 0.125$, providing 8 mesh spaces in the y direction and 16 in the x direction. This means that there are a total of 105 (7×15) interior points and thus 105 simultaneous equations to be solved, each of the form

$$u_{j,k} = \frac{1}{4}(u_{j-1,k} + u_{j+1,k} + u_{j,k-1} + u_{j,k+1})$$

We will discuss the adequacy of this mesh size later.

The first problem we face is that of choosing an initial guess for the unknown at each point. The simplest and most commonly used initial guess is a constant over the entire region, and we will take this approach. (It should be noted that a more sophisticated initial guess can result in faster convergence in many cases.) We will consider the effect of two different initial guesses, $u = 0$ and $u = 200$ in the interior of the region. Obviously $u = 0$ is a poor guess, and we would expect that more iterations would be required to satisfy a given convergence criterion than would be necessary for an initial guess of $u = 200$.

We employ an absolute convergence criterion of $\epsilon = 0.1$, and sweep through the region from left to right along lines parallel to the x axis, starting at $y = \Delta y$ and moving upward one line when the right-hand boundary is reached on each horizontal sweep. Using an initial guess of $u = 0$, 61 iterations through the entire region are required in order to satisfy the convergence criterion at every point. (To provide some perspective, this requires about 7.5 seconds of IBM 360/67 central processor time.) Some of the answers are shown in Fig. 11.11.

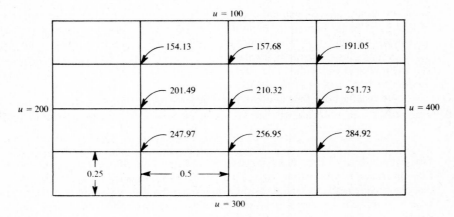

Fig. 11.11

With an initial guess of $u = 200$, only 36 iterations are required to yield essentially the same answers, and the advantage of the better initial guess should be apparent.

The exact solution at the center of the region is $u = 221.95$ as compared with the value from our numerical solution of 210.32. The numerical solution is in error by about 5% at this point, but it can be improved as much as desired by using smaller mesh sizes (and tightening the convergence criterion).

11.5 Solve Problem 11.4 by estimating and using an optimum overrelaxation factor.

We begin by using Gauss-Siedel iteration for the first few iterations. The initial guess is a uniform value of $u = 200$. The norm $\|Y\|$, and ω^2, which is the ratio of the norm on the present iteration to that on the preceding iteration, are shown below for the first 10 iterations:

Iteration	$\|Y\|$	ω^2
1	33.37	—
2	6.57	0.19674
3	2.90	0.44189
4	1.69	0.58114
5	1.12	0.66700
6	0.81	0.72215
7	0.62	0.75847
8	0.48	0.78341
9	0.39	0.80030
10	0.31	0.81305

By the tenth iteration, the value of ω^2 has settled down sufficiently that it is probably best to estimate λ_{opt} at this point, rather than to pursue what would appear to be a policy of diminishing returns in trying to obtain ω^2 more accurately. From (11.31), we find

$$\lambda_{opt} = \frac{2}{1 + \sqrt{1 - \omega^2}} = \frac{2}{1 + \sqrt{1 - 0.81305}} = 1.39628$$

Using overrelaxation with this value of λ, we find that the absolute convergence criterion of $\epsilon = 0.1$ is satisfied at all points in 14 more iterations. Thus a total of 24 iterations are required for this process as opposed to the 36 iterations required in Problem 11.4 using Gauss-Siedel iteration with the same initial guess.

The reduction in the number of iterations which can be accomplished by the use of an optimum overrelaxation factor is much more dramatic when mesh sizes are small, since small mesh sizes result in a large number of equations and a relatively slow convergence rate.

11.6 Formulate the solution to Laplace's equation on the region shown in Fig. 11.12.

The only new feature of this problem is the presence of gradient boundary conditions. Using the notation of Sec. 11.3, these conditions can be expressed in difference form as

$$\frac{\partial u}{\partial y}(x,0) \approx \frac{-u_{2,k} + 4u_{1,k} - 3u_{0,k}}{2(\Delta y)} = 0 \qquad \text{(written for } k = 1, 2, \ldots, n\text{)}$$

and

$$\frac{\partial u}{\partial x}(4,y) \approx \frac{3u_{j,n+1} - 4u_{j,n} + u_{j,n-1}}{2(\Delta x)} = 100 \qquad \text{(written for } j = 1, 2, \ldots, m\text{)}$$

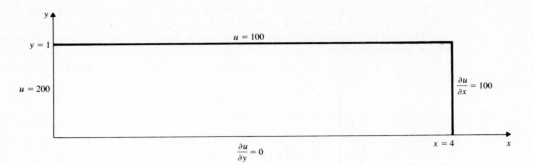

Fig. 11.12

The difference representation of $\partial u(x,0)/\partial y$ is forward and of error order $(\Delta y)^2$, while that of $\partial u(4,y)/\partial x$ is backward and of error order $(\Delta x)^2$. In our earlier consideration of elliptic problems, only the values of u on the interior points of the region were unknown, and corresponding to each of these unknowns was the difference form of the original differential equation written at that point. For this problem, the values of u along the boundaries $y = 0$ and $x = 4$ are also unknown, and the difference forms of the boundary conditions furnish the necessary additional equations. Solving each of the equations for the unknown which appears in it, we find

$$u_{0,k} = \frac{1}{3}(-u_{2,k} + 4u_{1,k}), \qquad k = 1, 2, \ldots, n$$

$$u_{j,n+1} = \frac{1}{3}[2(100)(\Delta x) + 4u_{j,n} - u_{j,n-1}], \qquad j = 1, 2, \ldots, m$$

These equations can now be solved along with the usual equations at the interior points by Gauss-Siedel iteration (or overrelaxation).

We should note that the other commonly encountered way of handling gradient boundary conditions is to use a central difference at the boundary along with an "imaginary" point outside the boundary. This approach was discussed in Problem 11.2 in connection with a parabolic problem, where the single additional unknown at the imaginary point was relatively insignificant. For the present problem, an entire line of additional unknowns would be added along the bottom and right boundaries. This could mean a significant amount of additional work.

The corner point at $x = 4$, $y = 0$ does not enter into any of the calculations, and, in fact, cannot be uniquely determined even after the solution is obtained, since *either* of the boundary conditions could be used to solve for it. Physically speaking, boundary conditions of the type considered here cannot be extended all the way into the corner, so this is a mathematical problem rather than a physical one. Similar situations are often encountered in the solution of elliptic equations on rectangular regions by analytical methods.

11.7 Devise an explicit finite difference representation for the wave equation

$$\frac{\partial^2 u}{\partial x^2} = \beta \frac{\partial^2 u}{\partial y^2}$$

and indicate the probable stability criterion.

Problems involving the wave equation are initial valued in one variable (we will assume it is y) and boundary valued in the other (x).   The initial values specified are usually $u(x,0)$ and $\partial u(x,0)/\partial y$.   We now impose a finite difference grid on the region of interest and associate the subscript j with y, and k with x.   If central difference expressions for the derivatives are employed about the point (j,k), then the differential equation can be represented as

$$\frac{u_{j,k+1} - 2u_{j,k} + u_{j,k-1}}{(\Delta x)^2} = \beta \left[\frac{u_{j+1,k} - 2u_{j,k} + u_{j-1,k}}{(\Delta y)^2} \right]$$

Solving for $u_{j+1,k}$, we find

$$u_{j+1,k} = [-1]u_{j-1,k} + \left[\frac{(\Delta y)^2}{\beta(\Delta x)^2} \right] u_{j,k+1} + \left[\frac{(\Delta y)^2}{\beta(\Delta x)^2} \right] u_{j,k-1} + \left[2\left(1 - \frac{(\Delta y)^2}{\beta(\Delta x)^2} \right) \right] u_{j,k}$$

This representation is clearly explicit, since we can solve directly for $u_{j+1,k}$.   At first glance, it might appear that this method is not self-starting, since u values with subscripts of j and $j-1$ are involved.   However, since one of the initial conditions is on $\partial u/\partial y$, a difference expression for this derivative will relate $u_{1,k}$ to $u_{0,k}$ and thus provide the necessary values of $u_{1,k}$ for starting.

Since we have not discussed the details of stability analysis, our only hope in this regard is to attempt to draw an analogy to the explicit representation of the parabolic one-dimensional diffusion equation (*11.14*).   Recall that this representation became unstable when the coefficient of $u_{j,k}$ was negative.   For the present problem, we might then expect the method to be stable only if

$$\frac{(\Delta y)^2}{\beta(\Delta x)^2} \le 1$$

A complete stability analysis reveals that this is indeed the correct stability criterion.

Problems

*11.8   Solve the following problem numerically:

$$\frac{\partial^2 u}{\partial x^2} = \frac{\partial u}{\partial y}$$

$$u(0,y) = 100, \quad u(10,y) = 300, \quad u(x,0) = 0$$

Use $\Delta x = 1$ and suitable values of Δy.   Use an explicit method up to $y = 5$; then shift to an implicit method and carry the solution to the "steady state."

*11.9   Given the following problem:

$$\frac{\partial^2 u}{\partial x^2} = \frac{\partial u}{\partial y}$$

$$u(0,y) = 50, \quad u(\infty,y) = 0, \quad u(x,0) = 0$$

Find $u(x,y)$ by any suitable numerical method.   Stop at the point where $u(1,y) \approx 40$.   (There is no "steady state" solution for this problem.   Why not?)

11.10   Convert the nontridiagonal sets obtained in Problem 11.2 to tridiagonal form.

*11.11 Complete the solution which was begun in Problem 11.2. Use $\Delta x = 0.1$ and an initial Δy of 0.005, increasing Δy as desired as the steady state is approached. Carry out the solution to the point where $u(1,y)$ reaches 95% of its steady state value. (You may use either of the matrix formulations discussed in Problem 11.2.)

11.12 Formulate an implicit method for solving problems involving the following parabolic equation:

$$\frac{\partial}{\partial x}\left(G(u)\frac{\partial u}{\partial x}\right) = \frac{\partial u}{\partial y}$$

where $G(u)$ is a known function of u.

11.13 Solve Laplace's equation numerically for the region shown in Fig. 11.13.
The boundary conditions are constant at the indicated values. Use two different approaches in obtaining your numerical solution:

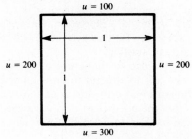

Fig. 11.13

(*a*) Gauss-Siedel iteration with a uniform grid size of 0.25 in each direction. *Do not* take advantage of symmetry.

(*b*) Repeat the solution as in part (*a*), but use the symmetry of the problem to reduce the amount of work.

*11.14 Solve the problem which was formulated in Problem 11.6. Use $\Delta x = \Delta y = 0.2$, and an absolute convergence criterion of 0.1 on u. The method should be one of the following:

(*a*) Gauss-Siedel iteration.
(*b*) Optimum overrelaxation.

If optimum overrelaxation is used, it will of course be necessary to first estimate λ_{opt}. In any case, use a uniform initial guess of $u = 150$ over the region.

11.15 Laplace's equation in cylindrical coordinates is

$$\frac{\partial^2 u}{\partial r^2} + \frac{1}{r}\frac{\partial u}{\partial r} + \frac{1}{r^2}\frac{\partial^2 u}{\partial \theta^2} = 0$$

Formulate a finite difference representation of this equation using central differences and indicate how Gauss-Siedel iteration could be used to solve the difference equations over any desired region.

*11.16 Solve by an appropriate numerical method the following problem involving Poisson's equation:

$$\frac{\partial^2 u}{\partial x^2} + \frac{\partial^2 u}{\partial y^2} = -10, \quad u(0,y) = 0$$

$$u(x,0) = 0, \quad u(1,y) = 0, \quad u(x,1) = 0$$

11.17 Using the Crank-Nicholson concept discussed in Sec. 11.2, formulate an implicit difference representation of the wave equation and discuss its probable stability characteristics.

Appendix

Interpretation of Flow Charts.

Tables of Weights and Zeros for Gauss Quadrature.

A FORTRAN IV Subroutine for Matrix Inversion.

INTERPRETATION OF FLOW CHARTS

We have adopted a very simple notation for the flow charts used in this book. Rectangular boxes are employed where actual arithmetic operations and substitutions are involved. Thus

$$\boxed{A \leftarrow B * C}$$

means that A assumes the value of B times C. Similarly,

$$\boxed{i \leftarrow i + 1}$$

results in the increase of the index i by 1.

Oval boxes are used for simple logic statements. The question "Is i greater than n?" is represented by

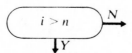

where the Y branch corresponds to an answer of Yes, and the N branch to an answer of No. For several reasons we have not adopted the diamond shaped boxes which are sometimes employed for logic statements.

Virtually every compiler has a suitable statement which should be used to carry out the actual computer programming of those loops which involve the incrementing of an index variable until it reaches a specified limit.   Typical examples are the FORTRAN DO statement and the ALGOL FOR statement.

A few flow charts are sufficiently complex that to put in all of the necessary connecting lines would result in a confusion of crossed lines or would require a large amount of space.   In these cases the following convention is used:

A connecting line between the circled numbers is implied, and the circled numbers may be physically separated by any vertical or horizontal distance.

Table A-1 Zeros and Weights for Gauss-Legendre Quadrature

n	$\pm \xi_k$	w_k	n	$\pm \xi_k$	w_k
2	0.5773502692	1.0000000000	12	0.1252334085	0.2491470458
3	0.0000000000	0.8888888889		0.3678314990	0.2334925365
	0.7745966692	0.5555555556		0.5873179543	0.2031674267
4	0.3399810436	0.6521451549		0.7699026742	0.1600783285
	0.8611363116	0.3478548451		0.9041172564	0.1069393260
5	0.0000000000	0.5688888889		0.9815606342	0.0471753364
	0.5384693101	0.4786286705	16	0.0950125098	0.1894506105
	0.9061798459	0.2369268850		0.2816035508	0.1826034150
6	0.2386191861	0.4679139346		0.4580167777	0.1691565194
	0.6612093865	0.3607615730		0.6178762444	0.1495959888
	0.9324695142	0.1713244924		0.7554044084	0.1246289713
7	0.0000000000	0.4179591837		0.8656312024	0.0951585117
	0.4058451514	0.3818300505		0.9445750231	0.0622535239
	0.7415311856	0.2797053915		0.9894009350	0.0271524594
	0.9491079123	0.1294849662	20	0.0765265211	0.1527533871
8	0.1834346425	0.3626837834		0.2277858511	0.1491729865
	0.5255324099	0.3137066459		0.3737060887	0.1420961093
	0.7966664774	0.2223810345		0.5108670020	0.1316886384
	0.9602898565	0.1012285363		0.6360536807	0.1181945320
9	0.0000000000	0.3302393550		0.7463319065	0.1019301198
	0.3242534234	0.3123470770		0.8391169718	0.0832767416
	0.6133714327	0.2606106964		0.9122344283	0.0626720483
	0.8360311073	0.1806481607		0.9639719273	0.0406014298
	0.9681602395	0.0812743884		0.9931285992	0.0176140071
10	0.1488743390	0.2955242247	24	0.0640568929	0.1279381953
	0.4333953941	0.2692667193		0.1911188675	0.1258374563
	0.6794095683	0.2190863625		0.3150426797	0.1216704729
	0.8650633667	0.1494513492		0.4337935076	0.1155056681
	0.9739065285	0.0666713443		0.5454214714	0.1074442701
				0.6480936519	0.0976186521
				0.7401241916	0.0861901615
				0.8200019860	0.0733464814
				0.8864155270	0.0592985849
				0.9382745520	0.0442774388
				0.9747285560	0.0285313886
				0.9951872200	0.0123412298

This table of zeros and weights for Gauss-Legendre quadrature has been excerpted from Ref. 15 and rounded to 10 decimal places.   More extensive tables can also be found in Ref. 14.

Table A-2   Weights and Zeros for Gauss Quadrature Applied to Integrals of Form $\int_0^1 f(x) \log_e (x)\, dx$

n	x_k	w_k
2	0.112009 0.602277	0.718539 0.281461
3	0.063891 0.368997 0.766880	0.513405 0.391980 0.094615
4	0.041448 0.245275 0.556165 0.848982	0.383464 0.386875 0.190435 0.039225

This table has been adapted from Ref. 15.

A FORTRAN IV SUBROUTINE FOR MATRIX INVERSION

The routine given here employs Gauss-Jordan elimination with column shifting to maximize pivot elements.   The routine is called by the statement

CALL INVDET (C,N,DTNRM,DETM)

where C is a square two dimensional array containing the matrix to be inverted, and N is the row and column dimension of the matrix to be inverted.   On return from the subroutine, the inverted matrix is stored in C in the same position as the original matrix (the original matrix is destroyed).   The magnitude of the determinant of the original matrix is returned in DETM, and this magnitude, divided by the Euclidean norm of the matrix, is returned in DTNRM.   There are no error exits, and attempting to invert a singular matrix will simply return erroneous results.   However, extreme ill-conditioning or singularity will usually be accompanied by a very small value of DTNRM.

The matrix C has been dimensioned as 70×70 in the subroutine.   This must be changed as necessary to agree with the dimensions of the corresponding array in the calling program.   The dimension of J must be at least 21 greater than the row or column dimension of C.   The value of N can be any integer less than or equal to the row and column dimension of C.

```
      SUBROUTINE INVDET(C,N,DTNRM,DETM)
      DIMENSION C(70,70),J(120)
      PD=1.
      DO 124 L=1,N
      DD=0.
      DO 123 K=1,N
  123 DD=DD+C(L,K)*C(L,K)
      DD=SQRT(DD)
  124 PD=PD*DD
      DETM=1.
      DO 125 L=1,N
  125 J(L+20)=L
      DO 144 L=1,N
      CC=0.
      M=L
      DO 135 K=L,N
      IF ((ABS(CC)-ABS(C(L,K))).GE.0.) GO TO 135
  126 M=K
      CC=C(L,K)
  135 CONTINUE
  127 IF (L.EQ.M) GO TO 138
  128 K=J(M+20)
      J(M+20)=J(L+20)
      J(L+20)=K
      DO 137 K=1,N
      S=C(K,L)
      C(K,L)=C(K,M)
  137 C(K,M)=S
  138 C(L,L)=1.
      DETM=DETM*CC
      DO 139 M=1,N
  139 C(L,M)=C(L,M)/CC
      DO 142 M=1,N
      IF (L.EQ.M) GO TO 142
  129 CC=C(M,L)
      IF (CC.EQ.0.) GO TO 142
  130 C(M,L)=0.
      DO 141 K=1,N
  141 C(M,K)=C(M,K)-CC*C(L,K)
  142 CONTINUE
  144 CONTINUE
      DO 143 L=1,N
      IF (J(L+20).EQ.L) GO TO 143
  131 M=L
  132 M=M+1
      IF (J(M+20).EQ.L) GO TO 133
  136 IF (N.GT.M) GO TO 132
  133 J(M+20)=J(L+20)
      DO 163 K=1,N
      CC=C(L,K)
      C(L,K)=C(M,K)
  163 C(M,K)=CC
      J(L+20)=L
  143 CONTINUE
      DETM=ABS(DETM)
      DTNRM=DETM/PD
      RETURN
      END
```

References

1. Salvadori, M. G. and M. L. Baron: *Numerical Methods in Engineering*, 2nd ed., Prentice-Hall, 1961.
2. Carnahan, B., H. A. Luther, and J. O. Wilkes: *Applied Numerical Methods*, John Wiley, 1969.
3. Ralston, A.: *A First Course in Numerical Analysis*, McGraw-Hill, 1965.
4. Conte, S. D.: *Elementary Numerical Analysis*, McGraw-Hill, 1965.
5. Froberg, C.-E.: *Introduction to Numerical Analysis*, 2nd ed., Addison-Wesley, 1969.
6. Forsythe, G. E. and W. R. Wasow: *Finite Difference Methods for Partial Differential Equations*, John Wiley, 1960.
7. Rice, J. R.: *The Approximation of Functions*, Addison-Wesley, 1964.
8. Meinardus, G., translated by L. Schumaker: *Approximation of Functions: Theory and Numerical Methods*, Springer-Verlag, New York, 1967.
9. Pugh, E. M. and G. H. Winslow: *Analysis of Physical Measurements*, Addison-Wesley, 1966.
10. Acton, F. S.: *Analysis of Straight-Line Data*, Dover.
11. Hamming, R. W.: *Numerical Methods for Scientists and Engineers*, McGraw-Hill, 1962.
12. Acton, F. S.: *Numerical Methods That Work*, Harper and Row, 1970.
13. Lanczos, C.: *Applied Analysis*, Prentice-Hall, 1956.
14. Stroud, A. H. and D. Secrest: *Gaussian Quadrature Formulas*, Prentice-Hall, 1966.
15. Abramowitz, M. and I. A. Stegun, eds.: *Handbook of Mathematical Functions with Formulas, Graphs and Mathematical Tables*, Dover, 1964.
16. Davis, P. J. and P. Rabinowitz: *Numerical Integration*, Blaisdell (now Xerox), 1967.
17. Henrici, P.: *Discrete Variable Methods in Ordinary Differential Equations*, John Wiley, 1962.
18. Crandall, S. H.: *Engineering Analysis: A Survey of Numerical Procedures*, McGraw-Hill, 1956.
19. Butcher, J. C.: "On Runge-Kutta Processes of High Order," *Journal of the Australian Mathematical Society*, Vol. 4, pp. 179–194, 1964.
20. Shanks, E. B.: "Solutions of Differential Equations by Evaluation of Functions," *Mathematics of Computation*, Vol. 20, pp. 21–38, 1966.
21. Hall, T. E., W. H. Enright, B. M. Fellen, and A. E. Sedgewick: "Comparing Numerical Methods for Ordinary Differential Equations," *SIAM Journal on Numerical Analysis*, Vol. 9, No. 4, pp. 603–637, 1972.
22. Gear, C. W.: "The Automatic Integration of Ordinary Differential Equations," *Communications of the Association for Computing Machinery*, Vol. 14, pp. 176–190, 1971.

23. Keller, H. B.: *Numerical Methods for Two-Point Boundary-Value Problems*, Blaisdell (now Xerox), 1968.

24. Bulirsch, R. and J. Stoer: "Numerical Treatment of Ordinary Differential Equations by Extrapolation Methods," *Numerische Mathematik*, Vol. 8, pp. 1–13, 1966.

25. Curtiss, C. F. and J. O. Hirschfelder: "Integration of Stiff Equations," *Proceedings of the National Academy of Sciences*, Vol. 38, pp. 235–243, 1952.

26. Wilkinson, J. H.: *The Algebraic Eigenvalue Problem*, Oxford University Press, London, 1965.

27. Rutishauser, H.: "Solution of Eigenvalue Problems with the LR Transformation," *National Bureau of Standards, Applied Mathematics Series*, No. 49, pp. 47–81, 1958.

28. Francis, J. G. F.: "The QR Transformation," *The Computer Journal*, Vol. 4, pp. 265–271, 1961 (Part I) and pp. 332–345, 1962 (Part II).

29. Bowdler, H., R. S. Martin, C. Reinsch, and J. H. Wilkinson: "The QR and QL Algorithms for Symmetric Matrices," *Numerische Mathematik*, Vol. 11, pp. 293–306, 1968.

30. Martin, R. S. and J. H. Wilkinson: "The Implicit QL Algorithm," *Numerische Mathematik*, Vol. 12, pp. 377–383, 1968.

31. Martin, R. S. and J. H. Wilkinson: "Similarity Reduction of a General Matrix to Hessenberg Form," *Numerische Mathematik*, Vol. 12, pp. 349–368, 1968.

32. Martin, R. S., G. Peters, and J. H. Wilkinson: "The QR Algorithm for Real Hessenberg Matrices," *Numerische Mathematik*, Vol. 14, pp. 219–231, 1970.

33. McCracken, D. D.: *A Guide to ALGOL Programming*, John Wiley, 1962.

34. Martin, R. S., G. Peters, and J. H. Wilkinson: "Symmetric Decomposition of a Positive Definite Matrix," *Numerische Mathematik*, Vol. 7, pp. 362–383, 1965.

35. Martin, R. S. and J. H. Wilkinson: "Reduction of the Symmetric Eigenproblem $Ax = \lambda Bx$ and Related Problems to Standard Form," *Numerische Mathematik*, Vol. 11, pp. 99–110, 1968.

36. Martin, R. S., C. Reinsch, and J. H. Wilkinson: "Householder's Tridiagonalization of a Symmetric Matrix," *Numerische Mathematik*, Vol. 11, pp. 181–195, 1968.

37. Rutishauser, H. and H. R. Schwarz: "The LR Transformation Method for Symmetric Matrices," *Numerische Mathematik*, Vol. 5, pp. 273–289, 1963.

38. Reinsch, C. and F. L. Bauer: "Rational QR transformation with Newton Shift for Symmetric Tridiagonal Matrices," *Numerische Mathematik*, Vol. 11, pp. 264–272, 1968.

39. Parlett, B. N. and C. Reinsch: "Balancing a Matrix for Calculation of Eigenvalues and Eigenvectors," *Numerische Mathematik*, Vol. 13, pp. 293–304, 1969.

40. O'Brien, G. G., M. A. Hyman, and S. Kaplan: "A Study of the Numerical Solution of Partial Differential Equations," *Journal of Mathematical Physics*, Vol. 29, pp. 223–251, 1951.

41. Fox, L.: *Numerical Solution of Ordinary and Partial Differential Equations*, Pergamon Press, dist. by Addison-Wesley, 1962.

42. Varga, R. S.: *Matrix Iterative Analysis*, Prentice-Hall, 1962.

43. Westlake, J. R.: *A Handbook of Numerical Matrix Inversion and Solution of Linear Equations*, John Wiley, 1968.

44. de G. Allen, D. N.: *Relaxation Methods in Engineering and Science*, McGraw-Hill, 1954.

45. Abbott, M. B.: *An Introduction to the Method of Characteristics*, American Elsevier Publ., 1966.

46. Zienkiewicz, O. C.: *The Finite Element Method in Engineering Science*, McGraw-Hill, London, 1971.

Answers to Problems

The number of decimal digits given for the numerical answers varies somewhat, but does not exceed 7, since this is the (single precision) word length of the IBM 360/67. Except as noted, these numerical answers are the results of actual computer runs using the specified method, and may not agree to all digits with the *exact* solution to the problem. The reader can in many cases expect to obtain results which differ slightly from the answers given here, depending on the computer and programming techniques employed.

CHAPTER 2

2.12 $\sinh x = x + x^3/3! + x^5/5! + x^7/7! + \cdots$

2.13 1.0215

2.14 Error bound = 0.0070518, actual error = 0.0050167. Note that the term involving x^4 is not present, so the error term must involve x^5.

2.15 $\sin x = (\sin \pi/4)[1 + (x - \pi/4) - (x - \pi/4)^2/2 - (x - \pi/4)^3/3! + (x - \pi/4)^4/4! + \cdots]$

2.16 $1/(1 - x^2) = 1 + 2x + 3x^2 + 4x^3 + 5x^4 + \cdots$

2.17 No. Not only is $\log_e(0)$ infinite, so are all of the derivatives of $\log_e x$ evaluated at $x = 0$.

2.18 $x - 2x^3/3$

2.19 $1 - x^2/2 + 5x^4/24$

2.20 The series is convergent. It is not necessary that the ratio of any two specific succeeding terms be less than one as long as one of the convergence tests is satisfied.

2.21 $g(x) = x + x^3/3! + x^5/5! + x^7/7! + \cdots$
$h(x) = 1 + x^2/2 + x^4/4! + x^6/6! + \cdots$

2.22 $1 + 3(x - 1) + 3(x - 1)^2 + (x - 1)^3 = x^3$

2.23 0.940316

CHAPTER 3

3.17 $\dfrac{d^6 f}{dx^6} = (f_{j+6} - 6f_{j+5} + 15f_{j+4} - 20f_{j+3} + 15f_{j+2} - 6f_{j+1} + f_j)/h^6 + \mathcal{O}(h)$

3.18 $f'(x) = (2f_{j+3} - 9f_{j+2} + 18f_{j+1} - 11f_j)/6h + \mathcal{O}(h)^3$

3.19 $f''(x_{j+1}) \approx \dfrac{\theta f_{j+2} - (1 + \theta)f_{j+1} + f_j}{\frac{1}{2}h^2 \theta(1 + \theta)}$

3.20 Exact answer $= -0.3826824$

for $h = \pi/10$		
forward $\mathcal{O}(h)$ -0.5203500	backward $\mathcal{O}(h)$ -0.2324857	central $\mathcal{O}(h)^2$ -0.3764178
forward $\mathcal{O}(h)^2$ -0.4018839	backward $\mathcal{O}(h)^2$ -0.3877978	central $\mathcal{O}(h)^4$ -0.3825588
for $h = \pi/20$		
forward $\mathcal{O}(h)$ -0.4535205	backward $\mathcal{O}(h)$ -0.3086988	central $\mathcal{O}(h)^2$ -0.3811097
forward $\mathcal{O}(h)^2$ -0.3866921	backward $\mathcal{O}(h)^2$ -0.3849109	central $\mathcal{O}(h)^4$ -0.3826741

3.21 4th degree polynomial

3.22 $f'(1) \approx 0.798$ for $h = 0.025$

3.23 $h = 10\pi$ for accuracy within a few percent.

3.24 $f'(x_j) = 0.2406 + \mathcal{O}(h)^2$
$f''(x_j) = -0.0618 + \mathcal{O}(h)^2$

3.25 If the function to be differentiated is a constant, then the difference representation of any derivative must yield zero.

3.26 Biased difference, first error term $= -\dfrac{h}{6} f''(x)$

Central difference, first error term $= -\dfrac{h^2}{6} f''(x)$

3.27 Actual error, biased difference $= 0.0152557$
Actual error, central difference $= 0.0008339$

3.28 $\mathcal{O}(h)^2$

CHAPTER 4

4.11   Third degree polynomial.   The coefficient of x^3 is 1.

4.12 $f(4.31) = 197.17$

4.13   (a)   10.909 (Bessel, 1.05 as base line)
           (b)   7.034 (Stirling, 0.9 as base line)
           (c)   25.708 (Gregory-Newton backward, 1.5 as base line)
           (d) -1.473 (Gregory-Newton forward, 0.3 as base line)

4.14 $f(4.3) = -0.007$

4.17 $f(1.3) = -411$

4.18 $f(6.3) = 0.226$

4.19   Results are virtually identical since the base lines of the tables used in 4.13 were almost full.

4.21 $f(3.4) = 13.745$

4.22 $f(9) = -12.953$

4.23 $f(3.0) = 36.769$ (polynomial extrapolation)

4.24 $f(5.0) = 5.04$ (polynomial extrapolation on a log-log scale)

CHAPTER 5

5.13 $\sqrt{3} = 1.732051$

5.14 $\sqrt[3]{75} = 4.217163$

5.15 $x = 1.23511$

5.16 $x = 0.73909$

5.17 $x = 0.567143$

5.18   Same root as 5.17

5.19 $x = 1.16556, 4.60422, 7.78988, 10.94994, 14.10172$

5.20 $x = 3.831698$

5.21 $x = -0.713967, 1.57251, 2.17178, 4.19268$

5.22 $f_{max} = 2.158887$ at $t = 0.374201$

5.23 $x = 2.70, 2.70, 3.40, 3.40$

5.24 $x = 1.87510, 4.69409, 7.85476, 10.99554, 14.13717$

CHAPTER 6

6.14 (a) $X = [100.3335, 28.66667, -32.66669]^T$
(b) $X = [1.0, 0.75, 0.25]^T$

6.15 (a) $X = [-21.86188, 11.46568, 2.376447, -8.514801, 0.7475478, -15.50981, 18.08498]^T$
(b) $X = [288.1675, -315.7456, -265.2044, -374.2180, -503.0234, 216.9468]^T$

6.16 See answers to 6.15.

6.17 $X = [8.705757, 7.823031, 7.586369, 7.522449, 7.503435, 7.491301, 7.461781, 7.355828, 6.961553, 5.490388]^T$

6.18 0.745

6.19 Magnitude of determinant $= 1.91 \times 10^{-2}$. Set is singular.

6.20 ($\epsilon = 10^{-4}$ for all problems)
(a) $X = [6.1656, 6.0191, -1.0892]^T$
(b) $X = [0.8119, 0.5638, 5.7390, -1.1630]^T$
(c) $X = [4.1992, 0.4955, -2.0308, 7.7589, 8.4767, 2.7424, 7.0443, 4.8825]^T$
(d) $X = [2.6943, 9.0222, -2.1541, 4.8317, 8.7579, 0.7241, -1.7160]^T$

6.21 See answers to 6.17.

6.22 Initial guess, $x_i = 10$ ($i = 1, 2, \ldots, 10$). $\lambda = 1$, 9 iterations; $\lambda = 1.3$, 12 iterations; $\lambda = 1.6$, 22 iterations; $\lambda = 1.8$, 44 iterations. ($\epsilon = 10^{-3}$ for all cases)

6.24 $X = [0.8890, -0.8126, 2.1419, 2.6497]^T$ ($\epsilon = 10^{-4}$)

CHAPTER 7

7.9 (a) $g(x) = 55.71671 - 5.301162x$
(b) $g(x) = 71.38016 - 1.503378x$

7.10 $g(x) = 1.130053 + 1.284786x - 0.0693512x^2$

7.11 $g(x) = 1.454021x^{2.014860}$

7.12 $g(x) = 1.27338e^{0.3894140x}$

7.13 $g(x) = 0.9999681x - 0.1664924x^3 + 0.0079856x^5$
Maximum error in $g(x) = 5.855 \times 10^{-6}$.
Maximum error using first 3 terms of Taylor series $= 1.984 \times 10^{-4}$.

7.14 $g(x) = 0.75y^2 - 0.75y - 6.132813$
Error bound $= 0.6328125$

7.15   Exact value $= 0.7853981$.
Continued fraction at sixth convergent $= 0.7853661$.
Error in continued fraction $= 3.2 \times 10^{-5}$.
Number of terms in Taylor series for comparable accuracy $= 15,625$.

7.16   Rational approximation $- 33.625 \mu$ sec
Taylor series$- 44.625 \mu$ sec

CHAPTER 8

All answers are exact except as indicated.

8.20   (a) $\log_e 3 = 1.098612$
(b) 3.749644
(c) $\pi/4 + \log(\cos \pi/4) = 0.4388245$
(d) $2/3$
(e) $\log(1 + e) - \log 2 = 0.6201130$

8.21 36.375 (4 points)

8.22 36.375

8.23   (a) 7.560909
(b) -0.8473821
(c) 1.449651 (computed)

8.24   (a) $\pi/8 \log_e 2 = 0.2721982$
(b) 0.828994 ($n = 24$ with Gauss quadrature)

8.25   (a) Let $y = e^{-x}$ and the integral becomes
$$\int_0^1 \frac{dy}{1 + y^2} = \pi/4 = 0.7853981$$
(b) $\pi/(2e) = 0.5778636$
(c) 1.033477

8.26   (a) $\sqrt{\pi}/2 = 0.8862269$
(b) -3.420544
(c) $\pi^2/8 = 1.243308$

8.27   (a) $1/(4e) = 0.0919698$
(b) 0.2546940 (50×50 Simpson's rule)
(c) 4.486770 (50×50 Simpson's rule)

8.28 (a) $\pi/2 = 1.570796$
(b) $\pi^2/4 = 2.467401$
(c) 0.185784 (Romberg $\epsilon = 10^{-6}$)
(d) 0.974302 (Special Gauss, $n = 4$)
(e) -0.5772157
(f) 6.0

8.29 58.39580 (Simpson's 1/3 rule + Simpson's 3/8 rule)

CHAPTER 9

For all problems where no method is specified in the problem statement, a fourth-order method has been used with sufficiently small step sizes to ensure good accuracy.

9.18

t	0.1	0.2	0.5	1.0	1.5	2.5
y	0.099668	0.197375	0.462116	0.761592	0.905146	0.986614

9.19

t	0.5	1.0	1.5	2.0	3.0	4.0
y	1.05785	1.21611	1.45636	1.76314	2.52248	3.40419

9.20

t	0.2	0.6	1.0	1.4	1.8
y	2.96714	2.73649	2.41648	2.16894	2.04838

9.21

t	0.5	1.0	1.5	2.0	2.5	3.0	3.5
y	1.11099	1.43438	2.06784	3.40014	7.01648	25.1192	5562.21

9.22

t	0.5	1.0	1.5	2.0	2.5	3.0	3.5	4.0
y	0.094709	0.512513	0.777002	1.09373	0.994983	0.732393	0.042280	-0.552708

9.23

t	0.8	1.6	2.4	3.2	4.0
y	0.937240	0.635519	0.107287	-0.785498	-3.66414

9.24

t	0.4	0.8	1.2	1.6	2.4	3.2	4.0
y	0.933176	0.739006	0.438683	0.071843	-0.637120	-0.990543	-0.825770

9.25

t	0.3	0.6	0.9	1.2	1.5
y	557.371	584.179	610.352	635.821	660.516

9.26

t	0.2	0.5	1.0	1.5	1.9	?
y	0.449335	0.135342	0.018331	0.0022586	0.001031	?

Using a standard method (4th order Runge-Kutta with $\Delta t = 0.05$), the solution reaches a minimum at $t = 1.9$ and (erroneously) starts to climb. This differential equation is "stiff," and as noted in the text, special methods are required.

9.27

x	2.0	3.0	4.0	5.0	6.0	7.0
y	-0.240197	-0.785408	-0.548954	0.084748	0.531348	0.457088

9.28 See answers to 9.27.

9.29

x	0.4	0.8	1.2	2.0	2.8	3.6
y	0.106119	0.420342	0.922318	2.30579	3.88034	5.47927
y'	0.529424	1.03352	1.45796	1.91102	1.99493	1.99991

($x = 6$ used as effective infinity.)

9.30 See Table 9.11.

9.31

x	0.4	0.8	1.6	2.4	3.4	4.4
y	0.088067	0.312440	0.979799	1.75527	2.75221	3.75210

CHAPTER 10

10.22 $L^{-1} = \begin{bmatrix} 0.2500000 & 0 & 0 \\ -0.7499998 & 0.3333333 & 0 \\ 0.1785714 & -0.0952381 & 0.1428571 \end{bmatrix}$

10.23 $L = \begin{bmatrix} 2.236068 & 0 & 0 & 0 \\ 1.788854 & 2.190891 & 0 & 0 \\ 0.8944272 & 0.6390096 & 2.965075 & 0 \\ 1.341640 & -0.1825730 & -0.0281048 & 3.341538 \end{bmatrix}$

10.24 (a) $\lambda_1 = 14.20680$
$X_1 = [1.0,\ 1.357335,\ 1.016850]^T$
(b) $\lambda_1 = 21.30525$
$X_1 = [0.8724071,\ 0.5400626,\ 0.9973493,\ 0.5643892,\ 0.4972264,\ 1.0]^T$

10.25 (a) $\lambda_1 = 4.361548$
(b) $\lambda_2 = 1.621394$

10.26 $\lambda_1 = 3.979469,\qquad X_1 = [1.0,\ 0.6929171,\ 0.4503604]$
Relaxation factor of 0.7 is near optimum.

10.27 (a) $\lambda_1 = 14.20680,\qquad X_1 = [1.0,\ 1.357335,\ 1.016850]^T$
$\lambda_2 = -6.568357,\qquad X_2 = [1.0,\ 0.0912823,\ -1.105274]^T$
$\lambda_3 = 4.361548,\qquad X_3 = [1.0,\ -1.332120,\ 0.7947350]^T$
(b) $\lambda = 27.99135,\ 13.86755,\ 10.97669,\ 8.711922,\ 5.988826,\ 4.463617$
$X_1 = [1.0,\ 0.9414426,\ 1.448744,\ 1.367083,\ 1.866736,\ 0.9641095]^T$
$X_2 = [1.0,\ -2.474414,\ -4.866274,\ -2.367334,\ 5.378862,\ 1.633608]^T$
$X_3 = [1.0,\ -0.5812529,\ 0.9383285,\ -1.139132,\ -0.617812,\ -0.1447591]^T$
$X_4 = [1.0,\ 0.6026523,\ -0.6093723,\ 0.1082658,\ -0.3642792,\ -0.1582096]^T$
$X_5 = [0.1954650,\ -0.4906382,\ -0.0703992,\ 0.2646958,\ -0.5129469,\ 1.0]^T$
$X_6 = [-0.4932583,\ 1.292125,\ 0.0521190,\ -1.171804,\ -0.0861762,\ 1.0]^T$

10.28 $\lambda = 21.52072,\ 8.704882,\ -1.002006,\ 5.448329,\ 5.327831$
$X_1 = [0.5558476,\ -0.2354614,\ -0.4953664,\ -0.5394152,\ 0.3150124]^T$
$X_2 = [0.3714356,\ 0.8916923,\ -0.1988552,\ 0.1641874,\ -0.0204547]^T$
$X_3 = [0.5347477,\ -0.0241771,\ 0.6851004,\ -0.2977896,\ -0.3942298]^T$
$X_4 = [0.4164587,\ -0.3702576,\ -0.3196153,\ 0.6266419,\ -0.4411753]^T$
$X_5 = [0.3060631,\ -0.1084728,\ 0.3788793,\ 0.4480103,\ 0.7418185]^T$

10.29 (a) Diagonal elements:
$h_{11} = 5.0,\qquad h_{22} = 8.230751,\qquad h_{33} = 6.769226$
Off-diagonal elements:
$h_{12} = 3.605552,\qquad h_{23} = 0.8461447$
(b) Diagonal elements:
$h_{11} = 7.0,\qquad h_{22} = 15.63634,\qquad h_{33} = 9.265319,\qquad h_{44} = 4.296923,\qquad h_{55} = 7.156559,$
$h_{66} = 1.644807$
Off-diagonal elements:
$h_{12} = 7.416199,\qquad h_{23} = 10.16117,\qquad h_{34} = 2.481489,\qquad h_{45} = 3.561502,$
$h_{56} = 2.923074$

10.30 (a) $\lambda = 3.414213,\ 2.000004,\ 0.5857906$
(b) $\lambda = 6.757132,\ 2.466472,\ 12.78438,\ 15.12421,\ -4.132152$
(c) $\lambda = 2.612795,\ 6.691607,\ 10.69557$
(d) $\lambda = 3.011776,\ -0.0415249,\ -1.685141,\ 7.941682,\ 10.53280,\ 25.24023$

10.31 $\lambda = 2.612795,\ 6.691607,\ 10.69557$

10.32 (a) $\lambda = 2.714084, -0.0765076, 1.227267, 0.5346729$

(b) $\lambda = 0.7497229, -1.791780, 2.600704, -0.4901396$

(Note: B is not positive definite and A must be decomposed instead.)

10.33 (a) $\lambda = 11.35097, 6.824839, 4.824121$

(b) $\lambda = 16.85295, 10.73615, 6.364584, 2.045894$

CHAPTER 11

11.8

$\frac{x}{y}$	2.0	4.0	6.0	8.0
0	0	0	0	0
1.0	17.97	0.39	1.17	53.91
5.0	56.69	38.98	69.26	160.95
10.0	85.49	90.56	128.99	202.95
15.0	105.82	124.49	164.24	225.41
20.0	118.83	145.71	185.67	238.76
25.0	126.93	158.85	198.84	246.92
∞	140.00	180.00	220.00	260.00

11.9

$\frac{x}{y}$	1.0	2.0	5.0	10.0	20.0
1.0	23.24	7.78	0.07	0.00	0.00
2.0	30.51	15.58	0.76	0.00	0.00
4.0	36.05	23.79	3.90	0.03	0.00
6.0	38.56	28.06	7.43	0.23	0.00
8.0	40.08	30.77	10.52	0.65	0.00

Since the right boundary condition is at infinity, the solution will simply tend to penetrate deeper and deeper into the region with increasing y, but will never reach a "steady state."

11.10 Consider first the formulation involving the backward difference form of the boundary condition. Subtracting the next-to-last equation (row n) from the last equation (row $n + 1$) changes the last equation to

$$[-4 - \beta]u_{j+1,n} + [2]u_{j+1,n+1} = 14(\Delta x) - \Omega u_{j,n}$$

The set is now tridiagonal. A similar treatment for the alternative formulation, this time involving the addition of the last two equations, results in

$$[\beta]u_{j+1,n+1} + [2]u_{j+1,n+2} = 14(\Delta x) + \Omega u_{j,n}$$

for the last equation. The resulting set is tridiagonal.

11.11

y	$u(0.3,y)$	$u(0.6,y)$	$u(1,y)$
0.1	5.126	2.463	3.079
0.2	6.941	5.090	5.820
0.3	8.098	7.080	8.213
0.4	8.972	8.629	10.118
0.5	9.653	9.839	11.613
1.0	11.381	12.919	15.417
∞	12.100	14.200	17.000

$u(1,y)$ reaches 95% of 17.000 at about $y = 1.26$.

11.12 Linear difference representation:

$$G(u_{j,k})\left[\frac{u_{j+1,k+1} - 2u_{j+1,k} + u_{j+1,k-1}}{(\Delta x)^2}\right] + \left[\frac{G(u_{j,k+1}) - G(u_{j,k-1})}{2(\Delta x)}\right]\left[\frac{u_{j+1,k+1} - u_{j+1,k-1}}{2(\Delta x)}\right]$$

$$= \frac{u_{j+1,k} - u_{j,k}}{\Delta y}$$

Various nonlinear difference representations are also possible.

11.13

x / y	0.25	0.50
0.25	235.71	242.85
0.50	199.99	199.99
0.75	164.28	157.14

11.14 (*a*) Table of u values from Gauss-Siedel iteration:

x / y	1	2	3	4
0	128.4	111.3	120.7	178.2
0.4	123.4	109.1	116.8	169.5
0.8	109.3	103.4	106.5	140.5

(*b*) Answers essentially as above, $\lambda_{opt} \approx 1.50$.

11.15 Difference representation:

$$\frac{u_{j+1,k} - 2u_{j,k} + u_{j-1,k}}{(\Delta r)^2} + \frac{1}{r_j}\left[\frac{u_{j+1,k} - u_{j-1,k}}{2(\Delta r)}\right]$$

$$+ \frac{1}{r_j^2}\left[\frac{u_{j,k+1} - 2u_{j,k} + u_{j,k-1}}{(\Delta \theta)^2}\right] = 0$$

Solving for $u_{j,k}$ yields

$$u_{j,k} = \frac{1}{\left[\frac{2}{(\Delta r)^2} + \frac{2}{r_j^2(\Delta\theta)^2}\right]} \left\{ \left[\frac{1}{(\Delta r)^2} + \frac{1}{2r_j\Delta r}\right]u_{j+1,k} + \left[\frac{1}{(\Delta r)^2} - \frac{1}{2r_j\Delta r}\right]u_{j-1,k} \right.$$

$$\left. + \left[\frac{1}{r_j^2(\Delta\theta)^2}\right]u_{j,k+1} + \left[\frac{1}{r_j^2(\Delta\theta)^2}\right]u_{j,k-1} \right\}$$

Gauss-Siedel iteration can now be applied in the same manner as for the rectangular coordinates case.

11.16

x \\ y	0.10	0.25	0.50
0.10	0.5196	0.9391	1.1582
0.25	0.9391	1.8051	2.2858
0.50	1.1582	2.2858	2.9370

These values were obtained using $\Delta x = 0.05$ and an absolute convergence criterion of $\epsilon = 0.0001$.   The values in the other 3 quadrants of the square can be found from symmetry.

11.17 $\dfrac{u_{j-1,k-1} - 2u_{j-1,k} + u_{j-1,k+1}}{2(\Delta x)^2} + \dfrac{u_{j+1,k+1} - 2u_{j+1,k} + u_{j+1,k-1}}{2(\Delta x)^2} = \beta\dfrac{u_{j+1,k} - 2u_{j,k} + u_{j-1,k}}{(\Delta y)^2}$

This difference representation is universally stable.

Index